WHAT THE CRITICS SAY:

D0878425

"The book's mix of small towr ... ...u ciegant restaurants makes for fun reading....An admirable gastronomic feat."

Mark Nixon, LANSING STATE JOURNAL

"One of those handy guides which every traveler should include in his glove compartment."

Lee Smith, Suburban Living Editor
ASSOCIATED NEWSPAPERS, INC.

"Marjorie and Duke Winters have already done the legwork. All you have to do is eat and enjoy."

Trudy Westfall, LANSING STATE JOURNAL

"Take time to experience some of Michigan's more unusual dining places."

CHICAGO SUN-TIMES

"Marjorie and Duke Winters set out to discover what's cooking in Michigan, and more than 7000 miles later, they're ready to tell you all about it."

ANN ARBOR NEWS

"A fascinating book of recipes from unusual, hard-to-find, and outstanding eating places in Michigan.... What a delight."

OKEMOS TOWNE COURIER

"If you love to eat and you love to travel, Marjorie and Duke Winters' book is an absolute must."

THE STATE NEWS

"Discover what's cooking in Michigan....Special interest and appeal."

ASSOCIATED PRESS

"Would-be diners are told how to get to each place, its hours, who runs it, and the specialties of the house--including recipes."

HOUGHTON DAILY MINING GAZETTE

"The story of the restaurants and the people who have built them into places where hospitality and good food meet."

Gay McGee, BAY CITY TIMES

"The first and still the best restaurant guide for the entire state--a remarkable book."

A. Winson Manters, Bon Vivant

"A book guaranteed to make eating in Michigan even more enjoyable....along with select recipes straight from the chefs' kitchens."

Mary Tinney, THE STATE NEWS

"An amazing culinary quest."

Mark Nixon, LANSING STATE JOURNAL

ADVENTUROUS EATING IN MICHIGAN

A Restaurant Guide and Cookbook

Marjorie and Duke Winters

BEECH TREE PRESS
Holt, Michigan

ISBN 0-9618424-0-7

 **ABOUT THIS BOOK**

Since our first edition, published in 1980, we've seen in Michigan and in the entire country a proliferation of Mexican eateries and menus, the Americanization of the croissant, the advent of Cajun cookin', the easy availability of fresh produce, and exotic ingredients, pasta in every form and color, the ebb of red meat and the flow of fish and fowl, and an emphasis on healthier eating while retaining a firm commitment to chocolate. All this is rather exciting to creative cooks and adventurous eaters, but it takes a long time, if ever, to trickle down to the public at large.

Humorist Erma Bombeck made a point recently about eating trends that come our way from California and New York: "The other 48 states wouldn't care if California ate its palm trees or New York tossed its graffiti in a wok with snow peas, they're going to eat like they've always eaten--fat! ....With all the flap about nutrition, Americans devoured 71 football fields of pizza a day last year. Wheels of Brie didn't even come close." Thus, for eaters who find the greatest adventure in the food itself and the creativity of the cook, this book has its limitations; large areas of Michigan haven't even an inkling of some of the things that are beginning to bore New Yorkers and Detroiters. In many less populated parts of the state the salad bar is on its way IN as a trend.

For this book, then, we couldn't use innovation in cooking as a criterion for inclusion. The only fair way to judge a restaurant is to determine whether or not it it's successfully meeting its own objectives, not our expectations. So this was a yardstick, as well as value received: the quality of food, service, and atmosphere in relation to price. Finally, we tried to achieve a balance in our listings, in price range and in geographical distri-

v

bution. The latter was a problem, but we did search equally hard for noteworthy places on the barren areas that appear on our maps as we did in populous and tourist-trod locales. The selection of restaurants is entirely our own, and we neither requested not received financial payment from any establishment. We only asked that the proprietors or chefs furnish us, if they wished, with recipes of their choice. Happily, most of them complied.

We've seen lots of changes in the state of the state's restaurants. This is a roller coaster of a business. We sadly saw the demise of some places that we had thought of as sure bets. And we had to omit some old timers for loss of imagination and cutbacks in quality. But we're pleased to see some of our favorites flourishing and excited by the number of newcomers. We've added almost 100 new eating places and revisited all those that appeared in our first book. We're aware that some deserving businesses may have been omitted and that some we've included may decline in appeal or quality. Even as we went to press, two restaurants and their chefs parted company and one eatery closed and reopened under different management. So we would most appreciate receiving your comments in order to make changes accordingly in future editions. One thing stays much the same, however. The chefs as a rule are young and enthusiastic and as talented or more so than those in any other state, and there's more adventure than ever to be found in the Michigan restaurant scene.

CONTENTS

Numbers on the left correspond to locations on the maps on the inside front and back covers. Page numbers are on the right.

Southwest Lower Peninsula

Southeast Lower Peninsula

Northern Lower Peninsula

Upper Peninsula

(1) *Tosi's*

It was in 1533, according to epicure M.F.K. Fisher, that "Fate and Pope Clement VII changed the table manners of Europe. The Holy Father, probably conscious less of the gastronomic importance of his act than of its political results, married off his niece Catherine de Medici to France's young Henry. And Catherine took her cooks to France with her. They were probably the first great chefs de cuisine in that land, and galling though the fact may be to those Frenchmen who mix patriotism with their love of fine food, they were Italians every one."

Exactly 449 years later Ginger and Charles Mostov brought their love of Italian cooking to Tosi's, a restaurant we had already been going out of our way for ever since 1966, when we saw it listed in Time magazine as one of the 22 best country eating places in the United States. Over the years it's changed hands, and today under the tutelage of the Mostovs it's not only as good as ever but better. And even though it no longer is the southwestern-most location on our map, we've put Tosi's first in our book out of special affection and admiration.

There are six rooms for dining: the VIP Room, very attractive for private parties and open to the public when not booked by groups; the New Walnut Room, with the best seating (the corner tables for six are choice); the Old Walnut Room; the Cypress Room, housing the charcoal grill (avoid the two

1

tables by the kitchen); the Venetian Room with white archways and murals; and the old, original bar. Except for the VIP Room the decor isn't appreciably better in one room or another. If you arrive early, have cocktails in the Sala Florentina, a pleasant lounge with overhead arborlike ceiling, slate floor, and a fountain. In warm weather you might prefer the patio or the garden adjoining it. We had one of our most memorable luncheons here one sunny afternoon at a glass-topped table in the corner, surrounded by green hedges, stone cherubs, and hanging geraniums; the conversation with our good friends and cruise ship experts Pat and Gary Manson over the outstanding food and wine combined delightfully for an unforgettable dining experience.

The evening menu at Tosi's has changed somewhat with the arrival of the new owners; as Ginger notes, "Just about every recipe has been adjusted." The Mostovs' aim is to present authentic Italian dishes cooked according to original Old World recipes and tasting "the way they were intended to." To that end, almost everything is wholly prepared on the premises. To that end, also, Italy itself has become a training ground for Tosi's kitchen and dining room staff. In 1986 the Mostovs guided 21 employees on a food and wine trip to Florence, Milan, and Venice. In 1987 four cooks and two managers worked in Italy at five different restaurants, one of them Batti Becco, a small place in Bologne whose cooks came to Tosi's on an exchange basis. The entire crew will again have a chance to tour Italy in 1988. Charles notes that "sales have increased about 50% since undertaking the education of the staff." And what a staff! The service we've had over the years by many experienced waitresses has always been friendly, helpful, and efficient. And we do mean experienced. In 1980 Elsa, a mere 83 years old, served us smashingly, and just recently we were fortunate to meet Barb, who's been at Tosi's for 15 years and looks forward to her next trip to Italy.

Among the soups are stracciatella and a wonder-

2

ful minestrone--not a vegetable soup with oregano but thick, sturdy, aggressive, and almost a meal in itself. Thirteen appetizers, most of them Italian, are on the menu. Truly magnificent is the Pietmontese agnolotti, pasta "pillows" stuffed with veal and served in a delicate butter-lemon-sage sauce. Also worth trying and offered generally only on week nights is the Ligurian pizza with parchment-crisp crust and a zesty topping of prosciutto, pesto, and cheese. The pastas include an interesting manicaretti a la Bolognese (filled with tortellini, ham, and cheese and baked in a balsamella sauce) and malfatti (spinach rolls with a creamy meat sauce and mushrooms). We especially enjoy the superbly prepared veal entrees at Tosi's, among them a lustier-than-usual Cordon Bleu in two sizes, scallopini with mushrooms and Marsala, and veal Valdostana (filled with prosciutto and Asiago cheese and grilled). The Italian chicken and shellfish entrees are also to be reckoned with as is the tasty beef preparation, filetto con salvia, a small filet with sage and prosciutto, brushed with garlic and olive oil, and grilled over charcoal. Steaks, prime rib, walleyed pike, and a few other old favorites date back to Tosi's earlier days.

One gratifying change the Mostovs have made is to offer lunch. And at Tosi's it's a special sort of midday repast, turning a usually mundane meal into something more exciting. Ginger is most proud of these offerings. "The kind of food I serve for lunch is not the kind you can serve to 800 people. Our lunch specials are more delicate and northern Italian. They're for people who like to experiment with good food." There might be pasta with smoked salmon and cream, a vitello tonnato appetizer (cold veal with tuna sauce), eggplant manicotti, shrimp raviolini, or an aromatic veal breast. Any item on the bill of fare is a delight, but it's always wise to try the specials at Tosi's. They invariably surpass your expectations. (Incredibly, this is a restaurant the starry-eyed people of Mobil Guide have consistently ignored.)

The wine list is well suited to both the cuisine and the oenophile. With about 250 selections, including many of the expected French, California, and German names, Tosi's offers the most carefully assembled and impressive collection of fine Italian wines we've ever seen. With numerous Barolos (11), Barbarescos (19), Chiantis (14), Amarones (5), and 10 of the prized Brunellos of Montalcino, among many others, the 17-page list is an adventure in itself. And within the Italian sections the wines from different districts are briefly described; in addition, the Mostovs identify wines of special value and quality. Added to this is a first page of 15 wines available by glass or carafe, some at remarkably low prices from two Cruvinet dispensers (expensive French wine storage devices that preserve opened bottles). In all, this is the best combination of first-hand knowledge, skillful selection, and good value in a restaurant wine cellar in Michigan.

Clearly one of the best country restaurants and getting better--superlativo!

TOSI'S, 4337 Ridge Rd., Stevensville, MI 49127. Exit 23 off I-94, north on the Red Arrow Hwy to Glenlord Rd., then west to Ridge Rd. Telephone (616) 429-3689. Hours: luncheon May 1-October 31, Monday-Friday, 11:30 a.m.-2:30 p.m.; dinner 5:30-11 p.m. (till midnight Saturday, earlier off season). Closed Sunday and from New Year's Day through March 9. Reopens March 10. Bit of Swiss pastry shop (great crusty breads and desserts, as served in Tosi's) open 8 a.m.-9 p.m. Full bar service. Valet parking (free). Credit cards: MC, V.

SKILLET PENNE TUSCAN STYLE
From Tosi's

First, cook the pasta. Bring 2 quarts water to a boil, add 2 cups penne, and boil until half done or about 8 minutes. (If cooking ahead, drain, chill

4

under cold running water to stop cooking.) Set aside.
In an 8-10-inch skillet brown ½ pound Italian
sausage links (with fennel) in 1/3 cup fruity extra
virgin olive oil. Add 1½ cups coarsely chopped onion
and 1½ cups coarsely chopped sweet red pepper.
Cook over medium heat till vegetables are just tender and onions are lightly golden. Remove sausage;
cut crosswise into ½-inch slices. Return slices to
the vegetables. Add 1 tablespoon minced garlic, ½
teaspoon black pepper, 1 tablespoon fresh minced
sage (or 1 teaspoon dried), ¼ teaspoon red pepper
flakes, 2 cups canned whole tomatoes (chopped),
½ cup dry Vermouth, and ½ teaspoon salt. Cook
until the liquid is reduced by half. Add the cooked
pasta. Saute, stirring occasionally, until all the
liquid is absorbed and the oil begins to crackle in
the bottom of the pan. Serve in the skillet, garnished with minced fresh parsley or strips of fresh
basil leaves. Serve freshly grated Parmesan cheese
on the side.

GINGER'S TEMPTING LITTLE BLUEBERRY SUNDAE
From Tosi's

Sometimes less is more. In Italy the way to say
it is "Poco ma buono." We definitely agree with
the Mostovs. The tasty result belies the simplicity
of this recipe. Mix together 1/3 cup chopped, salted, blanched roast peanuts and 2 tablespoons finely
chopped crystallized ginger. Place 1 scoop vanilla
ice cream in each of 4 attractive long-stemmed
glasses. Sprinkle liberally with the nut mixture. Top
with 1 cup (in all) fresh blueberries. Serves 4.

REDAMAK'S

Who can adequately describe the "hamburger that
made New Buffalo famous"? After hours of tossing

adjectives back and forth, we have given up in semantic frustration and must resort to cliches. "Big" (exactly one-third of a pound of beef chuck before cooking). "Juicy" (the menus are wisely encased in protective plastic). "Fresh" (the meat is cut and ground daily in Redamak's very own kitchen). "Popular" (why do hundreds of Hoosiers and Chicagoans stop here in 90-degree weather when they could as easily sit in air-conditioned splendor under the golden arches and spend less?).

So there it is, the enigma of Harbor Country, which is what this little corner of southwest Michigan is called locally. Redamak's, since 1948, has probably sold more hamburgers and cheeseburgers to outsiders from neighboring states than to its own. For most Michiganians, "Harbor Country is unknown territory," according to Clifford A. Ridley of the Detroit News. Yet Chicago vacationers, escaping the city heat, discovered this area around the turn of the century, and a number of the old resorts and cottages constructed then are still in operation.

Redamak's is now 40 years old, but it has been under the aegis of the Maroneys for the past 12 years. One waitress, Mae Burns, has been here 23 years. This is a place that got its start in the paleolithic, preinterstate era, when highways had only two lanes and travel took twice as long. Now and again, to escape the boredom of the concrete ribbon, we still like to get off the expressway and traverse the old, original roads. Yet sadly what motels and restaurants we've come across, constructed once with such high hopes, are usually now in ruins. But not Redamak's, that great survivor of the interstate system. Not Redamak's, which doesn't care a fig about the fast food franchises, because its hamburgers really ARE bigger and better.

Drivers make a point of getting off Interstate 94 in spite of the inconvenience. And we do mean lots of drivers. Redamak's serves 220,000 customers annually (not counting barflies); 78,000 pounds of ground beef are consumed every year. Could the decor have anything to do with it? We've thought about that. Inside, the knotty pine walls and the South Shore Railroad posters from the 1920s are the quietest things at Redamak's. What's much more apparent is the stereo set at high blare, several beeping video games, whirring ceiling fans, a slamming screen door, and occasional screaming kids. Crowded, noisy, lacking in privacy, no placemats, no silverware. Just waxed paper and baskets, naked catsup bottles, and salt and pepper shakers. And those hamburgers. (We should note that in the summer there's a good-sized patio for outdoor dining; waitresses communicate with the kitchen by walkie-talkies.)

Still, a hamburger does not a heaven make, in spite of teenage propaganda. Redamak's also offers deep-fried shrimp, chicken, lake perch, frog legs, and 11 pieces of smelt; an even dozen specially topped hamburgers, ten sandwiches, and nine hotdog variations; innumerable breaded and "batter dipt" things including the mysterious nacho nuggets and apple sticks. Wisconsin cheese, cream of potato, vegetable, chicken noodle, cream of broccoli, and clam chowder comprise the soups, all homemade. In a particular bit of perversity, Redamak's emphasizes on its menu that it does NOT offer lettuce or tomato on its sandwiches. We admire that sort of intransigence in a restaurant. Just as we admire owner Jim Maroney's clear-headed appraisal that "air conditioning is not part of the concept--let 'em sweat."

For your big Redamak attacks.

REDAMAK's 616 E. Buffalo St., New Buffalo, MI 49117. Take exit 1 (New Buffalo) off I-94; 4/10ths mile north of the downtown business district. Telephone (616) 469-4522. Hours: 11 a.m.-10:30 p.m. Monday-Thursday (bar till 2 a.m.); 11 a.m.-11 p.m. Friday-Saturday (bar till 2 a.m.); noon-1 p.m. Sunday. Open March 1-November 30. Full bar service.

No credit cards but accepts personal checks (and has "never been burned," according to Jim). Don't bother to reserve.

ANGIE'S HOME-STYLE CHILI
From Angie Maroney, Redamak's

Brown 1¼ pounds ground beef chuck in a small amount fat. Drain off grease. Mix in 1 handful coarsely chopped onion (about 1 cup), 1 heaping tablespoon chili powder, ½ teaspoon ground cumin, 24-28-ounce can whole tomatoes in their juice (previously mashed), and 12-16-ounce can hot chili beans. Simmer at least 30 minutes. Bring to 140 degrees just before serving.

 ③ Tabor Hill

It isn't every day that you can sip a glass of crisp, cold Vidal Blanc and at that very moment glance out the window and see the grape vines from where it originated. We visited Tabor Hill many years ago, when its tasting room had first opened. It was an eye opener then to come across a Michigan vineyard so dedicated to making premier wines. You can imagine, then, how pleased we were to learn that in 1982 the new owner, Dave Upton, opened the Tastings Cafe, a restaurant offering "new American cuisine" right where the wine is made.

The contemporary rustic building, overlooking the vineyards and countryside, consists of three main areas: the dining room and tasting bar, the screened porch, and an adjacent outdoor patio. Weathered barnwood walls, subtle artwork, and a stone fireplace add warmth to the dining area. The porch is especially pleasing in warm weather; the view here is wonderful--beautiful sunsets and a misty panorama of vine country in the distance. And the new and old blend effectively; modern cane chairs and paintings are a happy counterpoint to the table settings of antique porcelain and fluted wine goblets.

Chefs Paul Ewald and Don Smith emphasize light, fresh, healthy foods "with just a touch of California inspiration." The most popular entrees are the mesquite-grilled chicken and shrimp. But we think you'll also enjoy the filet of veal served with watercress sauce and the fresh sea scallops poached in champagne and served on pasta. An interesting appetizer is Brie cheese, wrapped in a grape leaf, grilled, and garnished with fresh fruit. Desserts generally focus on fruit, but we've heard good things about the chocolate mousse, too.

Wine (Tabor Hill, of course) is available by the bottle or glass. Most likely this is one of the top three premium wineries in the state. The vineyard's wines have been served by Presidents Ford and Reagan in the White House and were also chosen by Governor Blanchard for his inauguration dinner. Since it purchased Bronte, where it makes and bottles champagnes, Tabor Hill is also the third largest winery in the state. The printed tasting guide is a useful way to decide which wine to try since each is described and conveniently listed according to relative sweetness. We especially enjoy two of the sparkling wines, the Brut Chardonnay and the Vidal Blanc Demi Sec, which is, as the name indicates, not quite as dry. But with a tasting room nearby, you can decide for yourself what suits your palate and then order exactly that with lunch or dinner.

Today Tabor Hill comprises 15 acres planted in six varieties. Tours, conducted every hour, are interesting and informative. Of special note are the oak casks from Germany, still in use for either reds or Chardonnays. Elaborately carved by a local artisan (the same one who did Tosi's front door), each one is dated and depicts the first years of Tabor Hill's history.

During the year the winery hosts two special events, a Jazz Festival held usually the third week of July, and the Harvest Festival on the weekend after Labor Day, which drew 5000 people in 1986 for pig roasts, balloon rides, grape-stomping contests, and other events. If there's a disadvantage to Tabor Hill, it's in finding the place. No, it's not even close to Buchanan, its mailing address. And you'll see signs at the Bridgman exit of I-94 which will only lead you to a roadside tasting room. Our best suggestion is to find Baroda on the map and take it from there. Just be patient, enjoy the ride through the countryside, and you'll soon arrive at a very special place.

A winning winery and dinery.

TABOR HILL TASTINGS CAFE, 185 Mount Tabor Hill Rd., Buchanan, MI 49107. Three miles southeast of Baroda. Telephone (616) 422-1161. Hours: luncheon daily 11:30 a.m.-3 p.m., dinner Wednesday-Saturday 6-9:30 p.m., Sunday brunch noon-3:30 p.m. Closed January and February. Credit cards: MC, V.

④ *Little River Café*

For years all you could do in Paw Paw was visit the wineries and get into a heated discussion about the origin of the town's name (a paw paw is a fruit, if you care, and not an especially popular one). Sure, you could eat out, but only at a drive-in or else furnish your own picnic. Now Paw Paw has a restaurant worthy of its long tradition as a central community in southwest Michigan's wine country.

Like Phoenix rising from the ashes, the Little

River Cafe was built in 1984 on the site of an old A & W root beer stand. James Burkett is chef, and his wife Mara along with his brother Dan and Dan's wife Janet are managers of this successful family enterprise. There are two dining rooms and a barroom. We much prefer the main dining room for dinner, especially the four round green booths under the windows overlooking the patio (ask for tables 13, 14, 15, and 16 although it's not always possible to reserve one). Our second choice is the bar, which seems more welcoming than the somewhat austere second dining room. The simple green and white table settings and the wine theme throughout (framed, enlarged Michigan wine labels; table lamps made of cut-off wine bottles; doors carved with grape leaves) are effective and particularly appropriate here in Paw Paw.

Part of the adventure of wine is learning about new offerings and unusual sources. Though you can find the traditional and familiar on the wine list at the Little River Cafe, most of the more than 60 to choose from originate in the United States, and many of these in Michigan. Furthermore, the proprietors are especially knowledgeable about the various characteristics of our state's wines, so this is a good place to expand your appreciation on the basis of expert advice. And if you're still a bit chary, order one of the locally made wines with the Little River label, available by the glass at quite reasonable prices. Other wines can also be ordered by the glass, including a regularly changing special, as well as several after-dinner Michigan ports and sherries.

To be sure, all the customary dinner entrees are here: prime rib, steaks, broiled and fried fish, shrimp, and lobster. But the menu is infinitely better than these inclusions suggest. Current trends are given first-class treatment without verging on the outlandish as they sometimes do elsewhere. Homemade pasta dishes include chicken Parmesan with fettuccine, angel's-hair pasta with crab and lobster, and the highly praised shrimp and scallop

Romano, not to mention mesquite-flavored lake trout, swordfish, steak, and barbequed riblets. Two of the most popular main courses are the chicken stir-fried with vegetables abd cashews and the cranberry-glazed roast duckling with sage dressing.

Appetizers don't take a back seat, either. Among several traditional choices are three less common ones: country smoked sausage en croute, a smoked sampler (assorted foods smoked on the premises), and a combination plate of duck liver pate and Brie. Most of these, as well as smaller versions of the evening entrees, are offered on the luncheon menu, which also features sandwiches, soups, pastas, and an upbeat specialty: Mediterranean pizza bread (with artichoke hearts, black olives, Canadian bacon, Colby and Mozzarella cheeses). Prices are moderate. Service is generally good but sometimes still in the yearning process. At least they're trying. So should you.

A wine country winner.

LITTLE RIVER CAFE, 715 S. Kalamazoo St., Paw Paw, MI 49079. Exit 60 ("M-51") off I-94; across from St. Julian Winery. Telephone (616) 657-6035. Hours: Monday-Saturday luncheon 11:30 a.m.-2:30 p.m., dinner 5-9 p.m. (till 10 p.m. Friday-Saturday); Sunday luncheon noon-4 p.m., dinner 4-8 p.m. Closed Thanksgiving, Christmas Eve, Christmas Day, and New Year's Day. Live entertainment (country and Western and bluegrass) in the lounge Friday-Saturday evenings but no dancing. Full bar service. Credit cards: MC, V.

Nearby attractions: just across the highway are Michigan's oldest winery, the St. Julian Wine. Co., and its biggest, Warner Vineyards, with more than 300 acres devoted to a large number of grape varieties. Also, at 39149 Red Arrow Hwy. is Frontenac Vineyards. Tours are worth taking; no charge.

APPLE FRITTERS
From the Little River Cafe

Of all the desserts at the Little River Cafe, we were most impressed with the Burketts' 12-layer strawberry torte and the apple fritters, the popular house specialty. In a 2-quart mixing bowl, combine 2 eggs, 1/3 cup sugar, ¼ cup vegetable oil, and ¼ teaspoon vanilla extract. Mix thoroughly with a fork. Add, a little at a time, 2 cups flour, ½ teaspoon baking powder, and a pinch salt, stirring until completely incorporated. Mix in 3/4 cup milk, and stir until smooth. Peel, core, and cut into rings 3 medium-sized apples. Coat each ring with the batter, and fry in deep fat or oil heated to 350 degrees. Fry until golden, turning once. Serve hot with 1 or 2 scoops vanilla ice cream and your favorite topping (we especially like caramel or butterscotch with this).

black swan inn

This is a lovely place, with a very attractive exterior of wood and cedar shakes and an interior featuring dark woods and a contemporary decor with Mediterranean touches. The dining room's floor-to-ceiling windows overlook scenic Willow Lake and its resident black swans and Canada geese. A centrally located interior fieldstone fireplace has its own cozy seating area and provides contrast to the exterior view. The main dining area occupies a semicircle between these focal points. Some built-in seating and a slightly awkward traffic pattern in places may give some guests a feeling of being crowded on a busy night, but we believe this is a minor problem. You can also eat in the less dramatic lounge or ask for a sandwich menu here, but

13

if you're looking for a little adventure, you'll opt for the main room.

The Black Swan Inn nicely combines popular American fare and creative cuisine. For luncheon Chef David Kaufman offers several classically prepared appetizers and entrees, including a quarter of a roast duckling, veal parmigiana with fettuccine, and crab souffle. For dinner the most popular items are prime rib and beef Wellington (for two). Yet there's something here to please most palates: five excellent veal dishes, sauteed chicken Marengo, brandy-flambeed tournedos, steak Diane, shrimp Diana, and sole mousseline. Two experienced table cooks handle the theatrical numbers. Not on the menu but nearly always available are two to four fresh fish selections. Entree prices are moderately expensive, but they do include a vegetable and your choice of tossed or spinach salad.

The regular wine list has a pleasing selection, including about 20 offerings that can be bought by the glass and several carafes. These include Chateau Timberlay, a Chianti classico, and Mondavi Pinot Noir. Most diners will be pleased with both the varieties available and the prices charged. But upon request there is also a Captain's List, consisting of, among many others, five premiers grands crus at expected prices, an unusually large number of sparkling wines (the Moet and Chandon jeroboam is notable), quite a few well-selected California reds and whites, and even a special Black Swan house label bottled by Great Western. Wine lovers will enjoy reviewing the cellar list here. The Black Swan Inn is frequently cited in the yearly readers' choice surveys of West Michigan Magazine.

Graceful and gracious.

THE BLACK SWAN INN, 3501 Greenleaf Blvd., Kalamazoo, MI 49008. Three miles northwest of I-94 Stadium Dr. exit (E.); off Parkview Drive in the Parkview Hills complex. Telephone (616) 375-2105 and 06. Hours: luncheon 11:30 a.m.-3 p.m., dinner

4-10 p.m. (Saturday 5-11 p.m.), early bird special menu 4-6 p.m. Closed Sunday, most holidays. Full bar service. Valet parking. Casual dress okay but no blue jeans. Credit cards: AE, DC, MC, V.

⑥ OAKLEY'S AT THE HAYMARKET

Oakley's is located on the first floor of the Haymarket, a building which was once just that; it dates back to the turn of the century when it served as chief provider of hay to Kalamazoo's buggy-pulling horses. But Oakley's itself goes back only a few years and offers something a lot more aesthetic and sensuous than hay: probably the best cooking in town. The original structure has been renovated in such a way that the restaurant is built around a central atrium with the highest ceiling we've ever seen in an eating place. You can look up all the way to the roof of the six-story building.

Look up, too, at the exposed steel girders and ducts, at the graceful arched windows in the red brick walls. Look down and around at the contemporary decor: the plantings under the skylights, the arc lamps, the varied seating levels with arch-back Windsor chairs, the splashes of cinnabar and jade, the mix of paintings and prints--abstracts, landscapes, and still lifes. Then close your eyes and listen. Oakley's specializes in the quiet, soft, classical stuff that goes so well with dinner.

The food is likewise entertaining. We had a delightful conversation with Shawn Hagen, who assists Chef Terry Hagen, his brother and a graduate of the Culinary Institute of America. Shawn was named Apprentice Chef of the Year in 1982 after competing with 1500 contestants at the Kraft Foods competition. Young and enthusiastic, like so many chefs we've met, Shawn has much to do with creating the entrees and major presentations at Oakley's, and his work complements that of Chef Terry, who has won awards for his desserts and pastries and who is adept at the organizational aspects of kitchen management.

The experience and skill of these two are evident. On our last visit, everything from soup to dessert was perfectly seasoned and at the ideal temperature, which is not so common as one might think. The potato-dill soup with Gruyere cheese was a marvelous blend of satisfying flavors. The Cajun shrimp appetizer shouldn't be compared with Prudhomme's famous "Cajun popcorn." It's better: jumbo-sized shrimp sauteed with spices and finished with a beer-deglazed beurre blanc. We cannot speak highly enough about the veal and Canadian bacon mantled with a brisk blue cheese sauce or the duck sausage ravioli with green peppercorn sauce. And no short shrift is given to the appearance of food; our veal was accompanied by a colorful and savory saffron pilaf alongside bright green and barely blanched asparagus.

The dinner menu contains a number of such delicious and well-executed entrees and appetizers. Among the most popular are Oakley's cold pate (scallop mousse incorporating pieces of lobster and shrimp); linguine with Marsala and wild mushrooms; a hearty roast pork loin stuffed with apples and raisins and served with cider sauce; pastry-encased salmon with spinach and mushrooms; and several other veal, seafood, and beef dishes. Appetizers run $4 to $12; entrees range from $13 to $20. To finish, a dessert tray is brought to your table for your inspection, and it's certainly tempting: tortes, cheesecakes, and fruit plates decorated with fresh flowers. We include Terry's recipe for one of the most popular sweets, the seductively silken white chocolate mousse.

The wine list has over 200 entries, most from California and France. Offerings vary from moderately priced house wines to the understandably expensive five premier grand crus of Bordeaux.

16

Nearly all the wines here are post-1975, but the vintages selected tend to be excellent. With this large a list, you'll surely find something more than satisfactory. For example, a fine '78 Souverain Cabernet, a highly rated '78 Pommard, a magnificent '75 Brunello di Montalcino, and a gloriously fruity '82 Gloria are ready now. There's almost as good a selection of whites, including several Italian varieties at very affordable prices. Finally, a number of dessert wines are available plus Cognacs ranging from good to excellent (our favorite, the affordable Remy Martin VSOP) to an absolutely superb Remy Martin Louis XIII at $25 an ounce.

Hedonistic, and that ain't hay!

OAKLEY'S AT THE HAYMARKET, 161 E. Michigan Ave., Kalamazoo, MI 49007. Downtown, where Portage Rd. meets Michigan Ave. Telephone (616) 349-6436. Hours: luncheon 11:30 a.m.-2 p.m. and dinner 5:30-10 p.m. Monday Thursday; 11:30 a.m.-2 p.m. and 5:30-11 p.m. Friday-Saturday; early pretheater menu 5;30-6:30 p.m. Monday-Saturday at $15 per person. Closed Sunday and most major holidays. Nearby city parking lots. Full bar service. Credit cards: AE, DC, MC, V.

WHITE CHOCOLATE MOUSSE
From Oakley's at the Haymarket

In the top of a double boiler over barely simmering water, melt 7 ounces white chocolate. In a mixing bowl, whip 10 ounces heavy cream until stiff. In a second bowl, beat 4 egg whites until foamy; then gradually beat in 1/3 cup sugar, a tablespoon at a time until soft peaks form. Slowly add the melted chocolate to the meringue. Fold in the whipped cream. Chill until serving time. Serves 8.

What can you say about a place where, the moment you walk in, your nostrils are filled with tangy, spicy odors that get the juices rolling and invite you to try things you might not otherwise consider? The Italian aromas at Pasta Pasta are nothing short of irresistible. And we suspect that the owners, Pam and Wayne Deering, shrewdly planned that onslaught of the senses when they decided to open their kitchen to the public and provide a self-service sauce bar.

Customers can choose from fresh semolina or spinach spaghettini, linguine, penne, and either cheese- or meat-filled ravioli. The pasta is then cooked to order and brought piping hot to your table, whereupon you may serve yourself one or all of the half-dozen sauces, three cheeses, and other toppings at the bar. Four sauces are regularly on the menu: tomato and vegetable, meat, clam, and butter-garlic. Two additional chef's specials appear daily, such as eggplant or ricotta-nut sauce (see the recipe below). A pasta order is priced with or without salad, also self-serve; and either way it's gratifyingly inexpensive, about $6 with and $4 without. The spinach linguine, by the way, is the top seller.

And yes, Virginia, there is a chef; on our visit last November it was Steve Clawson, who studied at the Culinary Institute of America. But Steve will become head chef of the Deerings' newly opened Angelina's Ristorante, a beautifully decorated, classic Italian, fine-dining establishment located in the renovated historic State Theater, which saw its heyday in vaudeville times.

Steve's able assistant, William Canter, will move up as chef of Pasta Pasta and will, as Steve did, prepare two special entrees each day as an alternative to the pasta bar, dishes on the order of scallops "a la arancia" (scallops with orange-flavored pasta in a creamy cheese sauce) or "paglioe fieno" (prosciutto with peas and spinach tossed with semolina pasta and cream sauce). Meat or vegetable lasagne is also on the daily menu. And if you're lucky, you might be at the cafe when the "pasta monster" is at work--we watched it in utter fascination along with a dozen other customers. This enormous, unwieldy-looking robot is a La Parmigiana machine from Italy that mixes up to ten pounds of flour at a time along with other ingredients. And when it spews forth a sheet of ravioli, it's truly a formidable sight.

There's also a small but good range of appetizers at Pasta Pasta, including an insinuating number called "lumache repieno," snails encased in pasta and sauteed in seasoned butter. Fresh minestrone and chicken broth with ravioli are the house soups. Everything is done with gusto. And unless you have a tremendous capacity, desserts are mostly skippable. We'd opt for one of the espresso concoctions instead, perhaps laced with liqueur or brandy. Dinner wines are appropriately Italian and priced reasonably. Pasta Pasta is also open for breakfast, and you'll enjoy the unprecedented fare. Fried eggs and bacon, to be sure. But also Italian sausage, frittatas, rarebits, shirred eggs, asparagus crepes, peaches-and-cream French toast, assorted muffins and fruit, granola, and those admirable coffees.

Pasta Pasta is a thoroughly engaging little restaurant. We like the out-of-the-way location in a building that used to be a meat market south of town (it's upstairs from Sunshine Submarine, another Deering enterprise); the jaunty decor of brick and rough-plastered walls, Roman shades, bentwood chairs, and bare floors; and the changing displays of local artists' works scattered on the walls. We like the soft classical taped music and the tiny raised dining area at the windows. And we like the informal, relaxed ambience--which is exactly what we've always liked about Italy itself and every Italian we've known.

Pasta Pasta, buona buona!

PASTA PASTA, 816 S. Westnedge Ave., Kalamazoo, MI 49008. Four miles north of I-94's Westnedge exit; 8 blocks south of the city center. Telephone (616) 381-0358. Hours: 6:30 a.m.-11 p.m. Monday-Friday, 8 a.m.-11 p.m. Saturday, 8 a.m.-9 p.m. Sunday. Closed major holidays. Wines, beers, liqueurs, brandies. Parking on north side of building. Credit cards: AE, MC, V.

RICOTTA NUT SAUCE
From Chef Will Canter, Pasta Pasta

Here is a pasta sauce that our good friend, Marianne de Sua, a superb Italian cook, would commend. Saute 1 large clove garlic, 2 tablespoons finely chopped walnuts, and 4 teaspoons finely chopped pine nuts in 2 teaspoons olive oil about 5 minutes. Add $1\frac{1}{4}$ teaspoons basil, 2 teaspoons mint, 4 teaspoons dry white wine, and slightly less than $\frac{1}{2}$ teaspoon sugar. Simmer 5 minutes. Add 8 ounces ricotta cheese, and simmer 5 more minutes. Add one (1-pound) can crushed tomatoes or tomato puree and one (1-pound) can whole peeled tomatoes (put through blender or diced). Simmer 35 minutes. Makes a little more than $1\frac{1}{2}$ quarts.

⑧ ◆ *SOUTH STREET* ◆
CULINARY SHOPPE

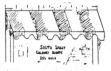

The Culinary Shoppe is a sunny and cheerful place (that is, when Michigan weather is sunny and cheerful), not much bigger than New York's eminent Silver Palate and with a food display just as appetizing, though less extensive. Four tables and a window counter with stools seat twenty in all, and the decor is disarmingly jejune, like so many little family-owned European-styled cafes. On the white walls are "Portraits in Pastels," originals by Nancy Shave, a local artist, and on the sound system are classical tapes. The crush of customers peaks at midday, so if you want a seat, arrive at either 11:30 or after 12:30 to avoid the business lunch crowd.

Rick Caruso, the owner/cook, hails from San Diego. He grew up learning about the fine aspects of food from his father, a professional chef. And, even though he studied political science at Pepperdine, the lure of the kitchen stayed with him. Now, after working in such swank communities as Malibu and Beverly Hills, California, Rick settled down in little old Kalamazoo, his wife's hometown, and opened the shop in August 1986. He's even initiated cooking classes in basic techniques.

Rick does a brisk business in catering, which, unfortunately, lets most of us visitors out. But you can easily compensate with a lunch on the premises (or take it out in nice weather and eat around the corner in Kalamazoo Mall). A changing daily menu of regional French and Italian specialties is chalked on a slate outside the restaurant and also above the counter. On our last visit Rick was offering poulet au citron (chicken with lemon sauce), herb-roasted Cornish hens, herbed tomato tart, and a really creamy and flavorful mushroom soup. But other items in the glass case are worth pondering, too: Sicilian stuffed artichokes, antipasto, manicotti, chicken-stuffed avocado, a number of salads, croissant sandwiches, tortes, and cheesecakes. Prices are very reasonable.

Little, likeable, and low priced.

THE SOUTH STREET CULINARY SHOPPE, 116 W. South St., Kalamazoo, MI 49007. Downtown, just off the main street (Kalamazoo Mall). Telephone (616) 385-0050. Hours: 11 a.m.-5:30 p.m. Monday, 11 a.m.-7 p.m. Tuesday-Friday, 10:30 a.m.-5 p.m. Saturday. Closed Sunday. No alcoholic beverages.

21

Street parking or two parking buildings within 1 block. Reservations not accepted.

SOLE WITH CAVIAR BEURRE BLANC
From Rick Caruso, South Street Culinary Shoppe

Here is a most elegant entree. Rick notes that "beurre blanc, used extensively in nouvelle cuisine, is a little tricky and does not 'sit' well," so plan to prepare it at the last minute.

For the sauce, place 4 ounces dry white wine and 3 ounces tarragon wine vinegar in a saucepan. Bring to a boil, and reduce to 2½-3 tablespoons of liquid. Over high heat begin to whisk in 1 cup of very cold butter which has been cut into small chunks. (Do not substitute margarine!) Reduce heat to medium high, and continue to whisk until sauce is thick and creamy and butter is almost totally incorporated. Remove from heat and continue to stir.

For the fish, in a large saute pan, poach 4 (8-ounce) fillets of sole in ½ cup white wine with a pinch of minced garlic and salt and pepper to taste. After 2 minutes on each side the sole should be done. Transfer to a serving platter. Top liberally with the beurre blanc and then with dollops of both salmon and black lumpfish caviar. Rick serves this dish with a warm asparagus vinaigrette salad and Champagne and follows it with a raspberry ice. Serves 4.

"THE IDLER"

⑨

From Mark Twain to Edna Ferber, from Daphne du Maurier to Jerome Kern, the Mississippi riverboat has caught the imagination of numerous

22

writers and artists. And when you combine the experience of being aboard an authentic 19th-century houseboat with the pleasures of well-cooked and inventive meals--voila! Instant adventure.

The Idler was built in 1897 at Clinton, Iowa, by a wealthy lumber baron who wintered aboard the boat in New Orleans and returned home each summer. After years of service by various owners, in 1981 Nichols Landing purchased the boat and arranged for its month-long, 760-mile journey down the Mississippi from Clinton to the Illinois River, north and east to Chicago, and thence across southern Lake Michigan to its present idling place on the Black River.

It's an enchanting little vessel, sprucely painted in white with green trim, a scheme carried over into the canopy over the gangplank and the uniforms of the young, enthusiastic "crew." On the upper promenade are the oak-paneled bar and lounge that open onto a larger breezy afterdeck, very pleasant for cocktails. Below, on the main deck are the galley, four dining rooms, and four saloon staterooms, each seating six persons for intimate but informal dining. Of the compartments we prefer the Garden Room in the stern; it's the most attractive and offers the best view of the harbor.

Highlights on the Continental menu include sea-food crepe casserole (shellfish baked in a crepe cup with Newburg sauce), perch Idler (pan fried, served over rice, and topped with Hollandaise), four exceptional pasta dishes (our choice the chicken prosciutto), and a lusty bouillabaise (the most expensive item on the menu). The southern French seafood soup-stew is something to behold--but to behold it, you'll need to shell out $26 per person. The hearty steak salad is another option but for lighter yet meat-oriented appetites. The ebullient Richard Hoscher, who trained at the Culinary Institute of America and whose labors won the Idler the 1985 Silver Spoon Award, also cooks up five weekly specials; on our last visit these included veal piccata, pasta with ham, and a winning chicken breast with mustard sauce. Prices for dinners are moderate to expensive.

If you'd like to treat the kids to a riverboat setting, lunches are geared to much more modest budgets. Sandwiches are large and tasty, especially the Texas club with roast beef, sauteed onions, and Swiss cheese. Salads, soups, and omelets round out the menu.

There's an adequate wine list, but it will probably be better when you visit. As we write this, the list is supposedly being expanded and improved. Last summer, the whites offered by far the best selections, reasonable considering the seafood and chicken dishes on the menu. No vintages were given, German wines were well represented, and 19 of 23 still whites were priced less than $15. Two somewhat unusual offerings were from Washington state and Australia, the latter a Chardonnay by Seppelt, which is produced in the southeastern part of that remote continent.

South Haven has about 35 restaurants, something for every taste and pocketbook. If you're unable to dine at the Idler (it's small so often there's quite a wait), stop across the river at the French-chateau-like mansion, Ruppert's for a more formal dinner of, we hear, food as good as any in the area. Or for a bustling informal atmosphere, try the popular Clementine's Saloon in the heart of town; specialties are "munchies, burgers, omelets, sandwiches, and basket meals." Both at Clementine's and the Idler are (in season) pick-up stations for the Black River Carriage Co., which offers four different horse-drawn carriage tours of South Haven; ask at either restaurant.

Down by the riverside on an authentic riverboat.

THE IDLER RIVERBOAT RESTAURANT, 515 Williams St., South Haven, MI 49090. On the river at Nichols Landing, downtown. Telephone (616) 637-7486. Hours: luncheon 11:30 a.m.-2:30 p.m. Monday-

Saturday; open deck casual lunch 2-5 p.m. Monday-Saturday weather permitting; dinner 5 p.m.-9:30 p. m. Monday-Thursday, 5-10 p.m. Friday-Saturday; brunch on deck 9 a.m.-noon Sunday weather permitting; Sunday dinner noon-6 p.m. (Call about off-season hours.) Full bar service. Credit cards: MC, V.

⑩ CRANE ORCHARDS
CIDER MILL AND PIE PANTRY RESTAURANT

U've seen the signs as U've headed along the interstate towards the Lake Michigan dunes, but U generally don't feel like picking--after all, this is vacation time. Still, U really mustn't miss a special treat in the heart of southwestern Michigan's fruit belt: a lunch or snack at Crane Orchards. At the family-owned and -operated fruit farm, athletic visitors can harvest their own fruit in season--raspberries, sweet and tart cherries, peaches, blueberries, Bartlett and Bosc pears, and apples in season--or else take the easy way out and eat in the Pie Pantry Restaurant amid a nostalgic array of antiques and memorabilia.

For six generations the Cranes have been fruit farmers. They purchased these 250 acres in 1916, and currently Bob and Lue Crane and three of their five children share in the family business. What started about 20 years ago as a small, locally popular cider and donut enterprise became a restaurant in 1972. The dining rooms, one a former workshop and one an erstwhile barn, and a newer weathered barnwood porch are decorated in early Michigania, an "atmosphere of yesterday" that reflects the Cranes' interest in history and respect for tradition. There's a simulated kitchen off one dining room, but the rea work of making all those pies and dumplings goes on upstairs in a

25

large modern kitchen, once the haymow of the 1879 farmstead.

Luncheon possibilities are limited but good. Everything is made on the premises, and, in the case of the fruit concoctions, grown here, too. Why not start with a cup of soup or chili and follow up with a sandwich made with the Cranes' own white, honey, whole wheat, or rye buns? Or have a tossed salad with a warm apple or blueberry muffin. Beverages include, of course, sweet apple cider, cold or hot and spicy. But sweets are the specialty. The old-fashioned apple pie--Ida Red with a hint of cinnamon--is a blue-ribbon winner; and just as good are the cherry, peach, and blueberry. Pumpkin and fruit mince pies appear in late fall and winter, perfect fuel for cross-country skiers who are here to follow one of the panoramic marked trails to Hutchins Lake. Other desserts include the popular apple dumplings, cider doughnuts, rhubarb tart, and apple walnut cake.

For families with children, for antique buffs, and for apple fanciers, Crane Orchards is made to order for a pleasant luncheon stop. Kids will most enjoy visiting on a Friday in the fall and winter, when cider is being pressed in the apple storage building that adjoins the restaurant. Expect, however, to wait up to 45 minutes for a table if you arrive during the fall harvest. What kind of apples? Mainly Red and Golden Delicious, Jonathans, and Ida Reds, the Cranes' choice for pies.

And did you know that our state ranks number one in production of Jonathans and Northern Spys and is third in the nation in production of all apples? It's no fluke that the apple blossom is the state flower.

While you're in the area, you might also visit the Fenn Valley vineyards and wine cellar, just south of the orchards. It's a small (230 acre) family-owned vineyard that styles its premium table wines after those of northern Europe. Something else you may not know about, as we didn't before our first visit, is that Canadian geese flock by the tens of thousands to the nearby Fennville State Game Refuge in early spring and fall and that in October of 1987 the city will host its third annual Goose Festival, with the memorable slogan "Get Your Goose in Fennville."

And get your apple pie at Crane Orchards!

CRANE ORCHARDS AND PIE PANTRY RESTAURANT, 6054 124th Ave., Fennville, MI 49408. Telephone (616) 561-2297. On M-89, 1½ miles west of Fenville, 4½ miles east of I-196, exit 34. Hours: in summer, Mother's Day to October 31, 9 a.m.-7 p.m. daily, 12 noon-7 p.m. Sunday; in winter November 1-March 31, 10 a.m.-5 p.m. Tuesday-Saturday, closed Monday; in spring April to mid-May, open Saturday and Sunday only, noon-7 p.m. No alcoholic beverages. Credit cards not accepted.

HOT SPICED CIDER
From Crane Orchards

This is so, so easy to make; but with cider fresh from the orchard in autumn, it's even more of a treat. Put 1 gallon cider, 6 sticks cinnamon, 3 teaspoons whole cloves, and a pinch of ground ginger into a large pot. Bring to a boil and let simmer 15 or more minutes. The Cranes note that this can also be made in a coffee percolator. We might add that it could be slowly simmered in a crock pot, on the lowest setting for about 3 hours. For a zestier final product, add a little fresh lemon and/or orange peel and a little rum to taste. Makes about 30 servings.

"Coleridge holds that a man cannot have a pure mind who refuses apple-dumplings. I am not certain but he is right."

....Charles Lamb

⑪ Billie's
Boathouse

Saugatuck has long been a major artists' colony
in the Midwest and a favorite destination of tourists.
Out of season, you could fool yourself into thinking
this is an untouched little waterfront village. But,
fair warning, in season it's not a place to get away
from it all. To be sure, Michigan has such places,
but rugged individualists would do well to aim for
the Upper Peninsula. Let's be sensible, however.
If you're starting out from Chicago or Detroit and
you only have a long weekend or even a week,
Saugatuck is a fine choice. It offers everything that
could possibly attract a vacationer: a sparkling
harbor with sailboats and yachts, scenic boat rides,
fishing charters, miles of nearby beaches, sand dunes
and dune schooners, summer theater, entertainment
and dancing, horsedrawn carriages, arrt galleries,
and shops and shops and shops. It's fun, it's cheerful,
and it's committed to separating you from your
dollars. But thousands of visitors each summer
don't seem to mind.

Eating places abound in Saugatuck and its twin
city Douglas, mostly more expensive versions of
fast food hamburger and pizza places and a few
steak houses. Since almost all of them have some
sort of view, we focused on the food. Our choice--
Billie's. A real boathouse it's not; that would have
been an adventure! But it's close enough to the
water to BE a boathouse.

Three dining areas offer the same menu. When
we want something cozy, we prefer the main room
nerarest to the bar and music (modern jazz nightly).
When we want sunlight and an airy garden atmosphere, we ask for seats in the newest addition, the
Patio. The decor throughout has a neutral color
scheme and an understated nautical theme with
rope-wrapped pillars and posts, brass ship's lanterns,

clocks and bells, and octagonal windows.

Chef Kevin Boerman's menu is Mexican/American and all that this implies: steaks, ribs, seafood, hamburgers, as well as a fair selection of Mexican appetizers and entrees, including either a crabmeat or beef and cheese enchilada with a rich cream sauce. Chicken fanciers might like the lemon chicken with Oriental overtones or an unorthodox version of chicken Florentine, and veal lovers will enjoy the veal scallops Dijonnaise (with artichoke hearts and mustard-cream sauce). Food trendies aren't ignored, either; a seafood linguine and Cajun catfish round out the already well-rounded menu. We also like the number and variety of salads, the two vegetable plates with either tofu or ranch dip, and the three "lite side" entrees. There really is something for every taste and budget—a smart way to do business is such a bustling tourist area. Billie's, by the way, was voted best restaurant in Saugatuck by readers of West Michigan magazine.

Both traditional and trendy, a tourist magnet.

BILLIE'S BOATHOUSE, 449 Water St., Saugatuck, MI 49453. Downtown, opposite the chain ferry and gazebo. Telephone (616) 857-1188. Hours: summer 11 a.m.-closing (usually around midnights on weekends, 10-11 p.m. on week nights). Closed the weekend after New Year's Day until March. Streetside meterless parking, but it's fun to walk the streets here. Full bar service. Credit cards: AE, MC, V.

Nearby attractions: Take a narrated scenic cruise of the Kalamazoo River and Lake Michigan on an authentic sternwheel paddleboat; the Queen of Saugatuck leaves from the Fish Dock, 716 Water St. Or consider one of a number of cruises available daily in the summer on the M/V City of Douglas, a 60-foot yacht docked at Tower Harbour. For a shorter and cheaper bit of fun on the water, cross the river on the 1838 Saugatuck Chain Ferry, the only hand-cranked ferry on the Great Lakes. Ring the bell at the landing for service (50¢ for adults, 25¢ for children—a bargain).

POINT
WEST
INN

(12)

Years ago we wrote that no restaurant in south-western Michigan had a lovelier setting than Point West. And that's still true even though it now has some competition from the nearby Sandpiper. We like both of these restaurants very much, for different reasons, but as for the most unobstructed view and most appealing patio area, Point West has the edge. The low, modern structure of brick, flag-stone, and dark wood lies at the extreme west end of Lake Macatawa, close to the water and over-looking a large yacht basin. The main dining room faces the lake and features beamed ceilings, a contemporary decor with a warm red and peach color scheme, floor-to-ceiling windows interrupted in the center by a massive fireplace. There are two levels to enhance the exceptional view. We prefer the lower, nearer the windows.

The luncheon menu is fairly conventional and in-cludes croissant sandwiches, a quiche of the week (seven years ago it was a quiche of the day--so goes a trend), a good mimosa salad, and a "king-sized burger" with an interesting choice of toppings. Breakfast is also available, and an early morning view of Lake "Mac" is a pleasure.

On the dinner menu are a number of tempting choices: tournedos Marchand de Vin (a New Orleans beef preparation with tarragon, shallots, and red wine sauce), pork Madagascar (herbs, wine, and green peppercorns), chicken Sacher (sauteed breast finished with mushrooms, tarragon, and cream), and veal financiere (scallops of veal sauteed with chanterelle mushrooms and Madeira wine), plus various well-prepared seafood, beef, and pasta dishes. There are some good, classic appetizers; and for dessert you might order the luscious French chocolate Pie (a house specialty for at least 10 years; see the recipe below), Koko Moko rum pie, cheesecake, or creme caramel.

On warm evenings we suggest that you arrive early and enjoy a cocktail on the shaded waterfront patio, as nice as any we've seen in Michigan (and as we write this, it's being expanded even closer to the water). Or, if it's cool, settle down near the second fireplace in the lounge, listen to the band, or dance. There's no dress code, but we recommend that men wear jackets to feel comfortable here.

A striking waterfront setting, inside and out.

POINT WEST, Macatawa, MI 49434. Seven miles west of Holland; follow South Shore Drive to the end. Telephone (616) 335-3358. Hours: breakfast 7-11 a.m., luncheon 11:30 a.m.-2:30 p.m., dinner 5:30 -10:30 p.m., Sunday brunch 10 a.m.-2 p.m. Closed Christmas Day. Full bar service. Credit cards: AE, DC, MC, V.

FRENCH CHOCOLATE PIE
From Point West

Bake 1 9-inch pie shell. In a mixing bowl combine 2/3 cup whipped butter and $\frac{1}{2}$ pound confectioners sugar. Whip for 2 minutes with an electric mixer on low speed. Scrape the bowl; whip again for 2 minutes on medium speed. Scrape again, and whip once more for 2 minutes on high speed. Scrape down the bowl. Add 2 ounces melted Bakers Chocolate and $1\frac{1}{2}$ teaspoons vanilla extract, and beat on medium speed 5 minutes. Scrape bowl, and beat on high speed 4 minutes. Turn mixer speed to high and add 3 eggs and 1 egg yolk, one at a time, while beating. Spoon into cooled, baked pie shell. This is terribly (and marvelously) rich. Plan on at least 8 servings.

(13) **SANDPIPER**

The usual steakhouses abound in the Holland area, but as far as we're concerned, there are only two choices for dinner: the handsomely redecorated Point West at the westernmost tip of Lake Macatawa and, almost too close for comfort--that is, Point West's comfort--but very different in cuisine and atmosphere, the Sandpiper. What's extra special about Point West is the building and the view. What's extra special about the Sandpiper is the food--the view of the marina and lake is a bonus. Built in June 1985, the restaurant adjoins the Eldean Shipyard and Yacht Sales business, which has been here since 1901. The main dining room is on the upper floor and is itself multilevel, affording all diners a view from the floor-to-ceiling windows. A fresh olive green and white color scheme is a counterpoint to the gleaming dark oak floors, and the shore bird motif is evident in a scattering of prints and sculpture.

Although the sandpiper theme, the view of the yachts just a few feet from the windows, and the flickering oil lamps on the tables all contribute to a feel of New England, the restaurant concept is country French. And the owners Pat and Herb Eldean were astute in calling upon the services of Chef Ed Westerlund. Chef Ed is a graduate of the Culinary Institute of America in Hyde Park, New York, as are so many of Michigan's bright young chefs. He brings a special flair to the Sandpiper. The menu, for example, changes every six weeks and features an eclectic array of taste sensations: baked artichokes piped with salmon mousse, hot pepper linguine with chorizo sausage, grilled strip steaks with caraway seed and akvavit, lamb chops with minted lingonberry butter, pastry-baked wall-eyed pike with chive mousse. None of these are ethnically confused dishes that can't stand up to critical scrutiny but instead are intelligently con-ceived and well executed. Changing daily specials also appear two or three times a week and quite often feature fresh fish. And we do mean fresh--freshly flown in from Manhattan or Fort Lauderdale. Chef Ed does them proud; imagine grilled red drum with almond-saffron sauce or king clip with basil-raspberry cream. Menus are geared to the seasons and availability of basic ingredients, for example, local mushrooms in spring, berries in summer, and game in autumn.

The Sandpiper has a nice way with wines, too. Your waiter will bring you a glass of the "wine of the day" at no extra charge; ours was a palatable '85 Chateau Regnon. We also like the splits of sparkling wines as an option for single diners. The prices for both food and wine are at the upper end of moderate. Our dinner last summer (pork tenderloin stuffed with sausage and fresh basil) couldn't be faulted , and our waiter Joel's service was expert and friendly. Finally, Chef Ed is someone to reckon with. We reckon it may be next November, when he again begins his search for both local and exotic wild game.

Promising provender in a nautical setting.

THE SANDPIPER, 2225 South Shore Dr., Macatawa, MI 49434. Seven miles west of Holland; drive to the end of South Shore Dr. If you're arriving by yacht, reserve dock space by calling the marina (616-335-5843). Telephone (616) 335-5866. Hours: luncheon 11:30 a.m.-2 p.m. Monday-Friday, dinner 5:30-9 p.m. Monday-Thursday (till 9:30 p.m. Friday-Saturday). Closed Sunday. Full bar service. Credit cards: MC, V.

ROAST DUCKLING, SAUCE OF FRESH FRUITS
From Chef Ed Westerlund, The Sandpiper

Chef Ed suggests that the ducks be prepared a day ahead. We find this a terrific recipe, and our only suggestion to the cook is to prick the duck's skin once, preferably two-three times during the first 1½ hours of roasting to facilitate draining off the fat.

Remove neck and giblets from the cavities of 2 (4-5 pound) ducks, and reserve. Cut wings at first joint. Trim skin off at neck (our note--also trim off skin and tail at the other end). Cut 1 orange in half, and rub outside of each duck with the ½-orange. Place orange half in cavity of each duck. Place duck on wire roasting rack 2 inches above the bottom of the roasting pan to allow fat to drip while cooking. Place in preheated 350-450-degree oven, and roast for 2-2½ hours. Roast until skin feels slightly crispy. When pressed with finger, the skin should touch the breast meat (this means that the fat "cushion" has cooked away from under the skin).

Remove and let cool on rack. When ducks are cool (best to bone the next day), split in half lengthwise, cut down center of duck and very carefully remove bones, leaving wing and thigh bone attached. Place bones in 2-4 quart stock pot along with carrots, celery, onions, and herbs for additional flavor. Simmer stock 2-3 hours. Strain and skim off fat. Bring back to a boil, and thicken with a mixture of cornstarch dissolved in cold water. Add, to taste, red or white wine, port wine, or orange juice. Simmer 10 minutes. Just before serving, add fresh fruit (one or more of your choice, for example, blueberries, melons, cherries, peaches, apricots, mangos, kiwi fruit, etc.).

To reheat duck, place semi-boneless ducks in baking dish. Reheat oven to 350-400 degrees. Roast but watch carefully so as not to caramelize skin. When ducks are hot and crispy, place on serving dishes with fruit sauce. Serves 4.

(14) **SCHOONER** RESTAURANT

If some spring or summer you're in Holland, Michigan, by chance or by choice, you won't be able to escape the Dutch Deluge. Hundreds, probably thousands, of tourists and passersby ignorantly, gullibly head towards nearby cutesy

34

little Dutch restaurants, because these are adequate eateries and, to be honest, tourists love cutesy little places. But the locals and knowledgeable visitors tend to seek out the Schooner, a small, immaculate restaurant off the beaten tourist path on the south side of town.

What a pleasure it is at 8 a.m. to walk into this shipshape dining room, to order an omelet, to barely get started on the newspaper, and in just minutes to receive your breakfast steaming hot from the kitchen. There's a steady flow of customers in the morning, but it doesn't seem to affect the service or the cheerful ambience. This little treasure of a place is only a year old, too. Recently remodeled, it retains a nautical decor, a legacy from its predecessor, the Wharf, and a scheme well suited to the shoreline city of Holland. Most noticeable are the bright sailing blue touches in tables and accents, described to us by a regular customer as a "warm blue."

The food is basic, honest, and unpretentious. The usual egg and meat varieties for breakfast are skillfully prepared, especially the omelets--we love the seafood version with shrimp and Swiss cheese, topped with crabmeat sauce (at less than $4). Among the luncheon choices are hamburgers with several intriguing variations, soups and chili (homemade, of course), and other good things--nothing fancy, everything delicious.

And all of this is presided over by, believe it, a 19-year-old. Lesa Yancy knew what she wanted and convinced a reluctant bank to back her up. She laughingly notes that she'll be 49 when the loan is paid off. We think it'll be paid off a lot quicker. Lesa knows exactly what she's doing. She's had four years' experience in restaurant work and handles the business like an old pro.

You really must meet Lesa when you visit the Schooner; she'll restore any lost faith you might have in teenagers and young people. A pretty, petite blonde, as feminine as can be, here is a young woman with vision, determination, and expertise. She manages her restaurant by day, and at night makes the soups and does all the prep work and baking. And what baking! We thought we'd never find cinnamon rolls as mouth-watering as those we savored many years ago in Linden, Washington. Lesa's are as good or better. Now we need to find excuses to visit Holland more often. You do, too.

And a child shall feed them.

THE SCHOONER, 393 Cleveland Ave., Holland, MI 49423. A few blocks south of the business district. Telephone (616) 392-6055. Hours: Monday-Saturday 6 a.m.-2 p.m., Sunday 8 a.m.-1 p.m. Closed major holidays. No alcoholic beverages. No credit cards or reservations accepted.

Nearby attractions: In Holland, the attractions are Dutch, naturally, and include Dutch Village on U.S.31 at James St.; Windmill Island, 7th St. and Lincoln Ave.; and two wooden shoe factories, one on U.S.31 at 16th St. and another at 12755 Quincy at U.S.31. The Tulip Festival is one of Michigan's greatest seasonal tourist attractions.

(15) THE OLD SCHOOL HOUSE

In 1924 the little Dutch community of Borculo objected to installing electric lights in the school building. Imagine what those village fathers would think of the place now--not only with lights and central heating but with Marion Boetsma in the kitchen dishing up steaming, aromatic plates of barbequed short ribs and meatloaf to the public at large. The Old School House no longer serves its original purpose but instead is fast becoming known as one of the best bargains in the state and for its combination of a nostalgic background and good American home-style cooking.

36

The wood-framed school, surrounded by massive oak trees, dates to 1908 and was built at a cost of $2900. It was closed down when the school system was annexed to nearby Zeeland and later purchased by Shirley and Hersh Weaver. The Weavers had never operated a restaurant before and, except for the charming old building with its towering belfry, started absolutely from scratch in 1977. Fortunately, they retained the old green chalk boards as originally installed, the maple flooring, and the high, embossed tin ceilings. And, fortunately, the owners for the past four years or so, John and Evie Smallegan, have the same vision and dedication as the Weavers, now semi-retired.

The three classroom-cum-dining rooms, still visited by former students and teachers, are now called the Lunch Box, the Kindergarten Room (with a collection of the school's class and graduation pictures from 1908 to 1970), and the Dutch Room. But the menus are the same in each. Marion has been doing most of the cooking since the business started, and she really does it well. The menus are displayed on old hand-held slates (the precursors of modern notebooks); and, in addition, the blackboards on the walls list soups, sandwiches, salads, and desserts of the day. When we last visited, the lunch menu included liver and onions, meatloaf, a number of sandwiches on homemade bread, salads (taco, banana split fruit, and others), and several soups--including the Dutch "buttermilk pop."

Popular dinner entrees (most in the $5-$6 range) include roast turkey, roast sirloin, pot roast, Swiss steak, barbequed short ribs, smelt and other fish, and a special baked chicken breast with rice. Also offered are delectable pies (the raspberry in season and the butterscotch are heavenly), old-fashioned bread pudding (see Marion's recipe below), and a full line of soda fountain treats.

Nostalgic Americana at bargain prices.

THE OLD SCHOOL HOUSE, 9354 Port Sheldon Road, Borculo, MI 49464. Six miles east of U.S.31; 9 miles northeast of Holland. Telephone (616) 875-7200. Hours: 8 a.m.-8 p.m. year round. Closed Sunday, holidays, and during the months of January and February. No alcoholic beverages. Credit cards not accepted.

Nearby is a charming craft and gift shop, Kissing Kousins, 5 miles east of the school house on Port Sheldon Rd.; take a look.

BREAD PUDDING WITH LEMON OR RUM SAUCE
From Marion Boetsma, the Old School House

This is an old-timey, heart-warming American dessert, a regional favorite in New England and the South. It's delicious both warm and cold.

In a large mixing bowl beat 10 eggs. Add 5 cups scalded milk and $\frac{1}{4}$ cup melted butter. Mix together and then add 1 3/4 cups brown sugar, $2\frac{1}{2}$ tablespoons cinnamon, 2 tablespoons vanilla extract. Stir in 10 cups bread cubes (first butter bread and grill it).Pour into a greased 9x13-inch baking pan. Place pan into a second pan with 1 inch hot water. Bake 50 minutes in a preheated 350-degree oven. Optional addition: you can add 1 cup each of raisins and chopped walnuts to the batter. Makes 20-24 servings. Halve the recipe if you'd like.

If no raisins or nuts are used, Marion serves this with a lemon sauce and whipped cream. In a small saucepan, stir together 1 cup sugar and 3 tablespoons cornstarch. Mix in 3 cups water, $\frac{1}{2}$ cup lemon juice, and $\frac{1}{2}$ teaspoon nutmeg. Cook until slightly thickened. Add $1\frac{1}{2}$ tablespoons butter, and stir till melted.

If raisins and nuts are used, serve the bread pudding with rum sauce and whipped cream. Mix together 3/4 cup sugar and 3 tablespoons cornstarch. Add 3 cups water, 2 tablespoons lemon juice, 3/4 teaspoon rum flavoring, and 1/8 teaspoon nutmeg. Cook until slightly thickened; add $1\frac{1}{2}$ tablespoons butter, and stir till melted.

16

This is one of those fascinating new places that looks like an old place. It opened in May 1981, and the owner, Roger Reister, had definite ideas about what he wanted for his restaurant--a Williamsburg tavern decor in a woodland setting. And what an enchanting hideaway he has created! The building's exterior is redwood clapboard siding, allowed to weather naturally. The two dining areas are small-ish and intimate with brown tones and soft candle-light. The walls of the larger, more formal room are decorated with 1732 Kensington Garden calendar prints, and the tables are set with gleaming brass candlesticks. The barroom features Oriental rugs, early American documents and maps, an old oak bar, and lots of dark wood. The unpadded chairs may seem hard and uninviting, but as Roger points out, "Some people at first complain about the chairs and then sit in them for more than two hours."

And that surely tells you something about the food at the Arboreal Inn. On any night of the week you can count on steaks, three versions of white-fish, and spicy boiled shrimp or crab legs; and the price of dinner includes soup, salad, and baked po-tato or wild rice. But food fanciers have even more choices than these; the restaurant has a se-cond enticing menu of "advance notice entrees," offered as a supplement and requiring a 24-hour notice. This special menu changes, and on our last visit consisted of beef Wellington; rainbow trout en croute; rack of lamb; lamb chops Pernod; and salmon steak stuffed with spinach mousse, covered with puff pastry, and served with sauce Nantua. These entrees, not surprisingly, cost more than those on the daily menu ($16 and up). But watch the signs, too; on our visit last fall veal Marsala, breast

39

of capon with Champagne sauce, and steak au poivre were additional choices. And for really personalized food and service, call Roger--he's very accommodating. By phoning far enough in advance, you can practically customize your dinner.

Oenophiles will like the list here: more than 100 different wine offerings, most from California and France. About a fourth of these are in the lowest-priced $10 to $11 range and include red, white, and sparkling. Many more are in the $20 to $30 range, with most French vintages dating from the finest years of the late '70s and early '80s. Finally, there are a few extraordinary wines at expected prices, such as a '78 Dom Perignon, a '77 Heitz Cabernet, a couple of German gems. And topping this premier list is a 1978 Chateau Lafite-Rothschild. So, even if you don't intend to spend a lot on wine, you'll enjoy analyzing the holdings here.

A woodsy retreat with Williamsburg overtones.

ARBOREAL INN, 18191 174th Ave. (Old Grand Haven Rd), Spring Lake, MI 49456. On the west side of Spring Lake; take U.S.31 to the Van Wagoner Rd. exit (north of downtown Grand Haven), drive west ½ mile to 174th Ave., then north ¼th mile. Telephone (616) 842-3800. Hours: luncheon Monday-Friday 11 a.m.-2 p.m., dinner Monday-Saturday 5-10 p.m. Closed Sunday, most holidays. Full bar service. Credit cards: AE, Dis, MC, V.

(17) Bil-Mar Inn

What's new and nice at the Bil-Mar is the open-air deck. What's old and still good is the deep-fried cauliflower appetizer, not to mention the prime rib and whitefish almondine. What's in between is the one-pound barbequed pork chop (shades of the

Embers?), the seafood gumbo (shades of Paul Prudhomme?), and the bay scallops au gratin. More importantly, what's still endlessly appealing is the location, right smack on the beach of Lake Michigan. The only view is of lake and sand, and the water is just 50 feet or less from the windows. In fact, the Bil-Mar is one of the very few restaurants where both beautiful sunsets and major storms on the lake can be enjoyed without any distractions.

Except for that sandy setting, not much at the Bil-Mar is surprising. The decor is semiutilitarian, a bit plastic, and with a slightly dated look. And the conventional American menu is interspersed with only one or two flourishes: escargots in the evening and croissants at noon. Favorite items for lunch are fried lake perch and "melon extraordinaire" (a half melon filled with tuna salad). For dinner the Bil-Mar serves up more prime rib, whitefish, and perch than anything else, but the variety is certainly adequate: steaks, seafood, frog legs, barbequed beef ribs, and the like. Entrees come with a garlic toast and cheese basket, salad, potato or vegetable, and bread. Prices are moderate.

The restaurant has two levels, but the lower is by far the best; it has the windows and that wonderful view. In fact, any table near the window on the lower level is fine. But avoid numbers 22, 23, and 29 by the bar entrance and the tables on the upper level near the main entry. Expect some traffic congestion, not only because the Bil-Mar is popular but because it's situated on a two-lane road just a short distance from a state park. The dress code: no swimwear or bare feet.

On the beach.

THE BIL-MAR INN, 1223 S. Harbor Avenue, Grand Haven, MI 49417. One mile south of town on Lake Michigan. Telephone (616) 842-5920. Hours: 11:30 a.m.-2:30 p.m. luncheon, 5-9:30 p.m. dinner (on Friday and Saturday till 10:30). Service expanded during the summer. Closed Sunday, New Years Day, Thanksgiving, and Christmas. Full bar service. Credit cards: AE, MC, V.

Drive around downtown Grand Haven for just ten minutes, and surely one building will capture your attention: Harbourfront Place, a new-fangled shopping center located in an old-fangled factory site. It's a great hulk of a building, with light brick walls and dark red awnings and canopies. And, yes, it once housed the Story and Clark piano factory, hence the name of Tari and Penny Smith's new restaurant that opened August 1985. Much of the decor is determined by that persistent architectural presence: the bare wooden floors dating to way-back-when, ceilings that make no attempt to hide ancient pipes and beams and heating ducts, and the modernized Windsor chairs spanning both time and aesthetics for the best of two worlds.

If there's a choice of seating, we'd opt for the booths along the windows in the main dining room or any of the tables in the Atrium, a cheery porch-like structure appended to the original building. The windows here overlook not only the ho-hum parking lot but several eye-catching old buildings in Grand Haven and the historic railroad station. In warm summer weather a table in the open-air patio in front is well worth reserving.

Tari Smith, chef-owner of the Piano Factory, and his wife Penny have some clear ideas what they want for their restaurant. It's even spelled out on the menu: "Dining should be a pleasant experience and a chance to try new things and enjoy yourself." How can we quibble with that? Tari is a graduate of the Culinary Institute of America, for two years was personal chef to an army general, and is an alumni of the Thornapple Village Inn in Ada (included in this book). His tracks are covered, as far as we're concerned. But what we most appreciate is his concern for the diner. Tari wants for his place "the feel of the Thornapple Village Inn but at a price for everyone."

First, let's take a look at Chef Tari's breakfasts. Omelets are filled not only with predictable ham, cheese, bacon, and mushrooms but also with spinach, crabmeat, chutney, and almonds. He offers apple pancakes with hot cider butter sauce and a "pocket" breakfast of scrambled eggs, cheese, and vegetables on pita bread. Lunch fares as well in Tari's hands: those same omelets plus salads, burgers and other sandwiches, including a terrific number he calls "East of the Channel"--deviled crabmeat patties on an English muffin topped with melted Havarti.

But dinner at the Piano Factory is our first choice. The somewhat unstructured menu changes weekly. Certain dishes are regularly offered, as long as both the clientele and the chef are happy with the results. Last summer the menu featured New York strip steak with Burgundy butter, seafood-stuffed chicken breast, sauteed pork medallions with piquante sauce, baked whitefish, and a mixed seafood saute, among other items. But daily specials are inked in on blank lines on the menu that Tari uses for his new and changing selections, for example, baked lake trout with Bearnaise sauce, tournedos with parsleyed demiglace and white wine, chicken breast Armagnac, and veal with basil sauce. All entrees are served with the fresh vegetable of the day and boiled redskin potatoes. There's also a lounge menu in effect for grazing latecomers.

The wine list, though not long, is amazing; 30 of 35 still wines cost less than $10! And these include a Glen Ellyn white and Trakia red for less than $7. Most bottles come from the United States, including several produced in Michigan. Though there's a '74 Lafite-Rothschild, also listed are some outrageously labeled Bully Hill wines from New York with names like "Love My Goat Red," "Miss Love White," and "Fishmarket White." Still, it's quite unusual to find so many low prices, and determining the best values is an adventure for wine lovers. And if you're not fully satisfied, who really cares when the investment is so small?

Play it again, Tari!

PIANO FACTORY RESTAURANT, 41 Washington St., Grand Haven, MI 49417. Downtown, corner of Washington and Harbor Ave. Telephone (616) 846-1221. Hours: 7 a.m.-9 p.m. (till 10 p.m. Friday-Saturday). Sometimes a jazz combo plays weekends (call). Closed Christmas, New Year's Day. Full bar service. Credit cards: AE, MC, V.

Nearby attractions: Ride the Grand Haven and Spring Lake Trolley to Grand Haven State Park, known for its 2500 feet of beach frontage and its pier fishing for perch and salmon. Or cruise down the river on the Grand Haven Harbor Steamer, a sternwheel paddleboat that leaves from the City Marina. In the summer, it's worth seeing the largest musical fountain in the world, just across the river from the restaurant; water, music, and colorful lights are "choreographed" for quite a show.

⑲BAY CAFÉ

The new Bay Cafe at the Lumbertown shopping complex on Muskegon Lake might be described as "bistro, Michigan style." And if anyone knows how to do it, it's Gina and Frank Lister, the talented couple who've become western Michigan's answer to Stafford Smith and Chuck Muer. Vision, flair, know-how--not to mention love and appreciation of good food--are as much apparent in the Listers' latest enterprise as in their other two highly successful Muskegon restaurants, the Hearthstone (see, in this book) and the Brownstone. But the style here is much different, both in setting and in cuisine.

Bay Cafe comprises a cheerful outdoor deck and two of three stories in the Lumbertown building, an old converted curtain-roll factory dating to 1885. The original heavy beams, century-old brickwork, and well-worn wooden floors are enhanced by an informal decor featuring Windsor chairs, a neutral and peach color scheme, framed menus on the walls, and an open, airy look between the two floors. The same casual, light-hearted approach is taken in the kitchen. The concept is "moderately priced contemporary California and Italian cuisine," focusing on lighter cooking techniques, pastas, and vegetables. Chef Steven Browe earned his degree from the Culinary Institute of America in Hyde Park, New York, and previously worked at Cygnus in the Amway Grand Plaza Hotel in Grand Rapids (also in this book). His cooking is inventive yet not intimidating, and his presentations are picture-perfect.

The menus are in effect all day and include an extensive array of appetizers, salads, and sandwiches. Among the better choices are the cheese-filled tortas with tomatillo sauce (a layered baked tortilla dish), grilled herbed bread served in warm Gorgonzola sauce, carpaccio (marinated rare beef tenderloin with a Worcestershire-mayonnaise sauce), Mediterranean tuna salad with artichoke hearts and fennel-seed dressing, and fusilli frittata with sundried tomatoes (an Italian omelet with salami). Prices for these start at $2.95 and top off at $7.95 (for the snow crab and shrimp salad).

Pastas include fettuccine tossed in dilled cream sauce paired with veal meatballs, cannelloni crepes with Italian sausage, and linguine with Creole shrimp. The catalogue of entrees features a classic veal saltimbocca, an irreproachable sauteed breast of chicken with Fontina cheese and mushrooms, top-quality barbequed baby back ribs, medallions of pork loin with apricot brandy cream sauce, and a fresh fish piccata of the day. Every entree comes with either of two house specialties: pommes frites (homemade matchstick French fries) or pasta sauteed in garlic and oil.

The wine list is small but good, consisting of three sparkling, six reds, and six whites from California, France, Spain, and Italy. Prices range from $7.50 to more than $30, with most less than $15. So you'll likely find something adequate and affordable. For example, you might enjoy one of the somewhat youthful but well-regarded '80 Nozzole Chianti Classicos for only $12.50.

Style and substance, a lakeside bistro.

BAY CAFE, 1050 W. Western Ave., Muskegon, MI 49441. At Lumbertown; take 9th St. off B.R. 31 (Seaway Dr.) 2 blocks north to Western, then west 2 blocks. Telephone (616) 728-7272. Hours: 11:30 a.m.-11:30 p.m. Monday-Thursday (till 12:30 a.m. Friday-Saturday), 11 a.m.-3 p.m. Sunday. Closed on Christmas and New Year's Day. Full bar service. Credit cards: AE, DC, MC, V.

RED SNAPPER WITH AVOCADO LIME BUTTER
From the Bay Cafe

In a noncorrosive saucepan, cook 4 ounces sauterne wine, 2 ounces Rose's lime juice, 2 medium peeled and minced shallots, 1 bay leaf, 1 tablespoon chopped fresh tarragon, and a pinch chopped fresh thyme over high heat until reduced, so that only about 2 ounces of liquid remains. Pour into mixer or food processor. Add 1 ripe peeled and diced avocado, and process till blended. Add 1 pound softened unsalted butter in small pieces, 1 teaspoon cracked black pepper, and salt to taste. Blend thoroughly. Dice 1 ounce each of red, green, and yellow bell peppers. Fold into butter mixture by hand. Roll in parchment paper (about 1-1½ inches diameter) and freeze until ready for use.

Season any firm-fleshed fish (red snapper, grouper,

swordfish) with salt and pepper and coat with vegetable oil. Grill over hot coals (or broil) until center is just opaque. Just before serving, slice 2-3 thin medallions of the frozen avocado butter, and place on fish. Put under broiler just until butter begins to melt. Transfer to serving plates. At the Bay Cafe this is served with seasonal vegetables and boiled redskin potatoes or garlicky peppered linguine with chopped herbs.

⑳ the hearthstone
food • spirits

We are only two among the throngs who are glad that Gina and Frank Lister turned from careers in psychotherapy to the culinary. There's a world of difference between shrinking heads and distending tummies. As a result, Muskegon boasts one of the very best soup and sandwich restaurants in the country. It's easy to drive past the place since the Hearthstone is half-hidden in a motel at a busy intersection. But don't miss it, even if you need to do a bit of hunting. And don't let the plain exterior mislead you. It doesn't reflect the convivial atmosphere inside.

The barroom is cozy and warm with flocked Victorian wallpaper, a number of black booths, and a few less comfortable center-room tables. Larger groups should reserve the circular seating area referred to as the Fireplace; it is indeed built around a gas fireplace and accommodates up to 12 diners. Two other dining rooms have the same comfortable though dated decor.

The menu, beautifully hand lettered by Gina Lister, offers a dozen substantial sandwiches (plus frankfurters), seven refreshing renditions of traditional salads, an innovative "sandwich of the week," an always extraordinary soup (or soups) of the day, several appealing appetizers, and a number of pastas. The breads are specially made for the restaurant in Grand Rapids. Of the sandwiches, we recommend the Hearthstone (corned beef, ham, onion, and melted Swiss cheese) or the sandwich of the week, alternating between various "exotic and unlikely combinations of smoked ham, roast beef, turkey breast, salami, relishes, fresh vegetables, and garnishes." All sandwiches are gratifyingly available in half portions or partnered with soup, a duo well worth ordering.

Appetizers include carpaccio (a northern Italian treat of thinly sliced rare beef drizzled with herbed olive oil), steamed shrimp with mango chutney sauce, chilled shrimp with "aioli" (the French Provencale garlic mayonnaise), a cheese and fruit assortment, and an expertly prepared pate or terrine of the day. All the pastas are great; we especially enjoy the linguine with pesto and walnuts (and other good things). You really will have some trouble choosing only one or two items from the mouth-watering menu. To make it even more difficult, the Hearthstone offers such monthly specials as fusilli pasta with artichoke-cream sauce, duck and pistachio pate, rotelle with Italian sausage and sun-dried tomatoes, as well as specialty drinks and desserts. This is a place where you might like to share several dishes.

But the soups are what most fill us with admiration. More than 90 different ones have been served at the Hearthstone over the years. They're always freshly and carefully made and range from the conventional to the remarkable--for example, beef barley, consomme with crepes, American cheese and beer, mulligatawny, and Kentucky burgoo. All receive the meticulous attention and TLC of the Listers. If you're not sure you'll like them, ask your waitress for samples (a wonderful custom here that we highly appreciate).

The Listers have opened a near-clone of the Hearthstone at the Muskegon County Airport, called the Brownstone. Your first choice should be the Hearthstone, but some locals tell us they head for the airport when the Hearthstone is too busy to give them quick service. Also new is a third Lister operation, the Bay Cafe, a very different kind of restaurant in an interesting location (see our review).

Michigan's best for soups and sandwiches.

THE HEARTHSTONE, 3350 Glade St., Muskegon, MI 49444. In the Cornerhouse Motor Inn, 3 miles east of town on B.R.96, across the highway from the Meijer Thrifty Acres complex. Telephone (616) 733-1056. Hours: 11 a.m.-2 a.m., Sunday 5 p.m.- midnight. Closed holidays. Full bar service. Takes all major credit cards.

DANISH HAVARTI CHEESE SOUP
WITH FRESH DILL AND POTATOES
From Gina Lister, the Hearthstone

In a small saucepan cook 2 medium potatoes (diced $\frac{1}{4}$-$\frac{1}{2}$ inch) until tender; drain and set aside. In a $2\frac{1}{2}$-3-quart Dutch oven add 1 cup water, $1\frac{1}{2}$ tablespoons dry granulated chicken base, 3 cups milk, and 2 cups heavy cream. Bring to boiling point but do not let boil. Meanwhile, in a small pan melt 3 tablespoons butter, and saute $\frac{1}{2}$ cup very finely chopped onions and $\frac{1}{4}$ cup finely chopped celery until very soft and tender (about 5-7 minutes). When soft, add 3 tablespoons flour and stir until it is absorbed. Cook the roux 1-$1\frac{1}{2}$ minutes, making certain not to let flour brown. Turn off heat and set aside.
In the stock pot with very hot milk, add 2 tablespoons minced fresh dill, $\frac{1}{2}$ teaspoon white pepper and $\frac{1}{2}$ pound Havarti cheese (cut into small cubes). Stir until cheese is completely melted and absorbed. Add the vegetable roux and cook until thickened, stirring fairly constantly (about 8-10 minutes). Remove soup from heat and puree in blender until smooth. Add cooked potatoes, and garnish with tiny homemade buttered croutons. Serves 6-8.

㉑ Mike's Kro

"Wholesome," "fresh," "homey"--all those good words about food that bring back childhood memories--all those words and many more apply to Mike's Kro ("Kro" is Danish for "restaurant" or "inn"). This is a dear little place, and that's something we wouldn't dare say about, for instance, the London Chop House. Mike's Kro is the one and only cafeteria we've included in this book. We don't as a rule like cafeterias or salad bars or any other do-it-yourself activity in a restaurant. If we feel like serving ourselves, there's always home. But we understand the economics of it. This is a favorite of senior citizens and families with small children. The prices are exceptionally reasonable, and the choice of food unintimidating.

With its colorful painted wood trim and peaked chalet roofline, the restaurant stands out in this quiet residential neighborhood of Muskegon. The bi-level dining room, decorated with Danish coats of arms and quaint wooden chandeliers, is immaculate. The menu changes twice daily for lunch and dinner; just check the chalkboard above the cafeteria line.

A typical selection is pasty, roast sirloin, karbo-nader (pork patties), Swedish meatballs, pork and/or beef barbeque, tuna-noodle casserole, baked scrod plus two or more soups, salads, rolls and muffins, and desserts. Tuesday evening is "Dutch night," and the special treat might be roast pork with potatoes, kale, and rutabagas--good earthy fare. Thursday's "Swedish night" might feature meatballs and rice pudding. Pasties are Mike's specialty, always on the menu and served plain or with gravy. The prices of most entrees are (gasp!) less than $3, which puts Mike's Kro on our list of the greatest bargains in Michigan.

In Muskegon our first choices for dining out are the perennially popular Hearthstone for super soups, sandwiches, and pasta; the new Bay Cafe at Lumbertown for upscale meals in an interesting setting; and Mike's Kro for the budget-minded. But there are two more possibilities to consider if you'll be in the area for a time: Dah Hu on Whitehall Rd., which specializes in Mandarin, Hunan, and Szechuan cuisine from China, and the Bear Lake Inn, an old-time favorite for hamburgers and fish fries at 360 Ruddiman Dr. in North Muskegon.

As for Mike's, high marks for Low Country treats, a bargain.

MIKE'S KRO, 1384 W. Laketon Ave. Muskegon, MI 49441. West on Laketon Ave. off U.S.31. Telephone (616) 755-4800. Hours: 11 a.m.-2:30 p.m., dinner 5-8 p.m., coffee and rolls 8 a.m.-8 p.m. Closed on Sunday. No alcoholic beverages. No credit cards.

DUTCH "SOEPEN BREI"
From Mike Hekkema, Mike's Kro

Cook 2 pounds pearl barley in 6 quarts water with 2 scant tablespoons salt about 1½ hours over low heat until most of the water is absorbed. Cool about 1 hour. Add 2 gallons buttermilk and bring back to the boiling point, stirring constantly. Traditionally served with brown sugar on the side.
Our hint: Obviously this will feed more people than you normally serve. For 4-6 servings substitute ¼ pound barley cooked in 3 cups water with 3/4 teaspoon salt; add 1 quart buttermilk to finish.

CROSSWINDS

(22)

Crosswinds was just getting under way when we first sighted her, and she barely held her course during some stormy weather since then. But we're pleased to report that she's finally found good sailing and a safe harbor under the ownership of Mimi and Otto Bouc. This is another of those admirable family operations: Otto, an orthopaedic surgeon, is rarely on the scene since he's usually off doing what orthopaedic surgeons do. Mimi, however, is on hand as manager, their son runs the marina next door, and their daughter keeps the books.

Whitehall was once a shipping area for a thriving lumber industry, and three freighters plying their trade here were called the Northwinds, the Southwinds, and the Crosswinds--hence the restaurant's name. For leisurely dining at the water's edge, Crosswinds has few rivals. Sailing boats and motor launches from many Great Lakes harbors tie up on the 100 yards of dock that flank the building on three sides. Of course, the best tables are by the windows, which wisely have been left unadorned. But in the summer you can also dine on the deck amid the pilings and have an unobstructed view of the water and vessels. And, as Mimi points out, "The sunsets alone are worth the trip" to Crosswinds. This is one of the few restaurants in Michigan where boaters can reserve a dock berth along with a table for dinner. And for the occasional boater and salmon fisherman, charter fishing boats are available here all summer.

Mimi has geared the menu toward stir-fries and the trendy Cajun/Creole cuisine that has taken the country by storm since Paul Prudhomme came up north to publicize his cookbook. Urbanites might yawn, but for this part of Michigan, Cajun is new. And it's packin' em in. Deservedly popular entrees are the Creole shrimp, Cajun blackened swordfish, and a beef and broccoli stir fry. Other "blackened" things are on the menu as are several standard main courses for the less venturesome. The appetizers are beguiling; we especially like the hot Cajun shrimp and the sausage-stuffed mushrooms. Another enticing choice is the confetti salad, Crosswinds' cold version of pasta primaverda. Prices are moderate. And if the trends move away from Cajun? Well, Mimi is prepared. "We're keeping a good pulse on what is going on elsewhere," says the former Chicagoan.

Nautically nice, on top of the trends.

CROSSWINDS OF WHITE LAKE, 302 S. Lake St., Whitehall, MI 49461. North of Muskegon, west of U.S.31; in Whitehall take B.R.31, turn south at the Mears Ave. stoplight, drive 2 blocks and turn west on Slocum one block. Telephone (616) 893-4655. Open for lunch and dinner; possibly closed in January (call to confirm this). Full bar service. Credit cards: DC, MC, V.

Nearby attractions: Visit the White River Light Station Museum, a lighthouse constructed in 1875 that now houses a collection of nautical artifacts. A climb to the top affords a glimpse of Lake Michigan's sand dunes stretching along the coastline. (Take U.S.31 to the White Lake Drive exit, turn right and drive to South Shore Drive; turn left on Murray Rd. and follow signs to the end.) Also on the shore of White Lake is the world's largest weathervane (48 feet tall, weighing 4300 pounds). It stands near the bridge joining Montague and Whitehall.

STUFFED PORK CHOPS CALVADOS
From Crosswinds of White Lake

For the stuffing, saute 2 pared and diced apples in 1-2 ounces butter. Add ¼ cup raisins and 2 ounces Calvados (or other apple brandy). Allow to cool. Pound 2 boned, butterflied pork chops (8 ounces each) until flat. Stuff with apple mixture, salt and pepper lightly, and fold over; pound edges to seal in the filling. Have three shallow bowls filled with flour, slightly beaten egg, and dry bread crumbs. Dip chops first into flour, then egg, then crumbs. Heat 3 tablespoons butter in saute pan, and pan fry the chops until brown on both sides. Place in a preheated 350-degree oven to finish cooking, about 10 minutes. Meanwhile, make walnut sauce. Saute 2 tablespoons chopped walnuts in 1 ounce butter. Add 1 cup heavy cream (whipping) and boil fast until reduced by half or to desired thickness. Salt and pepper to taste. Arrange chops on plates, scoop remaining apple mixture on pork. Pour the walnut sauce over. Makes 2 servings.

(23)

Here's a place that tugs on the heartstrings. It all comes back--your very first experience with ice cream. Ours, and it tells you how ancient and doddering we are, was the wonderful Tom-Thumb-sized sugar cone with orange ice cream (not sherbet) that cost three cents (!!!). Pekadill's costs much more, but it's a heckofalot bigger and a hundred times better. In Whitehall you don't have to settle for an ordinary or even a sugar cone; here you can order a homemade cone baked "fresh from scratch," and is it good? Filled with praline pecan ice cream, it is merely fantastic. Crisp and crunchy, it also takes some ingenuity to eat, but it's well worth every bit of spillage.

Just a few blocks off the main street of Whitehall, Pekadill's is a charming old house in a tree-lined residential area. Spiffily painted white with red trim, it has an outdoor terrace that beckons invitingly on warm summer days. The decor inside, too, is perfect for the concept of old-fashioned ice cream parlor: black and white tile on the floor, red tables and black wire chairs, white walls with red accents, and a few old signs and plants to soften the effect.

Though it's hard for ice cream freaks to keep in mind, all is not ice cream at Pekadill's. The little dining room also serves lunch. Owners Pete and Kathy Wessel have put together a nice menu of homemade soups, deli and combination sandwiches, and croissant sandwiches as well as a couple of salads and hot dogs. Most popular is the chicken salad on croissant, but you can't miss with any item.

54

To finish (and you really must finish here), the homemade cones, as already noted, are superb. The ice cream comes from Hudsonville, south of here, and aside from the praline pecan there are 31 other flavors, including the ultra-popular strawberry cheesecake and mint chocolate chip. Sundaes, sodas, and shakes are also available. If you enjoy delicious icy treats and nostalgic surroundings, you must visit this delightful old house in Whitehall.

Cold pleasures, warm atmosphere.

PEKADILL'S ICE CREAM AND SANDWICH SHOP, 503 S. Mears Ave., Whitehall, MI 49461. In downtown Whitehall, 5 blocks south of B.R.31. Telephone (616) 894-9551. Hours: 12 noon-5 p.m., year round. Second location at Lumbertown, 1050 W. Western Ave., Muskegon; telephone 616) 726-4625. No alcoholic beverages, credit cards, or reservations.

(24)

"IN KEEPING WITH A 100 YEAR TRADITION"

Clifford Lake Hotel

We might never have heard of Clifford Lake Hotel were it not for a chance meeting in Lansing with the owners, Dyanne and Norm Eipper, and a conversation about cooking: they wanted a recipe for noodles Alfredo, and we needed a new way to cook wild duck. So we exchanged recipes to our mutual satisfaction. And, of course, when the opportunity arose, we visited Stanton. What we found was a picture-postcard canary yellow inn with MSU green shutters, as pretty a bed and breakfast place as any we'd visited in England or Scotland.

The hotel in the village of what was once "Richard's Point" was in business in 1881, a year that seemed promising in the area. A U.S. post office was established, a horse-drawn bus line was put into service between Clifford Lake and Stanton, and a steamboat was launched on the lake. A news article a year later claimed, "Clifford...will eventually beat the world in progress." But it didn't happen, and today the hotel is the sole survivor of those eventful times. It's been in continuous operation ever since.

Designated an official historic site by the Michigan Historical Commission in 1983, the Clifford Lake Hotel is not only an inn (six quaint rooms, including four singles with shared bath plus a suite with cable TV and private bath) but a resort with three lovely lakefront cottages and a year-round restaurant offering a variety of "good American dishes." The rooms have neither television nor telephones, and as the manager points out, "There's nothing to do in Montcalm County." So, if you're looking for peace and solitude, here's the place to start.

On the luncheon menu are the favorite Clifford Char-burgers with olive sauce, sauteed mushrooms, lettuce, tomatoes, and melted cheese as well as other sandwiches and salads. It's a small but good menu; we like the turkey deluxe and fresh homemade croissant sandwiches and, when we're hungrier, the barbequed chicken breast and baked fish. Soups are inventive; try the BLT or Italian sausage. The dinner menu is more elaborate but not overly adventurous. Steaks, seafood, and prime rib are the rule. The exceptions are the chicken Cordon Bleu, London broil, and seafood sampler (everything baked or sauteed instead of the more common deep-fried selection). Daily specials are always worth considering. Sunday brunch is a winner, too--lots of entrees and a huge fruit tray, all for $6.95.

Four dining rooms serve the public: the Chart Room, warm and somewhat rustic with a cozy fireplace; the Porch, overlooking the lake with a crisp green and white color scheme; the main dining room, set back a bit with a small salad bar; and the adjoining Pantry. The latter two rooms are decorated in American country style with patchwork-printed table linens and shutters at the windows. Before or after your meal, browse in the Root Cellar, the hotel's well-planned gift shop. And stroll around the grounds or walk the beach. Better yet, take a ride on the Clifford Lake Clipper, a 22-passenger paddlewheel in operation Memorial Day-Labor Day (no fee, by donation).

A historic and country-casual setting.

CLIFFORD LAKE HOTEL, 561 Clifford Lake Dr., Stanton, MI 48888. Five miles west of Stanton (follow the signs). Telephone (517) 831-5151. Hours: in summer 11 a.m.-10 p.m. Monday-Thursday (till 11 p.m. (Friday-Saturday), 11 a.m.-9 p.m. Sunday; from Labor Day to Memorial Day 11 a.m.-9 p.m. Monday-Thursday (till 10 p.m. Friday-Saturday), 11 a.m.-7 p.m.; year round Sunday brunch 11 a.m.-3 p.m. Full bar service. Credit cards: AE, MC, V. As the hotel puts it, "Clifford Lake is just 45 minutes from Grand Rapids, 1 hour from Lansing, 2 hours from Detroit, 4 hours from Chicago."

WILD DUCK WITH ORANGE-RED WINE SAUCE
From the Clifford Lake Hotel

Skin 3 wild ducks, and remove the boned-out breasts. Dredge breasts with flour, and brown in 2-3 tablespoons butter or margarine (reserve the rest of the duck for soup or another use). Remove breasts and set aside. Add 1 cup coarsely chopped onion and 1 large clove minced garlic to skillet; brown. Remove from heat. Return duck breasts, salt and pepper to taste. Add 1 cup orange juice (preferably fresh), 1 cup dry red wine, 1 bay leaf, and $\frac{1}{4}$ teaspoon thyme. Cover and place in 275-degree oven, and bake for 4-6 hours OR cook in pressure cooker 50-60 minutes. Gravy may be strained or not, but do remove the bay leaf. Thicken, if desired, with a mixture of cornstarch and cold water (about 1 tablespoon of each or more depending on desired consistency). Six servings.

(25) **WINTER INN** RESTAURANT BAR ◄ HOTEL
A STATE AND NATIONAL HISTORIC SITE

How could we resist visiting a place with a name so similar to our own? The moment we saw the three-story brick building with numerous fluttering rust-colored awnings, we had a hunch it would be a winner. And we weren't disappointed. Unlike many restaurants in larger cities and busy tourist areas, the Winter Inn hasn't yet succumbed to yuppie food trendiness. Nary a stir-fry or pasta or Cajun concoction in sight. A basic dinner menu of steaks, pork chops, broiled chicken, and seafood is embellished, however, with a few more diverting possibilities: for example, sauteed veal with Madeira sauce and mushrooms, chicken breast stuffed with julienned carrots and celery and topped with Dijon mustard sauce, and broiled marinated pork tenderloin with rice pilaf. The fish and seafood selections are worth serious thought. Most popular are the pan-fried walleyed pike and the seafood au gratin, a combination of shrimp, scallops, and lobster baked in a wine and cheese sauce. We also like the fact that customers may choose to have their seafood deep-fried, baked, or sauteed. A daily featured entree is also available, such as chicken Cordon Bleu or spinach-stuffed sole. Prices, considering the quality of food and service and the generous accompaniments offered with main courses, are very reasonable. Only two entrees, both steaks, cost more than $11. Most regular patrons make room for dessert; the hot fudge sundae pie is becoming famous in Montcalm County, and almost as irresistible is the frozen tartufi, a rich confection of dark chocolate with cherries and almonds.

Since 1850 there's always been a hotel on this

corner in Greenville. The present Winter Inn was built between 1900 and 1902 by Thomas B. Winter, a prominent local citizen and county political figure. In its early days it maintained its own stagecoach to transport guests from the railroad station three blocks away. Restoration began under new owners John and Linda Stafford, and shortly thereafter the inn was designated as an official historic site by both the Michigan Historical Commission and the National Register of Historic Places. In 1984 the Winter Inn was purchased by the Everin brothers, with the goal of maintaining the warmth and appeal of Greenville's landmark building. It really is an inn, too, with 15 redecorated and refurnished rooms.

The focal points in the front dining room are the large windows capped with stained-glass insets and softened by lacy white cafe curtains. Also distinctive are the peach and bottle green color scheme and the waist-high drapery dividers on brass stanchions that separate a number of tables from traffic zones. Beyond this area is a second dining room with the same Victorian decor and boasting an impressive hand-carved antique fireplace. The table for eight in one corner is particularly desirable.

In the summer you can lunch or dine at umbrella tables in the nicely landscaped, brick-paved courtyard. And for cocktails we suggest that you visit the lounge. The solid oak floor, tin ceiling, shutters on the green walls all suggest a casual turn-of-the-century gentlemen's drinking establishment. The oak and mahogany bar, complete with brass footrail, was manufactured in the mid-1800s. And the three booths, each seating two people, are especially conducive to conversation. The Winter Inn prides itself on its "home away from home feeling," and we think you'll agree that the place has an easy, relaxed charm.

Traditional fare in a traditional setting.

THE WINTER INN, 100 N. Lafayette Street, Greenville, MI 48838. In the business center. Telephone (616) 754-7108. Hours: luncheon 11:30 a.m.-2 p.m. Monday-Friday, dinner 5:30-9 p.m. Monday-Thursday (till 10 p.m. Friday-Saturday). Closed Sunday and major holidays. Full bar service. There's entertainment (pianist or duo) in the lounge Friday and Saturday evenings. Credit cards: AE, DC, MC, V.

STUFFED MUSHROOMS SUPREME
From Robert King, the Winter Inn

This is an easy and tasty appetizer; if you're not concerned about browning, you can cook these in the microwave oven. Drain clams from a 4-ounce can minced clams, and reserve the liquid. Combine clams with 8 ounces softened cream cheese in a small mixing bowl. Add 1 teaspoon Lawry's seasoning salt. Stir until blended. Add a small amount of clam juice, enough to make the mixture smooth and workable.

Clean 24 medium to large mushroom caps. Remove stems with a twisting motion and reserve for another use. Brush caps inside and out with vegetable oil. Using a pastry bag fitted with a plain or star tip, fill mushroom caps with the clam mixture. Sprinkle with dill weed. Place stuffed mushroom caps on a rimmed baking sheet, and bake in a preheated 350-degree oven until slightly browned, about 10 minutes. Serves 4-6, depending on the size of the mushrooms, as a first course.

By The
River In Rockford
Restaurant
Bakery
Country Store
Gift Shop

The restoration of a grain mill (some historians say a bean warehouse), ravaged by fire in the late

1960s and renovated in 1970, was the first step in a proliferation of shops and studios known as Squires Street in the century-old village of Rockford. The Old Mill, a bakery and coffee shop, is one of three such restaurants owned by Arnie Fahlen, a graduate of a Swiss pastry school. His places have been winners of West Michigan magazine's readers' choice survey in three categories: best inexpensive eating place, best breakfast, and best desserts.

The Old Mill has a country kitchen atmosphere with a bare wooden floor, early American furniture, and a full measure of bric-a-brac on the walls. It's generally bustling--patrons have come here from every state in the Union and from dozens of foreign countries (check the guestbook). It becomes over-crowded at times, but that's part of the fun. Sociability is thrust upon you. There are two dining areas downstairs, one adjoining the kitchen and bakery and the other in the porch, as well as tables upstairs where you can escape the crowds if you wish. We prefer to stay downstairs with the tourists, watch the cooks at work, and smell the baking bread.

The Old Mill has a very limited menu, printed on a baker's bag. There are five options for breakfast, and at lunchtime until closing you have a choice of a few sandwiches and salads, followed by dessert, notably seasonal fresh fruit pie or the Old Mill's specialty, mile-high lemon meringue pie. The French dip roast beef sandwich is most popular, and we also like the Scandinavian Shuffle (thin grilled bread wrapped around ham or beef or turkey with Danish cheese) and the turkey and cheese with mushrooms. Sandwiches may be ordered in two sizes, worth considering if the pie tempts you. The soups vary; try the chicken corn chowder. On a warm, pleasant day you might prefer to buy carry-out sandwiches from the Old Mill and picnic beside the picturesque Rogue River dam. The Rogue, by the way, was intended to be named "Rouge," but the surveyor misspelled it on the first map and in 1983 his error was finally made official.

We like the Old Mill for its easy charm and as

a resting place while browsing in the interesting little shops on Squires Street, many of them antique or craft oriented: a toy train museum, clocksmith, apple and cider shop, rug hooking studio, hand-blown glass emporium, and others. Two yearly events in the village are a start-of-summer celebration in June and the October cider festival.

Historic Michigan recaptured.

THE OLD MILL, 31 Squires St., Rockford, MI 49341. About 10 miles north of Grand Rapids; 1 block west of Main St., near railroad. Telephone (616) 866-4306. Hours: breakfast 7-10:30 a.m., luncheon and snacks 11 a.m.-8 p.m. Closed Sunday and holidays. From the end of October to June 1, closed at 4:30 p.m. No alcoholic beverages. No credit cards or reservations accepted.

Nearby attractions: Just north on Main St. is the Rockford Factory Outlet Mall with the biggest draws Evan-Picone and Hush Puppies. Canoe trips and tube floats on the Rogue River can be arranged (call 86-9264). About 10 miles of Rockford is Cedar Springs, where you can tour the Red Flannel Factory, manufacturers of old-fashioned granny gowns and "drop seaters" (long johns).

How do we like Charley's Crab? Let us count the ways. We like the modern, spacious building, perched right over the Grand River and decorated as a tribute to Grand Rapids' industry with old photos and names of local companies in bas relief on the walls (Amway, Meijer, and many more). We like the high domed ceiling, the snappy brass rails and tile in the lounge (along with complimentary snacks), the white marble bar, and the upscale nautical-industrial decor, most suitable to Michigan's second-largest city. We like the view of the river from almost every seat. And if we break bread at Charley's before 6 in the evening, we like it even better when the check comes.

Charley, as surely most Michiganians know, is Chuck Muer, the enterprising fellow who brought us the Gandy Dancer, the River Crab (both included in this book), and a number of other places known for their visual effects and seafood specialties. The bill of fare changes daily and boasts at least a dozen different fresh fish--grilled, broiled, pan-fried, simmered, and "blackened." In addition to these are such featured main courses as bluefish en papillote, Charley's Bucket with all the Down East clambake fixin's, paella, scallops primavera, and a fairly recent and welcome addition to the Muer menus, fresh pasta. A few token beef and chicken entrees make an appearance, but clearly the emphasis is on the briny deep. Prices are moderate to expensive, and you get a lot for your money.

Bargain seekers might want to take advantage of the early dinner, served daily except Saturday. A more limited menu is in effect, but it's one that also consists of good fresh fish and about seven or eight other carefully chosen entrees. Dinners cost $8.95 to $10.50 (for the New York strip) and generously include Charley's Chowder, salad, bread, potato, vegetable, dessert, and beverage. For grazers, the lounge at Charley's Crab has a raw bar and its own menu of outstanding appetizers and snacks: stuffed clams, oysters Florentine, baked Brie amandine, mussels Dijon, and more. On Friday and Saturday evening there's a pianist, and during Sunday brunch a jazz trio. In the summer the Riverside Terrace offers outdoor dining and cocktails. Charley's received, we think deservedly, Grand Rapids Magazine's 1986 Award of Excellence as one of the city's top ten restaurants.

Great setting, great seafood.

CHARLEY'S CRAB, 63 Market St., S.W., Grand

Rapids, MI 49503. Downtown, on the river. Telephone (616) 459-2500. Hours: luncheon 11:30 a.m.-2 p.m., dinner 4:30-10 p.m. (till 11 p.m. Friday-Saturday), Sunday brunch 10 a.m.-2 p.m. The early dinner runs 4:30 to 6 p.m. Monday-Friday, 4:30-9 p.m. Sunday. Full bar service. Valet parking at the door if you wish, or park it yourself in the lot. All major credit cards.

Amway's multimillion-dollar renovation of the old Pantlind Hotel in Grand Rapids opened to great eclat in 1982. A year later, a sparkling new 2-story tower joined it to make this complex the most impressive hotel and convention center in western Michigan. And perched high atop this glass column is Cygnus, a restaurant at first promoted as a quantum leap into all the most luxurious and sybaritic pleasures of the table. In its earliest days food writers and gourmands excitedly converged on the celebrated new eatery, and so did visiting businessmen and somewhat wary city residents. But the reviews were mixed, and according to Al Mandar, then food and beverage manager of the Amway Grand Plaza, guests complained about the lack of beef on the menu. "They didn't understand or appreciate breast of partridge baked in clay, Alsatian style." The community, too, more and more favored Cygnus's less pretentious and less expensive sister restaurant, the 1913 Room on the hotel's ground floor.

So, after more than a year of stumbling over Midwest tastes and expectations, Cygnus is finally finding itself and standing tall. In 1987 it was named the best restaurant in the expensive category (along with the 1913 Room) by readers of West

Michigan magazine; it was also cited as best for view (of the city and Grand River), for atmosphere, and for romantic dinners. The menu, less esoteric than it once was, now includes prime rib roast, rack of lamb in pine nut crust, New York sirloin steak, smoked breast of chicken, seafood medley with mustard sauce, and a special entree and seafood of the day. An excellent Caesar salad is prepared tableside, and the highly acclaimed gin and tomato soup continues to live up to its reputation. Appetizers are more conventional than not, but perfectly prepared. (Try the sweetbreads and mushrooms in puff pastry or the tartare of smoked northern Michigan salmon.) An exceptional finale is the quenelle of chocolate mousse with vanilla and Port sauces. Or for some drama, order one of the flambeed desserts such as strawberries in Grand Marnier. Cygnus offers a good selection of wines, with prices skewed toward the middle and upper range. For example, from France you can get a '79 Gruard Larose, '79 Duhart Milon, '81 Eschezeaux, or '82 Vosne Romanee at the $25-$35 level. There are also American and German offerings, as well as several dessert wines, including the magnificent '71 Chateau d'Yquem, the queen of the list.

A talented team of culinary experts is attached to the Amway Grand Plaza. Daniel Hugelier, formerly with the Detroit Athletic Club and Win Schuler's, is Executive Chef; Paul Vining is the newly appointed Cygnus chef; and in charge of the hotel's breads, pastries, sorbets, cakes, and other sweet endings is Gilles Renusson, a member of Michigan's Culinary Olympic Team, which will travel to Frankfurt, West Germany, in 1988.

Like the Trillium outside Traverse City (see in this book), Cygnus offers not just a meal, but an experience. The room with mostly glass walls and ceiling is a visual delight. Plush claret-hued velvet chairs and tables with matching linens surround a pink marble dance floor, a midroom oasis accented by stylized white palm trees formed from papiermache and linen. Tables are set with dark red and silver service plates, Romanian crystal, and napkins folded like swans, a reference to the restaurant's namesake, Cygnus, the swan-shaped constellation that on the right clear nights may be seen overhead here. Up a flight of stairs on a higher level overlooking the dining room is the lounge, with the same stunning Art Deco decor: mirrored tables, attractive beveled-glass chandeliers, Walter de Roon prints, and potted "plants" and "flowers" fashioned from mother of pearl. Consider having hors d'oeuvre or dessert and capuccino here.

A grand setting on the Grand.

CYGNUS, Amway Grand Plaza Hotel, Pearl at Monroe, Grand Rapids, MI 49503-2666. Downtown. Telephone (616) 776-6425. Hours: dinner 5:30-11 p.m. Tuesday-Saturday. Closed Sunday, Monday. Full bar service. Complimentary valet parking. All major credit cards. Coats and ties required for men.

ROAST LOIN OF LAMB WYOMING
From Chef Daniel Hugelier, Amway Grand Plaza

This recipe was prepared by the Culinary Olympic Team at Frankfurt in 1984 and won a Gold Medal. It's been featured in Cygnus and for special occasions at the hotel.

Bone 2 double loins of lamb. Reserve loins, tenderloins, and all lean cap meat and trim meat. Reserve bones for sauce. Dice all trimmed meat (about 18 ounces) and 6 ounces fresh pork fat. Chill, and puree together in food processor until smooth. Add 4 egg whites, one at a time, processing till blended. Saute 2 ounces shredded carrots, 1 minced shallot, and 2 cloves minced garlic. Then add 3 ounces spinach (minced), 1 bunch minced scallions, $\frac{1}{4}$ cup minced parsley, 1 ounce pine nuts, 2 tablespoons duxelle mushrooms, 1 tablespoon salt, $\frac{1}{2}$ teaspoon black pepper, $\frac{1}{2}$ teaspoon coriander, $\frac{1}{4}$ teaspoon rubbed thyme. Saute until liquid evaporates. Chill in freezer. Add to processed forcemeat and just blend. (Note: save all vegetable scraps for sauce.)

Place tenderloin on top of each loin. Divide forcemeat in 4 and pack tightly around lamb. Wrap in 8 ounces caul fat, salt and pepper, and roast 20 minutes at 375 degrees. Let rest 5 minutes before slicing. For sauce, roast reserved bones with vegetable scraps until well browned. Add 1 tablespoon minced fresh ginger, 1 large minced clove garlic, 3 cups red wine, and 3 cups Espagnol sauce. Cook 30 minutes. Strain and finish with butter (swirl in tiny pieces off heat, 3 or more tablespoons).

Our hints: Recipes for duxelles and Espagnol sauce may be found in most good cookbooks, for example, Julia Child's French-cooking volumes. Makes 12 servings.

(29) Gibson's

Built about 1873, Paddock Place, named after its first owner, over the years became the home of several families who were instrumental in the development and growth of Grand Rapids. In 1944 it was sold to the Order of Franciscans and became known as St. Bernardine's Friary. The Italianate structure, with a low-keyed gray exterior embellished with deep burgundy awnings and accents, is situated amid mature trees and spacious lawns and surrounded by a high wrought-iron fence. Set off as it is in both time and space from the unimpressive buildings nearby, it really does capture the imagination. And its newest name, Gibson's, after the Gay Nineties illustrator, suits it perfectly.

In the main dining area are three rooms: the Clark Room near the entrance, the even prettier Wurzberg Room with subtle floral wallpaper and a lovely carved fireplace, and the more casual Porch.

The first two rooms, named after former owners
of the estate and furnished with period mahogany
and cherrywood, are decorated with crystal chandeliers, elaborate window treatments, and a changing
gallery of museum-quality paintings (for sale from
art dealer Stan Gohl on the second floor of Gibson's). We like the tables for two at the windows
in the Clark Room, though one table near the
service area and entrance to the Porch should be
avoided. And there's a wonderful table for eight
by the bay window in the Wurzberg Room.

In spite of this splendor, there's no pretentious-
ness or stilted ceremony here. Service is friendly
and efficient. Barbara Pugh, our young and enthusiastic waitress, couldn't have done a better job of
making us comfortable. Such hospitality along with
the fine Continental cuisine were surely deciding
factors in Grand Rapids Magazine's designation of
Gibson's as one of the city's top ten restaurants
in 1986. James Powell, the chef and an owner,
apprenticed at the Thornapple Village Inn and later
went to the 1913 Room at the Amway Grand Plaza
Hotel. You'll find that he's an exceedingly creative
cook.

Menu items that sound traditional, even banal,
are metamorphosed by a touch from Chef Powell's
magic wand. Escargots bourguignonne, for instance,
are baked in zucchini cups and served with herb
toast, and the tournedos are finished with cream
and Irish Mist. And though current food trends are
given a respectful nod, the cooking here is grounded
in solid classical technique. For proof of that, you
need only try the onion soup, Caesar salad, filet
mignon with Parisienne potatoes, or rack of lamb.
Menus change seasonally; prices are moderate to
expensive.

Luncheons are less costly, trendier, and just
as imaginative. "We try to stay on top of whatever is new nationally," according to Chef
Powell. You'll be tempted by the likes of mesquite-
grilled chicken Dijonaise, pork tenderloin with plum
sauce, California sushi roll, and orange roughy

Bangkok style. More traditional are the salads and sandwiches, including a BLT to end all BLTs: a third pound of bacon on toasted sourdough with potted mushrooms and artichoke hearts. Prices are $3.75 and up. Some great soups and snacks start at $2.75. Another alternative is to lunch or dine in the adjacent Grapevine, a barroom and lounge featuring live entertainment, a more casual atmosphere, and a lighter menu.

Modest house wine is available by both glass and liter at reasonable prices. The wine list is of much higher quality and interest, with about 150 offerings, many at less than $20 but also including a number of premier wines from Bordeaux. The selection from Germany (18) is relatively good for a Michigan restaurant, and California is well represented, too. A knowledgeable wine steward is on hand to provide advice. Before or after dinner, you might plan a visit to Gibson's Grand Cru Wine Cellar on the ground level; tastings are offered on Thursday, Friday, and Saturday. And if you find a wine you particularly enjoy, it can be specially ordered for your own cellar at a liberal discount.

A triumph of taste in setting and cuisine.

GIBSON'S, 1033 Lake Dr., S.E., Grand Rapids, MI 49506. Take Fuller St. exit from I-96 and go south to Lake Dr. Telephone (616) 774-8535. Hours: luncheon 11:30 a.m.-2 p.m., dinner 5:30-11 p.m. Closed Sunday, major holidays. Lunch not served on Saturday. Full bar service. Credit cards: AE, MC, V.

CHICKEN GALLANTINE
From Chef James Powell, Gibson's

We tried this for lunch one day and were enchanted. It looks like an elaborate creation, but a food processor makes a quick job of it. Skin 6 chicken breasts and remove bones. Place on cutting board, cover with parchment or waxed paper, and pound lightly with meat hammer until roughly $\frac{1}{4}$ inch thick. Oil or butter a 24-inch piece of aluminum foil, and place breasts end to end on it, with shiny side of foil down. Place 2 additional skinless, boneless chicken breasts, $\frac{1}{2}$ cup heavy cream, 1 egg, $\frac{1}{4}$ cup fine herbs (1 part each tarragon, parsley, and chives), and 1 tablespoon chicken base in food processor, and puree smooth. Spread filling evenly on top of chicken breasts. In long lines on top of the pureed chicken arrange $\frac{1}{4}$ cup julienned vegetables and 4 pieces blanched asparagus. Roll the breasts up into a long cylinder; try to completely enclose the puree. Fold the foil around the gallantine and bake 25 minutes at 350 degrees. Let cool, then chill. Slice and serve with raspberry vinaigrette and watercress garnish.

For raspberry vinaigrette, combine $\frac{1}{4}$ cup wine vinegar, $\frac{1}{4}$ cup raspberry vinegar, $\frac{1}{2}$ cup canned raspberries (in light syrup), 2 cups peanut or sunflower oil, $\frac{1}{2}$ teaspoon salt, 1 teaspoon chopped fresh parsley, 1 teaspoon dry basil, $\frac{1}{2}$ cup finely chopped fresh tomato. Serve at room temperature with cold chicken gallantine.

(30) Schnitzelbank

There's lot of variation in German restaurants. But generally the cooking style is hearty. One thinks of mounds of noodles and potatoes and dumplings; of thick slabs of dark bread, plump sausages, and rich meaty gravies; of pungent scents emanating from the kitchens of "hausfrauen." And they can occasionally offer "gourmet" cuisine, as does Karl Ratsche's in Milwaukee. But what we find appealing about the Schnitzelbank is the tasteful Bavarian decor (not too much schmaltz here) and the changing luncheon and dinner menus. The prices are most satisfactory, and everything is included, even dessert and coffee.

More important, there's a welcome consistency, both in excellent Teutonic cooking and in friendly, efficient service. The Schnitzelbank has been rated the best of moderate-priced western Michigan restaurants in West Michigan Magazine's readers' choice survey; it also received a 1987 Award of Excellence from Grand Rapids Magazine. The popular house specialties are wiener schnitzel, roast leg of lamb, baked spareribs, pot roast with potato pancakes, braised lamb shanks, and sauerbraten (see the recipe below). Other dishes worth considering, if offered during your visit, are the German pepper steak, beef rouladen, boiled pig hocks, smoked Mettwurst, and Viennese roast chicken. In addition, well-prepared steaks and chops are always available.

The restaurant was started in a building next door in 1932 by the grandfather and father of the present owner, Karl Siebert. It moved from its location within a drugstore to its current site in 1938 and was further expanded in 1954. Today the Schnitzelbank holds more than 350 people; and, we warn you, it generally DOES hold that many at serving hours. We believe that credit for its popularity must go to the highly professional management of Mr. Siebert. As we read in one review, "The place runs like clockwork." A minor disappointment is the rather limited wine list, with the best selection white dinner wines, especially and understandably the German varieties.

Wunderbar!

THE SCHNITZELBANK, 342 Jefferson Ave., S.E., Grand Rapids, MI 49502. Near city center, ½ block north of Wealthy St. Telephone (616) 459-9527.Luncheon hours 11 a.m.-2:30 p.m., afternoon menu in effect 2:30-5 p.m., dinner 5-8 p.m. Closed Sunday, major holidays. Full bar service. Credit cards: AE, DC.

SESQUICENTENNIAL SAUERBRATEN
From the Schnitzelbank

With a fork prick beef roast thoroughly (3 to 4

pound rolled rump roast, boneless chuck eye roast, or bottom round roast). Place meat in 4-quart glass bowl or earthenware crock. Mix together 2 cups water, 1 cup red wine vinegar, 1 medium onion (sliced), 6 whole cloves, 4 crushed peppercorns, $1\frac{1}{2}$ teaspoons salt, 1 bay leaf. Pour over the meat. Cover and refrigerate, turning several times each day, 2 to 3 days.

Remove meat from marinade; reserve liquid. Pat beef dry. Strain marinade, and reserve. Heat 3 tablespoons vegetable oil in Dutch oven until hot. Cook beef in hot oil, turning occasionally, until brown, about 10 minutes. Remove beef; pour off fat. Heat 2 cups of the marinade and $\frac{1}{2}$ cup water to boiling in the Dutch oven (reserve remaining marinade). Return beef to Dutch oven; reduce heat, cover, and simmer until beef is tender, about 2 hours, Remove beef to heated platter, and keep warm. Pour liquid from Dutch oven into large measuring cup; skim fat from liquid. Add enough reserved marinade to measure $2\frac{1}{2}$ cups. Return to Dutch oven. (If liquid measures more than $2\frac{1}{2}$ cups, boil rapidly to reduce.) Stir in 8 crushed gingersnaps (about 1/3 cup) and 2 tablespoons packed brown sugar. Mix 1/3 cup water with 3 tablespoons cornstarch; stir gradually into liquid. Heat to boiling, stirring constantly. Boil and stir 1 minute. Strain. The Schnitzelbank serves this with potato dumplings.

Grand Rapids boasts some impressive restaurants, the best of which we hope we've included in this guide. But for more old-fashioned food at old-fashioned prices, here's a small collection of our favorite bargain places.

LITTLE MEXICO CAFE, 401 Stocking St., N.W., Grand Rapids, MI 49504. Take Michigan St. (which becomes Bridge St.) west to Stocking. Telephone (616) 774-8822. Hours: 11 a.m.-2 a.m. Monday-Thursday (till 3 a.m. Friday-Saturday), noon-2 a.m. Sunday. Closed major holidays. Full bar service. Credit cards: MC, V. Reservations taken only for large parties.

The Southwest adobe-hut exterior does nothing to prepare you for what you'll find after you cross the threshold: elaborate and colorful carvings, murals, and paintings by William Bouwsema and rare, exotic furniture imported from the Yucatan jungles. Underwhelming it's not. Choose your own adjective (arcane, melodramatic, Kafkaesque?). Still, dining at Little Mexico is like spending two hours in another person's country. The place has as little in common with Taco Bell as the London Chop House has with McDonald's.

Make no mistake, it's not elegant. But a Friday or Saturday here savoring menudo, cactus salad, carne de puerco (pork and green chiles), or the especially delicious panchitos--all to the strains of mariachi music--is the closest thing in Michigan to Mexico City's famed Garibaldi Square. For almost 20 years Martin Morales has been mesmerizing Grand Rapids habitues with freshly prepared, authentic fare from his native land: all the dishes you've tried or heard about and more. Try the tacos al carbon (with broiled steak) or Martin's own tamales and beanfree chili. Wash it down with sangria or Mexican beer. And think picky. No chalupas on the menu? Ask and ye shall receive.

THE OYSTER HAVEN, 412 Fuller St., N.E., Grand Rapids, MI 49503. Just north of Michigan St. Hours: 11 a.m.-9 p.m. Monday-Thursday (till 10 p.m. Friday-Saturday). Closed Sunday. No alcoholic beverages. Credit cards: AE, MC, V.

Charley's Crab in downtown Grand Rapids can add up to an expensive night out. But for seafood almost (sometimes just) as good, the Oyster Haven won't chip away as much at your solvency. Discerning fish eaters will appreciate the wide variety here (including, goodness sakes, cod cheeks); the prices, averaging $5 to $8 and topping off at $13.95 for a steamed seafood platter; and the interesting preparations--a toothsome oyster stew in season, poor man's lobster pie (with monkfish), seafood omelet, fish kebabs, butter-crumbed scrod, and (ole!) a piscatorial chimichanga.

Up front is a fish market, lending credibility to everything served in the restaurant. The dining area is larger than it looks from the foyer, and most seats are in roomy booths. The big attraction here is the seafood salad boat--yes, indeed, an honest-to-gosh boat heaped full of ice and displaying caviar, shrimp, crabmeat, herring, vegetables, salads, and cold pasta creations. No one complains about the $6.25 tab at lunch or $6.95 in the evening.

THE WISLA SHOP, 644 Stocking St., N.W., Grand Rapids, MI 49504. Two blocks from Little Mexico Cafe. Telephone (616) 458-2903. Hours: 11 a.m.-8 p.m. Tuesday-Friday, 11 a.m.-2 p.m. Monday, noon-8 p.m. Saturday. Closed Sunday and major holidays. Parking lot in back or meterless street parking. No alcoholic beverages. No credit cards.

Once a pharmacy in an old Grand Rapids neighborhood, the Wisla Shop and Restaurant is a fetching little place with a simple and homey interior brightened up with posters, pictures, and other mementos from Poland. Mitch Szczepanczyk, owner and cook, prepares everything from scratch and says, "I love my customers and put everything into my work." His diligence has been rewarded; Grand Rapids Magazine has for several years bestowed special achievement awards on Wisla.

On the menu are such traditional Polish specialties as kielbasa, cabbage rolls, pierogi (some of the best we've tasted), pig hocks, potato pancakes, and borscht, along with Mitch's own renditions of baked chicken, pork chops, barbequed ribs, and fish. The combination plates, priced at $4.25 to $6.50, provide an opportunity to do some sampling. Six or more persons should order the all-inclusive family dinner at $7.50 per person (Also all you can eat, which is always too much). The truly voracious will opt for the "Warsaw Festival," a huge platter. Not on the menu every night but worth snapping up are the chrusciki, crisp angel-wing cookies. If you need help making decisions on anything new to you, call on the charming young manager, Margaret, also Polish and also apparently in love with her work.

YEN CHING, 3015 28th St., S.E., Grand Rapids, MI. From I-96 take the 28th St. exit west. Telephone (616) 942-9130. Hours: 11:30 a.m.-3 p.m. luncheon, 3-9:30 p.m. dinner Monday-Thursday (till 10:30 p.m. Friday-Saturday), noon-9 p.m. Sunday dinner. Full bar service. Credit cards: MC, V.

Yen Ching received the 1987 Award of Excellence from Grand Rapids Magazine as one of the top ten restaurants in the city. Located on the graceless strip of 28th Street, it has managed to create an atmosphere far removed from the steel, concrete, and exhaust fumes just a few feet from its doors. With its lacquered screens, Mandarin red table linens, vertical bead dividers, Oriental hanging lamps, lots of ormolu and Chinese pizzazz, the place sizzles with Asian ambience.

And the wok sizzles, too, primarily with the wonders of Mandarin, Peking, Hunan, and Szechuan cuisine. Owner Jack Kung and his capable Chinese chefs offer Michiganians some of the best of the East: moo shu pork with Mandarin pancakes, braised scallops, lobster with bean sauce, Mandarin king crab, pork with black mushrooms, and Jack's recommended house special, the hot and spicy Yen Ching shrimp. A number of combination dinners are available for small or large groups. To finish, try the hot caramelized bananas or apples. Everything you've heard about Chinese desserts was a lie.

CARTER'S CLAM SOUFFLE
From the Oyster Haven

Melt 2 tablespoons butter. Add 2 tablespoons flour and cook on very low heat 2 minutes. Gradually stir in ½ cup strained clam broth (fresh or canned), ½ cup heavy cream, 4 thin slices onion, 1 teaspoon minced parsley, ½ bay leaf, and pinch cayenne. Cook over low heat, stirring, till thickened. Add 3/4 cup minced clams (fresh or canned) and heat them. Remove pan from fire. In a large mixing bowl beat 3 egg yolks well; then add a little of the hot sauce and stir in. Blend in the remaining sauce. Let cool slightly. Beat 4 egg whites stiff with pinch salt and nutmeg. Gently fold into the sauce. Spoon into a 4-cup souffle dish buttered only on the bottom. Bake 25 minutes at 400 degrees or until well puffed and slightly browned. Serves 3-4, more as an appetizer.

An especially tasteful blend of old and new in both interior design and cuisine, the Thornapple Village Inn has established itself as one of the premier restaurants in western Michigan. There's an easy sophistication here in the apple green, white, and light oak of the walls and furnishings, in the superb use of space and subtlety of structural patterns, in the classical background music, and in the creative Continental and American cooking. Featured in the prestigious Interior Design magazine, this is certainly one of the most aesthetically appealing restaurants in the state. The exterior of the building conforms to the rather pedestrian style of the shopping center in which it's located and gives little hint of the three charming dining rooms on the ground level or the extremely well-executed wine cellar with its adjoining dining area.

If the Thornapple isn't busy, we suggest that you first look at all the rooms and then make a choice. For lunch we like the airy, brick-floored Solarium, with trailing greenery that evokes the sunny outdoors, even in cloudy Michigan weather. Our favorite room for dinner is the Harvest Room, a solid, warmer, and more formal setting with a cozy fireplace and an understated but effective use of stained glass. For semiprivate dining for four persons, try table 12 in the corner; two other somewhat secluded corner tables (numbers 4 and 7) that seat five or fewer are especially comfortable, with upholstered, sofalike seating. Large parties (up to eight people) should ask for Harvest 8 in the center of the room. The River Room, however, is the most popular dining room, with a view of lawn and the Thornapple River both day and night since the lovely grounds are lighted after sunset. It's tempting to be seated here at the chic green velvet banquette, accentuated by antique-framed mirrors overhead, but we still prefer the tables for four near the windows in the River Room.

On warm days lunch and cocktails are also served on the deck. And off the wine cellar on the lower level--which shouldn't be missed no matter where you dine--is the casual Vintage Room, with its wood-burning fireplace and latticed windows affording a look at the cellar itself, the most dramatic we've seen in a Michigan restaurant. Hundreds of well-organized bottles are kept at a constant temperature in a room specifically designed for both storage and observation. You might want to select your wine in the cellar before dinner. The inventory is impressive and growing larger (at least 300 to choose from; the wine list itself changes twice a week. Of our favorite red Bordeaux, there's a marvelous '79 Chateau Pichon Lalande (2nd growth Pauillac). California wines are well represented, and a rather good selection from Germany is available. You'll have no trouble finding what you want unless it's a low-priced wine at a bargain price.

The basic menu changes seasonally, making the

temptation to return irresistible. Let's look at just a few of the extraordinary dinner entrees served in late fall last year: roast pheasant or duckling, venison tenderloin, wild boar chops, baked partridge with a pear-white wine sauce, Camembert-stuffed chicken breast, and a fettuccine of the day. In addition, there are six fresh fish selections daily and occasional other specialties. Luncheon dishes, though less extensive, are just as rewarding. The tab is moderate to expensive, and the entree price includes salad, bread, and vegetables. At least two exemplary soups are regularly offered: Norman-style onion, for example, or Cheddar and crabmeat chowder. The appetizers are mouth-puckering: among others likely to be on the menu are Westphalian ham with fresh fruit and smoked rainbow trout with horseradish cream. As for desserts, there are sweets to satisfy the most demanding palate; the profit-eroles (tiny cream puffs) are very popular and the gateau chocolat (a rich flourless cake flavored with Grand Marnier) deserves a prize.

The restaurant is under the able management of Gregg Gilmore, whose family built the Thornapple Village Inn. Presiding over the kitchen is Chef Michael Whitman, who started here and then followed Jim Powell to the 1913 Room and Gibson's. His experience is apparent in the fine food served here. A great many professional chefs have commended the restaurant to us. In fact, aside from Southfield's Golden Mushroom with Chef Milos Cihelka, no place has been mentioned to us more often as a chef's training ground than the Thornapple Village Inn. We think you'll be as impressed as we are.

Distinctive dining and design--one of the best.

THE THORNAPPLE VILLAGE INN, 445 Thornapple Village Dr., S.E., Ada, MI 49301. Just to the east of Grand Rapids; take the Ada exit from I-96 or M-21 to Ada Dr. Telephone (616) 676-1233. Hours: luncheon 11:30 a.m.-2:30 p.m., dinner 5:30-10 p.m. Closed Sunday, holidays. Full bar service. Credit cards: AE, MC, V. You might dress up a bit, unless you're visiting the Inn's Tap Room, a casual dining area off the bar specializing in Chicago-style pizza.

SAUTE OF VENISON TENDERLOIN
WITH CURRANT-GOOSEBERRY SAUCE
From Chef Michael Whitman, the Thornapple
    Village Inn

Have about 6 ounces clarified butter ready for sauteeing. In large skillet saute 8 (1/3-inch) slices French bread in some of the butter until nicely browned on both sides. Set these croutes aside on paper towels to drain. Cut 32 ounces trimmed venison tenderloin into 4-ounce filets. Season with salt and freshly cracked pepper. Saute in very hot clarified butter in a pan large enough so they aren't crowded. (Cook in batches if necessary.) Saute to desired degree of doneness and place on the croutes, two per person.

Pour the butter out of the pan and deglaze with 4 ounces red Burgundy or Merlot. Add 8 ounces currant-gooseberry preserves (available from American Spoon Foods, Petoskey; specialty food shops carry it), 1½ tablespoon finely chopped shallots, and 4 tablespoons game glaze (made from a strong game stock, strained and reduced by 75%). Whisk sauce well. Cook over high heat until reduced by about half. Remove from heat and whisk in 2 ounces whole butter. Salt and pepper to taste. Pour over filets and serve immediately with vegetables of your choice. Serves 4.

Our hints: See any standard cookbook for information on clarifying butter. Mix equal parts currant and gooseberry preserves if you can't find American Spoon. You can make a game glaze by reducing canned wild game soup (if you can find it) or else substitute beef glaze.

③③ SAM'S JOINT

Something about Sam's makes you start tapping your feet. Maybe it's because it's in Caledonia (remember that old, old "hot jazz" number by Woody Herman?). Or maybe it's Fats Waller's tune and lyric that come to mind: "the joint is jumpin'." Whatever, when you drive up to Sam's Joint on a Saturday night, plan on letting down your hair, inhibiting your inhibitions, and setting aside all thoughts of calories and cholesterol. Sam's, which we think of as "Antler's South," deals in deep-fried appetizers (artichoke hearts, egg rolls, onion rings, chicken strips, Mozzarella "stix," and various battered vegetables) as well as deep-fried entrees (chicken, oysters, shrimp, lake perch, walleye). It also offers superburgers, corned beef subs, wet burritos, spaghetti, linguine, and lasagne. And you can, if you can, finish with apple or pecan pie, strawberry cheesecake, or a turtle sundae.

Still, there's more here than a quick glance at the menu might reveal. Actually some things (very few) are pretty healthy. You can opt for poached walleyed pike and steamed shrimp instead of fried, a number of broiled steaks at fair prices, and three giant tostada salads (use your judgment about the tortilla). The specialty of the joint is the "open-flame world-famous, succulent barbequed pork back ribs" at $10.95. Any entree comes with fries and slaw. The menu is in effect all day and evening. Prices range from $3.50 to a maximum of $12.95 for the extra-large cut of prime rib.

For tasty food at affordable prices, Sam's Joint is notable for its menu alone. But it offers even more to the adventurous diner. The corner building with weathered rustic exterior houses one of the finest collections of antiques we've seen in a restaurant. Part of the edifice was once the meat locker of Caledonia, now the bar at Sam's. The remaining area has become three dining rooms downstairs and four rooms and another bar on the second floor. Every room is worth studying. In the main bar are marble tables and bentwood chairs, old baseball masks and bats, Civil War lithographs, fishing nets, wooden boat propellers, musical instruments. On the stairway is a photo of the 1955 champion New York Yankees, and at the top of the stairwell are a copper diver's helmet and a stuffed black bear. The chairs on the second story are of woven leather and wood, and rooms up here have only two to four tables each. This is the best choice if you're seeking privacy (we especially like the American Indian room). But somehow privacy at Sam's is a non sequitur.

As we've hinted, you won't see a single soul in running togs and Reeboks or with an ID card from the Doctor's Weight Loss Clinic. What you will see are a lot of good-time folks out for an evening of fun and frolic. If that turns you off, go back to your wheat germ muffins, granola bars, and Gatorade. If it turns you on, you'll be pleased to learn that Sam Bravata, Jr., has been so successful that he's opened two more joints: one at Gun Lake near the state park entrance and one in Alaska, MI, on 68th St. (2 miles east of M-37). He's even opening a gourmet (!) food shop in what was once the Gun Lake Grocery.

A lively, old-time American tavern.

SAM'S JOINT, 107 East Main St., Caledonia, MI 49316. Three and a half blocks west of M-37. Telephone (616) 891-8325. Hours: 1 a.m.-11 p.m. (till 1 a.m. Friday-Saturday). Closed Sunday, Christmas, Thanksgiving, New Year's Day. Full bar service. Credit cards not accepted. Reservations taken only for parties of six or more.

(34) BAY POINTE

Let's start with the view: a placid lake beyond spacious, well-tended lawns and lovely, ancient shade

trees. Then visualize yourself and your dinner
partner seated at the window in the circular porch
of Bay Pointe. Or on a cooler evening nestled
together in "the booth," the most imtimate nook
in this exceptionally warm and inviting dining room
with its hard maple beams, massive staircase, and
crystal chandeliers.

Built in 1902 as a summer retreat by a Kalamazoo
paper tycoon, the Dutch Colonial mansion was
opened as a restaurant in 1983 by Jackie and Roy
Martin. Structurally, very little has been changed
from the original. So it's no wonder that Bay Pointe
was put on the State Register of Historic Buildings
in 1983 and the National Register in 1984 as an
architecturally significant edifice. Each room has
a different, though nostalgic, personality. We especially like the main dining room and porch on
the first floor, but there's also a smaller sun room
downstairs and three rooms on the second floor
for dining on weekends. Also on weekends the Upper
Deck, open only in summer, offers live music and
dancing in a relaxed patio environment--with that
great view of Gun Lake.

And, yes, there's food, too. Salads, soups, sandwiches, none of them unusual, appear on the luncheon
menu. But dinners are much more engaging, and
prices are moderate. Among the starters are a
memorable curried shrimp and carpaccio with
mustard sauce. And the seafood chowder is rich
and flavorsome. Entrees are eclectic and fairly
imaginative: sauteed scampi in garlic and white wine,
roast duckling with lingonberry-rum sauce, individual beef Wellingtons with sauce Bordelaise, cashew
and tarragon stuffed pork chop with blackberry
sauce, pecan-filled breast of chicken with raspberry
sauce. On Wednesday and Thursday Bay Pointe
features tableside cooking, presenting such specialties
as steak Diane or Monte Carlo and such desserts
as bananas Foster and strawberries flambe. Sweets
vary with the creative whims of the chef; there
are always ice cream drinks, but usually you'll have
a more tantalizing option, perhaps Grand Marnier
souffle or brandy Alexander cheesecake.

Get to the Pointe.

BAY POINTE, 11456 Marsh Rd., Shelbyville, MI 49344. Take exit 59 (Shelbyville exit) off U.S.131 and go about 7 miles east on 124th Ave. to the end (Gun Lake); turn right and drive 2 miles. Telephone (616) 672-5202. Hours: luncheon Tuesday-Friday 11:30 a.m.-5 p.m., dinner Tuesday-Saturday 5-10 p.m., Sunday brunch 11 a.m.-3 p.m. Open April 1 through December 31. Closed rest of year and on Monday. Full bar service. Credit cards: MC, V.

BROCCOLI SALAD
From Bay Pointe

In a large bowl gently combine 4 cups blanched broccoli flowerets, 1 cup raisins (plumped in hot water), 1 cup sliced mushrooms, ½ cup chopped red onion, and 6 slices crumbled crisp bacon. In another, smaller bowl, whisk together ½ cup mayonnaise, ½ cup sour cream, and 2 teaspoons lemon juice. Pour this dressing over the salad mixture. Toss well, and salt and pepper to taste. Serves 6.

(35) GILKEY LAKE TAVERN

In the bar area the worn wooden tables, moose horns on the backbar, bandstand, and pool table are probably the same ones we saw on our first visit more than 17 years ago. Oliver, the old bulldog, is now fitted with a pacemaker, and we hope he'll still be guarding the kitchen doorway when you make your first visit. Nothing much changes here. The entrance is still probably the least impressive of any restaurant's in the state: a plain brown battered door flanked by steel posts to protect it from rambunctious motorists. The most recent addition to utilitarian nondecor is an oil painting of the Old West with John Wayne's face peering down from the sky.

The Gilkey Lake Tavern, in business since the 1930s, ranks as a bona fide, off-the-beaten-track, rural gathering place, and for American home-style cooking, it's as consistently rewarding as any place of the sort in Michigan. We're pleased to report that Dorothy Leinaar, the owner, isn't even tempted to overmodernize; she realizes that the marvelous country atmosphere is what draws hundreds of people of all ages to her restaurant on weekends.

The menu includes more interesting selections than you might expect--for example, fried rabbit, an outstanding seafood platter, and terrific little frog legs ("the smaller, the better; large ones are stringy," Mrs. Leinaar notes correctly). This is not a place for dieters: beer-battered, deep-fried food predominates. But several fish entrees can be ordered broiled, if you prefer, and there are now two low-cal dinners on the menu.

The nightly specials are the drawing card here. On Tuesday an 18-ounce porterhouse is the featured item (possibly the best steak bargain in Michigan); on Friday it's a combination of shrimp, cod, and frog legs, all you can eat (the tavern typically sells about 300 of these in an evening); Saturday boasts prime rib or steak and scampi; and our favorite is the Sunday specialty, family-style chicken with homemade noodles and biscuits--all of these at very low prices.

If you stop at Gilkey Lake Tavern in the daytime, you might also plan a visit to the nearby Hickory Corners Antique Mall and the Gilman Classic Car Club of America Museum. Or take some of the pleasant walks at the Kellogg Bird Sanctuary of Michigan State University Biological Station, just south of Hickory Corners. If you're planning on a Friday or Saturday night dinner, you might want to stick around and dance afterwards. The band plays country and western and some light rock. Dress down here.

Best country tavern in the Lower Peninsula, a bargain.

THE GILKEY LAKE TAVERN, Rte. 2, Delton, Mi 49046. About halfway between Kalamazoo and Battle Creek; 2½ miles north of Hickory Corners. Telephone (616) 671-5870. Kitchen hours: 10 a.m.-9 p.m. (till 10 p.m. in summer and on Friday). Closed Christmas. Full menu in effect all day, but salad bar only in the evening. Full bar service. Jukebox; band starts 9 p.m. Friday-Saturday. No credit cards, but checks accepted.

SUMMER SALAD
From Dorothy Leinaar, Gilkey Lake Tavern

Gilkey Lake makes this salad in 25-gallon batches with Italian dressing from Gordon's Food Service in Lansing. We've adjusted the quantities and put together our own version of Italian vinaigrette. This is a very popular dish on the tavern's salad bar.

Mix vinaigrette; combine 1 cup vegetable oil or half vegetable and half olive oil, 1/3 cup red wine vinegar, 1 large clove minced garlic, 2 tablespoons minced onion, 1 teaspoon salt, ¼ teaspoon black pepper, 1 teaspoon lemon juice, 1 teaspoon basil, and 1 teaspoon oregano. In a large mixing bowl combine 2-3 cups cooked rainbow rotini pasta (cook 8-12 minutes until al dente, slightly chewy; drain and cool), 2 cups broccoli flowerets, 2 cups (1 pint) cherry tomatoes, 1 large sliced cucumber, and 1 cup whole pitted, drained canned black olives. Pour over Italian dressing, and toss to coat vegetables. Marinate 5 hours. Serves 8-12.

Cornwell's must be one of the few commercial enterprises (the only?) to rate its own green and white official sign on the interstate system--"Turkeyville Road," off I-69 north of Marshall. Here, city

families with kids who think that a turkey is born
and raised in a supermarket freezer can see the
real thing on foot and enjoy an inexpensive meal
at the same time. There's lots of shopping for
Mother, to boot, and it's a good thing for Dad that
Cornwell's is finally accepting credit cards.

The 180-acre turkey farm dates to 1848 and was
once the center of a thriving turkey business in
Michigan. Years ago the Cornwells realized that
the turkey sandwiches they sold at the Calhoun
County Fair by the thousands might be worth selling
at the farm itself. So in 1968 they established a
restaurant in a little one-room building behind the
farmhouse. By noon of the first day they'd taken
in only $26 and worried a bit. Now, Turkeyville,
USA is considered a tourist attraction, a fact that
surprises and amuses the Cornwells.

This is still a family-run business--truly, the
Michigan version of the Waltons. The owners Wayne
and Marjorie Cornwell live in the original farmhouse
across from the restaurant, and their sons and
grandson all contribute. Today only a few turkeys
are raised here at the farm; most are shipped in
from Booth's Poultry Farm in Indiana (though the
birds are raised especially to Cornwell feed specifications). On an average summer's day the Cornwells will roast about 50 large turkeys. All are milk
fed, and we think you'll agree that they're exceptionally moist and tender.

The large complex of buildings includes the Turkey
House, where assorted turkey dishes and excellent
homemade pies are served cafeteria-style; the Turkeyville Ice Cream Parlor with white tile floors,
striped awnings at the windows, and old-fashioned
soda parlor chairs (with the recent addition of a
fudge shop); an adjoining General Store, featuring
mainly candies and popcorn; a Christmas specialty
store a la Bronner's in the Ol' Granary; and an
antique shop in the barn across the road--not to
mention a field of some 200 white turkeys. What's
new since our last guidebook was published is the
addition of a banquet hall and, in 1984, the
"Country Junction," a concourse of little shops fea-

turing the quaint and the exotic, plus Cornwell's own canned and frozen turkey, pies, breads, and fruit butters (try the unusual beet bread or the prune-walnut and pumpkin butters).

The Turkey House dining room, decorated in early American style with ladder-back chairs and farm memorabilia, isn't air conditioned, but the large overhead fans are efficient. Or, if you prefer, you can eat at one of the very pleasant umbrella tables outside. Family dining is common here--even encouraged--and if the kids spill, it's not a crisis.

There are now 12 choices on the menu: five versions of what is modestly billed as "the world's best turkey sandwich" (buttered turkey, turkey salad, Sloppy Tom, smoked turkey, and turkey dog) and six lunch or dinner plates (turkey hot plate with gravy, potatoes, stuffing, cranberries; hot turkey and gravy on a bun; same thing on a biscuit; turkey and noodles; sliced smoked turkey salad; and the compete turkey dinner, the hot plate with the addition of cole slaw and roll); and a great turkey soup with barley and corn. The most expensive menu item is the full dinner with dessert and beverage for less than $7. Even though you'll probably need to wait in line, the food is served hot and quickly, and it's simple to go back for more. Do go back for a piece of pie. On our last visit the choice was fresh apple, rhubarb, and blueberry plus five cream pies--coconut, lemon, chocolate, banana, and the popular peanut butter.

Who wants to eat with a bunch of
turkeys? We do!

CORNWELL'S TURKEY HOUSE, 18935 15½ Mile Rd., Marshall, MI 49068. Five miles north of Marshall; ½ mile west on I-69, N Drive North exit; 4 miles north of I-94 and I-69 interchange. Hours: 11 a.m.-8 p.m. Open May 1 to September 30. No alcoholic beverages. Credit cards: MC, V. No reservations accepted.

ROAST TURKEY CHINESE STYLE
From Pat Manson, Williamston, Michigan

We have never tasted a juicier, more tender roast turkey than this version by a superb Williamston cook, Pat Manson. First, remove the gizzard, liver, and heart from a 12-14 pound turkey. Combine these in a saucepan with 1-2 ribs celery, and 1 quartered onion; add water to cover and simmer until tender, 1½-2 hours. Drain and chop; reserve for gravy.

Several hours or preferably the night before, rinse turkey inside and out with cool water. Season inside with 1 teaspoon salt. In a bowl mix together 1/3 cup Chinese plum sauce, ¼ cup soy sauce, ¼ cup sugar, ¼ cup chopped celery, ¼ cup chopped onion, and 1 clove smashed garlic. Coat the outside of the turkey with this, and allow to marinate 3-4 hours or overnight.

Place turkey on rack in roasting pan. Add ½ to 3/4 cup water. Brown bird without covering for 1 hour (or till golden brown) in 350-degree oven, basting frequently. Add 1-1½ cup water and cover pan. Bake 2 more hours, basting occasionally. When done (180-185 degrees internal), remove to warm platter. Strain pan liquids into a saucepan; bring to a boil. Mix about 3 tablespoons cornstarch and 3 tablespoons water until smooth. Add in a steady stream until desired consistency is reached. Add the chopped giblets, and simmer 2 minutes. Serve with either American or Chinese accompaniments.

The Casa Nova, first built in 1951 about a mile away on the same street, was forced by a highway expansion program to relocate to its present site. In a shrewd managerial move, the Italian Mediterranean decor, the amber lights in the chandeliers, the curved bar with comfortable armchairs, and even the too-small entryway were all transplanted with little change, as were the menu and prices. The result, we'd guess, is that Casa Nova has lost none of its popularity and still offers some of the best bargains in the Lansing area. Owner Bill Falsetta is to be commended for holding prices to a very reasonable level.

There are four dining areas: the main room with the most appealing seating at the booths along the wall, an elongated room parallel to it, a solarium, and the lounge. Reservations aren't accepted (you take a number upon arrival), but we think it's worth the extra wait for a booth or a corner in the bar area. But don't be fooled if there are only 10 or 12 people standing near the door. The large overflow waiting room and bar downstairs might be filled with others already on the seating list. Because of the usual crush, some tables--those near the main entrance and off the kitchen door--should be avoided.

Dishes we particularly like are the six "giant" sandwich specials ($2.20-$2.40), the thick cheesy pizza (you'll need a knife and fork), barbequed ribs (highly recommended; at $6.65 probably the best for the money in all of Michigan), prime rib ($5.95), either a thick strip or a large but thinner T-bone steak (both under $7), and very nice Alaskan King crab legs at $9.25. The French-fried onions are a good buy and much better than average. The Italian pasta entrees are somewhat pedestrian (the sauce a bit too sweet for our taste), but the veal scallopini is usually a standout and at $5.25 a steal. Soups here are canned, we'd prefer a crustier bread, and some seafood appears to be prebreaded and frozen. But if you stay with the items we mention above, you shouldn't be disappointed.

This is not a restaurant for intimate, quiet dining; and though once in a while you'll see even long, formal dresses here, more often it's bowling jackets and blue jeans. The Casa Nova is fine for families. There's no children's menu, but portions are large (ask for extra plates), and pizzas and sandwiches can be shared. The waitresses are cheerful and efficient for such a busy place, and some have been here for years. Brigitte Gogolin, from West Germany, has eight years in with Casa Nova and is such a great pie-baker that we wish she'd transfer to the kitchen. Hazel Oliver, our all-time favorite, came here from England as a World War II war bride and has been keeping things running smoothly for as long as we can remember, right alongside another sharp waitress, Bernie Wood, who's put in 25 years here.

Tops for pizza, ribs, steaks, crab--and a bargain.

CASA NOVA LOUNGE AND PIZZERIA, 3015 S. Logan St., Lansing, MI. Three miles southeast of the city center; 1 mile south of I-496, Logan St. exit. Telephone (517) 882-6697. Hours: 11 a.m.-2 a.m. Closed Sunday, holidays, the week of July 4. Full bar service. Credit cards: AE, CB, MC, V. Reservations not accepted.

VEAL SCALLOPINI
From the Casa Nova

The rich-tasting final product belies its origins in some "convenience" ingredients. We sometimes vary this by adding sage and Marsala to the sauce. Cut 2 pounds veal (from the rump or round) into 1-inch strips or cubes. Roll in a mixture of $\frac{1}{2}$ cup flour, 1 teaspoon salt, and $\frac{1}{2}$ teaspoon pepper plus a pinch of garlic powder. Heat 2 tablespoons oil and 2 tablespoons butter in a roasting pan. Add the meat, and brown in a hot oven (about 400 degrees) for 1-1$\frac{1}{2}$ hours, stirring occasionally. When nicely browned, remove from oven and add 5 tablespoons chopped fresh green pepper, $\frac{1}{4}$ cup minced onion, an 8-ounce can drained mushroom pieces, and 3 tablespoons sherry. If the mixture appears dry, add up to $\frac{1}{2}$ cup water. Cover with foil and return to a 250-degree oven. Bake slowly about 2$\frac{1}{2}$-3 hours until very tender. (Or cook in pressure cooker 12 minutes.) This much can be done ahead. For the final cooking, put meat in individual baking dishes. Top with mixture of 2 cans Campbell's cream of mushroom soup mixed with 2-3 tablespoons cream or milk. (We like to mix in the pan juices first.) Sprinkle with shredded Mozzarella cheese (about 2 cups in all). Bake about 20 minutes at 400 degrees. Serves 6.

㊳ SEVILLE'S

If you expect to see paella and tapas on the menu, dream on; Seville's specializes in northern Italian cuisine. Though everyone we've talked to at the Radisson thinks it's named after a town in Italy, we (and the six world atlases we've checked) beg to differ. But a second, more sensible reason for labeling it "Seville's" (in spite of the pointless possessive) is its identification with Buick-Oldsmobile-Cadillac, automobiles made in Lansing--the Cadillac Seville (pre-1980) is near the top of the line.

Although part of a national hotel chain, the restaurant has been designed as an entity unto itself. Decor consists of the geometrics and etched glass of Art Deco interrupted by neo-neon accents and traditional chandeliers. Shades of pink and muted aquamarine appear throughout the room and in the table settings. Adding further interest are plants and the modern Syd Kramer prints. Tables by the windows overlooking Michigan Avenue are especially pleasant in the daytime, but at any time we prefer to be seated far from the madding crowd in one of the three booths on the far rear wall. On the same wall to the south is the table favored by Governor Blanchard (ask for number 13). We least like the area just off the reservation desk, where incoming traffic can be distracting.

Chef Alfredo Kadapodis previously worked at La

Fontaine in Detroit's Renaissance Center and the Hermitage, a four-star hotel in Nashville. Assisting him is Rick Rienmen, also of La Fontaine and former chef of the State Room in East Lansing. Their expertise is apparent. Among the generally reliable beginnings are prosciutto and melon, baked escargots Sambuca, and pasta fresco--a triad of flavored pastas with different sauces. Most popular of the entrees are the pastas and veal options; we enjoy both the sage-scented saltimbocca and the piquant scallopini. Also offered are chicken Parmesan and piccata, a number of seafood specialties, and the predictable prime rib and steaks for diehards. A delicious medley of vegetables, perfumed with herbs, accompanies main courses. At lunch there's greater emphasis on salads (try the chicken pesto) and sandwiches. The latter are generous and a good value; most intriguing are an unprecedented Italian hamburger and a hearty Sicilian sausage number. The 36-item wine list is in need of careful editing and with one curious exception lacks vintage years. Possibly it will improve as the restaurant evolves. Even so, the variety of imported and domestic reds and whites, many costing less than $20, is adequate though not exciting.

As at many restaurants in Lansing, there may be undue waits for tables at prime time on Friday and Saturday evenings. But the enthusiastic personnel at Seville's is working hard to avoid or solve such problems. Gourmandism has yet to make much of an inroad in Lansing (or perhaps we're too close to judge fairly). Yet the promise and potential is here, and we hope that Seville's is, if not a bellwether, a harbinger of good things to come.

Downtown diversions.

SEVILLE'S, Radisson Hotel, 111 N. Grand Ave., Lansing, MI 48933. At Michigan Ave., one block from the Capitol; take Grand Ave. exit off I-496. Telephone (517) 482-0188. Hours: 6 a.m.-11 p.m. Monday-Friday, 7 a.m.-11 p.m. Saturday-Sunday.

Full bar sevice. Valet (fee) parking. All major credit cards.

For the Lansing area, we've included the moderate to expensive (Seville's, Beggar's Banquet, the State Room) along with a full-service restaurant known for its bargains (Casa Nova). But there are other options for diners who are looking for something a little different. We've chosen as samples the following places that, by virtue of site or cuisine, are atypical.

EL AZTECO, 203 MAC Ave., East Lansing, MI 48823. Just off Grand River Ave., downtown. Telephone (517) 351-9111. Hours: 11 a.m.-midnight Monday-Thursday, 11 a.m.-2 a.m. Friday-Saturday, noon-10 p.m. Sunday. Beer, wine, Margaritas. No credit cards or reservations accepted.

"El Az," as it's affectionately called by its collegiate habitues, is an East Lansing landmark. It pleases its patrons, however, in rather perverse ways: no placemats, no linens, no credit, no reservations, no air conditioning. The basement eatery is done up in neutrals, and you'll see lots of well-worn wood, brick, beer signs, amber lights, and facial hair. Amiable and animated conversation rises above the blatting radio and the clatter from the open kitchen. The food is Mexican and fairly authentic with, thank goodness, no "original wet burritos." Among dishes not yet offered in most fast food places are menudo (tripe and hominy soup), enchiladas de Jocoque (with sour cream and Monterey Jack cheese), and blue corn enchiladas with a spicy cheese filling. The flautas and chimichangas are especially good. Overheard: "This place has the best graffitti in town." El Azteco has a second location with the same easy-going informality but consi-

derably less hurly burly at 1016 W. Saginaw St.
near Logan St. (telephone 485-458). The menu is
almost the same but credit cards are accepted, cocktails are available, and there's an attempt at
Mexican decor. Students and aging flower children
are supplanted by business folk in suits and ties.
At either location, though, the purplish sangria
tastes like Kool-Aid; you're better off with one of
the Mexican beers.

JOHN D. NASH FISHERY-EATERY, 1820 S. Pen-
nsylvania Ave., Lansing, MI 48910. Take Pennsylva-
nia Ave. exit off I-496 and drive south. Telephone
(517) 484-7100. Hours: 11 a.m.-7 p.m. Monday-Thursday, 11 a.m.-8 p.m. Friday, 10 a.m.-7 p.m. Saturday.
Closed Sunday, major holidays. No alcoholic beverages. No credit cards, but personal checks accepted.
"We go to the source" is John and Sharon Nash's
motto. And if you want to savor some of the freshest of fish and seafood, your source should be this
thriving fish market on Lansing's south side. Cod,
perch, orange roughy, walleye, smelt, shrimp, clams,
catfish, frog legs, whitefish may be ordered a la
carte, in sandwiches, or as dinners that include
cole slaw, uncommonly good French fries, and excellent homemade bread or muffins. Or perhaps
you'd rather check the display case and choose
something else: salmon, swordfish, snapper, even
crappies and sunfish. For $1 per pound extra, the
Nashs will prepare just about anything you want.
Fish is either broiled or deep fried (the batter is
light and crisp). Prices range from 95¢ for a piece
of fish to $6.95 for the shrimp-scallop-clam com-
bination dinner. Also on the menu are Cajun fish,
oysters on the half shell, shrimp salad and cocktail, and clam chowder. The daily specials are
popular, and when John D. Nash sells all-you-can-
eat fish on Friday for $3.99, the line stretches
out into the parking lot. With such good food at
such reasonable prices, customers aren't concerned
with decor. In fact, the neatly arranged fish in the
display case and the occasional whiffs reminiscent
of the seashore are definite pluses.

94

THE PARTHENON, 277 S. Washington Square, Lansing, MI 48933. Downtown. Telephone (517) 484-0573. Hours: breakfast 7-11 a.m., luncheon 11 a.m.-5 p.m., dinner 5-9 p.m. Monday-Saturday. Closed Sunday, holidays. Full bar service. All major credit cards.

The baby blue stucco facade isn't especially attractive. But, inside, the vaguely Mediterranean furnishings, stylized pillars and arches, framed posters and murals, and Greek background music are quite pleasant. The oil lamps glow even at lunchtime on the first floor, but there are windows upstairs if you prefer natural light. The cuisine here is suitably Hellenic, featuring souvlakia (marinated skewered beef tenderloin, spanakotiropita (ask for spinach pie), moussaka (eggplant casserole), gyros (pita sandwiches), shrimp Scorpios, and most of the familiar national specialties. Uninspiring American entrees plus spaghetti and quiche flesh out the menu. The service is fast and efficient, and the prices are low to moderate. Zorba nights, feasts with bouzouki music and dancing, are held twice yearly. The Parthenon is arguably the best of Lansing's Greek eateries.

UNIQUE FOODS OF INDIA, 224 S. Clippert St., Lansing, MI 48912. One block south of east M-143 (Michigan Ave.); take Kalamazoo St. exit from north U.S.127, turn right on Kalamazoo, then left on Clippert. Telephone (517) 332-0664. Hours not available as we go to press (call). No alcoholic beverages. All major credit cards.

Somewhat secluded on a semiresidential street on the eastern edge of Lansing, Unique Foods of India started out mainly as a purveyor of the subcontinent's canned goods, rice, lentils, spices, breads, and occasional souvenirs and craft items. Today it's evolving into a full-fledged, albeit tiny, restaurant that takes pride in introducing uneducated palates to the pleasures of one of the world's great cuisines. For the uninitiated, "curries" vary widely in flavor, texture, and pungency. Neophytes would do well to discuss their trepidations with the owner/cook.

Start with mild or medium-hot dishes and spices you're familiar with. And do try the breads, served with ghee (clarified butter) and any of several wonderfully flavorful hot sauces. If you're familiar with the cooking style or if you've heard of a dish you'd like to try, make your wishes known. Accommodation is a trademark here. Prices are reasonable.

Just north of the restaurant in Frandor Shopping Center is an especially appealing place for food adventurers, Grande Gourmet, probably the best specialty food and cookware store in the state. Pat and Verne Alexander provide delighted customers from miles around with such delicacies as Godiva chocolates, Silver Palate condiments, expensive and hard-to-find exotica like Russian caviar and French truffles, homemade pasta, baked goods and pastries, coffees and teas, wines, deli meats and cheeses, and such prestigious equipment lines as Calphalon, Le Creuset, Chantal, Cuisinart, and Robot Coupe. Definitely worth your browsing time.

WOODY'S OASIS, 970 Trowbridge Rd., East Lansing, MI 48823. Trowbridge Rd. exit off U.S.127; at Harrison Rd. in Spartan Shopping Center. Telephone (517) 351-2280. Hours: 9 a.m.-9 p.m. Monday-Friday, 9 a.m.-6 p.m. Saturday, 3-8 p.m. Sunday. No alcohlic beverages. No credit cards.

On one wall are Ansel Adams photos, on another is the framed adage "God Bless Our Home," and on a third is a tapestry depicting an Arabian feast complete with belly dancer. As you see, decor tends to be unfocused. Cuisine, on the other hand, has a very clear identity at Woody's, which labels itself a "Mideast Deli." Here you can sample spinach pie, stuffed cabbage rolls, mujadara (lentils and wheat or rice), hashwi (beef, rice, and pine nuts), and many other items. But the beef rolls (zambuzi) and Lebanese pizza steal the show. Also, check out the desserts; the nut fingers are addictive. Prices range from 25¢ for one stuffed grape leaf to $2.50 for an order of foul mudamas (a fava bean concoction). Combination plates are offered on week days and consist of a main dish such as kibbee balls (lamb and cracked wheat) or falafel (chickpea) patties with tabouli salad, humous (sesame sauce), and pita bread for just $3. Turkish coffee is authentic and overwhelming; don't, like most Americans, swill down the sediment. Most of the business is takeout, but there are four little tables and two window counters for eating in. Look around while you're here; Woody Zamel carries a good selection of bulk dried beans and pulses, cracked wheat, olives, imported canned goods, and some great Middle Eastern breads--the crisp Iraqi flatbread is a find.

At the other end of Spartan Shopping Center is Goodrich's Shop-Rite, an outstanding supermarket. The produce section has always been a leader. Butchers here know how to butcher, not just hack away at meat. Specialty cookware and imported foods can be had at better prices than elsewhere, and unusual ingredients for foreign dishes are available here if nowhere else. At Goodrich's, too, are most of the area's best wines and wine buys; Steve Scheffel is the knowledgeable buyer and consultant.

⑩ beggar's banquet ✿✿✿✿✿
RESTAURANT AND SALOON

New Zealand green mussels, escargots, veal scallopini alla Marsala. These don't much sound like menu selections from an eatery popular with college students. The Richard M. Nixon Memorial Bologna, hard-boiled eggs, BLTs. Now, these do. Yet all of them are among the many offerings at Beggar's Banquet, a restaurant near Michigan State University that has become somewhat of an institution itself. The flexible menu meets all tastes. The clientele comes in all varieties. And the prices are for every pocketbook.

You enter through the often noisy and crowded bar that doubles as a waiting room during busy periods. Some first-time customers are most taken with the setting: old barn siding and beams, wooden tables and floors, numerous antiques, and an array of paintings by local artists. Other initiates to

Beggar's are fascinated by their fellow drinkers and diners, who tend toward a university-flavored avant-garde. Most patrons, however, forget all first impressions on later visits and concentrate on whetting their appetites for the rewarding American/French food.

Appetizers, snacks, and about 16 entrees are available day and evening and provide a less expensive option for dinner. Among the starters are salmon mousse, fried sesame chicken strips, petite souffle d'Alencon (Swiss cheese souffle baked in a taragon cream sauce), and shrimp quenelles, with prices in the $4-$5 range. Many of the entrees are homey and hearty, for example, braised short ribs, beef stew, roast chicken, and some Italian dishes. Prices for these top off at $6.95.

In the evening the list of entrees also provides a happy variety, ranging from four standard steaks to 10 or 12 more interesting items offered on a regular basis as well as three monthly specials and a fresh fish of the day. Over the years our favorite regular entree has been the near-incomparable chicken Kiev, which, like several items, can be ordered in two sizes. The veal rollatine is also most commendable as are the three trout preparations and the baked salmon. Prices start at $11.95 and reach $17.95 (for filet mignon), and everything but appetizer and dessert is included.

The lengthy wine list is 90% domestic, and these are largely Californian. A recipient of the Wine Spectator's Award of Excellence, the cellar boasts such bottles as a fine Edna Valley Chardonnay ('84), a Mayacamas Cabernet ('82), several Beaulieu George de Latour Cabernets ('74, '78, '79, '80, and '81) in three sizes, a Louis Martini 1958 Special Selection Cabernet, and a Sebastiani Casa de Sonoma 1941 (!). The aim here is to offer "good value for the money," and Beggar's allows a 10% discount to members of certain national wine clubs. Call on Michael Francisco for specific advice.

The best seating is in the north room, or "dining room," especially in the front. And if tables here aren't free, try for one of the more intimate booths in the "middle room." Above all, if you want a relaxing meal, avoid tables in traffic areas and especially those in the high-decibel, bustling bar. Reservations are honored quite promptly (though football Saturdays present problems); and once seated, you won't be rushed.

Doing its own thing nicely.

BEGGAR'S BANQUET, 218 Abbott Rd., East Lansing, MI 48823. In city center, ½ block north of intersection at Grand River Ave. Telephone (517)351-4573. Hours: 11 a.m.-2 a.m. luncheon and dinner, 10 a.m.-2 p.m. Sunday brunch. Closed Christmas and Thanksgiving. Full bar service. City lot behind the building, but no rear entrance. Credit cards: AE, Dis, MC, V.

CHICKEN BREAST WITH LEEK AND WILD MUSHROOM STUFFING
From Beggar's Banquet

Flatten 12 boneless chicken breasts by pounding or rolling them between 2 pieces waxed paper. For the stuffing, simmer 6 cups julienned leeks in salted water to cover until tender; drain. Saute them in 1 cup butter, along with 2 cups dried cepes (previously soaked in warm water 20 minutes or more), for 5 minutes. Cool. Place a little of the leek mixture on each of the chicken breasts and enclose stuffing as for chicken Kiev. Dredge rolls in seasoned flour; then saute carefully in clarified butter until lightly browned on all sides. Remove chicken to a casserole. Pour off the excess butter in the saute pan, and add 6 cups heavy cream and 1 split of Champagne. Simmer until slightly thickened; salt and pepper to taste. Pour over the chicken rolls. Serves 12.

Our hint: Cepes, or porcini as they're called in Italy, are available in Italian and food specialty shops.

The STATE ROOM

41

We admit a bias here, but we do believe that most visitors will agree with our assessment of the MSU campus as one of the most attractive in the country, especially in spring and fall. One way to enjoy it most fully is to eat at the State Room and then take a short walk through the beautifully landscaped grounds of the university. The State Room is housed in the Kellogg Center for Continuing Education, one of the foremost adult education centers in the United States. It's the headquarters for nearly all conferences held at Michigan State and also serves as the campus inn. Among many other facilities is its public dining room, the State Room.

As we write this, a renovation of the building is underway, but the State Room fortunately has already been completely revamped and revitalized along lines that are a great improvement over its former somewhat institutional (stodgy?) atmosphere. Where once it was somewhat dark and library-somber, now it's light and open and airy with white walls, dramatic rosewood panels here and there, and silvery metallic tiles along with a unifying but subtle Art Deco leitmotif of etched glass and mirrors. Most popular for seating is the new terrace area on a lower level near the windows.

Both luncheon and dinner menus change daily and offer interesting variations on basic American cooking at moderate prices. Over the years we've enjoyed the chicken salad plate, the homemade soups, and numerous delicious muffins. Daily specials are always worth considering, as are such regular menu items as cashew chicken, omelets, and beef teriyaki. Breakfast, too, is particularly agreeable at the State Room. We like the ground-to-order coffee, fresh fruits, and cheese blintzes.

At dinnertime entrees number only seven or eight, but there's a choice for all tastes: braised lamb shanks, chicken breasts with prosciutto and spinach, tempura shrimp with strawberry sweet and sour sauce, and a pasta and fish of the day. These come with a relish tray, salad, vegetable, potato or rice, and roll; and most are reasonably priced under $10. Usually there's a salad or dessert prepared at tableside, adding a bit of culinary fun and education. Desserts, by the way, have always been special here, but now, with pastry chef Laurie Boger at the helm, they're better than ever.

After your meal, we suggest that you take a leisurely walk out the rear entrance, cross the Red Cedar footbridge, pass Jenison Fieldhouse (who can forget Earvin "Magic" Johnson?) and the football stadium, all the way to Farm Lane bridge. Return on the opposite side of the river past the canoe livery; the Administration Building, named in honor of John Hannah, probably the university's most distinguished past president; and the library. Then stroll through Beal Botanical Gardens and cross the river again at the bridge near "Sparty" to return to Kellogg Center. This will take about an hour, but it'll give you an especially charming view of a splendid campus.

Number one in the Big Ten.

THE STATE ROOM, Kellogg Center, S. Harrison Rd., East Lansing, MI 4823. On the campus of Michigan State University. Telephone (517) 332-6571. Hours: breakfast 7-10 a.m., luncheon 11:30 a.m.-2 p.m., dinner 5:30-8 p.m., Sunday breakfast 8-11 a.m. and dinner noon-4 p.m. Closed holidays and holiday weekends. No alcoholic beverages (no wine-- a pity). Parking in adjacent pay lot (show stub at the State Room for reimbursement). Credit cards: AE, MC, V.

BANANAS FOSTER
From the State Room

This, a famous New Orleans dessert, is one of

the tableside creations that's often featured in the
evening at the State Room. In a flambe pan (or
any open skillet) melt ¼ cup butter over moderate
heat. Add ½ cup brown sugar (packed), and stir
until it dissolves. Add 4 ripe but firm peeled,
halved or quartered bananas. Sprinkle with ¼ teaspoon cinnamon. Cook, basting with the sauce, till
bananas soften, about 5 minutes. Warm ½ cup rum,
and add. Ignite. Then baste bananas with the
flaming syrup. Serve equivalent of 1 whole banana
with 2 scoops vanilla ice cream per person. Makes
4 servings.

(42) Acadian Fare Restaurant

When Paul Prudhomme, all 300 pounds of him,
burst onto the restaurant scene not too long ago
and zealously promoted Cajun cooking north of the
Mason-Dixon line, he was greeted by chefs with
welcoming arms, arms soon to be fatigued by hand-
ling those hefty cast-iron skillets. His blackened
redfish received the most attention from customers,
so much so that the federal government imposed
a ban on the harvesting of that species. But as
Chef Prudhomme notes about the blackening craze,
"A lot of it is terrible" (meaning, and we've seen
and tasted it, "burnt"). So it was not surprising to
hear about a new place in Albion calling itself
Acadian Fare, but we also had serious reservations.
    You can imagine our pleasure, then, to discover
a restaurant that specializes in bona fide southern
Louisiana cooking. The proprietors are Jan and Steve
Pittman, the latter a native of Hammond, Louisiana,
about 50 miles from New Orleans. Everything here
is home cooked by Jan and her assistant. Among
the menu choices are shrimp Creole, coconut beer
shrimp, a blackened fish of the day, oysters en

brochette, fried catfish, baked chicken with corn-bread stuffing, and Cajun-style steak and prime rib. The house specialties are combination plates (Shrimp Fare, for example, consists of 14 shrimp prepared in five different ways), available in two price ranges: $17 a la carte and $20 including appetizer and dessert. And what bewitching desserts! Save room for the spectacular three-layer cheesecake or the down-home goodness of sweet potato pecan pie.

We highly recommend the seafood gumbo, a robust and chunky soup based on roux (cooked flour and oil) and shrimp stock. And if you're here for lunch, there's a flavorful Cajun meat pie, a spicy beef mixture baked in a slightly sweet crust. Breads are exceptional. The liquor license is too new for us to judge the wine selection. We would, however, suggest red wines with some of the nippier seafood selections.

The setting of Acadian Fare is nearly as appealing as the food. The three-story house, built in 1904, was once owned by Audrey Wilder, retired Dean of Women at Albion College, birthplace of the famous fraternity serenade "The Sweetheart of Sigma Chi." On the first floor are three dining rooms and a parlor-cum-lounge, all boasting lots of the original old oak and each with only two or three tables. We prefer the Porch in back and the Green Room as a second choice. The Front Room is too close to the entry for our tastes. The atmosphere is only slightly formal, and the Southern hospitality is most engaging.

The best of the bayou.

ACADIAN FARE RESTAURANT, 202 S. Monroe St., Albion, MI 49224. Two and a half blocks south of B.R. 94. Telephone (517) 629-6827. Hours: Tuesday-Friday 11 a.m.-2 p.m. luncheon, Tuesday-Saturday 6-10 p.m. dinner Full bar service. No credit cards.

THE HISTORIC HOMER MILL

There is no one thing special about the Historic Homer Mill; there are lots of things: a fascinating old restored building listed on both the Michigan and National Registers of Historic Sites, a resident professional acting troupe, a profusion of authentic Americana, fine food and drink, and good prices. The theater restaurant is located in a white-painted mill by the bridge over the Kalamazoo River at the east end of the little town of Homer. The mill, built in 1887, was in use until 1969, when graining operations ended. If local historians are to be believed, it almost became a casualty of World War I, when the U.S. government wanted to condemn the building and use the beams to make airplane propellers.

T he restaurant is furnished with innumerable antiques. Overhead are hand-hewn oak and black walnut beams, hung with chandeliers fashioned from the old mill's drive wheels. The effect throughout is cordial and inviting. The main dining room is the dinner theater, but there is also a large lounge and restaurant, the Bin Room, where one may eat even if eschewing the theater. It should be noted, however, that you cannot see the play without having dinner here.

The True Grist Dinner Theater opened its doors to the first professional musical revue in December 1975 and has been in continuous operation ever since. Dinner-theater packages feature American country cuisine. At the start, hearty homemade soup, salad, and rolls are served at the table. A buffet follows, consisting of roast round of beef, a more inventive chicken entree, and one revolving item along with a selection of vegetables. These might include glazed carrots with Bourbon, hot German potato salad, or scalloped corn. A la carte menus on Friday and Saturday afford a choice of the buffet, prime rib, or orange roughy. Among the desserts are the celebrated "Death by Chocolate" (brownie, chocolate mousse, whipped cream, hot fudge, and nuts) as well as New York cheesecake, Viennese walnut cream layer cake, shortcakes, and sundaes. The Bin Room is open all week long, and its menu leans to sandwiches designed for the hearty appetite (the turkey bacon croissant is a favorite) and, in the evening, broasted Broadway chicken, orange roughy, New York strip steaks, and shrimp. The specialty of the house is a huge chef's salad.

We recommend the package for a pleasant evening's entertainment. The theater staged its 100th production in April 1987, which coincides with the mill's 120th anniversary as a viable business entity in south-central Michigan. Actors come from all over the country. About 500 are auditioned each year, from which 60 are hired. They live and work in the second-floor storage area. Depending on the size of the expandable stage and type of show, the theater can seat 155 to 230 people. Viewers are never more than 30 feet from the stage. Reserve two to four weeks in advance for the best seats.

Old mill, new ideas.

THE HISTORIC HOMER MILL, M-60, Homer, MI 49245. Telephone (517) 568-4151. Hours: luncheon 11 a.m.-4 p.m., dinner 5-9 p.m. Closed Thanksgiving and Christmas. Full bar service. Credit cards: MC, V. Write or call for theater schedules.

BEEF BURGUNDY
From Chef Russell Camp, the Historic Homer Mill

Have 2 cups brown sauce prepared (make with diced carrots, onions, and celery; beef stock; basil, thyme, marjoram, garlic, sugar; tomato paste and

105

Burgundy--see any standard cookbook for directions).
Heat 2 ounces butter in large saucepan, and brown
2 pounds cubed top round of beef. Season to taste
with salt and pepper; sprinkle with thyme and basil.
Add 1¼ cup red Burgundy wine, 1 sliced onion, and
12 ounces quartered mushrooms. Cook until liquid
has reduced by half. Add the 2 cups brown sauce.
Simmer 20 minutes. Serve on noodles or rice. Makes
8-10 servings.

(44) BILLINGSGATE

101 Main Street, P.O. Box 13
Horton, Michigan 49246

   In a picturesque, erstwhile Methodist church built
in 1906 and now designated a state historical site,
Billingsgate is one of Michigan's most original and
enjoyable restaurants. But perhaps that's the wrong
word; it's really a dinner club. Lunching and dining
here are mainly possible by appointment and for
groups. But Billingsgate is also open to the public
on Saturday. And it's worth a phone call any time
to see if a table's free.
   The red brick building, overgrown with ivy and
surrounded by a brown picket fence and graceful
birches and evergreens, is an example of the Romanesque style of the noted American architect
Henry Hobson Richardson. The interior is mellow
and clublike with subtle earth tones and soft lighting.
On the upper level in what was once the nave of
the church, with a resplendent stained-glass window,
grand piano, and comfortable antique settees, diners
can enjoy cocktails and appetizers before descending
to the lower level for dinner. A third room lower
still called the Pub Room may be rented by groups
that wish more privacy.
   James Beck, the owner, has a degree in architectural design from the University of Michigan.
He lived in England for a few years, hence the
name of the restaurant (ironic, of course--this is

hardly a place that recalls Billingsgate, the venerable and lowly fish market of London). James and his wife Karen do most of the cooking, and his mother is the chef du boulangerie (her breads are exceptional). Four-course dinners are price fixed very fairly for the quality of the offerings and the individualized attention ($16.50 as we go to press), but you will pay slightly more than the affordable going rate for certain more elaborate dishes (such as beef Wellington and baked Alaska). The procedure is to choose in advance from an extensive repertory of dishes that should appeal to the most discriminating diner. And, if you wish, you can make arrangements for an entirely personalized feast for your family or friends.

Among the starters are several pates, tomato Provencale, sausage pie, vichyssoise, gazpacho, and classic quiche Lorraine. Salad choices consist of Caesar, spinach, or mixed greens vinaigrette. The catalogue of entrees includes, among others, beef Bouguignonne, tournedos Chasseur, coconut shrimp, chicken Cordon Bleu and Florentine, seafood au gratin, and Cornish game hen. Accompaniments may be selected from a list that embraces such engaging items as curried fruit or vegetables, spinach Parmesan, corn souffle, onions mornay, and glazed carrots Grand Marnier.

Dinner wines are an afterthought, but thankfully they're inexpensive: beaujolais villages, Valpolicella, Blue Nun, and Soave. That's all, folks. Still, $7.50 to $9.50 per bottle is fair. House wines are Chablis, Rhine, and Paisano. We much preferred the prelicensed days here, when we could bring our own. For the number of beef entrees, Billingsgate is remiss in not providing at least one full-bodied red. The desserts, however, are dazzling: pies and cakes, meringues, sherry trifle, creme caramel, cherries jubilee, and the extremely popular dessert trolley with assorted sweets arranged on a 100-year-old serving cart.

For your own private culinary congregation.

BILLINGSGATE, 101 Main St., Horton, MI 49246. Take Spring Arbor Rd. (M-60) southwest from Jackson to Moscow Rd., which goes to Horton. Telephone (517) 563-2943. Luncheon and dinner, mainly by prior arrangement. Group dining; $35 deposit required to hold reservation. Open to public on Saturday until 11 p.m. Full bar service.

CHICKEN NEPTUNE
From Billingsgate

This is an unusual combination of fish and fowl that works well. Poach 12 skinned, boned whole chicken breasts in chicken stock to cover for 20 minutes. For stuffing, saute 1 pound scallops in butter till tender. Poach 1 pound each monkfish and cod separately in fish stock. Drain these and place in mixing bowl. Stir in 3/4 cup chopped sauteed onions and ¼ cup chopped parsley. Prepare bechamel sauce by heating 3/4 cup butter in skillet. Blend in 3/4 cup flour, and cook slowly 2 minutes. Gradually add 6 cups fish stock (from poaching); season to taste. Stir in ½ cup catsup and 2-3 tablespoons caraway seeds. Stuff chicken breasts and place in shallow baking dish. Thin remaining bechamel with half-and-half, and pour over enough sauce to coat chicken. Sprinkle with grated Parmesan and sauteed bread crumbs. Bake at 375 degrees for 45 minutes. Pour over the last of the sauce. Garnish with lemon slices, chopped green pepper, and parsley sprigs. Serves 12.

BRANDYWINE

(45)

The Brandywine Pub, since its opening day, has attracted quite a following of loyal regulars in the Jackson area. The exterior was once a modern version of American roadhouse style without a single window; but the latest owners, Bob and Lois Peterson, have opened it to the sunlight and yet retained its warmth and intimacy. The interior has always had panache: barnwood siding and brick on the walls as well as old posters and photographs, a gleaming brass church rail in the lobby, and a calculated, almost theatrical use of stained glass throughout.

There are four fashionable and fetching dining rooms. The Tiffany Room was our first choice for years, with its fireplaces and several semiprivate booths. The adjacent LaSalle Room, once rather too cool and contemporary, now has large picture windows and the same decor as the rest of the restaurant. The Lower Lounge felicitously has become a dining room instead of a seating area and, with its expansive fireplace wall of cut fieldstone, is particularly inviting. And the most recent addition is a trendy solarium called the Greenhouse, bedecked with potted and hanging plants and more of those notable Tiffany lamps.

Entrees, served with soup or salad, vegetable, muffins and soft whole-grain breadsticks, consist of the usual steaks and chops, a good chicken Cordon Bleu, meltingly tender veal liver, and some eloquent seafood and fish. The latter are just as popular, if not more so, as their red-meat counterparts. Fish is flown in fresh from Boston; some items are regularly offered (steamed mussels, scallops in butter sauce, and fried haddock), but at least three other alternatives are possible. Daily specials, too, are worth considering, such as pasta, stir-fried dishes, or something earthy like roast pork with baked apple. Servings are generous, but at least a dozen entrees may be ordered in smaller-sized portions. Prices are moderate.

A special characteristic of the Brandywine Pub is that vegetables are treated with the respect they deserve. The restaurant even adds a line in its advertisements--"fresh steamed vegetables"--right up there with the heavy hitters like prime rib and seafood. One entree, the variety casserole, is a most successful (and popular) melange of fresh vegetables and mushrooms baked in cheese sauce. Receiving top billing with classic appetizers is a crunchy and colorful vegetable cocktail. And the salads and vegetable side dishes are prepared with meticulous care and comprise only the best and freshest of seasonal produce.

Among the tempting desserts are cream puffs, a warm blueberry house dessert, deep-fried ice cream, and a dessert of the day, quite often the popular hot chocolate pudding ("We sell a ton of it," says Bob Peterson). California house wines are available by the glass, and the list contains about 20 offerings. None are extra special, except possibly the Moet and Chandon Champagne, but all are reasonably priced, most between $10 and $15. For nondrinkers, the pub carries a full line of New York Seltzers.

Superior seafood, voluptuous vegetables.

THE BRANDYWINE PUB, 2125 Horton Rd., Jackson, MI 49203. Southwest of city center; take 4th St. south; near corner of Horton and Jackson Rds. Telephone (517) 783-2777. Hours: luncheon 11 a.m.-4 p.m. Monday-Friday, dinner 4-10 p.m. Monday-Thursday (till 11 p.m. Friday-Saturday). Closed Sunday and most major holidays. Full bar service. Credit cards: AE, MC, V.

Your first hint of what's to come is on U.S.12 some three miles east of M-50: a shabby twin-towered lighthouse overlooking the highway. A half mile farther east is the Prehistoric Forest, with grotesque tree trunks, piles of artificial bones, replicas of ancient monsters (including our favorite, a friendly looking woolly mammoth)--all of them gaudily painted and perched on a blatantly bogus rocky hillscape. And you need not merely marvel passively at these wonders; you can "ride the Scout

Train on an exciting tour of a lost world that existed millions of years ago. Also visit [and we tend to think this is more important] the beautiful Mammoth Gift Shop." Or you might prefer the 400-foot Jungle Rapids Waterslide ("breathtaking turns"). Or, best of all, keep on driving east. You'll pass, in order, the Mystery Hill ("the amazing force of gravity"), Stagecoach Stop U.S.A. (of which more later), and most remarkable of all, Fantasy Land, a jumble of distorted buildings and weird, convoluted creatures that seem to have stepped out of a surrealistic nightmare. Finally, if you haven't had enough, take a look at the Bear's Lair Fun Park and the Go Cart Raceway. This, folks, is Irish Hills entertainment. Kids love it (but have you ever met a kid with good taste?).

To be fair, the Irish Hills is chiefly known for its rolling glacial topography and many sparkling lakes, not its plaster dinosaurs and other commercial attractions. It's a very popular vacation spot, and for that reason we'd like to acquaint you with the Golden Nugget saloon and steak house and the most worthwhile theme park in the area, both under the same able management. The latter is a facsimile of an 1890s Western town. More than 10,000 genuine period collectibles lend realism to the project; and the gunfights, jail breaks, train robberies, and runaway mine cars add further authenticity plus fun.

The Bahlau family has paid as much attention to details in its restaurant across the street. The Golden Nugget was designed and built in the tradition of the grand saloons of the California Gold Rush era. Antique buffs will appreciate the leaded glass chandeliers and windows, the gaudy Western stage and backbars, the collection of Gay Nineties' artifacts throughout. We especially like the Fireplace Lounge with its large round fireplace table in the center and its wealth of honky-tonk memorabilia. Just off this room is the Old Caboose, a railroad car seating up to 24. For an unusual people-watching vantage point, ask for a table on the balcony of

111

the Livery Stable. Or, if you want to be close to the dance floor, request seats in the Red Room.

All these rooms, combined with the downstairs Barbary Coast Room, seat a total of 500 people--and that's big.

Also big are the portions of good, sturdy American food: the Comstock Lode (two charbroiled pork chops served with barbeque sauce), hefty steaks, prime rib, fried chicken, and the popular catch of the day. A big winner here is the River Boat Gambler for $11.95, which includes a 7-ounce sirloin butt steak and a "heapin' helpin' of deep-fried ocean clams." Other entrees are frog legs, haddock, and crab legs--all dipped in beer batter and deep fried. If you're watching calories, you have only three choices: the Slim Sally hamburger plate, Big Mama's Delight (chef's salad), and the broiled catch of the day. If you couldn't care less about calories, the menu lists ice cream, strawberry shortcake, and cheesecake. But there's probably more; on our last visit we were lucky enough to tour the spotless kitchen and found ourselves spellbound by some gorgeous lemonade pies.

Bauer Manor, a couple of miles east of the Golden Nugget on U.S. 2, is another restaurant option. Situated in historic Davenport House, an 1839 former stagecoach inn, it's registered with the Michigan Historical Society. We've heard positive things about the food, and if you're vacationing in the Irish Hills, you might want to give it a try, too. A more sedate setting and more formal dining experience provides a contrast with the Old West atmosphere of the Golden Nugget.

A first-rate kitchen in the state's kitsch capital.

BAULAU's GOLDEN NUGGET STEAKHOUSE, 7305 U.S.12, Irish Hills area, Onsted, MI 49265. Twelve miles east of U.S.127; 4½ miles east of M-50. Telephone (517) 467-2190. Hours: Tuesday-Thursday 5-11 p.m., Friday-Saturday 5 p.m.-2 a.m., Sunday 12 noon-11 p.m. Closed Monday. Full bar service. Modern country band and dancing Friday and Saturday evenings. Credit cards: MC, V. Reservations accepted only for large groups.

Nearby attractions: Hidden Lake Gardens, managed by Michigan State University, is a 670-acre arboretum that includes a nature center and greenhouse amid a natural and developed landscape; it's spectacular in the fall color season. Located on Munger Rd. near Tipton (call 517-431-2060).

(47) Hathaway House

Entering their 25th year of operation, the Weeber family--Art, Mary, and Mike, the chef--are dedicated to making their guests feel welcome and very special. Though there are a few Continental and Oriental dishes on the menu, Hathaway House is 100 percent American, from the 1851 building to the furnishings, from the table settings to the service. Originally a private residence, the stately Greek Revival home hasn't changed much since its construction. Though converted to a restaurant in 1961, the feeling here is still that of a warm, friendly, and relaxing home, albeit a magnificent one.

The building is worth studying. The monumental facade is representative of the architectural movement that swept over the South and Midwest prior to the Civil War, a revival of the Doric Order of Greece that dates to four centuries before Christ. Some typical features incorporated in Hathaway House are the fluted columns and the triangular tympanum they support. It's an imposing exterior--those large white pillars, the crisp green canopy over the entrance, the low wrought-iron fence surrounding the grounds, and the manicured lawns and shrubbery. Imposing, but inviting, too. There are six gracious dining rooms, each with a different color scheme, and the decor is essentially early American, though the fireplaces and woodwork retain the classical lines of the building's architectural design.

The menu is dominated by good American cooking and goes far beyond limited steakhouse fare. Yes, the steaks, chops, and lobster are here (and are very well prepared), but there is much, much more. At least 20 entrees make an appearance: shrimp and scallops Parisienne, blackened sirloin, veal scallopini, traditional prime rib of beef, baked ham with brandied raisin sauce, and the famous fried chicken. Included with all dinners are homemade soup and an extraordinary salad table.

At luncheon the daily buffet is usually the focal point, consisting of six hot dishes, soup, the full salad table, and rolls. You can count on Chef Michael for an ever-changing, appetizing variety in his noon buffet. And on Sunday there's a smorgasbord featuring roast beef and ham, complemented by six other hot dishes and at least 25 salads. Though we're not enamored of salad bars or buffets, they work well here. The tables are in a separate room so that seating is not disrupted by traffic to and fro. The breads are mouth-watering (try the wheat mead). And the desserts should be forbidden, but we're glad they're not: ice cream drinks, lots of good coffees (Jamaican, Irish, Spanish, etc.), six-layer carrot cake, chocolate-peanut-butter pie, and deep-fried ice cream.

While at the Hathaway House you'll want to visit the numerous specialty shops on Main Street and possibly drop in at the Main St. Stable and Tavern in the restored carriage house in back. This second restaurant is publike, casual, and inexpensive. It's a good choice if you're feeding a big family. Directly across from Hathaway House is the latest addition to the complex: the Hiram D. Ellin Inn (bed and breakfast), offering fine overnight accommodations in a renovated 1883 Victorian red brick house. With the new inn, Blissfield becomes a great getaway destination.

114

There are lots of nice touches at Hathaway House. On the tables are pressed-glass stemware, fresh flowers, and petal-folded napkins. The children's menu is a prize winner--literally. We've seen lots of placemats and coloring books, but for the Little Guests here are magic slates; on the back the dishes (good selections, too) are named after famous Americans of the Revolutionary War period. The menu won a silver medal from the National Restaurant Association.

Deserves a gold medal for all-American cuisine.

HATHAWAY HOUSE, 424 W. Adrian St. (U.S.223), Blissfield, MI 49228. About halfway between Ann Arbor and Toledo, Ohio. Telephone (517) 486-2141. Hours: luncheon 11:30 a.m.-4 p.m., dinner 4-9 p.m. (till 10 p.m. Friday-Saturday); luncheon buffet 11: 30 a.m.-2 p.m.; Sunday brunch 11:30 a.m.-4 p.m. Closed Monday, December 24 and 25, and New Year's Day. Full bar service. On Saturday in the Ballroom Eddie Bogs, country/rock recording star, sings and entertains; book well ahead ($3 cover). All major credit cards.

CHOCOLATE PEANUT BUTTER PIE
From Chef Michael Weeber, Hathaway House

First, make the piecrust dough. Place 1 cup flour and ½ cup solid shortening in food processor with metal blade. Process until the consistency of coarse meal. Add 3-4 tablespoons water and process until dough begins to hold together. Chill 1 hour. Roll dough and fit into a 9-inch pie pan. Place waxed paper over the dough in the pan and weigh with dry beans or commercial pie weights. Bake 15 minutes in a preheated 400-degree oven. Remove weights and paper, and return to oven to finish browning.

For the filling, heat 1½ ounces unsweetened chocolate in microwave oven until melted. Mix together

1 cup sugar, 7 tablespoons flour, $\frac{1}{4}$ teaspoon salt,
2 eggs, and the melted chocolate. Slowly stir in
$1\frac{1}{2}$ cups scalded evaporated milk. Return the mixture
to low heat, and stir constantly till it begins to
boil. Reduce heat to simmer when boil is reached,
and cook 2-3 minutes more. Remove from heat,
and add 1 tablespoon vanilla. Mix $\frac{1}{4}$ teaspoon gelatin
with 2 tablespoons warm water until gelatin
dissolves. Stir into the hot pudding. While it cools,
mix the topping. Combine $1\frac{1}{2}$ cups confectioner's
sugar, $\frac{1}{2}$ cup peanut butter, and $\frac{1}{4}$ cup melted butter
in food processor; process till crumbly. Cover the
bottom of the baked pie shell with all but $\frac{1}{2}$ cup
of the crumbs. Pour in the cooled pudding. Chill
about 2 hours. Top with whipped cream and sprinkle
with reserved crumbs. Our hint: Try not to eat the
whole thing in one sitting.

Cousins Heritage Inn

48

Owners Paul and Pat Cousins call their restaurant
"a 19th century home serving 20th century European
cuisine." The description is terse, pointed, and perfectly true. But it gives no indication of the
adventurous eating experience in store for you at
the Heritage Inn. The house itself is a charmer:
a Greek Revival structure dating from 1855 and
once the residence of President Millard Fillmore's
brother (doubtless much more sedate that Billy
Carter). The Cousins have completely restored it
with discretion and taste. The subtly patterned
papers, dadoes, and hand stenciling on the walls
blend harmoniously with the bentwood chairs and
antique lamps. There's an unusual ceiling fixture
in the entryway, a combination gas and electric
light, marking the transition from old to new. Note,
too, the scattering of framed lithographer's proofs,
the work of Thomas Cole from an 1890-1900
magazine.

The restaurant seats only 45 diners. As a Cousins ad puts it, "Our dining room only seats 10--but then, our living room seats 16. And then there's the front parlor, or perhaps you'd prefer the study." We find it difficult to choose one room over another (although in the right kind of summer weather we're partial to the tiny screened front porch). The muted mauve and rose colors throughout are enhanced, even dramatized, by the elegant table settings: white and eggshell linens, gilt and burgundy rimmed service plates, crystal, candles, and bouquets of altamarius.

The talented chef at Cousins Heritage Inn is Greg Upshur, who worked at the Golden Mushroom with Milos Cihelka and at the erstwhile Tweeny's with Yvonne Gill, two exceptional training grounds. The dinner menu is revised at least every two weeks, and the luncheon choices change daily. Though Continental cuisine is featured here, menus eschew foreign labels. As Paul Cousins says, "We don't want our restaurant to be threatening." We agree; one sure threat to many American diners is the incomprehensible menu.

Entrees at dinner generally number just four: a seafood, poultry, game, and meat dish. The soup of the evening and several appetizers and desserts flesh out the small but captivating bill of carte. Seasonal fresh vegetables accompany the main courses. On our visit in the fall, among the first-course options were poached salmon terrine with crabmeat and capers and foie gras with Madeira sauce and apples. Comprising the entrees were poached sea scallops and shrimp with lobster sauce, roast pheasant with Armagnac sauce, New York strip steak sauteed with mushrooms and green peppercorns, and roast whitetail venison with sour cream sauce and glazed shallots. Prices ranged from $16 to $19.50.

The wine list here is like the menu, limited in number but offering excellent quality and a reasonable choice. The whites include five German selections, four French (three of them lovely Burgundies), five from California that should certainly interest you, and four sparkling possibilities. Sixteen reds, with only one older than 1979, are split between French and Californian and include a rich, marvelously colored 1982 Lalande-Borie with the flavor of black currants (but not the second wine of Ducru-Beaucaillou as many believe), a good '81 Figeac from St. Emilion, a very nice '80 Talbot, an underrated '79 gem from Chateau Meyney, along with nicely priced Burgundies (one a Beaujolais) and a good-valued Rhone. But the sleeper and bargain on the list is a terrific Chateau Verdigan, which will improve for years, though you can drink it now. The Californias are half Cabernets and one each of Pinot Noir, Petite Sirah, Merlot, and Zinfandel.

To return to cuisine, almost everything is done on the premises, including home-grown herbs, house-made ice creams, and cold-smoked meats and fish (the sturgeon is outstanding). Duck, beef, and venison are barded with backfat before smoking; and local apple wood from a nearby farmer's orchard is used in the process. We are impressed by such scrupulous attention to detail. But when we're leisurely dining in the lovely front parlor, with soft classical music to bind up the wounds of care, it's easy to forget all the hard work that goes on backstage.

Deft Dexter doings.

COUSINS HERITAGE INN, 7954 Ann Arbor St., Dexter, MI 48130. Two miles from exit 167 off I-94; on the town's main street. Telephone (313) 426-3020. Hours: luncheon 11 a.m.-2 p.m. Monday-Friday, dinner 6-9 p.m. (last reservation) Tuesday-Saturday. Closed Sunday, New Year's Day, Christmas Eve, Christmas Day, July 4. Full bar service. Credit cards: MC, V.

"Man wants but little here below, but likes that little good--and not too long in coming."
....Samuel Pepys

⑭ The Earle

Handsome and stylish, the Earle in Ann Arbor is a place to see and be seen, although there are a few less obtrusive recesses on the upper level around the perimeter of the room for those who wish to hide. But "upper level" is deceptive; everything here is below ground. The restaurant itself, when we visited it, was playing cat and mouse: the only identifying sign was small and inside a fairly dimly lit lobby. Luckily we knew what corner the eatery was on. Also, we looked for one of the oldest buildings downtown, an 1885 registered historic site--a hotel for most of its life and now called the Earle Building, hence the name of the restaurant. Though showing some wear and tear, it's attractively done up in steel blue and neutrals: tweed upholstery, brick and stone walls, bare wood tables--all warmed in the glow of candlelight. For several years this was a well-known jazz center in town. These days meals have taken on greater importance, but there's still a solo pianist Monday through Thursday and a combo that starts at 10 p.m. on Friday and Saturday.

The cuisine is described on the menu as "country cooking from the provinces of France and Italy." And the chef is Shelley Caughey Adams, who trained at the Culinary Institute of America, apprenticed at the London Chop House, and was sous-chef at the Money Tree. Her talent and resourcefulness are apparent in the frequently changing and always mouth-watering menus. On a visit last fall we we were impressed with the choice of appetizers, including such classics as saucisson en croute (pastry-wrapped sausage) and polenta baked with pancetta ham and Fontina cheese.

On the catalogue of entrees were a fragrant and hearty cassoulet (Provence's answer to pork and beans), duck breasts sauced with winter fruit compote and served with turnip-potato puree, scallops and shrimp sauteed with fennel, among other tanta-

119

lizing possibilities. Most popular with the Earle's regular customers are the lamb and, when it's on the menu, the coulibiac, a Russian-derived salmon filet with dill encased in puff pastry. It's a wonderful dish, and we highly recommend it. We also enjoy the veal sweetbreads in sorrel cream sauce served on a puff-paste shell; on a recent visit it was faultless. And if you're a pasta fancier, you needn't look elsewhere. Chef Adams has a magic touch; if you have the chance, try her fettuccine with garlicky sun-dried tomatoes and steamed mussels. Salads, too, are terrific, always made up of the freshest greens and vegetables. Our favorite: the romaine tossed with walnuts, Gorgonzola cheese, and a perfect vinaigrette. All portions are generous, and prices are moderate to expensive, depending on how judiciously you order.

In addition to some of the best menus we've seen in Michigan, the Earle has an absolutely outstanding wine list. With hundreds to choose from, you can easily find something quite satisfactory, possibly an old favorite, and only a few cost more than $30! Try the '82 Potensac for $20, any of the three Cos d'Estournels for about $40, the two best wines ever produced ('75 and '82) at Chateau Meyney for $30, a good LeBoscq at $13, a fine '80 Langoa Barton ($22), the supple and mature Terrey-Gros-Cailloux of 1979 ($17), and on and on outside of Bordeaux to other areas of France, then Germany and California. This is, in our opinion, the longest list of wine wines at reasonable and even bargain prices to be found in Michigan.

Prime provincial provender.

THE EARLE, 121 Washington St., Ann Arbor, MI 48104. Downtown, 1 block west of Main St. on the corner of Washington and Ashley. Telephone (313) 994-0211. Hours: 5:30-10 p.m. Monday-Thursday, 5:30 p.m.-midnight Friday, 6 p.m.-midnight Saturday, 5-9 p.m. Sunday. Closed Sunday in the summer (Memorial Day-Labor Day) and most holidays. Full bar service. City parking building and lot across the street. Credit cards: AE, DC, MC, V.

TORTA DI BERNARDONE
From Chef Shelley Caughey Adams, the Earle

This is a great dessert recipe from Tuscany in
Italy. Peel 2 pears and 2 tart apples, and slice
thinly. In mixing bowl cream together 9 ounces unsalted butter and $2\frac{1}{4}$ cups sugar. Add 5 eggs, one
at a time, beating after each addition. Sift together
3 cups flour, and 1 tablespoon baking powder. Add
to butter mixture, and blend just until mixed; do
not overbeat. Add 1 teaspoon vanilla and $\frac{1}{2}$ cup
Pernod. Pour into a buttered 12-inch springform
pan. Decorate top with fruit slices, pushing them
slightly into the cake. Bake at 350 degrees until
golden brown and center springs back when lightly
touched. Serve at room temperature with warm
cream. Chef's note: All ingredients should be at
room temperature before you begin. Do not overbake;
this is a soft, almost pudding-like cake.

The first thing to remember about Escoffier is
to choose your companion for the evening with
roughly the same care as you choose your house-
mate or your slippers (someone or something you'll
be warm and comfortable with). It's an intimate
place without too much light, and this of course
makes it an attractive spot for those evenings when
you just want to groove with someone close. Still,
the approach is in the grand formal tradition of
crystal chandeliers, immaculate linens, Bavarian
china, European stemware, and haute cuisine at
pretty much haute prices. So do plan on an evening
of it.

We were impressed with Escoffier from the moment we heard about it from two dear friends,
Jane and Georges Joyaux, who a few years ago
showed us much of the best of France (and were
instrumental in arranging a visit in Bordeaux with

wine authority Alexis Lichine). We were impressed more recently when we learned that another Frenchman, Marcel Marceau, sat in the back dining room raving--and not just with his hands--about the food here. But what overwhelmed us with its improbability was the East Lansing connection. Chef Charles Solomon hails from the MSU University Club and Beggar's Banquet, and owners Maureen and Tony Perault once attempted to educate the outlanders in wine and cheese at the Vintage Year shop in downtown East Lansing. We consider it sheer treachery that they located in Ann Arbor.

The bill of fare changes every two to three weeks and leans, as you'd expect from the name, to classic French cuisine along with some regional specialties. Dinners are price fixed at roughly $24 to $30 and include four courses, with surcharges for certain items. For example, your choice of first courses might include duck and pistachio pate, pear tart, or fried Camembert. Soups provide a Gallic gamut: for instance, black beans and shrimp or a rich chicken consomme. Some half dozen entrees are available each evening to please the most fastidious tastes. There's usually a good balance of seafood (salmon, lobster, langostinos); beef and lamb (beef tenderloin tournedos with wild mushrooms or saddle of lamb with Madeira sauce); veal; and poultry. As a refreshing finish, in the French manner, is your choice of salad, generally a "verte" (mixed greens) or at an extra charge some inspired creation featuring artichokes and peppers, watercress, or Chevre cheese. All items are available a la carte. You'll pay a bit more but don't skip dessert. Escoffier is particularly proud of its expert patissier, Carol Pryor. The mousses, cheesecakes, and hazelnut torte are exquisite.

The wine cellar is being expanded and much improved. As we write this, according to Tony Perault, some 700 wines will be offered, including red Burgundies of vintages '66, '69, and '70 and some really old Bordeaux, among them classic 1961s, occasional venerable bottles from 1947, and the like. About 250 different Bordeaux will soon be available from a wine cellar prepared to hold about 4000 bottles. If all this comes to fruition, Escoffier might have the best wine selection in the state.

C'est si bon.

ESCOFFIER, 300 S. Thayer, in the Bell Tower Hotel, Ann Arbor, MI 48104. Between downtown and the U-M campus. Telephone (313) 995-3800. Hours: 6-10 p.m. Tuesday-Thursday, 5-11 p.m. Friday-Saturday. Closed Sunday, Monday, and major holidays. Parking in building next door. Full bar service. All major credit cards.

HUITRES EN CHAMPAGNE
From Chef Charles Solomon, Escoffier

These oysters in Champagne sauce are a favorite hors d'oeuvre at Escoffier. We could make a meal of them! In a heavy covered saucepan, sweat 2 cups sliced mushrooms and ½ cup finely chopped shallots until mushrooms are wilted and shallots transparent. Add 2 cups Champagne, and reduce over high heat until evaporated. Add 2 cups heavy cream, and cook until starts to thicken. Strain. Season with salt, pepper, and cayenne pepper. Shuck 48 oysters, and place on an ovenproof platter. Bake at 400 degrees until the edges start to curl (about 5 minutes). Transfer to 6 serving plates (6 oysters per plate) and top with Champagne sauce. Serves 6.

For railroad buffs and admirers of Victoriana, the Gandy Dancer is a must. The building is a designated Michigan and national historic site, and while that sounds a trifle flat, it does convey a very special aspect of this restaurant. Conversion of old railway stations into eating places is becoming nearly ubiquitous, but in this case both the station itself, which dates to 1886, and the restaurant, a Chuck Muer seafood house, are worth going out of your way for.

The depot was known in railroading days as "the finest station between Buffalo and Chicago." And today, we conjecture, it's one of the finest stations in the country. Lending authenticity and even greater appeal to the Gandy Dancer is the auxiliary stone building on the west that now serves as the Amtrak station on the main line between Chicago and Detroit. Yes, the trains are still rumbling by. When the restaurant opened in 1969, customers applauded somewhat self-consciously at the sight of a passing engine and its entourage. Now they cheer in vociferous appreciation, and the bells start ringing.

The interior has been handsomely restored by the Muer Corporation, and the patina of age and character remains untouched. The main--and what for years was the only--dining room occupies the site of the original waiting room. Adjoining is a newer addition, and now the favorite of customers: the Garden Room, with floor-to-ceiling windows, trailing foliage, and effective track lighting on the expansively high ceiling. The tables for two along the windows, just 15 feet from the railroad tracks outside, are our choices. Each room in the restaurant is so interesting and well designed that we hope you'll stroll all the way from the upstairs dining room on the west side of the building to the small, intimate Wolverine Room on the east.

Seafood and New England dinners predominate here, as at the other colonies of the Muer empire, and this is reflected in the emphasis on whites in the adequate but not elaborate wine list. Chuck Muer's restaurants are noted for their seafood, and it is indeed very good as a rule. Prices border on the expensive, but the high quality justifies this. You might start with a cheering bowl of Charley's

Mediterranean-style fish chowder (see the recipe below) or any of several choice shellfish appetizers. Entrees include various fried, poached, and broiled fish and shellfish as well as bluefish baked in parchment, red clam linguine, seafood mixed grill, stuffed lobster, and a couple of obligatory Cajun blackened fish.

Two dinner specialties are Charley's Bucket (a down-east clambake comprising Maine lobster, Dungeness crab, mussels, steamers, corn on the cob, and redskins) and bouillabaise with or without lobster. Bowing to current tastes for lighter fare, many of the fish are now served poached or broiled; the Gandy Dancer has gone from three deep fryers to one. Also, a number of pastas are now on the menu.

To put a bit more adventure into your experience with the Gandy Dancer, there's an easy round-trip train ride on the Amtrak from Detroit to Ann Arbor. It'll drop you off for about four hours, long enough for a leisurely meal and a relaxing time listening to the Gandy Dancer's pianist before the return train arrives.

Depot dining at its best.

THE GANDY DANCER, 401 Depot St., Ann Arbor, MI 48104. Six blocks north of the business district. Telephone: (313) 769-0592. Hours: Monday to Thursday 11:30 a.m.-11 p.m., Friday 11:30 a.m.-12 midnight, Saturday 5-12 p.m., Sunday 3-10 p.m. Full bar service. Pianist in lobby nightly at 7 p.m. All major credit cards.

CHARLEY'S CHOWDER
A Chuck Muer signature soup

Heat ¼ cup olive oil in a large pot until very hot. Add 3 minced medium cloves garlic. Cook until golden in color. Add ½ finely chopped medium onion and cook a minute or two. Add a pinch each

125

of basil, oregano, and thyme and cook 1 minute.
Add 1 rib finely chopped celery, and cook until
translucent. Add 6 ounces stewed tomatoes, chopped
very finely (can use canned stewed tomatoes, either
a 6-ounce can o r half a 16-ounce can). Cook 20-
25 minutes, stirring.

Add 12 cups water, 1 pound boneless fish (tur-
bot or pollack), 2 ounces clam base, and cook for
15 minutes. (If clam base is not available, substitute
12 cups clam juice for the water.) This last 15
minutes of cooking should be on high heat with the
pan uncovered. Add salt to taste, cover the pot,
and cook on low heat for 20 minutes, stirring frequently to break up the fish and blend the flavors.
Just before serving, add 2-3 tablespoons chopped
parsley. Serves 6.

⑤② raja rani

Raja Rani takes its name from the East Indian
words for "king" and "queen," a translation quite
appropriate to the regal fare regularly served here.
According to owner Loveleen Bajwa, originally from
the Punjab state (not to mention being the great-
great-granddaughter of Majaraja Ranjit, once king
of all India), the restaurant does mainly a word-of-
mouth business. And the word seems to be getting
around more and more. This is a good place to find
out what Rudyard Kipling was raving about all
those years.

On our first visit some time ago, Raja Rani was
housed in a small box of a building where Washtenaw meets Huron, and even then it was a magical
spot where we're sure genies were at work in the
tiny kitchen. Today the restaurant has found a home
in an impressive old Victorian mansion, with an
interior done up in shades of peach, persimmon,
and burgundy and softly lighted by the same shiny
pierced-brass lamps.

East Indian cuisine is one of the greatest in the
world, and the use of spices and herbs is its most

126

distinctive characteristic. Unfortunately too many people group all Indian dishes into a homogeneous "curry" and have no idea of the wide variety of flavors that result from the centuries-old craft of blending spices. First-time customers here usually order the Raja Rani special dinner for two: Mulligatawny soup, tandoori chicken, egg and vegetable curries, pullao (rice), dal (lentils), chapati (unleavened bread), papadams, and chutney relish. It's almost impossible not to become enamored of the chicken, which has been marinated in an amalgam of spices, citrus, and yogurt and then cooked to reddish golden perfection. The color alone, from the saffron and turmeric, is aesthetically satisfying. As for the papadam, Americans--who spend millions each year on potato chips--should be delighted with this paper-thin, crisp delicacy made from lentil flour.

Habitues at Raja Rani are particularly fond of the fiery hot Madras-style lamb vindaloo and the tandoori chicken masala (served with a creamy tomato sauce; "masala," by the way means "sauce"). We can also vouch for the shrimp biryani, the tandoor mixed grill, and the chef's special, Bataera Keema Mattor, a quail curry with ground lamb and peas. Order raita with the more incendiary dishes; this is a yogurt and mint sauce that acts both as a palate refresher between tastes of different dishes and as an almost essential tongue cooler after an injudicious mouthful of vindaloo.

Another way to try several Indian dishes at one meal is to lunch at Raja Rani, which now offers an excellent buffet of curries, pullao, lentil fritters, dal, vegetables in yogurt, meatballs, tandoori chicken, nan (tandoor-baked bread), and a fruit custard dessert (a good value at $5.95). Mrs. Chalal, the dining room manager, most likely will greet you at the restaurant. This charming lady in 1985 was chosen "most hospitable person" in a poll of restaurant customers by AAA and the Michigan Restaurant Association. If you're nice to her, she'll probably show you the tandoor, an authentic Indian clay oven, in effect a deep oval charcoal pit set into firebrick and concrete and glamorized by a glazed tile exterior. The temperature reaches about 1000 degrees, and it's quite a sight to watch the chef reach bare handed into that inferno to slap a round of nan dough directly onto the oven wall.

Food fit for a majaraja.

RAJA RANI, 400 S. Division St., Ann Arbor, MI 48104. Three blocks east of Main St., just south of the business district. Telephone (313) 995-1545. Hours: luncheon 1:30 a.m.-2 p.m. (buffet) Monday-Friday, dinner 5:30-10 p.m. Monday-Saturday. Closed Sunday and some holidays. Full bar service. No credit cards. Reservations taken only for parties of 6 or more.

EAST INDIAN SAMOSAS
From our files

These are spicy little turnovers served as appetizers. Mix together 2 cups flour and ½ teaspoon salt. Cut in 2 tablespoons cold butter and 1 tablespoon shortening. When mixture resembles coarse crumbs, gradually add ½ cup water, stirring with a fork until it holds together. Gather dough into a ball and set aside.

For the filling, saute ½ pound ground beef in a small amount shortening, along with 1 medium chopped onion, 1 clove minced garlic, 1 teaspoon salt, ¼ teaspoon each of cayenne, ground cumin, and ground ginger. When brown, stir in 3 medium boiled diced potatoes and 1 cup cooked peas. Cool. Divide pastry into small balls, and roll out into 4-inch circles as thinly as possible. Cut each in half. Moisten edges with water and place filling on each ½-circle. Fold to form triangles and press to seal. Fry, a few at a time, in 1-1½ inches of oil heated to 375 degrees.

"Strange to see how a good dinner and feasting reconciles everybody."

....Samuel Butler

Like most university towns, Ann Arbor has its share of low-priced eating places. But unlike many such towns, it's also the hub for lots of up-and-coming high-tech businesses and it's close to a major medical facility. The restaurants decribed below are not student hangouts or beer parlors, though an occasional undergraduate might inadvertently wander in.

ARGIERO'S ITALIAN RESTAURANT, 3900 Detroit St., Ann Arbor, MI 48104. At Catherine St., a few blocks north of the city center. Telephone (313) 665-0444. Hours: luncheon 11 a.m.-2 p.m. Monday-Friday, dinner 5-9 p.m. Monday-Thursday (till 10 p.m. Friday), 11 a.m.-10 p.m. Saturday. No alcoholic beverages. No credit cards.

Brick walls, red-and-white-checked tablecloths and curtains, seductive Italian music, travel posters from Roma and Firenza, and seats for only about 30 diners--fortunately Argiero's hasn't been tempted into cut-throat restaurant competition. It remains instead a small family enterprise. Rosa and Tony Argiero head the family and the restaurant, and their children--Sam, Amelia, Carmine, and Michael--all contribute. The cafe is located in an old section of Ann Arbor and was once a gas station and later a fish market. Now it's taken on a settled Italian flavor and has begun to look much older than it is.

The menu is simple and special. There are just two antipasti: a primo at $2.50 and a supremo at $4.25, depending on the number and quantity of

Italian smoked meats. Soups are minestrone and tortellini in chicken broth. Entrees include huge, filling portions of spinach fettuccine, generous slabs of spinach lasagne, chicken alla cacciatore, and a delicious garlic-laden pasta di giorno. The menu is dominated by pasta: fettuccine, lasagne, rotini, ravioli, spaghetti, mostaccioli, and fidelini. And with it we much prefer the Parmesan butter and pesto sauces to the tomato. You can order meatballs or Italian sausage on the side. Dinner prices range from $3.50 to $5.95. At lunchtime look at the list of panini (sandwiches); the pane in carrozzella (prosciutto, ham, melted provolone on toasted bun) is a standout. For either lunch or dinner, check the blackboard at the entryway: on our last visit the specials were eggplant bracciole, veal parmesan, and manicotti. One criticism--we wish the bread were crustier.

AFTERNOON DELIGHT, 215 E. Liberty, Ann Arbor, MI 48104. Downtown, corner of Liberty and 5th Ave. Telephone (313) 665-7513. Hours: 8 a.m.-8 p.m. Monday-Friday, 8 a.m.-5 p.m. Saturday, 9 a.m.-3 p.m. Sunday. Beer and wine only. No credit cards or reservations accepted.

Afternoon Delight is, first of all, well known in Ann Arbor as a morning delight, featuring freshly squeezed citrus juices, homemade muffins, waffles, blintzes, and omelets. But it's also a delight at any hour of the day. The exterior is eminently forgettable: big windows on a corner with a plain, black and white sign. But step in, and listen to the crowd waiting for tables and the line cooks at work in the open kitchen. Then look at the menu and the prices, and you'll see why this may be the most popular restaurant of its kind in Ann Arbor. It's not a place for claustrophobiacs, but no one seems to mind. In fact, a sort of camaraderie develops as you look at the posted specials with your fellow standees. "Have you tried the pecan chicken with wild rice?" someone might ask. Down the line a bit an answer will come: "No, I come for the sandwiches." The juices start to flow as you wait. The pecan chicken is a teaser, as is the seafood crepe. Most customers come for the salads, sandwiches, and soups. Good things on the list include the albacore grill (tuna on whole wheat muffin topped with Cheddar cheese and garnished with broccoli and tomato), the veggie nacho, and the elaborate house salad. Aside from the crabmeat salad, nothing costs more than $4.75.

KANA KOREAN RESTAURANT, 1133 E. Huron St., Ann Arbor, MI 48104. On B.R.23, at Washtenaw; less than a mile east of Main St. Telephone (313) 662-9303. Hours: 10:30 a.m.-9 p.m. Monday-Friday, 4:30-9 p.m. Saturday. Closed Sunday. No alcoholic beverages. Credit cards: MC, V. Reservations accepted for parties of 5 or more.

The exterior recalls a forties dinette. The interior is much as it was when Raja Rani was here, and if that's an omen, good things are in store for this little Korean eatery. Some dishes that might be new to you include the hot and spicy fish soup; the crunchy vegetable and beef dumplings (Kun Man Du); a pungent pork stew (Ho Bak Chige); and Kim Chee--incidentally, a pickled cabbage, and not John Kim's brother-in-law. Cold noodles make an assertive appearance at Kana: as an appetizer mixed with vegetables and hot sauce and as an entree with pork or chicken. Prices for entrees range from $3.99 to $9.95, with most items about $4.50 to $5.50. A hard-working Korean family works diligently to make your meal as pleasant as possible.

THE PALM TREE, 216 S. 4th Ave., Ann Arbor, MI 48104. Downtown, between Liberty and Washington. Telephone (313) 662-2642. Hours: 11 a.m.-9 p. m. Monday-Thursday, 11 a.m.-10 p.m. Friday-Saturday. Closed Sunday. No alcoholic beverages. No credit cards or reservations accepted.

"Ahlan wa sahlen!" are the Arabic welcoming words at the Palm Tree. Nameh and Dawin Sahem are your hospitable hosts in this little storefront eatery. Small round oak tables and captain's chairs and an etagere on one wall highlighting Mideastern copper and brassware are the distinctive aspects of the decor. But the delicious, freshly cooked Lebanese food is what encourages customers to return again and again. On the menu are such items as kibbeh (ground beef and cracked wheat), kafta (broiled spiced beef), baba ganooj (eggplant), falafel (a fried chick pea concoction served in pita bread), fatoush (spiced tomato, cucumber, and toasted pita bits), and tabouli (cracked wheat salad). Better known are the lamb and chicken shish kebab and lentil soup. But two specialties beg for mention: the vegetarian rakika (an eminently palatable combination of noodles, sesame paste, sesame seeds, tomato, and cauliflower) and the broiled baby lamb chop dinner, the most expensive menu item at $7.50. Most offerings cost less than $4.

SOUTHSIDE GRILLE, 640 Packard Rd., Ann Arbor, MI 48104. At State St., just south of the U-M campus. Telephone (313) 662-7811. Hours: breakfast 7-11:30 a.m. Monday-Saturday, luncheon 11:30 a.m.-2:30 p.m. Monday-Saturday, dinner 5-10 Tuesday-Saturday, 7:30 a.m.-2 p.m. Sunday. No alcoholic beverages. No credit cards.

When you hear the words "hash house," what do you visualize? Vinyl booths, Formica tables, windows opening on a busy street, austere furnishings and decor, coffee-stained menus? The Southside Grille comes very close to this image. The surprise here is that there's nothing imitation about the food. Breakfasts do indeed boast predictable though well-cooked eggs and bacon with your choice of toast, but also on the morning menu are chocolate-almond waffles with creme anglaise, Mexican huevos rancheros, French toast made with Grand Marnier batter, chorizo and linguica sausages, and omelets filled with such exotica as cappicola and Montrachet cheese. Lunches (starting at $3.75) and dinners ($5.25 and up) are just as startling, especially the beautiful salads; envision, for instance, marinated duck breast with poached fruits and raspberry-hazelnut vinaigrette.

ZINGERMAN's DELICATESSEN, 422 Detroit St., Ann Arbor, MI 48104. Near 5th Ave. and Kingsley, about 4 blocks north of the central business district. Telephone (313) 663-DELI. Hours: 7 a.m.-8:30 p.m. Monday-Saturday, 9 a.m.-8:30 p.m. Sunday. No alcoholic beverages. No credit cards or reservations accepted.

Our favorite deli in the world is Zabar's, on the upper west side of Manhattan. But takeout is the order of the day there. True, people do take out at Zingerman's, but a heckuvalot eat in and stay on and on. Yet the constant crush of customers is what makes this Ann Arbor landmark so colorful. On one wall is the meat and cheese case; a number system is in effect, and the young man behind the counter keeps up a running line of patter with the patiently waiting patrons. On the wall farthest from the door is the sandwich counter, and nearby the salad case, which also displays such deli classics as chopped liver, blintzes, and potato knishes. But let's go back to the sandwiches. More than 30 "singles" are available (meaning one basic ingredient like liverwurst or curried turkey salad) on your choice of bread (rye, pumpernickel, challah, whole wheat, onion or Kaiser roll, or sourdough). These comprise the wimp's list. Heavy hitters at Zingerman's choose one of the 50 esoterically named "combos"--to mention just two, Randy's Routine (whitefish salad, scallion cream cheese, and tomato on pumpernickel) and Monahan's Irish Lament (cream cheese and Irish smoked salmon on a bagel). A note on the menu points out that almost 2000 pounds of corned beef is cooked and sliced at Zingerman's every week. Prices range from $1.95 for a Kosher hot dog to $6.50 for a "Montreal smoked meat combo." Plan on $4 to $5 for a hefty sandwich.

At first glance you might think that Zingerman's is only a store and deli with a long line of customers and eye-high pyramids of imported foods.

But no, it's even more than that. Tightly wedged into the last vestiges of space are six little marble tables. Good luck on getting one.

AVOCADO DIP WITH CAVIAR
From Zingerman's

Mash 1 large ripe avocado. Stir in $\frac{1}{4}$ cup sour cream and 2 tablespoons lime juice. Season to taste. Spoon back into the shells, and make a cavity in the middle. Spoon in 2 ounces American golden caviar. Serve with unsalted tortilla chips.

THE MAYFLOWER HOTEL

"Community," with all its connotations, is the one word that's most applicable to the Mayflower Hotel. It was founded in 1927 by 234 stockholders who had faith in the hotel and the then tiny community of Plymouth. Managed since 1939 and owned since 1964 by Ralph and Mabel Lorenz, it's still true to its original mandate as, first and foremost, a community hotel. In fact, in 1981 Vice-President Bush presented Mr. Lorenz with a national award from the Small Business Administration for his "leadership and contributions to the city." This sense of community has been extended to the hotel's gracious dining rooms and London Pub. For, after all, what is more communal and traditional in this country than Thanksgiving?

Ralph Lorenz, himself an immigrant from Austria, has become an eloquent spokeman for those immigrants who arrived in 1621 at another Plymouth. Accordingly, during the entire month of November each year, he offers to groups a re-creation of the first Thanksgiving feast, complete with narrated films and souvenirs. On Thanksgiving Day itself, the hotel serves 1000 people in the Meeting House and 500 in the main dining room. And throughout the month, busloads from all over the country make the pilgrimage.

In a warm English-style setting diners partake of food as early American as you can get: authentic dishes based on recipes that Native Americans provided to the bereft Pilgrims in the 17th century. Pumpkin soup is served in hollowed out acorn squash. There are "fruits of the sea" (oysters, scrod, shrimp), and nut and squash breads, a taste of venison, and of course turkey served over a sage-scented cornbread stuffing with sides of succotash and cranberry relish. The succotash is not the expected corn and lima bean mixture but a stewlike amalgam of corned beef, chicken, turnips, potatoes, white beans, and hominy. To finish, guests are treated to a luscious corn custard and "Priscilla Mullen's Cranberry Torte."

Almost as celebrated is the Sunday brunch served across the street in the Mayflower's Meeting House. For $8.50 you can gorge yourself on cinnamon rolls, corned beef hash, chicken stew, omelets, potato and buttermilk pancakes, blintzes, waffles, sausage, ham, ad infinitum. (Call to reserve a table.) Incidentally, the Mayflower is a family operation, and at one time or another all six of the Lorenz children have worked here. One of them, Kirk, owns two top-notch new restaurants, both recommended in this book: the Hotel Frankfort and the Brookside Inn in Beulah.

Native bounty, thanks to Ralph.

THE MAYFLOWER HOTEL, Main and Ann Arbor Trail, Plymouth, MI 48170. Downtown. Telephone (313) 435-1620. Hours: Mayflower Room 4-10 p.m. daily; Meeting House brunch 10 a.m.-2 p.m. Sunday; Steak House luncheon 11 a.m.-2:30 p.m., dinner 4-10 p.m. Full bar service. Credit cards: AE, MC, V.

SQUASH BREAD
From the Mayflower Hotel

We've adapted the recipe to make it more specific. To 1 cup mashed, cooked winter squash (acorn or Hubbard are good), add 2 tablespoons sugar, 1 teaspoon salt, 1½ cups scalded milk, and 1 tablespoon butter. When still warm but not hot, add half a cake of yeast and enough flour to make a soft dough (5-6 cups). Knead 15 minutes, adding flour as necessary. Place in buttered bowl, turn to coat, and then let rise in a warm place to double its volume, about 2 hours. Punch down, knead briefly, and shape into 2 loaves. Place in 2 greased 9x5-inch loaf pans and let rise again. Bake about 50 minutes in a preheated 370-degree oven.

It's fast changing, but we in the United States still too often gain our first impressions of Chinese food from chop suey, chow mein, fried rice, and egg foo yong without appreciating the centuries-old tradition of Chinese cuisine, one of the greatest in the world. But somewhere between our first taste of chop suey and our first taste of Peking duck, we begin to recognize the signals to all our senses that this cuisine, almost beyond any other, offers. Texture--crisp young vegetables, silky sauces. Aroma--sometimes assertive, sometimes subtle, even elusive. Color--the golden clarity of consomme, the brilliant greens of a fresh bok choy. And flavor-- from the almost endless condiments and spices of the Orient: ginger, coriander, sesame oil, hoisin and soy, red chili peppers, mustard, star anise and garlic, perhaps the most versatile cross-cultural herb in existence. Though the style varies from one province to another, Chinese at its best is an artistic study in sensual contrasts.

And Ah Wok is a place of which even our perfectionist friend Jimmy Wang would approve. The shopping-center location might at first put you off, but once inside you'll find a modern, trim decor with globe lighting, well-spaced tables and booths (best for two persons) along the walls, partitioned by Chinese import crate lids--the only obviously Oriental accessories in the room. The service is courteous and helpful, and the food exceptional.

The chef/owner Gam Moy, a native of Canton, came to this country via Hong Hong in 1932, making him surely the elder statesman of Michigan chefs (most of whom are in their 20s or 30s). He opened his restaurant more than 10 years ago and specializes in Mandarin and Cantonese dishes. The Mandarin is hotter, spicier, and the ingredients more finely cut than in south China's more familiar Cantonese. The menu here is quite comprehensive and features many such seldom-seen Chinese treats as the always wonderful shark's fin soup (the Chinese equivalent of caviar, truffles, and foie gras wrapped up in one), sizzling soups (chicken and shrimp), fried taro nests, and velvet chicken. The Szechuan hot and sour soup is outstanding. On three days' notice Chef Gam Moy will provide you with that great shark's fin soup as well as Peking duck, one of China's most prestigious dishes, served at feasts all over the country. It must be prepared well ahead to assure a skin free from fat and perfectly crisp and yet a flesh that's moist and flavorful.

The luncheon menu offers many of the same dishes along with several combination plates. Prices are moderate. And don't just rely on the menu; if the ingredients are in the kitchen, Gam Moy will be glad to whip up something special. Furthermore, if you can get 10 people together and call ahead, the restaurant will arrange a lavish banquet of 11 courses or more. It's a way to savor Chinese cooking and service at its most enchantingly characteristic.

Ah, the winning wok.

AH WOK, 41563 W. Ten Mile Rd., Novi, MI 48050. Take exit 162 off I-96; go south 1 mile on Novi Rd., then east 1 mile on Ten Mile Road to Novi Plaza. Telephone (313) 349-9260. Hours: 11 a.m.-9:30 p.m. (till 11:30 p.m. Friday-Saturday), noon-9:30 p.m. Sunday. Closed Monday and most major holidays. Full bar service. Takeouts. All major credit cards.

STEAMED FISH
From Chef Gam Moy, Ah Wok

Clean one 2-2½-pound walleyed pike or black bass and place on a platter that will fit inside your steaming kettle. Mince ½ cup fermented black beans and mix with 1 tablespoon vegetable oil. Add 3 ounces finely minced pork, 2 ounces julienned fresh ginger, 1 tablespoon soy sauce, ½ tablespoon Chinese molasses, ½ teaspoon salt, ¼ teaspoon white pepper, and 4 whole diced green onions. Spread this on top of the fish. Put the platter in a steamer over boiling water, and steam for 25 minutes. Near the end of that time, heat 5 tablespoons vegetable oil till very hot. Remove platter of fish from steamer, and pour over the oil.

Our hints: You can improvise a steamer by putting a rack (or even an upturned cake pan) in any large kettle. For even steaming of fish make 3 to 4 diagonal slashes on each side with a knife.

(56) Periwinkles
FOOD AND SPIRITS

The vibrant periwinkle blue awning smartly sets the restaurant apart from the other buildings on Brighton's Main Street. The interior is even more appealing and welcoming, done up in a stylized floral fabric, carved oak chairs, dark muted rose upholstery, brass railings, silk flowers, pink and white table linens. Periwinkles, by the way, are

138

ground-hugging evergreen plants that bear pretty blue blossoms in the spring. The name also refers to tiny saltwater snails, and both kinds of periwinkles are pictured in the restaurant's logo. But the briny ones remind us of an occasion a few years ago when we snorkeled for the little devils in a bay off Mykonos, a Greek island in the Dodecanese. We collected a good bucketful to feed nine people as an appetizer; we steamed them as we would mussels or clams, and wound up with one shriveled, absolutely tasteless mouthful. Fortunately, Periwinkles doesn't serve periwinkles.

What it does serve is the likes of salmon en croute, escargots with garlic-spinach puree, brandied duck livers, Cognac shrimp, and other exciting edibles as first courses. Then come such entrees as filet of beef Matignon (with a choice of Bearnaise or green peppercorn sauce); Dover sole with mushrooms, tomato, and creme fraiche; duckling and fresh fruits; and a classic cassoulet de Toulouse. But the menus change, at least seasonally. In the fall, for example, game is served more often; one excellent dish is the sauteed venison with red wine and peppercorns. Presentations are carefully conceived; accompanying an entree might be a wonderfully artistic vegetable arrangement: carrot flowers, onion cups filled with peppers, miniature pattypan squash, beets vinaigrette, and more. Indeed, vegetables are so well treated here that we highly recommend the vegetarian platter offered every evening. We found it just as tempting as many of the delicious protein-rich options. The soup, pasta, and fish of the day are also worth considering. In all, there's a good variety of choice and a good price range from moderate to expensive.

In charge of the kitchen is the talented chef, Peter Veach, who trained with Daniel Hugelier at the Detroit Athletic Club and later Win Schuler's. At his side is an able pastry chef, Laurie Thomas Joransted, who bakes all the breads, onion-dill rolls for sandwiches, croissants, and some great cheesecakes, pastries, and tortes (do try, if possible, the apple or pear rougemont).

Wines are selected with care, mostly by Paul Terzano, the maitre d'hotel. There are many in the $10 to $15 range along with some great ones for special occasions. For those who haven't been here since May 1987, you should know that plans are under way to expand the wine list considerably from such attractive offerings as a splendid '76 Leoville Las Cases for about $40 and a fine '81 Beaumont for only $12, a real bargain. You'll most likely have no trouble finding a wine of satisfactory quality and price here.

Brighton's brightest.

PERIWINKLES, 400 W. Main St., Brighton, MI. In city center. Telephone (313) 229-4115. Hours: 11: 30 a.m.-2:30 p.m. luncheon Tuesday-Friday, 5-10 p.m. dinner Tuesday-Saturday. Closed Sunday, Monday, most major holidays. Full bar service. All major credit cards.

BLUE CHEESE MOUSSE WITH CHIVE CREAM
From Chef Peter Veach, Periwinkles

This is a superb appetizer and would also serve well as an accompaniment to certain entrees. Soften 12 ounces cream cheese in mixing bowl. Add blue cheese to taste, and mix until smooth. Add 2 eggs and 1 egg yolk, one at a time, scraping bowl down after beating in each egg. Season with ½ teaspoon salt, pinch each of cayenne pepper and nutmeg. Slowly add ½-1 cup whipping cream, while beating, until well blended. Adjust seasoning if necessary. Spray timbale (or custard) molds with nonstick spray, and fill molds 3/4 full. Bake molds in a pan of hot water in a 350-degree oven for 15-20 minutes, or until done (as for custard).

For chive cream, in saucepan combine 2 tablespoons white wine and 1 tablespoon snipped chives. Cook over high heat until reduced by half. Add 1 cup whipping cream and cook to reduce until sauce is thick. Salt and pepper to taste. Serve with blue cheese mousse.

(57) JENNIFER'S CAFE

When you drive into the Bay Pointe Plaza, a mini-mall on a busy intersection, you'll think, "Oh, oh, Marjorie and Duke really goofed on this one." And, just looking at the outside of Jennifer's Cafe won't dispel your doubts. Sure, it's neatly painted and the windows are clean and the sign is intact. Actually it's much nicer in front than most cafes in shopping plazas. But it looks just like a typical American sandwich shop--where's the adventure? Once inside, the trepidations may remain, but only for a short while. The decor is modest: Formica, paper, plastic. But there's carpeting underfoot and a compensatory color scheme of pale blue and deep lavender. What's more, the place is immaculate. Still, an adventure?

Yes. When you look at the menu and taste the food at Jennifer's, we can assure you of a culinary event. American sandwiches are indeed on the menu: classic Reuben, Monte Cristo, club, ground sirloin, as well as several succulent mixtures wrapped in pita bread. And the sandwich of the day on our first visit was a memorable ground veal patty with Swiss cheese and grilled onions on rye. The house soup is chicken and rice with lamb meatballs, and a second soup du jour is offered. One unusual touch at lunchtime is the home-cooked potato chips that accompany the sandwiches--wonderfully thin, crisp, and tasty.

Dinners, however, are even more dynamic. There's a choice of spinach tortellini tossed with ham or shrimp, sauteed chicken breast topped with Canadian bacon and Cheddar or with prosciutto and Havarti cheese, chicken fettuccine, sauteed beef tenderloin tips. Our own preferences lean towards the veal Amaretto with toasted almonds, the lingonberry veal, and the sauteed chicken and shrimp with Havarti and white wine sauce. Prices are low to moderate, ranging from $8 to $10.

Quite an international menu, don't you think? But, wait; there's more: baked kibbeh, shish kafta, stuffed grape leaves, baba ghanooj, falafil. And leading all other entrees in popularity is the chef's combination platter, comprising six such Middle Eastern specialties at a very reasonable $8.45. Your serving person will be happy to explain all the nuances of these delightfully aromatic dishes. And do save room for dessert. The Mideast pastries are unusual and good, and two other tempting options include French vanilla ice cream with piz-zelle (a crisp Italian cookie-crepe) and "ataiif," the house specialty--a light pancake filled with walnuts and pistachios and napped with vanilla sauce.

Chef-owner Jack Suidan has cooked at the Holly Hotel (see our review), Truffles, and the Bay Pointe Golf Club. The restaurant is, in fact, right across the highway from that club. A sweetly sentimental attachment resulted in the cafe's nomenclature; Jack and his wife Jayna named their restaurant after their first-born child, Jennifer, since, according to her parents, "she is a breath of fresh air and a continuous source of new experiences that is our goal here."

Yessir, that's our baby.

JENNIFER'S CAFE, 4052 Haggerty Road, Walled Lake, MI 48088. At the intersection of Haggerty and Richardson Rds., north of town in Commerce Township. Telephone (313) 360-0190. Hours: noon-9 p.m. Sunday-Thursday, 11 a.m.-10 p.m. Friday-Saturday. Closed most holidays. No alcoholic beverages. Credit cards: MC, V ($15 minimum). Reservatins not accepted.

TABOULEE
From Jack Suidan, Jennifer's Cafe

This is a great, refreshing salad; and Jack

142

Suidan's version is one of the best. The recipe he sent us served 3C; we've reduced all quantities to come up with eight mouth-watering servings.

Place 1/3 cup cracked wheat in a colander or sieve and wash under cold running water. Drain and put in a small bowl. Stir in 2 tablespoons lemon juice and 2 tablespoons cold water; let set until the wheat absorbs the liquid. Into a large mixing bowl, put 2 bunches washed, well-drained, chopped parsley along with 2½ medium cucumbers (peeled and diced), 2 diced green peppers, and 3 diced tomatoes. Mince ¼ medium oniion and stir into mixture in bowl. Add the cracked wheat (be sure all the liquid is absorbed; if it's not, wait a while). Add ½ cup vegetable oil, ½ cup freshly squeezed lemon juice, and 1½ teaspoons salt. Mix thoroughly. Serves 8-10.

(58) LA FAMILIA MARTINEZ

To judge Mexican food on the basis of a taco is like judging Italian cuisine from a pizza. Both are popular snacks (and full meals can be made of them), but Mexican cuisine, like that of other countries, has a long history and comprises a wealth of varied dishes, many of them going back to Montezuma, the famous emperor of the Aztecs, and many others derived from the Spanish. The finished products are rooted in native bounty: chiles (more than 140 varieties grown in Mexico alone), corn, tomatoes, avocados, cocoa, pineapples. In an early survey of MSU students, of all the Mexican restaurants in Michigan, three were consistently recommended: the Beltline Bar in Grand Rapids and the more authentic La Familia Martinez and Trini and Carmen's, both in Pontiac.

The Pontiac restaurants are, as you've guessed, managed by the Martinez family, Trini and Carmen and their 12 children. La Familia has been open since 1966 and shows some of the wear and tear, but the effect is comfortable and relaxed all the same. The main dining room is adjacent to a long bar that seats about 20, and there's an overflow room in back. But the action is up front in the American-tavern-like setting with a few Mexican touches (including Latin music on the jukebox).

Trini and Carmen's opened its doors in 1978 and seats about the same number of customers (up to 150) but is roomier and modern and has more personal touches, mementos from Mexico brought back by the family. Though neither place is quite the equal of Mexico City's El Refugio, they're both worth visiting if you like or want to try some genuine Mexican food.

"Desayuno" isn't served, and we're sure that the Martinez women make some great huevos rancheros. Maybe these will come in the future. But you can have a fine "comida" (dinner), "cena" (late supper), or "merienda" (light snack). All the familiar items are here: tostadas, burritos, tamales, nachos, and enchiladas. We suggest the combination dinner if you'd like to sample more than one. We find the "crispa con queso" appetizer especially delicious. For the "postres" try the Mexican cookies or "munuelos" (deep-fried flour tortillas with cheese and honey, similar to "sopapilla"). Specialty drinks include imported Mexican beers and Margaritas.

Por una comida excelente.

LA FAMILIA MARTINEZ, 848 S. Woodward Ave. (B.R.10), Pontiac, MI 48053. About 3 miles south of the business district. Telephone (313) 338-8477. TRINI AND CARMEN'S, 1715 N. Telegraph Rd., Pontiac, MI 48055. Telephone (313) 332-6851. Hours at both: 11 a.m.-midnight, Saturday noon-midnight, Sunday 4-11 p.m. Closed most holidays. Full bar service. All major credit cards. No reservations.

⑤⑨ MITCH'S

Mitch's opened its doors in 1952 as a tavern serving only beer and wine, but within three years, not by the choice of the Mitchells but by the demand of their customers, pizzas went on the menu. Today Mitch's is practically an institution in the southern end of the state and serves, in addition to its famous pizzas, some of Michigan's best barbequed ribs, Italian pasta, and salads.

Oldtime Mitch's patrons recall the scaling paint and sagging structure; the building was described as looking like it was slowly slidng into the lake. As sentimentalists we were sad to see the old place doomed to destruction. But the newer building on the same site is similar enough to make us feel at home. The exterior is a lot different--dark red brick, roughsawn siding, and a Western-style veranda. But inside there are still two levels and the same knotty pine walls and wooden floors. The roomy booths with dark wood and stained-glass dividers afford privacy and comfort.

So, then, what's so special about Mitch's? The portions are stupendous, the quality high, the atmosphere cheerful and casual, the food straightforward and mouth-watering, and--if you order wisely--it's a bargain. You'll like the liter bottle full of ice water on each table. And while you're waiting, you'll be served a basketful of salt bread--chewy and buttery hot bread sticks: fables in flour. These are addictive and, unless you're careful, guaranteed to ruin your appetite for what's to come. Hard as it is to believe, there's more to Mitch's than the salt bread. The Greek salad, for example, is by far better than any we've had in Athens. It accompanies certain dinners, or you can order it instead of the tossed salad at a slight additional charge. And you really should plan on sharing it; one salad is enough for two and could suffice for four.

The barbequed baby back ribs are the best we've had in Michigan (though ribs tend to encourage controversy among their devotees). Toby, our waiter, showed us the eight-foot, glass-enclosed barbeque grill in the kichen. It takes 100 pounds of charcoal just to get it to cooking temperature, and Mitch's uses up 500 pounds of briquettes in one night of grilling. As they say in the South, this is a hog heaven. Also on the menu are baked and barbequed chicken, steaks, chicken parmigiana, and a good selection of seafood and fish. Pastas include spaghetti with several sauces, linguine with clam sauce, lasagne, and a superb "special rigatoni." Again, share. There's a lot of sharing here, so much so that Mitch's even has a "sharing charge" of $2 per table--and it's worth doing.

The service is fast and attentive. We suggest beer with the ribs or pizza and Chianti or Burgundy by the glass with the pasta. "Come as you are" seems to be the dress code, although a sign above the front door forbids bare feet and motorcycles. Mitch's II has opened at 6665 Highland Road (M-59) in Pontiac and has much the same offerings but was mainly established for banquets and private parties. Mitch's I on Cass Lake is our choice.

Pure pleasure.

MITCH'S, 400 Cass Elizabeth Rd., Pontiac, MI 480 54. In Waterford Township, just west of Cass Lake Rd. Telephone (313) 682-1616. Hours: 10 a.m.-10 p.m. Monday-Thursday (till midnight or later Friday, Saturday, and Sunday). Closed Christmas and Thanksgiving. Full bar service. Carryouts, across the road; call 681-3400 (salt bread, anyone?) Credit cards: MC, V.

(60) The Pike Street Company

Pike Street, okay--that's its address. But "Company"? The name, trendy as it sounds, was sensibly chosen. The building actually did once house a company, a really big company; it was a Michigan State Telephone Exchange. And the owners of the restaurant are also part of a bona fide company, which just a few years ago purchased four square blocks in downtown Pontiac in an effort to revitalize the city with an entertainment center along the lines of Detroit's Trapper's Alley. An initial enterprise was the Pike Street Company Restaurant, a handsome red brick structure with green-painted frame trim, situated in what was the retail and cultural hub of Oakland County in the 1900s and which is now listed in the National Register of Historic Places. Coming soon will be Baker Street North, a jazz club and luncheon spot. And we can envision lots of upbeat, interesting things happening now that Pike Street Company has begun sprucing up the neighborhod.

The dining room with a beige, burgundy, and blue color scheme, has two especially nice circular booths, each seating up to five persons and surprisingly in the middle of the room. The porch is more casual and is decorated in green and cream shades. And it's worth stopping in at the lounge, Cassidy's Tavern. There's a great old horseshoe bar and some before and after photos of the building. A piano and bass play during lunch, and a small group provides entertainment Wednesday through Saturday evening.

As you see, Pike Street Company has some good ideas. But its best idea recently was to acquire an outstanding chef, Brian Polcyn, who spent five years working and training under one of Michigan's finest cooks and teachers, Certified Master Chef Milos Cihelka of the Golden Mushroom in Southfield. Then followed a year and a half as chef of the sophisticated Lark in West Bloomfield and lately of the Austrian Pine Farm in Grand Blanc. Chef Brian, half Polish and half Mexican, has his roots in two of the world's heartiest cuisines, and he retains a healthy respect for sound, basic food and the use of the best fresh ingredients (which is, after all, the essence of that abused phrase "gourmet cooking"). "He was the best assistant I ever had," according to Chef Milos.

For openers, there might be a choice of mushrooms with Madeira, poached shrimp with Cajun remoulade, escargots sauteed with toasted filberts, and the pate of the day. Look for such entrees as beef medallions with sherry, caramelized onions, and bacon; breast of capon stuffed with crabmeat and partnered with Champagne sauce and asparagus; and Michigan brook trout with shiitake mushrooms. The house salad is a decorative composite of spinach, julienned pear, and mushrooms with honey-mustard dressing. We imagine that Chef Brian, as he has done elsewhere, will offer special "chef's dinners" that focus on certain foods or cuisines at fixed prices for several courses. But this may still be in the planning stage, as is the wine list, sure to be updated and improved along with the opulent new offerings in the culinary line. And for Lions' fans, Pike Street Company presents a real treat, the Sunday "BST," a combination of buffet brunch ("B") at the Pontiac restaurant, a shuttle ride ("S") to and from the Silverdome, and a ticket ("T") to the game. The cost of the package is based on stadium rates; in 1986 it was $23 per person. Tickets go like hotcakes, so call well ahead.

You're in good company on Pike Street.

THE PIKE STREET COMPANY, 18 W. Pike Street, Pontiac, MI 48058. Downtown, 2 blocks south of M-59 (Huron St.). Telephone (313) 334-7878. Hours: 11 a.m.-11 p.m. Monday-Thursday, 5-11 p.m. Saturday, bar till midnight. Closed Sunday (except for Lions' season), Christmas, New Year's Day. Full bar service. Valet parking. Credit cards: AE, DC, MC, V.

LOBSTER BISQUE
From Chef Brian Polcyn, Pike Street Company

This exemplifies a few techniques that Chef Brian teaches in his classes. "Some people think this is hard to do; that's not true," he says. Keep this recipe in mind when you cook any kind of bisque. In a large stock pot melt ½ stick butter; in this sweat 1 onion, 2 ribs celery, 3 carrots, and ½ head chopped garlic. Add 2 quarts light fish stock or canned clam juice, and bring to a boil. Add 2 bay leaves, 1 tablespoon thyme leaves, and 1 tablespoon black peppercorns. Drop 4 (1½-pound) live Maine lobsters into the boiling stock. Bring water back to a boil, cover tightly, and turn off heat. Allow to finish cooking in stock 20 minutes. Remove lobsters; strain stock and set aside. Remove meat from lobster shells (reserving shells and all juices), and set meat aside. Grind shells in meat grinder or pound with mortar and pestle until a fine pulp.

In a stock pot sweat the ground shells along with ½ head chopped garlic until all the moisture has evaporated. Add ½ cup brandy and ignite. When flames die down, add strained stock. Bring to boil, and then simmer 1 hour, stirring occasionally so it won't stick. Strain twice, once through a large-mesh screen and then through a fine screen. Reduce stock if necessary. Add 1 cup heavy cream. Dissolve some arrowroot in cold water, and add gradually, stirring, until desired thickness is reached. Season to taste with salt and white pepper. Cut lobster meat into bite-sized pieces, and add. Garnish with finely chopped chives.

Our hints: "Sweating" means cooking at high heat until vegetables exude their moisture. You can use several layers of cheesecloth instead of the screens Chef Brian calls for. Substitute cornstarch for arrowroot if you wish.

⑥⑴ MEADOW BROOK HALL
beauty in all seasons
history for all ages

This is the stuff of dreams. A blend of Tudor and Elizabethan architecture, the 100-room mansion is one of the most impressive buildings in the state. Set within rolling, glacially formed hills, Meadow Brook Hall was completed in 1929 for $3½ million (imagine what it would cost today, if it could be built at all) by the Alfred G. Wilsons--Matilda

Wilson was the widow of auto pioneer John Dodge).
In 1957 the Wilsons donated their estate and
surrounding farm land to Michigan State University
for the establishment of another campus, which in
1970 became an independent institution, the present
Oakland University.

The exterior of brick and sandstone, with windows inset with decorative stained glass, is enhanced
by 42 brick chimneys extending from the gabled
tile roof to serve 24 fireplaces, all of individual
design, as suggested by those at Hampton Court,
Henry VIII's summer home outside London. It's like
stepping into another century as you enter the
Great Hall, with its needlepoint draperies, stone
arches, and oak ceiling beams. Leading from this
room is our favorite, the Main Gallery, patterned
after that of England's Knole House, with the inside
wall consisting mostly of windows that open onto
the magnificent Grand Ballroom on the floor below.
For the children, there's even a secret staircase--
but no dungeon.

The Christopher Wren Dining Room, accented by
walnut paneling, ornate lighting fixtures, and an
elaborately carved ceiling, seats 36 at the gleaming
inlaid table and, with the smaller tables in the
room, will serve up to 84 persons. Throughout the
manor house are priceless antique furnishings in a
variety of periods and styles as well as paintings
by such masters as Rembrandt, Gainsborough, Con-
stable, Turner, Van Dyck, and many more , all
personal choices of the Wilsons for what was, after
all, their home. And this fact is what lends Meadow
Brook Hall the fascination, but not the coldness,
of a museum.

And, yes, visitors may dine in this splendor. In
July and August the Summer Tearoom is open, and
on pleasant days there's outdoor dining nearby. Exceptional buffets are served on Sundays throughout
most of the year in the stately Wren dining room,
but in July and August it offers the same menu
as the tearoom: mostly soups, salads, sandwiches
(try the Polish sausage with Provolone cheese).

However, dining at Meadow Brook is only possible in conjunction with tours and conferences. You might even consider arranging your own group tour, available year round by appointment and including lunch or dinner. Luncheon tours require a minimum of 20 persons; dinner tours are arranged for 30 or more.

Chef Laurie Dorch's dinner entrees include a number of chicken preparations (in wine sauce with artichoke hearts, for example), veal tenderloin with mushrooms and Cognac sauce, and medallions of pork with a bacon-onion-wine sauce. The menu is quite extensive and will please most tastes. A series of stately seven-course dinners offers another possibility; seven of these, each focusing on a single European cuisine, were scheduled for the 1986-87 season at $60 per person. And for the ultimate fantasy, consider staying overnight at Meadow Brook; accommodations (though not in Matilda's room) along with meals may be arranged for a group of at least ten persons (the house can sleep up to 38).

A special annual event is Christmas at Meadow Brook Hall in early December. The mansion is stunningly decorated by florists for the occasion, the fireplaces are glowing, and light lunches are served in the Carriage House. Is it worthwhile and popular? Just ask any of the more than 30,000 visitors who showed up in 1986.

Our own magnificent obsession.

MEADOW BROOK HALL, Oakland University, Rochester, MI 48063. Telephone (313) 377-3140. Tour hours: 10 a.m.-5 p.m. (last tour at 4); tours last at least an hour. Dining hours: Summer Tearoom open July and August 11 a.m.-3:30 p.m., Sunday buffet 1-5 p.m. year round except in July and August (when it has same menu as tearoom). Group tours, including luncheon and dinner (and rooms for the night)available year round by reservation. Alcoholic beverages offered only in group plans. No credit cards or reservations for the Summer Tearoom.

GREEK CHEESE TRIANGLES
From Meadow Brook Hall

These are great appetizers, and the finished
product looks much more involved than the actual
work that goes into producing them. For the filling,
Make ½ cup very thick bechamel sauce (or make
American white sauce of 1 tablespoon butter, 2 tablespoons flour, and 1 cup milk). Add 2 egg yolks
and 1 pound Feta cheese. Purchase 1 box prepared
filo dough for this amount of filling.

Brush 1 sheet filo with melted butter. Place
second sheet on top, and brush with butter. Cut
this double layer into strips (5 across). Place 1
tablespoon cheese filling at the end of each strip
so there's room to fold a triangle of dough over
it. Continue to fold triangularly (like folding a flag)
until each strip is a closed triangle. Brush front
and back with butter, and place on baking sheet.
Repeat this process until all the filo and filling have
been used. Bake triangles 5 minutes at 425 degrees
until lightly browned. Watch carefully while baking;
Remove immediately if filling starts to ooze out
or triangles may burst.

Painted barn red and with a pine green canopy
over the doorway and a cursive neon sign, "Darby's,"
the building stands out jauntily among the other
commercial establishments nearby. It's at least 100
years old, and for 20 years before the arrival of
its present owner, Mary Beth Darby, it was a
restaurant with nothing much worth going out of
one's way for--barbequed ribs and a blue-jeaned
clientele. Now this culinary caterpillar has found
its butterfly wings. Darby's opened in January 1985,
and perhaps "pragmatic" best describes it. The

modest menus of its earliest days met with a more and more sophisticated response from its customers. And Mary Beth rose to the occasion and now presides over what may be the finest dining establishment in Macomb County.

There are three small main dining rooms plus another little one off the bar. We like the front parlor facing Cass Avenue, especially the round table for four at the window. A fireplace is the interior focal point, but the room glows red year round from the lighted sign outside. People often request seats in the "neon room." Just as pleasant, though, is the largest dining room with only ten tables or so, a second fireplace, and an eye-catching French tapestry on one wall. Furnishings are Victorian but with a mix of other periods (more pragmatism), and the color scheme throughout of forest green, terra cotta, and beige is subtle and soothing. The general effect is the homey hospitality of an earlier, more genteel era.

Dinners are a la carte and fairly expensive, boasting such inventive entrees as Michigan pheasant with dried-cherry vinaigrette sauce and wild rice patties, Norwegian salmon with oyster mushrooms and roasted red peppers, sauteed partridge with spinach and black chanterelle mushrooms, and baked Dover sole with rosemary-lobster sauce. Prices generally start at $16 or $17. You really needn't order anything else, except, of course, wine from one of the best lists we've seen. But it's hard to avoid gilding the lily at Darby's. How can you resist a soup like puree of red bean or an appetizer of wild mushrooms in puff pastry?

Luncheon is less spectacular but also much less expensive. Still, don't count pennies here. This is a place to enjoy a leisurely hour or so, savoring the delectable creations from Chef William Wolf's kitchen. (Wolf, by the way, is a member of the Michigan Culinary Olympic team, which will travel to the 1988 Olympics in Frankfurt, Germany.) The menu, which changes daily as it does in the evening, might offer a venison veal ragout with fettuccine, roast leg of lamb with pear chutney and spinach angel-hair pasta, or sauteed ginger-glazed Hawaiian marlin.

Now for some words about that wine list. How would you like to choose from, among others, 13 Californian Cabernets, 17 Champagnes (including a nine-liter bottle), 18 red Burgundies, and a spectacular selection of nearly 50 Bordeaux dating back to 1945 (the year of the victory)? And the list ends with about 10 different Cognacs, none lesser than a VSOP, including the incredible Remy Martin Louis XIII. The emphasis is clearly on quality rather than economy so plan accordingly. Surprisingly, the magnum of '76 Branaire-Ducru at $75 may well be the greatest bargain here, so get together with another couple or two and enjoy this very good red wine.

Macomb's most marvelous.

DARBY'S, 45199 Cass Ave., Utica, MI 48087. Two short blocks north of M-59, one block west of Van Dyke Rd. Telephone (313) 731-4440. Hours: 11:30 a.m.-10 p.m. Tuesday-Saturday (till 11 p.m. Friday-Saturday). Closed Sunday, Monday, and major holidays. Full bar service. Entertainment: music to look at (a computerized piano that plays all by itself). Credit cards: AE, DC, MC, V.

PARSNIP AND PEAR PUREE
From Chef William Wolf, Darby's

Chef Wolf notes that this is an excellent accompaniment for fish, poultry, pork, veal, or wild game. We tried it with One Water Street's pheasant (see)-- fantastic! In a 12-inch skillet warm 1 tablespoon butter or margarine. Add 2 medium-sized parsnips (peeled and sliced ½-inch thick), 1 medium pear (peeled, cored, and sliced ½-inch thick), and ½ of a small red onion (peeled and thinly sliced). Cook slowly for several minutes. Add 3 tablespoons white wine (not too sweet), 2 teaspoons honey, ½ teaspoon sugar, 1 teaspoon cider vinegar. Cover, and cook slowly until parsnips are tender, about 30 minutes. Remove from pan, and puree in food processor or blender. Salt and pepper to taste. Serves 4.

(63) JOHNSON'S

If you'd like to recapture the atmosphere of the wood-framed roadhouses so common four or five decades ago, stop in at Johnson's, outside of Mount Clemens. Sure, there's a new screen door out front and someone jammed a room air conditioner into one of the windows as well as improving the parking lot with a couple of loads of crushed rock, but thankfully the old Johnson's remains. On the outside of the building is waterfront-weathered wood, painted blue with a large neon sign spelling out the owner's name. The place started out as a gas station-cum-grocery store and after several additions evolved into an eatery. A long, old, well-stocked bar extends along the west wall, and eight or ten tables occupy the remaining area (avoid the table for two nearest the kitchen). Some of the furnishings are new, but most first-time visitors over age 45 will probably be impressed by the nostalgic aura of a place that opened in 1937 and has stayed much the same.

For lunch Johnson's offers about 20 sandwiches, including a low-cost homemade grilled frankfurter and a liverwurst on dark bread (ask for an onion slice). Soup and chili are always available, and a creamy New England clam chowder (the real article) is served in weekends. About 20 dinner entrees are on the menu, two-thirds of them "seafood." By far the most popular, and deservedly so, is the broiled Boston scrod with lemon butter (less is often more where fish is concerned; see the recipe below). Some 400 pounds of it is consumed each week at Johnson's. Also outstanding are the deep-fried lake perch and pickerel (walleyed pike), and the beef is prime.

Do consider the daily specials, too: simple but well-prepared things like broiled orange roughy, sword-fish, and fried trout strips.

We wish we could tell you that prices are low, but "moderate" is a better description. Still, the value increases as you come to appreciate the authenticity of the place. This is one of those half-hidden marvels that you're glad to know about. Even getting there is a small adventure as you drive east from I-94 along North River Road and pass Selfridge Air Base with its variety of planes and an occasional takeoff or landing and as you notice the increasing clutter of all kinds of boats in sundry stages of repair both in and out of the water along the nearly continuous row of marinas and docking facilities on the shores of the Clinton River and Lake St. Clair.

Finally, if you glimpse a tall, white-haired, handsome septagenarian, it's probably Fred Johnson himself. Born in Masachusetts and later a runaway with the Ringling Bros. circus, he's now a member of the local "Old Crowd." He's run a good restaurant for years, and if you enjoy your meal, we're sure he'd like to hear about it. If you're a circus buff, ask him about Emmett Kelly; if you're a seafood buff, he can tell you the difference between scrod and schrod.

A remarkable roadhouse.

JOHNSON'S, 32003 North River Rd., Mt. Clemens, MI 48045. North River Rd. exit (number 237) off I-94, eastbound about 3 miles. Telephone (313) 469-9656. Hours: 11 a.m.-3 p.m. luncheon, 5-10 p.m. dinner, 1-9 p.m. Sunday. Closed Christmas, New Year's Eve, New Year's Day. Full bar service. Credit cards: MC, V. Reservations not accepted.

BROILED BOSTON SCROD
From Johnson's

We've all heard scrod described as a sort of poor

156

man's lobster. But we think it deserves recognition on its own merits. This recipe is good for any fleshy fish. Ideally, use freshly caught fillets of scrod weighing under 2½ pounds. Johnson's uses only the thickest part of the fillet and trims away the small part of the tail and the belly part.

Cut the fillet in half; brush the skin side with lemon butter; and place, skin side down, in a pan of flour. Shake off loose flour, and lay fish in in a greased broiler pan with floured side down. Brush the top of the fillet with lemon butter (melted butter mixed with fresh lemon juice), and dust lightly with paprika. Broil about 10 minutes per inch. Test with fork; it should flake easily. Served with melted butter.

Even if you're a discriminating diner-out, sometimes you need a respite from creative American cuisine and other dynamic approaches to cooking. Sometimes wild rice crepes, balsamic vinaigrette, and Chevre with pear puree cannot quite warm the soul--or balance the budget--like, say, a mountain of smelt for $3.95 or (are you ready?) a 12-ounce slab of prime rib for $5.99. Welcome, then, to Terry's Terrace in Mount Clemens.

Terry Owens, who graduated from high school in Mount Clemens, is the young and enthusiastic owner. He enjoys doing business in his hometown because he's able to chat with old friends among the regular clientele. He also loves to eat, which is why he piles the platters so high; apparently he thinks everyone's capacity approaches his own. We were first attracted to Terry's place when we read Marcia Biggs' review in the Detroit News: "OK, so it is smoky and the band plays a little loud for a little too long. Terry's Terrace is still the best cheap eats in Macomb County, one that keeps my circle of friends returning over and over again."

It is, indeed, an eye-opener of a restaurant. The menu is extensive, the food unsophisticated and basic, and the portions and prices guaranteed to please. It's a lively and likeable place. And tremendously popular, with boaters in the summer and people of all ages year round; we've seen it three-quarters full at 5:30 on a Monday night. Look in one direction, and you'll see a small television set and jukebox. Look towards the bar, and there's a huge TV screen and two more jukeboxes. Look almost anywhere, and you'll see endless wall and ceiling adornments--the results of Terry's 20 years of collecting antiques.

One particular old collectible has taken a beating over the years: every toddler who comes in here falls in love with the four-foot-high Yogi Bear doll near the bandstand. The little ones have squeezed his nose so often that it's charcoal gray and misshapen; Terry's made arrangements with a tolerant dry cleaner to spruce him up. As for seating, the gold Naugahyde chairs are more comfortable than most of this ilk, but our own preference is for one of the seven semiprivate booths in the stylish bar area.

But back to those bargains. That 12-ounce prime rib costs $5.99 only on Wednesday and Sunday, but on other evenings it's $6.95, still a steal. Sixteen-ounce cuts are regularly $9.95 and on special nights $8.99. The zesty barbequed ribs come in two portion sizes, also: a whole rack for $11.95 and a half for $6.95. Steaks, hamburgers, lake perch, walleyed pike are other favorites, as are the baked lasagne (an enormous serving, enough for two, at $5.25) and the occasional weekend special, a creamy seafood fettuccine at $5.69 (see Terry's recipe below).

Appetizers and side orders at Terry's Terrace reach heroic proportions, so be forewarned. The Nachos Supreme at $4.95 could be shared by a dozen hungry people as a starter; a half order is a more-than-ample, foot-long platterful. The "side" of spaghetti and meatballs ($1.50) is as large as a dinner portion would be elsewhere. We now know why the restaurant pictures two whales in its logo.

In case any food snobs are reading this and turning up their educated noses, we should note that one regular customer is none other than Dan Hugelier, Executive Chef of the celebrated Amway Grand Plaza Hotel in Grand Rapids and head of a Culinary Olympics team. Chef Dan likes the fish and chips and veal Parmesan, according to Terry, and recently left a note that read, "Food and service at the Terrace are always great." That's some compliment. Maybe even well-known chefs need to warm their souls and balance the budget.

Blue light specials every day.

TERRY'S TERRACE, 36470 Jefferson St., Mount Clemens, MI 48045. About 3 miles east of town; take Crocker St. east to the end. Telephone (313) 463-2671. Hours: Monday-Friday 9:30 a.m. to 2:30 a.m. (breakfast served till 11 a.m.), Saturday-Sunday 8 a.m.-2:30 a.m. Closed Christmas Day. Full bar service. "Easy-listening" entertainment Wednesday-Sunday evenings. Credit cards: AE, MC, V. Reservations not accepted on weekends.

SEAFOOD FETTUCCINE
From Terry Owens, Terry's Terrace

Melt 2 tablespoons butter in medium-sized saucepan, and saute 2 teaspoons finely chopped onion and 1 clove minced garlic. Cook a few minutes until tender. Add 1 pound mixed shellfish (shrimp, crabmeat, scallops, lobster), 2 tablespoons chopped parsley, ½ teaspoon seasoning salt, ¼ teaspoon white pepper, ¼ teaspoon oregano, 2-3 teaspoons sweet Marsala wine. Cook 5 minutes 'on moderate heat until the shrimp curls and turns pink. Add 1½ cups half-and-half, just to cover seafood, and set over

159

low heat. Dissolve 2 teaspoons cornstarch in 2 teaspoons cold water. When sauce is hot, stir in cornstarch mixture until sauce thickens.

Cook about ½ pound each of egg and spinach fettuccine. Pour a small amount of the sauce on each serving, and pass the remainder at the table. Serves 4-6.

Only a few establishments that are part of a larger chain are included in this book, because one of our objectives is to identify places with a special distinction. In the case of Michigan's Chuck Muer restaurants, though the menus are virtually the same in most of them, each retains its own individuality. The River Crab has a reputation for quality, a continuing popularity, and a fine setting where you can watch the lake vessels being navigated through the swift St. Clair River. Since our first edition, the view is even better; the Crab has added a bilevel patio near the dock.

If you have nautical interests, you should take time to look at the rowing shells hanging from the open rafters of the enclosed porch; both are from the Detroit Boat Club, which claims to be the oldest rowing club in the Western Hemisphere (and for which Chuck Muer once rowed). One of them, the "Doc Raynor," qualified for a slot in the 1956 Olympics at Melbourne, Australia, where the team won a silver medal.

Menus are fairly extensive and focus on seafood, but a limited number of other dishes are offered. Smaller late evening "suppers" are also available, and customers flock to the elaborate Sunday brunch (be sure to try the Bavarian apple dumplings). Many of the Muer specialties are on the menu: baked stuffed lobster Larry, Charley's Chowder (see the recipe following our review of the Gandy Dancer), and several good shellfish appetizers. Two of the

160

most popular entrees are Charley's Bucket (of shellfish, a clambake for two) and Dungeness crab, but about 20 others are available, including several homemade pastas and the less frequently seen paella (a Spanish rice dish). Paella can reach gastronomic heights; the best we've had was as guests of Juan Calvo in Jeresa, Spain. Some day we hope to get his opinion of this one.

If you're on a limited budget, come here for lunch or for the light dinners offered in the lounge. Many of the items served at dinner are available (often in smaller portions) at a considerably lower cost. And if you want something other than seafood, the linguine primavera, lamb chops, and barbequed ribs are especially good. The light menu in the lounge features seafood stews and Provencales--your choice of shellfish braised in a zesty, garlicky tomato sauce and served with rice pilaf.

The wine list, as in other Muer restaurants, is often presented in a delightful replica of the standard-sized U.S. passport. From 40 to 50 wines are offered as well as a house carafe at relatively low prices. The cocktail lounge (with an appealing snack menu) is cheerful and made especially pleasing by pianist Silas Walker; he's been entertaining people here for years.

At times seating is a bit of a problem for those who want to enjoy the view or be out of the traffic pattern. It may be worth an extra wait if you're particular. (Table 56, seating four to six, is well situated in all respects). There's ample parking with valets, or you can arrive by boat; the Crab has convenient docking facilities.

More Muer magic.

THE RIVER CRAB, 1337 N. River Rd., St. Clair, MI 48079. Two miles north of town on M-29. Telephone (313) 329-2261. Hours: June to Labor Day, luncheon 11:30 a.m.-4:30 p.m., dinner 5-10 p.m., Sunday brunch 10 a.m.-2 p.m.; rest of year opened in evening only, 5-9:30 p.m. Tuesday-Thursday, 5-

10:30 p.m. Friday-Saturday, 3:30-8:30 p.m. Sunday.
Full bar service. All major credit cards.

SCHROD WITH CRABMEAT STUFFING
From the River Crab

This is a popular Chuck Muer specialty, served
at the River Crab on a rotating basis. Starting with
the thickest end, split one (8-ounce) skinned fillet
of fresh schrod horizontally from end to end, leaving the two halves attached along one side. Place
stuffing (see below) between the 2 halves, and roll
slightly to shape the fish. Place on broiler pan, dust
with paprika, and drizzle with oil. Broil 5-6 minutes.
Garnish with parsley and lemon wedge, and serve
with tartar sauce.
For the crabmeat stuffing, first saute 2 ounces finely
chopped onions in 8 ounces margarine until translucent. Let cool and then mix with 8 ounces crabmeat (Maryland lump or crab leg), 6 ounces cream
sauce, and 3 ounces plain fresh bread crumbs.
Recipe serves 1. Our hint: To assure perfect timing,
measure stuffed fish at its thickest and allow 10
minutes per inch in cooking time.

ST. CLAIR INN

Here is a place with a grand old tradition. The
Tudor-style inn was built in 1922 on the site of
the old St. Clair sawmill on the riverfront and is
charmingly decorated in Old English, with many
furnishings to interest the collector. The grounds
are attractively landscaped, and in the rear are a
very pleasant boardwalk and patio near the water
for outdoor relaxation and cocktails.
Both the River Lounge and the Coach Room
serve drinks and light dinners and are warm and
comfortable. There are four other, more formal

162

dining rooms, but our favorite is clearly the South Porch with windows on two walls that offer, aside from the patio, the best view of the St. Clair River and its water traffic.

Michael LaPorte, the manager, is experienced, personable, and helpful. We think you'll be well satisfied with the friendly and efficient service. But one person you won't meet but will admire is busily at work in the kitchen--Evelyn Mary Cowan, who has been making the inn's famous strawberry pies since 1944.

The St. Clair Inn is open for three meals a day and leans to American cooking. The dinner menu includes such interesting entrees as duck with raspberry glaze, shrimp Provencale, and baked whitefish in parchment. Customers' favorites are the prime rib, sauteed frog legs, walleyed pike, and, of course, Evelyn Cowan's fresh strawberry pie. And the scallops may be the best in the area. On Friday and Saturday evenings in the summer, steaks are grilled outdoors on the patio and served with corn on the cob and a salad bar. Prices are upper moderate (entrees with accompaniments average $13.50). The inn maintains a good wine cellar, and connoisseurs may wish to ask for the special wine list. The dinner menu includes a less extensive selection of mainly California, French, and German wines. Carafes are also available.

Sophisticated, scenic, serene.

THE ST. CLAIR INN, 500 N. Riverside, St. Clair, MI 48079. Near city center; 1½ blocks north of St. Clair on M-29. Telephone (313) 329-2222 or Detroit 963-5735, MICH WATS (800) 482-8327. Hours: 7 a.m.-10 p.m. (till midnight Friday-Saturday). Sing along in Coach Room Wednesday-Friday; dancing in the River Lounge Tuesday-Saturday. Closed December 24-25. Full bar service. All major credit cards.

The rambling frame building with its many-gabled roof and circular piazza was not too long ago a bleak house by any standard. Then in June 1983 two Port Huron couples showed up with great expectations. In the following six months, for Vicki and Ed Peterson and Lew and Lynn Secory, it was both the best of times and the worst of times. The original intention was to establish just a bed and breakfast inn. But it was a far, far better thing they did to concentrate on the restaurant. Another aim, according to Vicki, was to "create the feel of a home rather than a commercial establishment." Now, thanks to their efforts, we can enjoy the grandeur and serenity of an authentic Victorian mansion as well as an exceptional luncheon or dinner.

An outstanding example of Queen Anne architecture, the Victorian Inn was built in 1896 by James A. Davidson, a Scottish immigrant and owner of a prosperous home furnishings store in Port Huron. The second owner was James and Helen Davidson's only child, the unmarried Eusebia, who lived here until she died in her 80s. Two other families later occupied the place; and the present owners, the Petersons and Secorys, bought it in June 1983. Fortunately the original woodwork and leaded glass windows were still intact. Fortunately, too, the plans, drawings, and specifications by renowned architect Issac Erb were passed on to the new owners so that their ambitious restoration could be as accurate as possible.

The three dining areas feature a forest green and soft peach color scheme inspired by documented Victorian wallpaper samples. Burnished old carved wood, assorted antique chairs, ornate lambrequins at the windows, and splendid lighting fixtures all contribute to a gracious and hospitable ambience.

The main dining room is our first choice; but
Eusebia's Room, the mansion's original dining room,
and a third room off the lobby are only slightly
less appealing. And for cocktails before or night-
caps after dinner, stop in downstairs at the inn's
Pierpont's Pub, a pleasant bar and lounge with fieldstone walls, fireplace, and easy-listening entertainment Thursday through Saturday evenings. The
Victorian Inn is also proud of its four guest rooms,
some with original pedestal sinks and claw-footed
bathtubs.

The menu here changes monthly. On our visit last
December soups were Polish dill and broccoli curry,
both lovely. Dinner entrees, just five of them, included the popular beef tenderloin with Bearnaise
sauce; filet mignon with sauce Diane; walleyed
pike ("pickerel") topped with crabmeat and sauce
mousseline; a succulent chicken breast stuffed with
Havarti cheese and leeks, wrapped in puff pastry,
and sauced with lemon cream; and "three French
hens," a Christmas-season specialty of three quail
with cranberry-walnut stuffing, served with brandy-
cream sauce and garnished with blushed pears. On
the luncheon menu the same day were mushroom
strudel, chicken crepes Florentine, and the locally
acclaimed baked seafood (in this case, a breaded
walleye fillet served with rice pilaf). Both domestic
and imported wines are available by the glass and
carafe, and the list includes a good mix of seven
reds, eight whites, three roses, and several sparkling
wines including some splits. All are fairly priced
with a nice selection in the lower range.

Everything is presented attractively on mixed or
matched settings of antique china, glasses, and silverware. And the waitresses, costumed like 19th-
century housemaids, are reminiscent of television's
"Upstairs, Downstairs." Dinner prices are a trifle
expensive but fair: $15 to $19 with everything but
dessert included. And do consider one of the
Victorian Inn's sweet endings; on our visit we found
it hard to choose from among apple crisp, creme
de menthe mousse, hazelnut torte, and the inn's own
ice creams and sorbets.

165

Vital Victoriana--we ARE amused.

THE VICTORIAN INN, 1229 Seventh St., Port Huron, MI 48060. Exit 271 off I-94 (Downtown Port Huron), then north on Seventh St. about 4 blocks. Telephone (313) 984-1437. Hours: Tuesday-Saturday luncheon 11:30 a.m.-2 p.m., dinner seating 5:30-8: 30 p.m. Closed Sunday, Monday, December 21-29, major holidays. (Guest rooms available daily.) Full bar service. Credit cards: AE, MC, V.

CHOCOLATE PECAN PIE
From the Victorian Inn

This is one of the inn's most popular desserts. Vicki Peterson sent instructions on preparing it in the food processor, but for the convenience of all our readers, we've written this more convention- ally. For the pastry, mix together 1 1/3 cup un- bleached all-purpose flour, 1 tablespoon sugar, and $\frac{1}{2}$ teaspoon salt. Cut in 1 stick cold unsalted butter until mixture resembles coarse crumbs. Combine $3\frac{1}{2}$ tablespoons ice water and $\frac{1}{2}$ teaspoon lemon juice, and add. Stir until mixture holds together. Roll out to a 14-inch circle on a lightly floured board. Fit into a 10-inch pie plate, trim the over- hang, and crimp the edge. Chill 20 minutes. Line the shell with foil and fill with pie weights or dry beans. Bake at 425 degrees for 10-12 minutes till just set but not brown.

Meanwhile, prepare the filling, which is by far most efficiently done in blender or processor. Finely chop 5 ounces broken-up bittersweet chocolate combined in the machine with 1 cup plus 2 table- spoons sugar. In a small saucepan melt 1 stick un- salted butter in 1 cup light corn syrup. With the motor on, pour butter mixture through the feed tube and run machine until chocolate is completely melt- ed, stopping once to scrape down. Add 4 eggs and $\frac{1}{4}$ cup dark creme de cacao. Blend well. Remove to a bowl and stir in 2 cups pecan halves (chopped).

166

If using a processor, add nut halves along with eggs to the work bowl, and process so pecans are still in fairly large pieces. All of this can be done by hand, but chocolate will need to be melted and nuts chopped in separate steps.

Reduce oven temperature to 350 degrees. Remove weights and foil from pastry. Pour in chocolate mixture; place pie on baking sheet, and bake 1 hour, covering edge of crust with foil if it browns too much. Cool to room temperature. Garnish with $\frac{1}{2}$ cup cream, whipped. Serves 10.

(68) THE LAPEER FAMILY INN

"Family inn" is a mundane but most appropriate name for this informal, crowded, noisy, animated restaurant. On our last visit we saw at least six or seven grandmothers and a veritable host of small, wriggling, happy children--and just about everything imaginable in between. We arrived at 7 p.m., and the little ones were still struggling with their pizzas, dropping napkins, playing video games, or watching the large screen at one end of the dining room showing cartoons and "G"-rated old movies. We could, however, visualize the later college crowd enjoying pitchers of beer and deep-dish pizzas at perhaps the same or even greater noise level.

When you enter the Family Inn, you'll first notice the hanging ferns, brick walls, wooden booths with red tables, and large metallic chandeliers. Walk right in, stake out your booth, and go to the "Order Food Here" sign to pick up a menu. There's also a "Pick Up Drinks" sign, and your best bet is to emulate the regular clientele, most of whom tote pitchers of beer or water or soft drinks to their tables. When you've placed your order, a loudspeaker (yet more noise) will let you know when it's time to pick up your food (and paper plates).

The American-Italian menu features three kinds

of pizza: the Round House Special, a souffle-like creation made with two layers of dough like a pie; the Regular Round, with a nice thin crust and your choice of 22 different toppings; and the Italian-style Deep Dish Pizza (try the Lapeer Special). Also on the menu are several homemade pasta dishes, veal Parmesan, chicken, steaks, seafood, some very appealing sandwiches, minestrone, and assorted deep-fried side orders. We like the pizza and the pasta best.

The most popular menu items, besides pizza, are the lasagne, ribs, chicken, and spaghetti, the last two at really low prices (be sure to try the restaurant's recipe for its sauce, below). In fact, if you order the right thing, the place is a bargain. The hard wooden booths are surprisingly roomy and comfortable. Don't look for privacy or the "best" table; don't expect niceties. Just enjoy the food and marvel at the generational melting pot.

Family fun, Italian bargains.

THE LAPEER FAMILY INN, 325 East Imlay City Rd., Lapeer, MI 48556. On Route 21 east of the business district. Telephone (313) 664-5983. Hours: 11 a.m.-2 p.m. (till 3 a.m. on Friday and Saturday). Closed Easter and Christmas. Full bar service. Credit cards: MC, V. Reservations not accepted.

Nearby attraction: Near downtown Lapeer is the county courthouse, built in 1839, the oldest in the state and still in use; it's an outstanding example of classic Greek Revival architecture.

SPAGHETTI SAUCE
From the Lapeer Family Inn

In a large pot heat 2 tablespoons olive oil and 2 tablespoons butter. Saute until wilted: 1 medium diced carrot, 1 medium diced onion, 1 diced rib of celery, ½ diced green pepper, and 4 minced cloves garlic. Add 3/4 pound ground beef (or combined beef and pork) and $\frac{1}{4}$ pound seasoned sausage, preferably Italian. Cook until color changes, stirring constantly. Add 1 cup dry red wine such as Chianti or Barolo, and cook 4 minutes. Add four 30-ounce cans of whole tomatoes (chopped, with juice), 1 tablespoon dry basil, 1 teaspoon pepper, 2 tablespoons sugar, 1 teaspoon dry oregano, and 1 teaspoon dry rosemary (chop dry herbs together for best flavor). Simmer 1 hour. If liquid reduces too quickly, thin with chicken or beef stock. When sauce is done, it will have a smooth appearance; do not overcook or it will taste too acidic. When done, stir in 2 small cans tomato paste and salt to taste(about $\frac{1}{2}$ to 1 tablespoon). Enough sauce to serve 8-12.

(69) Clarkston Cafe

From setting foot into the snugly warm lounge to seating yourself either here or in the homey, welcoming adjacent dining room to your first glimpse of the menu and chalkboard specials, you'll probably have the same feeling that we do, of somehow stumbling upon a hidden treasure. The building has an agreeably publike and Victorian facade. Inside are worn and comfortable solid oak rustic armchairs, a pendulum wall clock and assorted odd plates, pictures, and agricultural implements on the walls. Over the bar is the original sign of the Clarkston Cafe of many, many years ago. And in the dining room, a glowing fire (get a table here on a wintry day), well-stocked China hutches, and converted hobnail milk-glass parlor lamps. Throughout are nuances of the early days of Michigan with the still clinging flavor of country living. Little touches are integral, such as the tiny bouquets or pots of fresh seasonal flowers on the tables.

The luncheon menu offers omelets (strawberry or herb-tomato) some exceptional soups, several interesting salads and sandwiches, as well as a few praiseworthy cafe specialties: chicken cassoulet on spinach noodles, pork loin California, and grilled chicken breast with lemon-sage butter. The appetizer list is brief but satisfying: steamed mussels, smoked salmon with dill sauce, escargots Chablisienne, fettuccine Alfredo or carbonara or sausage-tomato (the last three also available in entree portion sizes). In the dessert category are strawberry shortcake, parfaits, chocolate velvet pie, tortes, and sometimes a heavenly raspberry pie.

At dinnertime many of the same dishes prevail. But beef makes a more commanding appearance, and the entrees are even more rewarding, among them veal medallions with morels, double-rib lamb chops with beurre rouge, sauteed or deep-fried baby frog legs, chicken breast sauteed with fresh peaches and ginger, beef tenderloin tips Marsala, and some sort of tournedo (sauteed and sauced beef tenderloin). Prices are moderate (from $12.95), considering that entrees are accompanied by soup, salad, potato or vegetable, and breads. But no reservations are accepted in the evening, and by 8:30 or so you may need to wait quite a while; here, it's best to come early for dinner.

Chef Gary Grzywacz (pronounced "Grizz-wack") follows in the footsteps of his two predecessors at the Clarkston Cafe, Tom MacKinnon and Greg Goodman, who now own their own restaurants. Like many of Michigan's finest chefs, he trained with Milos Cihelka at the Golden Mushroom in Southfield. The cafe's owners, Don Hayes and his daughter, manager Lee McNew, describe him as "the best we've had." He does his own butchering, smoking, curing of meats, pasta and pastry making; and apparently he's meticulously well organized as well as creative. The restaurant is also fortunate to have three apprentice chefs under Mr. Grzywacz; and that adds up to four innovative minds in the kitchen, not that common in the food business. The menu changes every six months or so, but you can expect to see both homey traditional fare and exciting new American cuisine.

A main street marvel.

THE CLARKSTON CAFE, 18 S. Main Street, Clarkston, MI 48016. In city center on M-15, south of I-75. Telephone (313) 625-5660. Hours: 11 a.m.-midnight Monday-Saturday (dinner served till 11 p.m. Monday-Thursday, till closing Friday-Saturday). Closed Sunday, holidays. Full bar service. Entertainment 8:30-1:30 p.m. Thursday, Friday and Saturday (easy-listening piano by Jim Bajor). Free parking in rear or on street (no meters). Credit cards: AE, MC, V. Reservations taken for lunch only.

TURKEY BREAST WITH RASPBERRIES
From Chef Gary Grzywacz, the Clarkston Cafe

Slightly flatten 12 small medallions of turkey. Saute in 6 tablespoons butter. Remove from pan and keep warm. To the saute pan, add 1 tablespoon chopped shallots and cook until transparent (do not allow to brown). Add 3 ounces raspberry liqueur (for example, framboise) and 1 ounce raspberry vinegar. Cook over high heat until the liquid is reduced by 2/3. Add a small handful of fresh raspberries. Then add 1 cup heavy cream. Cook to reduce the mixture until it coats a metal spoon. Serves 6. The chef notes that chicken may be substituted for the turkey.

The Holly Hotel isn't a hotel at all but a fine restaurant that retains the original name of the historic building in which it is housed, a restored turn-of-the-century railroad hotel. The lounge is unadulterated Victoriana: a nostalgic old bar labeled the "Dispensing Department," high-backed red plush chairs, floral carpeting, embossed metal ceiling, marble tables, and the obligatory reclining nude on the backbar (two-dimensional and framed, of course). This was a place that Carrie Nation raided in 1908. It's now mainly a waiting area for dinner customers.

Two tiny rooms for dining are the Depot Room, with brick walls, cascading ferns, and ceiling fans, and the nearby Dining Car, where patrons are seated on old train seats with luggage racks overhead. But the third and main dining room is by far the most appealing and gracious, with a Victorian decor similar to that in the lounge. The tables for two hugging the walls might seem attractive for tete-a-tetes, but the plushy low chairs that were fine for cocktails earlier are a little impractical at a dinner table. The tables for four have far more suitable chairs.

Chef Brad Smith and his young staff are to be highly commended for the execution and presentation of some of the state's finest culinary offerings. On the luncheon menu are such appetizers as farci of duck, shrimp-stuffed mushrooms, chicken liver pate, salads and soups, and four creditable entrees: tenderloin tips, sole meuniere, chicken strudel with Hollandaise, and sauteed chicken breast. The dinner menu, too, is small but by no means inadequate. The same appetizers as on the luncheon menu appear, as well as two soups. Entrees regularly comprise, among others, veal estragon (with tarragon pasta), filet of beef Wellington, tenderloin beef medallions with morel mushrooms, breast of chicken with green peppercorn sauce, and broiled New York sirloin steak. Specialties are also offered, including such interesting dishes as pan-fried perch with toasted pine nuts and scallions in citrus-butter sauce and broiled smoked pork chop with strawberries and Kirsch-honey glaze. Desserts include enticing daily creations prepared by the pastry chef. Prices, for this quality, are fair.

Plush Victoriana.

THE HISTORIC HOLLY HOTEL, 110 Battle Alley,

Holly, MI 48442. Downtown. Telephone (313) 634-5208. Hours: luncheon 11 a.m.-3 p.m. Monday-Saturday, dinner 5-10 p.m. Monday-Thursday (till midnight Friday-Saturday), Sunday dinner noon-8 p.m. Full bar service. All major credit cards. Reservations expected. Last reservations taken for week nights are 9:15 p.m., on Friday and Saturday 10.

RHAPSODY TORTE
From Chef Brad Smith, Historic Holly Hotel

Make walnut dough. Cut 1 pound butter into small bits. Add 4 cups flour and ½ cup sugar. Rub together with fingertips until mixture resembles corn meal. Add 3 cups ground walnuts and combine well. Mix in 4 egg yolks. Roll out dough on a lightly floured board, and line bottom of a 9-inch springform pan. Line sides with dough to come up 1½ inches. Coat bottom of pastry with raspberry preserves, and pour in filling (see below). Bake 30 minutes at 350 degrees; reduce heat to 300 degrees and continue baking about 20 minutes. Test with toothpick for doneness. Chill at least 4 hours. Before serving, coat top with beaten currant jelly. Serves 12-16 persons.

For filling, beat 3 eggs and 1¼ cups brown sugar together for 10 minutes with an electric mixer. Combine 3/4 cup flaked coconut, ¼ cup flour, ½ teaspoon baking powder, a pinch salt, and 1¼ cups chopped walnuts. Add to egg mixture. Beat at low speed for 3 seconds, enough to fully combine ingredients.

⑦ MICHIGAN BEAN CO.

There once was a Mr. Dibble, who was so important in a little crossroads of a town that the residents decided it should be named Dibbleville. And so it was called until in the mid-1800s Colonel

Fenton and his business associate, Mr. Leroy, purchased all rights to the village and its sawmill from Mr. Dibble and then reportedly played a game of poker to determine which of them the town would be named after. We assume Col. Fenton won, and at about that time, in 1865, the railroad tracks came in, an economic turning point for the area. The grain elevator was built that same year; and later, beginning in 1922, it functioned for 45 years as the home of the Michigan Bean Company, in its heyday the premier grain storage center for the entire Thumb of Michigan.

Today, thanks to the present owners, orthopaedic surgeon Rick Hamilton and his wife Linda, this Fenton landmark has not only been renovated and protected from possible destruction, but it has also become an exceptionally good eating place and entertainment center. Huge, hand-hewn timbers and oak beams, restored to their natural color, are the focal points of the restaurant. The main dining areas feature period furnishings, brass light fixtures, stained glass windows, and a rich deep plum and teal blue color scheme. Off to one side of the main room is the Fireside Room, which you might prefer for more intimate dining. And farthest from the entry is the smaller Scale Room, with the original grain scale on display. Upstairs is the Col. Fenton Room, an elegant private dining room with fireplace, chandeliers, and swagged floral draperies.

There's less formal dining, too (though nothing is stiffly formal here). Downstairs is Raspberries, a pub with a sparkling urban ambience and a touch of Art Deco. Here, in elevated booths amid raspberry and turquoise walls and upholstery, you can hear some of the best jazz in the area. The room is open for lunch Tuesday through Saturday, and a bar menu (mostly appetizers) and raw bar are also available. At the front of the building is the Company Store, which supplies freshly made pasta, pastries, truffles, breads, sausages, and other food products to the restaurant. Under the direction of pastry chef Randall Robbins, a Culinary Institute of America graduate, this is also a retail outlet and cafe.

Meanwhile in the main kitchen, the executive chef is Kirk Sutliff, who trained at the Philadelphia Culinary Institute and was formerly attached to the Dickens Inn in that city and the Hyatt-Regency in Flint. The food concept is creative American cuisine, described by Sylvia Medlen, Jill of all trades for the Hamiltons, as food of wide ethnic diversity with "a tad of French" thrown in "plus Yankee ingenuity." Only certified Angus beef is used, only fresh produce and seafood. The menu changes daily, with entrees priced from $10 to $22. Look for traditional favorites (steaks, prime rib, Caesar salad); ethnic fare (Oriental stir-fries, Cajun oysters, French ballotine of duck, Italian minestrone); and some new fangles (baked salmon with mussel cream sauce and caviar, veal-stuffed beef tenderloin sauced with artichoke cream).

The wine list reflects the restaurant's intention to offer a good, well-rounded selection at affordable prices but not to tie up a huge inventory. Five by the glass; 7 sparkling types; 14 French reds and whites at fair prices; 6 cost-unlisted premium collectibles from 1966 and 1970; 2 Michigans; a mix of 10 to 12 Californian, 4 German, and 5 Italian including a very promising '79 Chianti Classico Reserva from Gabbiano combine in a most presentable list, skillfully put together with a reasonable concern for your pocketbook.

Haute bean cuisine, and much more.

MICHIGAN BEAN CO., 234 N. Leroy St., Fenton, MI 48430. Downtown. Telephone (313) 629-0440. Hours: luncheon Tuesday-Saturday 11 a.m.-3 p.m.; dinner Tuesday-Thursday 5:30-10 p.m.; Sunday 11 a.m.-6 p.m. Closed Monday. Full bar service. Valet parking ($1). Credit cards: AE, MC, V.

BLACK BEAN SOUP
From the Michigan Bean Co.

You can buy the beans and seasoning packet at

the Company Store; or follow this recipe, using ingredients from the supermarket. Soak 1 pound dry black turtle beans overnight in water to cover well. (Or cover with water, bring to a boil, and simmer until tender.) Set aside. In a large stock pot melt 3 tablespoons butter. Add 2 cups chopped onion, 2 cups chopped carrots, ½ cup chopped celery, and 2 teaspoons minced garlic. Cook until onions are translucent and carrots and celery are soft. Stir in 4 pounds diced cooked ham, and saute lightly.

Add 16-ounce can peeled stewed tomatoes, 10-ounce can chicken broth, and 2 quarts water. Stir in beans and seasonings (2 bay leaves, 5 whole cloves, 12 whole black peppercorns, 3/4 teaspoon oregano, ½ teaspoon thyme, 1½ tablespoon salt). Cook to desired consistency. Remove cloves and peppercorns. Reduce heat, and cook gently over low heat. to thicken or add chicken stock to thin. Salt and pepper to taste. Ladle into 16 serving bowls and mound 2 tablespoons shredded Cheddar cheese over each serving (2 cups in all). Set under broiler, and broil until cheese melts. Garnish with parsley sprigs. Serves 16. Our hint: You can easily cut this recipe in half, but leftovers are so good you won't want to. Also, the soup is freezable.

(72) **Little Joe's**

Here's a tavern atmosphere with style, as well as delicious pizza, ribs, and fish; frothy pitchers of beer and soft drinks; and relaxed, informal dining. If this is what you're after, especially when out with the family or friends, Little Joe's of Grand Blanc will more than fill the bill. The tavern has a long tradition as a local gathering place. It started as a grocery store in the 1930s, and later Joe Dewey (the Little Joe in the name) opened the restaurant and began to serve sandwiches. For years the village's oldtimers played euchre here in their free hours. And today, under the able management of Pat and Kathy Hughes, it has come into its own as a cheerful, noisy magnet for all age groups.

There's a late 19th-century flavor, with leaded windows, Tiffany lamps, walls of shake siding, bentwood chairs, and pseudo-slate tables. If there's a disadvantage, it only add a bit more noise to the already bustling place: the Grand Blanc Fire Department is right next store.

Many MSU students are very appreciative of Little Joe's, as we are. The menu is versatile: excellent pizzas (you can order a thick crust, if you prefer); a few other Italian favorites; sandwiches; steaks; deep-fried seafood (cod, clams, and shrimp); or for a special treat, zesty barbequed ribs in four cost categories--full and half dinner portions with salad and potato or by the pound and half-pound for the real aficionados. New to the menu since our first edition came out are some Mexican offerings and such trenditions as potato skins, cheese sticks, chicken fingers, and breaded mushrooms and cauliflower. The prices are, for these days, astonishingly paltry, mostly in the $4 to $6 range. The service is efficient, friendly, and experienced; Arlene has tended bar here since 1969, and you may be lucky enough to be served by Ruby, a 20-year veteran with Little Joe's.

Light hearted, low prices.

LITTLE JOE'S, 11518 S. Saginaw, Grand Blanc, MI 48430. In city center. Telephone (313) 694-8391. Hours: 10 a.m.-12:30 a.m. Full bar service. Entertainment Friday-Saturday 8 p.m. Park in the rear (almost everyone uses this entrance). Credit cards: MC, V. Reservations accepted only for large parties during the week.

STRAWBERRY COLADA
From Little Joe's

Try this for dessert, too. Combine 1½ jiggers

($2\frac{1}{4}$ ounces) Cream de Strawberry, 1 jigger ($1\frac{1}{2}$ ounces) Coca Casa (cream of coconut), 3 jiggers ($4\frac{1}{2}$ ounces) pineapple juice, and 1 jigger ($1\frac{1}{2}$ ounces) cream. Pour over ice in a large glass. Garnish with a chunk of pineapple and a maraschino cherry or fresh strawberry when in season. Serves 1.

73) Figlio

Something's cooking every minute at Figlio. There are extensive lunch, dinner, and late menus; there are also a happy hour menu, a bar menu, a "zap lunch" served especially fast, and a Sunday brunch menu. Oh, yes, and daily specials on the chalkboard at the entrance. Italian is the lingua franca, as you might guess from the name. And what's really fun about the cooking here is that you can watch it all being done. The open kitchen off the main dining room boasts an authentic hardwood-fired European grill and a wood-burning oven. (Just maybe that's why Figlio's rosemary rolls are so good.) You can even watch the bread doughs being kneaded and the pasta being rolled and cut on a manual machine.

But don't expect a cozy, Old World kitchen with Papa Luigi hovering anxiously over the sauce Bolognese. Figlio (pronounced "feel-ee-oh") is an upscale and amiable eatery that intentionally attracts a clienele of grazing yuppies and would-be Gatsbys. The decor is a contemporary blend of brick walls, shining oak floors, and soft coral accents along with nailpolish pink neon in the bar area. Chairs are just uncomfortable enough not to crease the dress-for-success suit of either gender. But what really defines the restaurant is the architecture: the plethora of beams and rafters, lintels and posterns, painted metal girders, bare black track lighting, and dozens of windows overlooking the shops and shoppers on the lower level. In certain respects but on a small scale, it reminds us of the avant-garde Centre Georges Pompidou in Paris with its radical exoskeletal design and somewhat industrial look.

Most of the atmosphere here derives from Figlio's location in the uppermost part of the Water Street Pavilion, a building with 60,000 square feet of restaurants and stores patterned after Baltimore's Harborplace. Built in 1985 by the Enterprises Development Co., like its sister structure McCamley Place in Battle Creek, the two-story, block-square building is a highly effective urban answer to the suburban mall. Adjoining parking makes it convenient. And unlike typical malls hereabouts, the pavilion houses 80% local merchants and no national chains. So don't look for a Radio Shack or Waldenbooks. Instead, watch the candy bubbling in a copper pot at Here Come the Fudge; take a look at the unusual Soar-N-Dipity Kite Shop; or look for MSU and U-M souvenirs in The Great Divide. Lots of food emporia are here, too, the most popular being Steak of the Art. But for dinner or for something beyond fast food, take the elevator to Figlio.

Standouts among the starters are the deep-fried squid, steamed mussels, and carpaccio (marinated raw beef). Of the pastas we lean to the ziti with Italian sausage sauce and the angel-hair noodles with spinach and pine nuts. Individual pizzas are prepared Calabrian style and baked in the wood-burning oven. Sandwiches are notable for the homemade focaccia buns or sourdough bread. On a more elaborate scale are such luncheon and dinner entrees as chicken parmigiana, scampi, steak spiedini, and for those less enamored of Italian fare, grilled fresh salmon, pork chops with tarragon-apricot sauce, and the trendy blackened redfish. There are some good desserts (including gelato and pizzelle), but you'll probably have trouble saving room for them. Portions are large, and prices moderate.

The rather short wine list (20) has none over $25, and most cost between $9 and $15. Here we'd most likely order a Verdicchio or an Italian Chardonnay (Lungarotti) for a white or, better yet, either a Viviano Chianti Classico or a favorite of ours, Rubesco, if we're drinking red. But you'll find an adequate selection other than Italian if you wish, and it won't cost much either. And not to worry if you're not a yuppie. You'll be graciously attended to by any one of several attractive and friendly young waitpersons.

The peak of chic.

FIGLIO, Water Street Pavilion, Flint, MI 48502. In city center. Take exit 136 off I-69; take Saginaw St. north, turn right on Kearsley, then left on Harrison to the parking entrance. Telephone (313) 767-0000. Hours: 1 a.m.-midnight Monday-Friday, noon-midnight Saturday, noon-10 p.m. Sunday. (Luncheon served till 4 p.m., dinner 4-10 p.m. special late menu after 10 p.m.) Dancing to a DJ Wednesday and Friday 10 p.m.-1:30 a.m. Full bar service. Credit cards: AE, DC, MC, V.

CHICKEN MARSALA
From Chef Mark Weston, Figlio

In a shallow dish blend together 1 cup flour, 1 teaspoon salt, and 1 teaspoon white pepper. Prepare 4 boneless, skinless chicken breasts; halve each one (8 pieces in all) and flatten somewhat between pieces of waxed paper until uniformly thick. Coat chicken well on both sides with flour mixture. Add 2-3 tablespoons oil to a skillet, and heat until surface ripples. Add chicken, and saute until golden brown on both sides. Add 1 cup sliced fresh mushrooms and 1 cup semisweet Marsala wine. Simmer until chicken is done. Remove chicken to warm platter. Off heat, add 2 tablespoons butter (in tiny pieces) and swirl into pan juices until butter melts and sauce is thickened. Pour over chicken. Serves 4.

Makuch's Red Rooster

Tableside cookery is billed as a specialty, but at the Red Rooster it's done as it should be done, not just to impress the naive or to intimidate the timorous or to provide mere entertainment, but to bring the diner into closer contact with the pleasures and rewards of cooking. The Makuchs like to cook and enjoy sharing their own enthusiasm in creating exciting dishes for their guests. In business for more than 25 years, this is another admirable family operation. Arthur senior and his two sons Arthur and Kenneth own and manage the Red Rooster; Kenneth is also the chef and tableside wizard.

There are lots of inviting nooks and crannies, banquettes and booths, for semisecluded dining. The red and black decor is warm, enhanced by barnwood, soft lighting, and paintings by local artists. The table settings are tasteful and most attractive: pewter service plates, fresh flowers, red and white linens. It's especially crowded for lunch here; in fact, reservations are a must for the midday meal. The menu is a typical roster of American favorites: steaks, shellfish, salads, sandwiches, several entree combinations, and three daily specials. It amounts to a good choice of hearty food to satisfy the hungry auto workers who fill up the restaurant at noon.

But the dinner menu is what most appeals to us. The appetizers include two shrimp and three oyster preparations as well as baked stuffed clams and crabmeat remoulade. Other starters are an onion soup, gratineed and encrusted with a delightful blend of four cheeses, and the ever-popular Caesar salad. Entrees on the regular menu consist of commendable steaks and seafood, but we prefer the chef's specialties: veal Marsala, steak Robert with a zesty wine-tomato-mushroom sauce, and chicken

181

with crabmeat Hollandaise and spinach sauce. Among the tableside cookery choices are pepper steak with brandy and wine sauce (Chef Kenneth takes justifiable pride in this), steak Diane, crab-stuffed filet of beef with Vermouth sauce, and veal Olympic (scallopine with Madeira, brandy, and a creamy mushroom sauce). Some half-dozen specials are also offered each evening; these, too, are standouts.

Also flambeed at the table are a few desserts: bananas Jamaica (like Foster, with a dark rum sauce), crepes Suzettes, cherries Jubilee, crepes Fitzgerald (filled with Grand Marnier-flavored cream cheese and topped with strawberry sauce), and banana strawberry Royale. Other possibilities include toasted almond ice cream pie, crepes Kirsten, two coffee concoctions, and a liqueur parfait. As for wine, the list emphasizes Californian, but there are also some top Bordeaux from France; the Burgundies, however, are thin. You might wish to see the private list.

Tres bon, le rouge chanticleer.

MAKUCH'S RED ROOSTER, 3302 Davison Road, Flint, MI 48506. One mile northwest of I-69, Center Rd. exit. Telephone (313) 742-9310. Hours: 11 a.m.-10 p.m. Monday-Friday, 5:30 -11:30 p.m. Saturday. Closed Sunday, major holidays. Full bar service. Credit cards: MC, V. Reserve for lunch and on weekends.

VEAL MICHOLE
From Chef Kenneth Makuch
Makuch's Red Rooster

Here is a delightful veal dish that Chef Kenneth created in honor of his new bride Michole. The recipe serves one, but feel free to double, triple, quadruple as desired. Dredge one 5-ounce thinly sliced veal scallop in seasoned flour. Saute lightly in 2 tablespoons butter. Add 2 tablespoons Cognac and ¼ cup dry white wine. Simmer 1 minute. Add 1/3 cup medium-thin white sauce, 1 ounce morel mushrooms (or substitute 2 ounces sliced button mushrooms), and salt and pepper to taste. Simmer an additional minute. Serve on a warm platter, sprinkled with chopped parsley.

JIMMY LUM'S ALOHA LOUNGE

Wedged tightly between the Musical Memories shop and the Petras Electric Company on the busy strip of Dort Highway, the Aloha Lounge looks exactly like a cedar-shake roof without a building. Only the door in the center tells you that the place hasn't fallen halfway into a crevasse formed by a wayward earthquake. Yet there is a method to the mad exterior design. Envision dried grasses instead of wood shakes, and you might notice a fleeting similarity to a Polynesian thatched-roof communal hut.

Opened in March 1984, Jimmy Lum's Aloha Lounge has steadily attracted a stream of faithful customers. For its Hawaiian decor? No, the bar and dinette-style tables and chairs in front are hardly exotic, although the two small rooms in the rear are rather nicely done up with grasscloth on the walls and South Pacific hanging light fixtures. For the Hawaiian food then? No, the cooking is essentially Chinese (as is Jimmy Lum). A popular luau dinner for two to six persons is on the menu, but it's not much different from a combination dinner at a typical Cantonese restaurant. Nor are the shrimp in lobster sauce, egg rolls, pressed duck, sesame chicken, and fried rice--good as they all are. The drinks, we admit, are the fancy fruity sort representative of the islands: Mai Tais, Volcanoes,

Scorpions, and the like. But, no, they aren't what makes this place click either.

The drawing card at Jimmy Lum's is something we haven't seen elsewhere in Michigan, the Mongolian barbeque. Here in a front corner of the restaurant, diners line up and serve themselves from bins of frozen, paper-thin curls of beef, lamb, pork, and chicken; then from containers of scallions, green pepper, carrots, mushrooms, cabbage, celery, onion, and bean sprouts; and finally from assorted flavorings such as oyster, hot chili, barbeque, and curry sauces. At this point the Chinese chef cooks the food to order on a huge circular cast iron grill. It's a fascinating production of sizzle and smoke, somewhat like the theatrics at a Japanese steakhouse but without the swordplay. It's a freshly cooked, delicious Chinese treat. And it's a bargain: $5.50 at lunchtime, including rice, and $8.95 for dinner. In the evening accompaniments are relish tray, rice, and Mandarin pancakes and the policy is all you can eat. We like to make two or three visits to the grill and try various combinations.

Lum's for your tummy.

JIMMY LUM'S ALOHA LOUNGE, 429 Dort Highway, Flint, MI 48503. One-half mile north of exit 136 (Dort Hwy) off I-69. Telephone (313) 233-7081. Hours: 11 a.m.-2 a.m. Monday-Saturday, 11 a.m.-9 p.m. Sunday. Entertainment Tuesday-Saturday evenings by Bob Adado on the synthesizer. Full bar service. All major credit cards.

⑯ GRACIE'S COUNTRY INN

Downtown New Lothrop hasn't changed a bit since our guide first came out in 1980. The cows are still nibbling the grass along the Misteguay River. And Gracie Yott's place still stands out as the most imposing building on Main Street. An old brick structure once occupied by a bank (the safe's still there) and an antique store and now painted firehouse red and black has for 15 years been the home of one of the best-known steak houses in the area.

But don't expect "country inn" to carry the usual connotations. Here there are neither rural charm nor that dull roadhouse nondecor. Instead, the main dining room boasts Tiffany-style lamps, and the bar has new hanging fixtures reminiscent of some of Las Vegas' most tasteful. A third dining area, the Crystal Room, is characterized by mirrored walls and tabletops, ornate chandeliers, decorative leaded glass, and lace (honest) tablecloths. All of this glitz and glitter is a far cry from the utilitarianism of years past.

Gracies's is not for the epicurean, the gourmet, or the connoisseur, but simply and unpretentiously caters to those who want good steaks at good prices and a generous salad bar with at least 30 choices and even more than just salads: cheeses, snacks, baked beans, soups, soft ice cream, pies, cakes, and cinnamon rolls. On Saturday nights the waiting line stretches into the street, and most people leave here with doggie bags.

On Mondays through Fridays from 11 a.m. to 2 p.m. Gracies's features an all-you-can-eat luncheon buffet in addition to a simple sandwich menu. The most popular dinner steaks are the 3-pound sirloin for two persons and the porterhouse. Six other steaks are listed as well as steak and ground sirloin sandwiches. You might also consider the barbequed beef ribs, another specialty and one that sells out early. Other popular items are the shrimp, frog legs, seafood platter, and combination dinners. A number of entrees may be ordered in smaller portions (priced $2.75-$6.95), and the Thursday special of 12 ounces of prime rib at $8.95 is a top seller. The wine list is modest; carafes are available.

Don't plan on an evening at Gracie's. The bar is used mainly for eating; there's no music (except an occasional jukebox selection) and no entertainment. We include Gracie's as a special place, not for its setting or for its inventive menu--but because, relatively, it's a bargain and is extremely popular locally.

A country American bargain.

GRACIE'S COUNTRY INN, 9483 Genessee Street, New Lothrop, MI 49460. Two miles west of M-13 in village center. Telephone (313) 638-5731. Hours: luncheon 11 a.m.-2 p.m., dinner 3-10 p.m. (Friday- and Saturday 11 a.m.-11 p.m.), Sunday 12 noon-10 p.m. Closed Christmas, New Years Day. Full bar service. No credit cards.

⑦ CHESANING HERITAGE HOUSE
"On The Boulevard"

Once you're in Chesaning, you won't need to ask directions to the Heritage House. Just look for a magnificent old building on Broad Street. It is, quite simply, the most beautiful restaurant of its style in the state. What style is that? Southern Mansion of the "Gone with the Wind" era--envision a majestic white colonnade, fanlights, balconies, carved pediments, and, inside, an impressive rotunda opening above the foyer and three floors of superbly decorated rooms. To sum up, the architecture is Georgian Revival, and the interior decor is tasteful early Victorian.

The Chesaning Heritage House was built in 1908 by a lumber baron, George Nason. The fourth and present owners, Bonnie and Howard Ebenhoeh, purchased it in 1980 and four months later opened the restaurant. Their entire family is involved in the operation, and the enthusiasm and dedication come through when you visit. Thus, in spite of the opulent surroundings, a warm domesticity prevails.

There are seven dining areas in regular use, each with aesthetic and historic interest. We especially like the rather formal Dining Room and Living Room, both featuring bay windows, lovely hand-

186

carved fireplaces, and curved Louis XV side chairs upholstered in blue velvet. But our first choice is the stunning Rose Room on the second floor. It's completely glass enclosed and richly decorated with floral carpeting and old rose and pink fabrics. Still, you won't be disappointed no matter where you're seated in this stately and stylish place. And you won't feel intimidated. It's posh, yes, but not a bit pompous.

The Ebenhoehs' avowed purpose is to offer "generous portions of home-cooked food at family prices." And this they do very well. On the dinner menu are the expected array of steaks and seafood along with some unexpected additions: half a roast duckling with dressing and spiced baked apple, an especially flavorful stuffed pork tenderloin served with fried apples, pan-fried chicken livers, and scallops "cipollone" (wrapped in bacon and broiled in garlic butter sauce). The dessert listing leans towards ice cream concoctions but also boasts cheesecakes, pies, and hot caramel apple fondue (enough to share). And you know that families are welcome when you see some of the beverage offerings: pop, hot chocolate, and milk shakes.

Before or after your meal you might take a look at the Rathskellar bar and lounge in the basement and the Carriage Shop directly behind the restaurant, which specializes in unusual gifts and reproductions of antique furniture. At any time of the year you'll find it worth taking a stroll. On Broad Street, where the Heritage House is located, is the "Boulevard Area," a three-block stretch with historic turn-of-the-century buildings, many now gift and antique shops. And, if you want to make an event out of your trip, visit Chesaning in July for the showboat festival. The 1937 showboat, the only one in Michigan, is as of 1987 in its 46th year (excluding World War II), and the outdoor stage features well-known professional entertainers. Finally, if at all possible, plan some time to dine at the Heritage House during the Christmas holidays. No less than 10,000 lights blaze nightly, and the effect is truly spectacular. If there's a problem with this place, it's that, after dinner, you want to move in.

Blue velvet and a rosy future.

CHESANING HERITAGE HOUSE, 605 W. Broad St. Chesaning, MI 48616. On M-57 just west of the business district. Telephone (517) 845-7700. Hours: 11 a.m.-4 p.m. luncheon Monday-Saturday, 4-10 p.m. dinner Monday-Saturday, noon-9 p.m. holidays and Sunday. Rathskellar hours: 11 a.m.-midnight Monday-Thursday, 11 a.m.-2 a.m. Friday-Saturday, 12 noon-12 midnight Sunday. Entertainment on weekends. Full bar service. Credit cards: MC, V.

ICE CREAM PIE
From Bonnie Ebenhoeh, Chesaning Heritage House

Whirl 20 Oreo cookies in blender or processor until fine crumbs are obtained. Mix well in a bowl with ½ cup melted butter. Press onto bottom and sides of a 10-inch pie tin. Freeze until firm. Spread 1½ quarts slightly soft French vanilla ice cream in the shell. Top with 1 cup chocolate fudge sauce, then 1 cup pecans. Add another layer of 1½ quarts ice cream, 1 cup fudge sauce, and 1 cup pecans. Wrap pie with plastic film, and freeze until firm, 6 hours or overnight. Serves 10-12.

Bonnie notes that you can use caramel sauce instead of fudge or strawberry sauce instead of fudge (in which case she omits the nuts). Mint chip or peppermint stick are good substitutes for the vanilla ice cream (again, omit nuts).

The Bavarian Inn, along with its near relative across the street, Zehnder's, is practically an insti-

tution in Michigan. In a village fairly overflowing
with colorful Bavarian motifs and tourist attractions,
the two restaurants amiably compete for customers
who may have driven miles with the sole purpose
of treating their families and friends to the generous chicken dinners featured here. As for choosing
between the two, it's mainly a matter of taste in
decor or offerings other than chicken on the menus.
The Bavarian Inn's seven dining rooms and Koffee
Haus are expectedly Germanic in theme, and the
food here includes such entrees as wiener schnitzel,
sauerbraten, kasseler-rippchen (smoked pork loin),
and German sausages.

You may also order the weekly or monthly special
as well as several seafoods and sandwiches, all at
modest prices. Everything is prepared and cooked
on the premises, and you'll find some excellent
breads, soups, and desserts--our favorite is the apple
strudel, topped with whipped cream and caramel
sauce. During the Frankenmuth Bavarian Festival
in mid-June, there is also outdoor dining in the
rear. Along with bratwurst and beer, you might
even catch a glimpse of Michigan's famous "Polka
King," Fred Rieger.

The famous family-style, all-you-can-eat chicken
dinners comprise soup, relishes, breads (try both
the white and the fragrant dark rye), krautsalat
(sauerkraut salad), heaping bowls of noodles and
mashed potatoes and gravy, beverage, and ice cream.
There's a limited wine selection, none distinguished,
not even the German. But probably the most popular drink here is beer.

The Bavarian Inn was founded as a boarding
house in 1888 and, aside from its German-American
cooking, has become well known for its Glockenspiel, a 35-bell carillon that plays daily at noon,
6 p.m., and 9 p.m., followed by a figurine movement portraying the legend of the Pied Piper of
Hamelin. With bells from Holland and mechanism
from Germany, the intricate device is housed in
the clock tower rising above the parking lot. It
draws milling crowds, and kids seem to love it. On
our first visit, the Mayor refused to come out of

the Glockenspiel. But that's the only thing that didn't work, as far as we could see, at the Bavarian Inn.

We were fortunate to tour the working part of the inn with Bill Zehnder, the owner, as our guide. This is a spectacular, large-scale restaurant operation, of which the thousands of tourists who visit here are probably unaware. Efficiency, cleanliness, and quality control are predominant. The chickens, we found, are superchicks--weighing $3\frac{1}{4}$ pounds each at the age of only 7 or 8 weeks. On a busy day the Bavarian Inn uses 1500 of them and serves 5000 dinners. In an average year it cooks 250,000 chickens, weighing 325 tons.

New since our first edition is the Holz-brucke, a 230-ton wooden covered bridge over the Cass River that connects the Bavarian Inn with the recently built 100-room, $7 million motor lodge, another Zehnder family enterprise. It's a welcome addition to Frankenmuth, Michigan's number-one tourist attraction. The lodge also features a dining room with a menu and atmosphere comparable to those of the Bavarian Inn. In sum, all three of the Zehnder restaurants provide fine quality and fine food; you can expect to get your money's worth.

Always gemuetlich.

THE BAVARIAN INN, 713 S. Main St., Frankenmuth, MI 48734. On M-83 in village center, 7 minutes from I-75. Telephone (517) 652-9941. Hours: 11 a.m.-9:30 p.m. daily February through December. Closed on Monday January through mid-February. Full bar service. Credit cards: AE, MC, V.

CRANBERRY-ORANGE RELISH
From the Bavarian Inn

This is still the recipe customers ask for most frequently. Sort 6 pounds cranberries, removing any bad ones. Core 6 pounds apples and 6 seedless

oranges (or 7 or 8 if small), leaving on the peel.
Grind the apples, cranberries, and oranges, using
the medium blade on a grinder. Mix well. Add
sugar to taste (about 3 pounds) and 1 tablespoon
red food coloring. Refrigerate; this keeps well.
Serves 12-15. The recipe can be increased or cut
quite easily.

(79) Zehnder's

Rumor has it that both Zehnder's and the Bava-
ian Inn are under one management and that waiters
bear their enormous burdens of steaming, crusty
chicken from a kitchen located under Main Street
that serves both restaurants. In truth, the two
establishments are each separately managed, though
owned and operated by the Zehnder family, and re-
lated mainly by the fact that both specialize in
the chicken dinners for which Frankenmuth is noted.
It is estimated that nearly 3 million tourists visit
the American/Bavarian community each year and
that at least half of them order the celebrated
family-style dinners.

At Zehnder's the theme is colonial American.
Unlike at the Bavarian Inn, the accompaniments
to the chicken include old-fashioned fruit bread,
poultry dressing, chicken livers, and cabbage salad.
The dessert specialties here are homemade pies and
European pastries. Other entrees are grilled steaks,
prime rib, ham, duckling, smoked pork loin, barbequed ribs, and seafood. In addition, soups and sandwiches and weekly lunch and dinner specials are
available in the Coffee Shop; lighter appetites and
tighter budgets might prefer this room (although
all prices are moderate).

Zehnder's is an outgrowth of the Exchange Hotel,
built in 1856, and it's about 32 years older than
the Bavarian Inn. It accommodates 1300 visitors
at a time and serves more than 4500 meals every
Sunday--about 80 percent of them the famous chi-

cken dinners. There are nine dining rooms, each furnished in Early American and each with its own atmosphere. If it's not too busy, you might visit each room and decide what appeals to you before asking for a table. The "Original" dining room is more than a century old and located in the center of Zehnder's, where the old hotel once stood. You might wish to have cocktails (or eat) in the quaint and nostalgic Tap Room, where the early history of Frankenmuth is depicted on the walls in rustic photographs. But Zehnder's, like its neighbor across the street, is generally packed and requires your patience if you want much choice in dining area.

Both restaurants in Frankenmuth have gift shops and bakeries. And there are plenty of other things to see and do in town, so you might plan a day's outing. Pick up a brochure in one of the restaurants and take your choice: the art gallery; the Schnitzelbank Woodcarving Shop; Bronner's, where you can stock up on Christmas decorations; the Chippewa cemetery; the Clock Haus with what may well be the world's largest cuckoo clock (Guiness is looking into it); and the local breweries and wine-tasting rooms.

18th-century flavor, 20th-century amenities.

ZEHNDER'S, 730 S. Main Street, Frankenmuth, MI 48734. On M-83, 7 minutes from I-75. Telephone (517) 652-9925. Hours: 11 a.m.-9:30 p.m. daily; 7 a.m.-9 p.m. in Coffee Shop. Closed Good Friday. Full bar service. Credit cards: AE, MC, V. Reservations taken on availability.

HOME-STYLE ROSETTES
From Zehnder's

This is a recipe Zehnder's bakery provides its customers. The bakery has been greatly expanded and was chosen Retail Bakery of the Year by a trade magazine. Don't miss the almond tuiles and

rosettes. As for the latter, try making them yourself. Beat 2 eggs slightly. Add 1 tablespoon sugar,
¼ teaspoon salt, and 1 teaspoon flavoring of your
choice. Add ½ cup milk and 1 cup flour (measured,
then sifted), and stir together. Add another ½ cup
milk and stir (do not beat). If foamy, set aside.

Place oil and rosette mold in fryer, and heat to
385 degrees. Shake excess oil off mold and touch
it on paper toweling to absorb oil. Dip hot mold
into batter almost to top. Place in hot oil, and
when it holds its shape, remove the mold. Allow
rosette to brown, then turn over to brown other
side. Drain on absorbent paper.

(80) OLD TOWN WAREHOUSE

Old Town Warehouse is one of the many renovations and successful businesses in "Old Saginaw City,"
which is, as you'll find, light years ahead of new
Saginaw city in style and atmosphere. The three-
story yellow brick structure was owned from 1881
to 1982 by the Stenglein family, who over the years
manufactured furniture, store fixtures, restaurant
and bar supplies, and finally Spic and Span, the
patent of which was eventually sold to Proctor and
Gamble. After an ambitious restoration, requiring
extensive sand blasting, the restaurant opened in
April 1983.

Structural elements such as wooden ceiling
supports and heating ducts are all original. Seating
has been added on two levels; we like the tables
on the upper level and the double bank of booths
in the center of the room. The color scheme is
derived from the rose, peach, and green floral
fabric on brass standards used as dividers between
areas and levels. Other cosmetic touches include
some stained glass, hanging plants, and old photographs of historic Saginaw.

The menu, in effect for both lunch and dinner,
is a yuppie's delight, leaning to international

experiments and current grazing trends. Appetizers include Cajun popcorn (fried crayfish tails), chicken won tons, cheese croquettes, and potato skins. Among the six pasta selections are our recommended pasta primavera and seafood fetuccine; the lobster shells, which we haven't tried, sound wonderful. Big meat eaters will enjoy the char-grilled steaks and back ribs and, on Friday and Saturday nights, the prime rib. There's also the obligatory assortment of Mexican and Cajun "blackened" things and enough traditional and trendy soups, salads, and sandwiches to appeal to most tastes. A lighted slate at the entry lists daily specials, which always include a fresh fish and stir fry. Entrees are accompanied by salad, vegetable or potato, and breads. We love the sticky pecan rolls and soft garlic bread sticks but wish the butter weren't whipped to a tasteless froth.

The wine case near the door to the lounge is generally almost empty, a hint of the management's attitude toward the noble grape. But the prices are reasonable, and even wine snobs can find something palatable. House wines include the typical lineup of Chablis, rose, Burgundy, Lambrusco, Liebfraumilch, and Piesporter Michelsberg. Slightly better choices are "premium" wines by the glass: Bollini Chardonnay and Cabernet Sauvignon and Parducci white Zinfandel. On the limited wine list are a fair Beaujolais Villages by Drouhin for $10, a Soave for $8.75, Vouvray at $10.50, and, probably most acceptable of all, Great Western Extra Dry Champagne for $13.

From Spic and Span to soups and sauces.

OLD TOWN WAREHOUSE RESTAURANT, 500 S. Hamilton, Saginaw, MI 48602. In Old Saginaw City, just south and across the river from downtown Saginaw. Telephone (517) 790-7330. Hours: 11 a.m.-9 p.m. Monday-Thursday, 11 a.m.-10 p.m. Friday, 4-10 p.m. Saturday. Live entertainment Friday and Saturday. Closed Sunday, some holidays. Full bar service. Credit cards: AE, MC, V.

194

(81) montagueinn

At the turn of the century, Saginaw's historic Grove district was the center of an opulent, glittering social life. Even a casual look today at the impressive mansions in the area calls up an earlier, more gracious era. Here is a sequestered island of the past in a Michigan locality known mainly for the bustle of industry. And standing out as a showplace in the district is a restored red brick Georgian manor house, the elegant Montague Inn. The building, south of downtown Saginaw on Lake Linton and nestled in eight acres of spacious, landscaped lawns and gardens, opened as an inn and meeting center in 1986. The clublike atmosphere and setting are ideal for both business conferences and special family occasions. But the inn is fast gaining a reputation for fine dining as well.

What is perhaps most memorable about a meal at the Montague is the disarmingly friendly approach taken by the staff. There's the feel here of a small European luxury hotel. Imagine having cocktails and hors d'oeuvre in the library at one of the settees in front of the fireplace or in the game alcove. Then imagine your first glimpse of the dining room: the mahogany sideboard, brass chandelier, and sconces, gilt-framed paintings, silver serving pieces, and the rosy soft-focus color scheme of a Renoir. The room seats only 30, and the focal point is the bay window framed by a lambrequin of raspberry-hued draperies. Table settings are delicate white-on-white Bavarian porcelain, sparkling crystal stemware, and shell-pink napkins fanned out on white tablecloths. Envision food and service just as gratifying as the visual effects. And, finally, imagine settling down after dinner in a resilient wingback chair in front of the huge living room fireplace with a glass of something entertaining in your hand. The entire experience is like going to a friend's (a rich friend's) home for dinner--and that's exactly how the management wants you to feel. The Montague Inn, as a newcomer to the Tri-Cities, however, is still finding itself. Menus are in the embryonic stage, awaiting patron response and approval. On our visit last winter, appetizers included the soup of the evening, a fruit and cheese selection, sauteed dilled mushrooms wrapped in phyllo and served with a sherry cream sauce, shrimp turnovers with sauce Dijon, baked Brie with caramalized almonds, and a fresh pasta of the evening. The six entrees, accompanied by fresh vegetables, consisted of salmon with hazelnut cream sauce, Cornish game hen with apple-sausage stuffing, a house version of beef Wellington, lobster tails in sherry cream sauce, roast leg of lamb, and veal with Gouda, prosciutto, and Marsala sauce. Considering the small number of diners, the selection was well rounded and perfectly satisfying. Entree prices start at $12.95 and top off at $21.95.

The wine list, too, is just now being developed, and its final outcome is still in question. Yet the present selection is, considering the cuisine, small but adequate, with among others, seven reds and nine whites. You may also order five different wines by either the glass or carafe.

Luncheons are down to earth, filling, and flavorful. Usually there's a sandwich on homemade bread served with the soup of the day or a salad that might surprise the palate, for example, a medley of turkey, apples, smoked Gouda, and glazed pecans tossed with a curried vinaigrette. A few other options might appear, such as beef Burgundy stew or smoked salmon quiche. Guests at the inn also receive complimentary Continental breakfasts and high tea in the afternoon.

Secluded and serene surroundings, a timeless inn.

THE MONTAGUE INN, 1581 S. Washington Ave., Saginaw, MI 48601. On M-13 just north of M-46; across from the entrance to Hoyt Park. Telephone

(517) 752-3939. Hours: luncheon 1:30 a.m.-2 p.m., dinner 6-10 p.m. Thursday-Saturday. Closed on Sunday, Monday, Christmas, New Year's Day. Full bar service. Credit cards: AE, MC, V. Reservations essential. Dress up a bit.

PARMESAN CHEESE FANS
From the Montague Inn

These are house favorites at the inn, passed each evening before dinner. They're easy to make and delicious. Blend together 1 cup sour cream, 2 cups unsalted butter, and 3 cups all-purpose flour. Gather into a ball, wrap in waxed paper, and refrigerate for 1 hour. Roll dough out on a lightly floured board into a rectangle 10 by 15 inches. Sprinkle with freshly grated Parmesan cheese. Roll both of the longest sides into the center. Slice crosswise into thin "fans." Place on ungreased baking sheets, and bake 10-12 minutes at 425 degrees.

(82) Embers

The Embers is another of those de rigeur stops for vacationers traveling north or south on U.S.27. And if you're not too far from Mount Pleasant, it's worth the extra drive to dine here any time. The dining room is large and the tables well placed and well spaced. It's an attractive contemporary room with lots of rusts and black, dark wood and brick, an open-hearth charcoal grill, and an interesting papered ceiling. We suggest that you reserve one of the appealing alcoves, each opening onto the main room through a brick archway and affording seclusion for parties of six or eight.

The menu suits most tastes. Appetizers are mostly traditional; for a change, try the broiled

cheese bread. From the charcoal grill come such
entrees as steaks, lobster tails, swordfish, and
shish kebab. Other possibilities include chicken
Divan, trout amandine, Chinese shrimp, sole de
jongh, and medallions of pork tenderloin Oscar. But
the piece de resistance is the Embers' "Original
One-Pound Pork Chop," created by the dedicated
owner Clarence Tuma. Although some diners may
not be charmed by large pork chops, we think this
might change their minds. Thankfully, Mr. Tuma
has provided this recipe to his customers for years;
we include it here for you to try at home.

All dinners are served with a relish tray, bar
cheese and garlic toast, Caesar or another salad
of your choice, potatoes, homemade bread, sweet
rolls, and coffee or tea. After dinner you might
wish to choose something from the dessert cart--
the chocolate angel torte is exquisite.

The Embers has a second and very popular location in Traverse City called Embers on the Bay.
The menu is much the same but the decor is quite
different, and the restaurant has an outstanding
waterfront view. We recommend it highly.

Glowing better than ever.

THE EMBERS, 1217 S. Mission St., Mount Pleasant
MI 48858. South of city center on B.R.27. Telephone (517) 773-5007. Hours: dinner 5-9 p.m. Monday-Thursday, 5-10 p.m. Friday-Saturday, Sunday
brunch 10 a.m.-2 p.m., Sunday dinner noon-7 p.m.
Closed major holidays. Full bar service. Credit
cards: AE, MC, V. Reservations not taken on Saturday.

THE ORIGINAL ONE-POUND PORK CHOP
From Clarence Tuma, the Embers

This recipe is most versatile. Omit the final charcoal grilling and broil instead if you wish. Smaller
sizes of chops may also be cooked this way. These

chops are great as a Chinese entree served with rice and stir-fried vegetables.

Combine marinade ingredients in large saucepan: 2 cups soy sauce, 1 cup water, ½ cup brown sugar, 1 tablespoon dark molasses, and 1 teaspoon salt. Bring to a boil. Let cool. Pl ace 6 (1-pound) pork chops vertically in a deep pan with the bone side up. Pour marinade over. Let stand overnight in re-frigerator. The next day, remove chops, place in baking pan, and cover tightly with foil. Bake at 375 degrees until tender, about 2 hours.

Meanwhile, make red sauce: combine in saucepan 1 tablespoon dry mustard, ½ cup brown sugar, 1/3 cup water, 1 (14-ounce) bottle Heinz catsup, and 1 (12-ounce) bottle Heinz chili sauce. Bring to a boil, and remove from heat. When chops are tender, remove from oven, dip each into red sauce, and return them to the baking pan. Bake 30 minutes at 350 degrees or until slightly glazed. For addi-tional flavor, place chops on hot charcoal grill, and let cook slowly, no more than 15 minutes. Serves 6. Chef's note: both marinade and red sauce can be reused if brought to a boil and then refrigerated or frozen.

(83) 園 竹
Bamboo Garden

The enterprising Evangeline Chow has done it again. When we heard that her exquisite Midland restaurant, the Shanghai Peddler, had closed, we were convinced that someone had been tampering with her fortune cookies. Though we haven't heard the story about the undeserved fate of her earlier undertaking, we're pleased that she is once again bringing the best of Oriental food and atmosphere to her grateful customers. The Bamboo Garden opened in 1980 in as deceiving and graceless a location as the Shanghai Peddler's. The building is an utterly drab brick and stucco box, enlivened a bit by the Mandarin red canopy and Chinese characters on door and wall.

Ah but, inside, the Chow magic remains at work. Rattan armchairs, blond hardwood tables, grasscloth and Oriental paintings on the walls, and a sophisticated neutral color scheme most resembling what the Japanese call "shibui" and what eminent designer Carleton Varney calls the transcendent "Zen approach." Everything is contemporary, subtle, and stylish. No fire-breathing dragons or garish multicolored paper lanterns. Even the soft Asian background music contributes to the comfortable serenity of the Bamboo Garden.

The menu features all the regional cooking styles of China, although it specializes in the more assertive Szechuan and Hunan cuisines. Each main dish is labeled according to origin, and hotly sesoned dishes are printed in red. Items that we haven't seen often in Michigan include paper-wrapped chicken, velvet chicken and corn soup, various duck preparations, and glazed fruits for dessert. Daily or monthly specials are also offered to take advantage of seasonal ingredients and to provide variety. Recently the Bamboo Garden has served tea-smoked duck, Peking chicken, braised stuffed tofu, spiced tangerine steak, and spareribs with black bean sauce. On Sunday and Tuesday you can try an authentic dim sum for lunch. Literally "delight your heart," dim sum consists of a variety of dainty delicacies: crescents and buns filled with meat and seafood, steamed dumplings, pearl rice balls, taro fritters, crispy won tons, and packages of sticky rice wrapped in lotus leaves. And for the most elaborate Chinese meal you're likely to eat outside of Peking itself, you can arrange with Mrs. Chow for a banquet, a feast of 10 to 15 courses (8 persons minimum) These are dishes that require prolonged preparation and personal attention from the chef. Last, for a Chinese eatery, the wine list is exceptional, including a '67 Latour that, if stored properly, should still be magnificent since it was likely the best Medoc made that year. But for one-tenth of the price, you can get a $10 Chianti Classico and a carafe for even less. And then there are always tea and beer, which are both perfect for this kind of dining.

Chow down at Madame Chow's.

BAMBOO GARDEN, 2600 N. Saginaw Rd., Midland, MI 48640. Take Eastman Rd. exit south from U.S. 10, then west to Saginaw Rd. Telephone (517) 832-7966. Hours: Monday-Thursday 11:30 a.m.-9 p.m., Friday 11:30 a.m.-10 p.m., Saturday 5-10 p.m., Sunday noon-8 p.m. Full bar service. Credit cards: MC, V.

CHUNG KING PORK
From the Bamboo Garden

The best hint we can offer on Chinese cooking is to read through the recipe carefully and plan to prepare all ingredients ahead so that you won't be in the midst of stir frying and suddenly need to stop to slice up the water chestnuts.

Simmer 1 1/3 pounds pork hind leg (fresh ham; or substitute another lean cut) in water for 30 minutes. Remove and drain. Slice thinly into pieces about 2x3 inches. Remove the stem and seeds from 3 green peppers; then slice. Cut 1 large clove garlic into small dice. Stir fry the pork in 3 tablespoons oil 1 minute. Add 1 tablespoon hot soybean paste, 2 teaspoons sugar, $\frac{1}{2}$ tablespoon sherry, and 1 tablespoon soy sauce. Stir fry quickly over high heat for less than a minute. Remove and serve. Enough for 2 to 4, depending on the number of courses being served.

Rarely have we visited a restaurant where the exterior has so little in common with the electrifying culinary skills demonstrated inside. From the outside this might as well be the Chatterbox Cafe in Lake Wobegon. Yet its windowless American roadhouse facade in no way suggests the sophistication and chic of its interior. And it certainly doesn't indicate that this is one of the state's finest dining establishments. One Michigan magazine has described it as an "improbable outpost of gastronomy." Improbable, presumably because of its distance from Detroit. Not so improbable when you consider that Midland is one of Michigan's wealthiest areas.

There's a bold and sleek, rather masculine decor with gray tweed, dark wood, brass chandeliers, and deep-toned patterned carpeting. Except for the two tables nearest to the kitchen, all the seating in the two dining rooms is good; we especially like the two booths in the front room and the three in the back, each with its own chandelier and botanical print. Table settings are pristine, each one boasting a perfect rose, the restaurant's logo.

The menu changes seasonally, and prices cover everything from canapes to truffles. On a visit last fall, for appetizers we had a choice of Chef Michael Tuma's rabbit fricassee vol-au-vent (in puff pastry case), steamed mussels with Cognac and cream, goose saucisson (sausage) with brioche and lingonberry juice, snail and herb tart, poached oysters with salmon caviar and buckwheat blini, and many more just as prepossessing. It was by far the most extensive and engaging catalogue of starters we've seen in Michigan.

Entrees are limited to half a dozen or more "preparations of the evening" (for example, the chef's current inspiration on lamb or beef tenderloin or veal) in addition to possibly a chicken breast or duckling creation. When we visited in fall, we could have opted for a saute of venison with "jus Cabernet Sauvignon," grilled buffalo steak with "jus spiced wild blueberry," and two appealing seafood offerings. Desserts include heavenly house-made ice creams and fresh fruit sorbets. The chocolate mousses (dark chocolate, white chocolate, and mocha) are luscious. And the chocolate cake with creme anglaise and fresh fruit tart with ice cream should be illegal. Prices are high and worth it.

About 200 wine selections--including a number of half bottles and within a wide price range many in the $10-$25 bracket--are available, making this one of Michigan's best cellars. The largest numbers fall within the sparkling wines (18), California Cabernets (20) and Chardonnays (20), French red and white Burgundies (a total of 32), Bordeaux (26), and German whites (23). Wine "specials" and "special rare selections" are also identified in a tastefully presented and skillfully compiled list. As an added attraction for anyone discovering a new favorite here, Justine makes all wines available for take-out purchase at a substantial discount.

Midland magic.

JUSTINE, 5010 Bay City Rd., Midland, MI 48640. Just off U.S.10, southwest of city center. Telephone (517) 496-3012. Hours: 5-10 p.m. Closed Sunday. Full bar service. Credit cards: AE, MC, V. Coats and ties required for men.

MAINE LOBSTER EN BRIOCHE
From Chef Michael Tuma, Justine

This is one of the most elaborate recipes we received. The lobster is magnificent; and if you are willing to expend the time and money to serve this to guests, your reputation will be made.

Have ready 4 ounces of brioche dough (recipe in most standard and French cookbooks) or substitute your favorite flaky pastry crust or commercial puff pastry. Dismember 1 ($1\frac{1}{4}$-$1\frac{1}{2}$ pound) lobster, removing tail, claws, and body from shell. Gently remove coral and green matter, keeping intact. Remove meat from tail in one piece, saving tail fins and the main body and head shell. Poach the claws (meat in) in 1 quart water with red wine vinegar, salt and pepper to taste, until they turn orange. Remove from liquid and cool quickly in ice water. Drain and remove meat from claws, keeping claw and meat intact. Keep claw meat cold till ready to use. (Needle-nose pliers and scissors are useful.) In same liquid poach body shell and tail fins till color is bright orange. Drain, and split main body shell in half, saving one half. In 3 ounces poaching liquid, quickly cook 5 large spinach leaves. Drain, spread flat, and pat dry on lint-free towel. Salt and pepper tail meat and wrap tightly in the spinach leaves. Roll out half the brioche or other pastry lengthwise. Place spinach-wrapped lobster tail on top. Roll out remaining dough lengthwise, and drape over tail. Press down to enclose it. Brush excess pastry surrounding tail meat with egg wash (1 beaten egg), and roll up tightly. Preheat oven to 500 degrees.

Begin sauce. Combine chopped lobster body pieces, 1 tablespoon chopped shallot, and 2 ounces dry white wine; bring to a boil. Reduce over high heat until a glaze. Add 2 ounces heavy cream and reduce by $\frac{1}{2}$. Lower heat and add 2 ounces butter, stirring constantly. Strain into a small pan and set on low heat. Do not boil! Add salt, pepper, and lemon juice to taste. Paint lobster tail with egg wash; place on parchment-paper-lined baking sheet. Brown lightly in oven 3-4 minutes. Rotate baking sheet. Turn oven to 450 degrees. When pastry is golden brown, remove from oven and let stand at room temperature a few minutes. Bring poaching liquid to a slight simmer. Add claws and poach to heat gently. Add coral and green matter to sauce, and turn heat to medium. Stir vigorously but do not boil. When roe turns red, remove from heat.

Presentation: Paint lobster head shell and tail fins with butter to make shiny. Place head at top of plate (11 o'clock), fins at 5 o'clock. Remove claws from liquid, drain, and paint with butter. Place claws on both sides of head. Slice pastry-wrapped tail into 5-6 pieces and arrange on right

204

side of plate in fanned, natural shape. Pour sauce in center of plate and serve with fresh vegetable accompaniment. Serves 1.

(85) Krzysiak's House

Don Krzysiak (and how's that for an authentic moniker?) is one of those capable restauranteurs who's been in business for years. Gourmet magazine and even the Detroit News probably don't know who he is, but, hey, that's okay with Don because he's doing exactly what he wants and loving it. Recently in one of those articles that lists the current "ins" and "outs," one restaurant trend was noted as coming "in" in 1987: home cooking. We imagine that Don would be both pleased and amused to be considered a trendsetter. But if home cooking is really the wave of the future, his place has a big edge on the competition.

Once known as Doc's Tavern and later as Big Dan's Bar, Krzysiak's House is at first noteworthy for the number of cars parked in front. Inside are three dining rooms, a bar and lounge that serve mainly as a waiting area, and a bakery-confection-ary-emporium at the entryway. Furnishings and table settings are modest, of the oilcloth and silk-flower school. What comes through is the Polish pride. On several walls are huge hand-painted murals that Don commissioned after his two trips to the mother country.

The food here is hearty and satisfying. The menu is extensive, but most things are simply prepared: grilled steaks, roast beef and prime rib, steamed crab legs and lobster tails, fried and broiled fish, frog legs, honey-fried chicken, baby beef liver, and Southern-fried rabbit among others. In both quality and quantity, there are some remarkable bargains, for example, the Jumbo Seafood Platter at $7.25, consisting of cod, shrimp, walleyed pike, whitefish, scallops, frog legs, lake perch, and smelt. Most entrees range from $5.95 to $7.95, even for good-sized steaks. Included in the price are soup, salad bar, potato, and bread. Budgeters will also be tempted by the hot buffets offered at lunchtime for $3.49 (among other bargains) and in the evening for $4.95 (all you can eat, of course). To wash it all down, consider one of the great German brews or a bottle of Polish beer or "Don's famous 2-oz. Duze Piwo" ("big beer" from the tap). Wine seems to be an afterthought here (only three, only in carafes). But Don has a few Polish wines for sale in the front retail shop; maybe he could open one for you.

But the most interesting section of the menu is "A Taste of Poland." Other ethnic options aside, the Polish Platter would be our first recommendation because it's a way to sample some dishes that might be unfamiliar. For $6.95 you'll start with an appetizer and czernina, a fruity duck soup. The platter itself contains golabki (stuffed cabbage), bigos (the Polish national stew), pierogi (filled turn-overs), Polish sausage, and potatoes with cheese sauce. And you'll finish with "Don's famous nale-sniki, marvelous stuffed, rolled crepes with whipped cream. We were able to tour the kitchen (neat as a pin) and were most impressed by the pierogi waiting in the cooler for their final hot bath in butter and the 20-gallon stock pot of chicken kluski (noodle) soup. Don tells us that customers go through 10 gallons at lunchtime and another 20 gallons in the evening. These figures rise to 40 or 50 gallons on Sunday. The aroma, not to mention the glorious golden color, told us why. For many of the Polish specialties, credit must go to Elizabeth Kubica, who came to Krzysiak's two years ago from Poland. Don himself butchers the meat and makes his own sausages. There's a sense of adventure here that the best home cooks bring to their work.

Proud Polish presentations.

KRZYSIAK'S HOUSE, 1605 Michigan Avenue, Bay City, MI 48708. About ½ mile east of M-13, just off Cass Ave. Telephone (517) 894-5531. Hours: 6:15 a.m.-9 p.m. daily. Closed Christmas, Thanksgiving. Full bar service. Credit cards: AE, MC, V.

POLISH STEAK ROLL-UPS
From Krzysiak's House

This is a favorite of Don's, a recipe he received from his aunt when he visited her in 1986; she has operated a restaurant in Zakopany for more than 40 years. It's one of those free-wheeling recipes that most of us have received from our mothers or grandmothers, requiring us to use our own judgment as to quantities.

Cut round or flank steak into 1x2-inch rectangles; pound with meat mallet until very thin. Spread with filling of your choice: (1) chopped onions simmered in butter with bread crumbs and seasoned with salt and pepper, (2) mushrooms sauteed with chopped onions, put through meat grinder, and salted and peppered, (3) a slice of uncooked bacon, dill pickle, and onion, (4) a slice of uncooked onion and sharp brown mustard. Roll up meat tightly, fasten with 2 toothpicks, dip in flour, and brown in hot lard on all sides. Place in roaster, sprinkle with pan drippings, add 1-2 cups broth or water. Cover and roast 2 hours in a preheated 350-degree oven. Fork-blend 1 cup sour cream with 1 tablespoon flour. Remove meat and keep warm. Stir sour cream into pan drippings. Add enough water to obtain a pourable gravy. Serve with beef rolls along with cooked buckwheat groats (kasha) and cooked beets.

"Benvenuto" to Terry and Jerry's, and that's exactly how you'll feel--welcome. A family-owned restaurant for more than 35 years in downtown Bay City, O Sole Mio has a faithful clientele of regulars who enjoy its special cheerfulness and well-worn comfort as well as the memorable and generous assortment of Italian specialties. If the restaurant's name puzzles you, you should know that Terry and Jerry (Teresa and Jerardo) were musical and comedy entertainers before turning to entertaining of another sort. Chef Jerardo died a number of years ago, but his proteges are serving up the same wonderfully hearty Italian dishes. And his widow Terry, ever the gracious hostess, will probably stop by your table with a greeting and infectious smile.

The decor is an attempt at classical Italian, but decor isn't really important to management or guests. The table settings? When we first visited, along with paper mats over a bandanna-printed oil-cloth were a red Victorian pressed-glass sugar bowl and a Perrier bottle with a fresh daisy in it. Last winter we noticed new red-checked plastic table-cloths, but everything else was much the same. The dining room adjacent to the bar and kitchen , we must note, has an awkward traffic pattern, and we urge you to reserve a table in La Vinezia, away from the salad bar and entryway.

Dinner, if you don't order a pasta dish, includes entree, soup, salad bar (refreshingly labeled "antipasto buffet"), and a spaghetti course. We had a tasty seafood chowder and ordered at an extra charge (well worth it) a small loaf of delicious homemade garlic bread. Especially popular entrees are the beef tenderloin with parsley sauce, the scampi dishes, and various pasta "speziale," including mussels marinara over linguine, potato gnocchi, manicotti, and a tantalizing Sicilian "calimari" (shrimp-stuffed squid with pasta). There's a limited wine list, and the prices are fair; different-sized bottles are available, and you can order Californian and Italian wines by the glass; connoisseurs won't be disappointed.

One warning--go to O Sole Mio hungry. You'll be served enough food to please the most famished longshoreman. And you might even have room for the cappuccino, made with your choice of chocolate mint, almond liqueur, or Amaretto (take home your cup as a souvenir).

Let them entertain you.

TERRY AND JERRY'S O SOLE MIO, 1005 Saginaw St., Bay City, MI 48706. In city center. Telephone (517) 893-3496. Hours: 5-10:30 p.m. daily, 4-8:30 p.m. Sunday. Closed Monday, most holidays. Full bar service. Credit cards: AE, DC, MC, V.

FRAGOLI UMBRIACOTTO
From Terry and Jerry's O Sole Mio

Literally, this means "drunken strawberries." A strawberry never had it so good. Clean 1 quart strawberries. Reserve 4 whole ones for garnish, and cut remainder in half. Toss berries in a bowl with 1 tablespoon light brown sugar until all are coated. Add 1 ounce Grenadine syrup, 1 ounce Triple Sec, 2 ounces Galliano. Marinate in refrigerator 2-3 hours. Pour berries and marinade into 4 wine glasses to serve. Float 1 tablespoon Sicilian Gold wine on top of each serving (optional). Top with whipped cream and reserved berries. Vary by adding one of the following to the berry mixture: 2 ripe peaches, 1 pineapple, or 1 ripe papaya (each peeled and cut in the same size as the berries). Serves 4.

(87) THE BANK 1884

Port Austin, at the tip of Michigan's Thumb, is known as "grindstone city" after the era in which it once produced most of the world's grindstones. You can visit the former quarries, but from what we've heard, you'll be a lot more interested in visiting the Bank 1884. This is the only "hearsay" restaurant entry in our book. And if you go to Port Austin, in itself most unlikely, you are hearby being warned. We didn't get there either, mainly because we couldn't meet the Bank's seasonal schedule. Yet everything we've heard about it from people we trust implicitly tells us that it would be a shame to omit it in our guide. So, then, here are the rumors.

Th e two-story brick building (a former bank, of course, and you can guess in what year it was built) dates to the Victorian era and was a shambles when it was purchased in 1981 by Tony and Marilyn Berry, a teacher in Ubley and librarian in Bad Axe, respectively. Now handsomely restored, it's been a restaurant since 1984 and is furnished with old church pews and a brass teller's cage and is adorned with early photographs of the town. The Berrys (Tony's a native of California) have introduced some sophisticated and tasty new things to Port Austin, for example, rainbow trout in dill sauce, steak Diane, oysters Rockefeller, and walleyed pike baked in parchment. There's also a good house salad, tossed at tableside with a buttermilk-herb dressing. Prices are in a reasonable $8.95 to $14.95 range, and the wine list is nicely selected.

Bank on a good dinner.

THE BANK 1884, 8646 Blake St., Port Austin, MI. Telephone (517) 738-5353. Hours: dinner 5-10 p.m. Tuesday-Saturday, 2-9 p.m. Sunday, July 4 to Labor Day; 5-10 p.m. Thursday-Saturday, 2-9 p.m. Sunday, spring and fall. Closed January-April. Full bar service. Credit cards: MC, V.

(88) THE BIG PAW

Here is home-style cooking as good as you'll find in a beautifully kept, simple rustic dining room overlooking the shore of Lake Huron. The resort, nestled amid 70 acres of pine forest and reached

210

after an adventurous drive down a narrow, winding old logging road, now blacktopped, has been in operation since 1940, and three generations of the Yokom family have worked here and contribute to making the Big Paw ideal for quiet relaxation and seclusion in the charming log cabins and for superior meals in the small, immaculate lodge.

The kitchen at the resort is much like your own, with the addition of a 10-burner gas range. The spotless dining room has three large windows facing the lake and woods nearby. To take full advantage of all the Big Paw's meals and activities, you might want to stay overnight (or longer) in one of the cottages, each with its own fireplace, small fridge, and private path to the lodge and beach. Aside from swimming and boating, there are lighted tennis courts, lawn sports, and a game room. The Big Paw is one of only 24 state resorts and hotels to receive AAA's four-diamond accommodation rating, along with such notables as the Dearborn Inn and Mackinac Island's Grand Hotel.

But the fine food is the main attraction for us. A single menu is offered for breakfast and dinner, the latter including juice, entree, potatoes, vegetable, salad, freshly baked bread or rolls, dessert, and beverage (no wine). Particularly popular is the unusually tender pan-fried New York strip steak, and for dessert you might be lucky enough to be served deep-dish apple pie or an uncommonly good chocolate fudge cake. Other main dishes are likely to be baked chicken, Swiss steak, or roasts. On Sundays the Yokoms host a weiner roast on the beach (they bake their own hot dog buns). Meals are served family style and price fixed at one rate. You must either be an overnight guest or make reservations well in advance to eat at the Big Paw. But the lack of selection and the bother of planning ahead are minor problems when you consider the quality of food, hospitality, and pleasing surroundings.

Genuine food, genuine hospitality.

THE BIG PAW RESORT, Route 23, Harrisville, MI 48740. Between Alpena and Tawas City on Lake Huron, 1½ miles north of town. Telephone (517)724-6326. Hours: breakfast 8:30-10 a.m., dinner 6 p.m. only. Closed November 1, open again on Memorial Day weekend. No alcoholic beverages. Reservations required. Credit cards: MC, V.

SOUR CREAM MUFFINS
From Nancy Yokom, Big Paw Resort

This has become our all-time favorite muffin. Combine 1¼ cups flour, 1/3 cup sugar, 1 teaspoon baking powder, ½ teaspoon baking soda, 1 teaspoon salt. Add 1 tablespoon vegetable oil, 1 egg, and 1 cup sour cream. Stir (do not beat). Fill well-buttered muffin tins half full. Bake 20 minutes in preheated 350-degree oven. Makes 12. Our hint: after 20 minutes remove or test with toothpick. Don't wait for them to brown; they stay quite pale.

The present establishment has been around since 1961, but the large authentic log cabin was also an inn prior to that. Today the exterior of the Rustic Inn is coated with a new preservative that gives it a greenish color and more modern look. The interior is knotty pine, and the table settings are characterized by black vinyl, red and white paper, and heavy amber glass. But what best defines the Rustic Inn's "personality" is the colorful John Wayne clock above the bar. This is he-man country, and this is a he-man's restaurant--where hard workers, hard players, hard drinkers, and their women come for red meat and lots of it, not to mention the

212

loud country/rock music and dancing.

Unlike many of the more remote restaurants in this book, the Rustic Inn has almost as busy a season in winter as in summer. In weather, to be sure, it attracts fishermen and golfers from the nearby Garland Golf Course. But it begins to come into its own with the hunting season, and it really swings when it's snowmobile time. Try to envision great numbers of Ski-doos and Arctic Cats roaring up to the back door of the Rustic Inn. Yes, the trails from Mio and Luzerne run just behind the restaurant, and for some drivers dinner here after a frenzied day in the snow and cold has become a tradition.

If you're overly concerned about cholesterol, finesse, and elegant dining, you'd best go elsewhere. But if your appetite is up and you'd like to glimpse a slice of life you don't often see, give the Rustic Inn a try. The food is as good as that of many of the fancier steak houses throughout the state and as unimaginative. Even here, far from Lake Michigan, broiled whitefish is popular along with steaks, lamb and pork chops, liver and onions, fried chicken, crab and lobster. On Friday there's a fish fry (cod) for only $5.50, the outdoorsman's favorite, and on Saturday, prime rib. Slightly more interesting are the frog legs fried in a garlic-flavored batter and the sauteed bay scallops with mushrooms and scallions.

Three inexpensive specials appear on Sunday (fried chicken), Wednesday (ground sirloin), and Thursday (barbequed ribs). Curiously, the appetizers include "escargots," but read further--they're described as "mushroom caps with garlic butter." And the mushroom soup is defensively sublabeled "truly our own recipe." As you see, no one aspect of the Rustic Inn qualifies it for this book. It's a combination of fine food in its own realm, good value, and the marvelous northwoods rural recreational scene that makes this place special. And it reveals a fascinating and often captivating life style that we think most of you will enjoy unless you're already having fun as a part of it.

A retreat for roisterers.

THE RUSTIC INN, Rte. 1, Box 364, Lewiston, MI
49756. Seven miles south of town on county road
491. Telephone (517) 786-4790. Hours: summer 5-
9 p.m. (till 10 p.m. on weekends), closed Monday;
winter 5-9 p.m. nightly, opens at noon Saturday,
Sunday for light lunches, closed Monday, Tuesday.
Full bar service. Credit cards: MC, V. Reservations
not accepted.

Nearby attraction: If you're here in winter, stop
at the curling rink in Lewiston, one of the few in
Michigan; curling is an ancient Scottish gentleman's
game played on ice.

(90) GATES' AUSABLE LODGE

"The AuSable is justly famous as a trout stream--
the best in the world--but if you're a fisherman,
you already know that and have probably fished
there. If not, you should because one of the best
ways to experience the AuSable is by wading in
it thigh-deep with a fly rod swishing in the air,"
according to Robert C. Wilson, special writer for
the Detroit News. Well, we HAVE experienced the
AuSable, thigh-deep and also even more intimately,
when we upended a canoe in it one summer.

But what has all this to do with adventure? With
eating? The first is easy: the greatest thrill in
fishing may be to see a trout take a surface fly
at exactly the point you expect. As for eating, what
caught our eye in Mr. Wilson's article was the line
"Gates' AuSable Lodge...is a small, out-of-the-way
restaurant that serves the finest rainbow trout I've
ever had." That's pretty decisive, but still he goes
on: "It provides one of the finest dining experiences,
period." This time, WE were hooked.

Scenically things seem all backward here. You

drive up to an apparently charmless white building surrounded by crushed stone, and all your expectations of something remote, rustic, and woodsy fly out the car window. But don't be disappointed or deceived. You're actually entering at the rear; buildings and cottages here, as along so many riverfronts, face not a straight city street but a winding and scenic water highway. Behind that facade is a lovely little dining room with appealing soft greens in carpet and upholstery that blend with the forest setting outside the wall of windows overlooking the beautiful and fast-flowing AuSable River.

AuSable Lodge has been in the Gates family for 20 years and bills itself as a "full service fly-fishing lodge run by fly fishermen for fly fishermen." By full service is meant 16 adjacent motel rooms at reasonable rates, fishing guides, custom fly tying, and a top-of-the-line Orvis pro shop (a favorite of John Hehr, fisherman par excellence), which contains all the tackle of a fly fisherman's dream. And, of course, breakfasts and dinners in the Fishermen's Dining Room. At least 60 percent of the Gates' business comes from out-of-staters, and almost all are repeaters. Maybe because the place is located smack dab near the middle of the part of the river that's designated for fly fishing only. But our guess is that some also come for the food.

The cooking style is basic, hearty, and homey. The dinner menu features steaks, honey-dipped fried chicken, baby beef liver, smoked pork chops, fisherman's platter (shrimp, walleye, scallops), and "locally grown" rainbow trout, baked or pan fried. Accompanying are homemade soup, salad, freshly baked bread, and potatoes (try the AuSable hash browns). There is also a daily special, allowing the cook a bit more creativity, and some pies and other goodies warm from the oven.

Breakfast is available, too. Outstanding among the predictabilities are the French toast, about two inches thick and made from one of Mary Gates' delectable breads, and those wonderful hash browns-- ground potato patties seasoned with sour cream, onion, and parsley. But no lunch at the lodge, presumably because fishing folk are either off wading in the stream or picnicking in the woods or sacking out in their rooms in anticipation of a fine dinner and some night hatches.

The dining room is open to the public, but the overnight guests are given priority. You'll have the hardest time getting reservations in May and June. At any time, though, it's essential to call ahead (you can do this from Grayling along the interstate, about 15 minutes away). If you don't fish, just dress casually, talk about trout and tackle (you can study an Orvis catalogue ahead), and no one will guess you're there just to eat.

An AuSable adventure.

GATES' AUSABLE LODGE, Rte.2, Box 2336, Grayling, MI 49738. At Stephan Bridge; 6½ miles east of Grayling on M-72 (S. Down River Rd.), then 1½ miles north on Stephan Rd. to bridge. Telephone (517) 348-8462. Hours: breakfast 8-11 a.m., dinner 5-8 p.m. Open mid-April through October. No liquor license. Credit cards: MC, V. Must reserve.

Nearby attraction: Hartwick Pines State Park, seven miles northeast of Grayling, should definitely be visited; here are 49 acres of virgin white pine, living reminders of the way Michigan looked when blanketed by magnificent forests.

LEMON BREAD
From Gates' AuSable Lodge

Cream ½ cup shortening until soft. Beat in 1 cup sugar and 2 slightly beaten eggs. Stir together 1½ cups flour, 1 teaspoon baking powder, and ½ teaspoon salt. Add these dry ingredients to the shortening mixture alternately with ½ cup milk, beating constantly. Stir in ½ cup chopped pecans and the grated peel of 1 lemon.

Pour batter into a greased 9x5-inch loaf pan (or 2 smaller bread pans). Bake 1 hour in a preheated

216

325-degree oven (30 minutes for smaller loaves).
While still warm, mix a glaze of ½ cup sugar and
the juice of 1 lemon. Poke holes in the top of the
bread, and pour the glaze over.

We're sure residents of Marquette and Houghton
chuckle when they hear Clare mentioned as "the
beginning of the North." Still, for years our stop
at the Doherty either going to or coming from
points north in Michigan has been traditional.
Depending on our travel schedule, we've breakfasted,
lunched, and dined there innumerable times and have
always enjoyed it. The place is a short and convenient side trip off the freeway; it's open daily all
year; it's reliable and consistent; the prices are
moderate. And for a restaurant of this quality
there are even some bargains.

At breakfast the smoked pork chops, bacon, and
toast from homemade bread are favorites of ours.
The luncheon menu offers something to please most
tastes. In the evening the popular specialties are
prime rib and broiled whitefish, but the menu is
more reassuring than this suggests. Try, for instance,
the broiled pork tenderloin on rice, Chinese pepper
steak, tournedos, or marinated steak kebab with
curried rice. Steaks, seafood, baby beef liver, Chateaubriand for two, fried chicken, spaghetti, some
hearty sandwiches and salads round out the versatile
menu. Dinners include soup , potatoes or wild rice
or vegetable, rolls, beverage, and a generous salad
table. Wines can be had at very attractive prices.
No great chateaux are offered, but the Doherty
has a fine selection, practically all under $20.

The Doherty Hotel was opened in 1924 by the
first A.J. Doherty, grandfather of the present owner,
A.J. Doherty the third. It has always been success-
ful--even in the Depression years, since oil was

struck in the area. It has even been touched by notoriety: in 1938 a member of Detroit's Purple Gang was shot here. But the notorious has now become the nostalgic--A.J. Doherty guesses that at least 500 people have claimed to have been in the bar on the Saturday night that Isaiah Leebove was shot and killed.

It's fun reading the Clare Sentinel of May 20, 1938; on the same day as the shooting, the paper felt it was worth printing that "120 air mail letters have been sent out from Clare in observance of National Air Mail Week" and that the weekend special at Chaffee's Grocery was pecans at 21¢ a pound. The special edition of the Sentinel came out in 1979, and another item caught our interest: on April 10, 1919, "Michigan did well...burying the Wine and Beer amendment abomination by a majority of more than 100,000. It may just as well be understood now that this state is done with the saloon and will have no more of it." If that prophecy had been accurate, there might have been no Purple Gang shooting, and there certainly wouldn't have been the famous Doherty Bloody Marys. So much for history.

The hotel has four dining rooms, though two are generally used for private parties. The main dining area, the Four Seasons Room, has minimal and unobtrusive decor, most notably hand-painted murals. In the evening we prefer the Leprechaun Bar for its comfortable banquettes and cozy atmosphere. The best tables here are numbers 2, 3, and 5 for parties of two to four and number 4 for groups of six. In the winter the Doherty features special ethnic nights and puts on an occasional dinner stage show. For New Year's Eve it arranges an overnight champagne-food-music extravaganza (the packages sell out months ahead). There's nothing elegant about the Doherty (yes, come as you are), but it has the appeal of a solidly established, perennially popular hostelry. And we hope it will continue that way--sure and begorrah, there IS an A.J. Doherty the fourth.

218

One of the last good downtown hotel restaurants.

THE DOHERTY HOTEL AND CONVENTION CENTER, 604 McEwan St., Clare, MI 48617. On B.R. 27 in city center. Telephone (517) 386-3441.Hours: 7 a.m.-10:30 p.m. (Friday-Saturday till 11 p.m., Sunday till 9 p.m.). Full bar service. Credit cards: AE, DC, MC, V. Reservations not taken for Easter or Mother's Day.

THE FAMOUS DOHERTY BLOODY MARY
From the Doherty Hotel

Interestingly, according to James Beard, from 1929 to about 1945 the Bloody Mary was made with gin instead of vodka (and was a creation attributed to the comedian George Jessel). It generally incorporates one constant, a dash or two of Worcestershire sauce; this recipe is an exception. For each drink, fill a 14-ounce glass with ice cubes. Add 1½ ounces vodka, a good pinch celery salt, and about 1/9 ounce or 1 teaspoon Smither's Beef Tea. Fill to the top with V-8 juice, and add a lime wedge and celery rib. Our hint: We like this a bit hotter; try adding a drop or two of Tabasco or use Spicy-Hot V-8.

⑨² *Hermann's*

EUROPEAN CAFE•775-9563

Chef Hermann Suhs is a relatively new Michiganian with more than his fair share of old European culinary tricks. And in spite of the respectable and pragmatic menu here, there's a Continental touch to all that passes his well-trained eye. Chef Hermann, born and raised in Vienna, Austria, earned his first certificate in a Viennese konditorei (pastry shop) and his chef's certificate at the celebrated Hotel Sacher. After receiving his master chef's credentials in Sweden, Mr. Suhs worked in numerous hotels and resorts worldwide and became the personal chef to the King of Nepal. In 1978 he accompanied the Austrians' expedition to Mount Everest--as cook, of course. So one does feel compelled to ask, "Why Cadillac" for a European cafe? And why would such an eminent and talented chef burrow himself away from the glittering urban lights and glow of public recognition? "Simplement." Mardi Suhs, Hermann's wife, is a Cadillac resident, and both of them highly appreciate, as we do, the charms of Michigan's northern woodlands.

What is special about Hermann's is that the cooking is grounded in century-old techniques and standards, which many restaurants today bypass in favor of profits and fleeting praise. International specialties on the menu range from expertly prepared wiener schnitzel to veal Marsala to chicken breast Francaise to seafood curry and so it goes. But there is also a daily-changing "gourmet" dinner menu on the blackboard at the entrance. On our last visit the cafe offered an elegant Swedish-style poached rainbow trout with dilled cream sauce and baby shrimp and a wondrous dish of veal scallops with morels and chanterelles, flambeed with brandy. On a luncheon visit the slate boasted ham loaf with almond-raisin sauce, accompanied by new potatoes and braised cabbage--"good old-fashioned food," according to Chef Hermann. And the dessert of the day was peach cream meringue pie; on other days it might be Austrian apple strudel or Napoleons. Can you miss?

On the first Friday of each month Hermann's puts on an international buffet. It could be a mixture of various cuisines of the world, or it might focus on, say, Cajun, Greek, or German. And each November wild game specialties are featured every evening. But "we are not a gourmet restaurant," insists Chef Hermann, who deplores the overuse and misuse of the word "gourmet." Service, by the way, is personally supervised by Chef Hermann, and he's put together a thoroughly proficient staff.

The exterior is notable without demanding much attention--creamy wood siding complemented by blue and white awnings. And the interior is not much more obtrusive. Decorated by Mardi, it has a homey atmosphere with brick walls, dark oak chairs, lace curtains, basketry, dried flowers, a domestic accent of handmade quilts on the walls, and a warm beige, rose, and burgundy color scheme. And do take a look at the massive old backbar, made in Grand Rapids in 1901. Next door to the restaurant is the Chef's Deli; we recommend it for bakery goods and takeouts.

Agreeable Austrian antics.

HERMANN'S EUROPEAN CAFE, 214 N. Mitchell St., Cadillac, MI 49601. On the main street downtown. Telephone (616) 775-9563. Hours: 11 a.m.-10 p.m. Monday-Saturday. Closed Sunday, Christmas, and New Year's Day. Free municipal parking lot a block away off Pine St. Full bar service. Credit cards: MC, V. Reservations necessary only for parties of 10 or more.

MOROCCAN STEAMED CHICKEN
From Chef Hermann Suhs,
Hermann's European Cafe

Rinse and pat dry 1 roasting chicken (about $3\frac{1}{2}$ pounds). Sprinkle inside and out with salt. Mix together 4 cups steamed couscous (or brown rice, kasha, or buckwheat groats), $\frac{1}{2}$ cup chopped walnuts or pine nuts, $\frac{1}{4}$ cup seedless raisins, 2 tablespoons melted butter, 3 tablespoons honey, and 2 pinches each of cinnamon, garlic, cloves, turmeric, cumin, and pepper. Stuff chicken with half the mixture, and close cavity. Tie legs together and place chicken in a steamer or rack an inch above boiling water in a roasting pan. Put remaining couscous mixture in aluminum foil, seal, and place next to chicken on rack. Cover roasting pan tightly, and steam chicken about 40 minutes or till tender (when fork tested, juices will run clear if done). Remove chicken. Pat dry with paper towels. Heat $\frac{1}{4}$ cup peanut oil and 2 tablespoons unsalted butter in a large skillet over high heat. Lower heat to medium, and cook chicken, turning to brown all sides. Serve at once, garnished with mint sprigs or watercress; surround with remaining couscous. Serves 4.

⑨③ M°GUIRE'S

There's not much that's Irish about McGuire's except the name and the cozy Irish Pub, serving as cocktail lounge. In the past, we always wondered why the dining room was called the Viking Room (maybe Jim McGuire married a Norwegian?), but that problem is now solved. The room has been remodeled and renamed the Terrace Dining Room, and it's lovely. With light oak and trelliswork and a soft peach and forest green color scheme, it provides dining on three levels; most appealing are the seven tables for four on the lower level near the window walls overlooking the golf course and the city of Cadillac. The view doesn't equal that of Shanty Creek, but at night the flickering candlelight indoors and the twinkling city lights in the distance are an enchanting combination.

Three meals a day are served here, but dinner is a special treat. McGuire's is especially popular for its fine, fairly priced Saturday evening buffet and the Sunday brunch served from 11:30 a.m. to 3 p.m. On Sunday through Friday evening, the dining room offers rather predictable fare ("the best prime rib in town") but with a few nice additions: oysters Florentine, turtle soup New Orleans, chicken Panache (stuffed with wild rice), and frog legs sauteed with garlic butter. Entrees are accompanied by a choice of potato or fresh vegetable, soup (good hearty soups here--see the recipe below), salad bar, and fresh breads. Prices are moderate. Pay a bit more for something

222

fattening from the enticing dessert cart. The wine list is modest; house wines by William Wycliff of California are acceptable, and a best bet may be the B & G Vouvray at a reasonable price.

The attractive contemporary lodge is the center of a resort complex that offers year-round recreation packages (its own 27-hole golf course, tennis courts, heated indoor pool, Finnish sauna and whirlpool baths, snowmobile warmup trails, cross-country skiing) and is only minutes away from the famous Caberfae ski area. Set high on a glacial moraine amid 230 acres of pine trees and well-maintained landscaped grounds, McGuire's is fast becoming a major convention center. It's hard to believe that it started in 1948 as a hamburger stand with only four stools. And, yes, burgers are still on the menu.

Fine food, seasonal sports.

McGUIRE'S MOTOR LODGE AND RESORT, 7880 Mackinaw Trail, Cadillac, MI 49610. South of the city 1½ miles; ½ mile south of M-131. Telephone (616) 775-9947. Hours: 6:30 a.m.-10 p.m. in the summer, 7 a.m.-9 p.m. in the winter (till 10 p.m. on Friday and Saturday). Closed Thankgiving, Christmas Eve and Christmas Day. Full bar service. Entertainment in lounge Tuesday, Friday, Saturday by a disc jockey. Credit cards: AE, DC, MC, V.

BEEF SHORT RIB SOUP
From Chef David Smith, McGuire's

In a 6-quart saucepan, heat 2 pounds beef short ribs (cut into 2-inch pieces) and 8 cups water to boiling. Skim off foam. Add 1 cup fresh or frozen chopped onion, 4 teaspoons salt, ½ teaspoon pepper, and ¼ teaspoon monosodium glutamate (optional). Heat to boiling. Reduce heat to low; cover and simmer 1½ hours.

Add 3 medium potatoes (peeled and cut in bite-

sized pieces), 3 medium carrots (sliced), and $\frac{1}{2}$ of
a small head of cabbage (cut in bite-sized pieces).
Heat to boiling. Reduce heat to low; cover and
simmer 30 minutes or until meat and vegetables
are tender. Add 2 large tomatoes (peeled and cut
into bite-sized pieces) and heat through. Serves 12.

94 CLUB 37

Most newcomers to Lake County are struck by
the seemingly endless miles of highway flanked
by seemingly endless forest land. It's a place where
you start worrying about running out of gas or
finding a rest stop or starving to death. This is the
heart of the Manistee National Forest and the Pere
Marquette State Forest, after all. So when you
come upon the Club 37, set back a bit from the
highway (M-37, of course) and see dozens of cars,
you wonder where all these people come from. In
this part of the state, one tends to have a sense
of remoteness, of being in an untamed wilderness
area. But unlike what we think of as "the Felch
experience" (in the U.P., see Solberg's Bar), where
there really isn't anything out there in the woods
except trees and animals, here if you were to
crash through the underbrush, you'd come upon
numerous lakes and campgrounds teeming with
tourists and sportsmen. You just can't see them
from the highway.

Club 37 prides itself as being one of Lake
County's most popular family restaurants; we would
guess it's THE most popular. (Or can you think of
anything better in Luther, Idlewild, or Peacock?)
A good proportion of the habitues are not only
locals but regulars who drive fairly long distances
(even from Ludington and Manistee) because they
can get a good hearty meal here at surprisingly
low prices. The exterior is unmemorable country
roadhouse style, and the interior features lots of

basic black and Scottish plaid. A notable touch is a number of deer photographs, appealing to the many hunters that frequent this place. Come early or late on Friday and Saturday if you don't like long lines. And come as you are--you'll see unshaven types in flannel shirts and old men who keep their hats on at the bar. If you're dressed up, they'll stare at you.

Tables are decorated with catsup, Heinz 57, A-1 Sauce, and Worcestershire; are you beginning to get an idea of the cuisine? Club 37 cooks claim to be the "prime rib experts of the north," and if prime rib is the name of your game, why order anything else? If it isn't, there are lots of steaks and other simply prepared but fresh main courses to choose from--the walleyed pike is second in popularity to the prime rib, and steaks come in third. We like the frog legs and steamed scampi, too. Dinners, mostly in the $10 range or less, include a relish tray, liver pate, salad, potato, and bread.

The lunch menu offers a number of predictable sandwiches, many at an amazing $1.50. We splurged and had the crab sandwich--LOTS of steamed crabmeat (not canned, either) piled on a toasted English muffin and topped with a really good Hollandaise--at only $3.50. And if you're in this area at lunchtime, take a few minutes to stop in at the Shrine of the Pines, two miles south of Baldwin. It's a state historic site that's a lot more fun to see than the words "shrine" and "historic" suggest. This is a memorial to the white pine tree and Michigan's lumbering era and, as it turns out, Lake County's answer to the Leg's Inn in Cross Village (see)--a log cabin boasting, for example, a table made from a 700-pound stump, a fireplace constructed from 70 tons of native stone, and a bootlegger's table with a hollow leg (open May 1-November 1).

Dine by the Shrine of the Pines.

CLUB 37, Route 2, Box 2677, Baldwin, MI 49304.

Ten miles north of Baldwin on U.S.37. Telephone
(616) 266-5601. Hours: Monday-Thursday 10:30 a.m.-
10 p.m., Friday and Saturday 10:30 a.m.-11 p.m.,
Sunday 11 a.m.-10 p.m. Closed Easter, Christmas
Eve, and Christmas Day. No credit cards. Reserve
for parties of 10 or more.

FROZEN DAIQUIRIS
From Arthur G. Flint, DeKalb, Illinois

Since Club 37 is a favorite of outdoorsmen, for
drinks as well as food, this is an appropriate
opportunity to include a great recipe we received
from our friend Art Flint, one of the most accomplished sportsmen we know. This is simplicity itself
and perfect to keep on hand for summer entertaining. Mix together 1 (6-ounce) can frozen lemonade
concentrate, 2 lemonade cans of light or dark rum,
2 tablespoons sugar, and 1 small (10-ounce) bottle
of 7-Up. Freeze until mushy. Serves 6-8. Increase
proportionately if you wish.

(95) **TUGBOAT ANNIE'S**

"Getting there is half the fun." This is a cliche
that works so well for Tugboat Annie's that it
proves once again that cliches are still around
because they can make sense. There are three
ways to get to this restaurant, and we've purposely
left out "by foot" as ludicrous: first, by your own
water-going vessel; second, by automobile; or third,
by a no-kidding tugboat, the most fun of all. It is,
admittedly, the shortest cruise on record--five or
six minutes, depending on the wind--and it costs
only a dollar, making it the cheapest scheduled
cruise on record. But how often can you set foot
on a genuine tugboat?
At the helm of the little red and black "Annie"
is Captain Denny Atherton, a former chief engi-

neerman in the U.S. Navy who served aboard landing ships, a destroyer, and a battleship in the Pacific during World War II. Sharing duties in the pilot house is Fran, his wife, who is licensed to operate vessels up to 50 gross tons on the Great Lakes.

And when this little workhorse of the water gets you to where you're going for lunch or dinner, what will you find? Luckily, it's not all a gimmick. There's something for everyone here, and it's served in a very attractive little restaurant with high domed ceilings and skylights, dark brick and light oak, and a neutral color scheme softened with hanging plants. In sunny weather there's also a nice patio--all of this overlooking the bay, the marina, and across a short stretch of water the city of Ludington.

On the menu for kids of all ages are nachos, potato skins, hot dogs, good soups and sandwiches, and mostly ice cream desserts. At lunch salads are the standouts. We especially like the fresh fruit plate (in season). At dinner are a few more sophisticated possibilities: huge marinated pork loin chops, roasted rock Cornish game hens, prime rib (on weekends), and a good selection of fish and seafood. It's not a fancy menu, but it's quite acceptable, agreeable, and appealing to customers of all ages. The prices are so reasonable that you won't quibble about the cost of a tugboat ride, even for the entire family.

Don't miss mess with Annie.

TUGBOAT ANNIE'S, 501 S. Lakeshore Drive, Ludington, MI 49431. Telephone (616) 845-0210. Tugboat leaves from city docks in downtown Ludington Monday-Thursday 11:30 a.m.-3 p.m., 6-9 p.m.; Friday-Saturday 11:30 a.m.-3 p.m., 6-11 p.m.; Sunday 1:30 a.m.-7 p.m.; leaves on the hour and half hour. Restaurant hours: Monday-Saturday luncheon 11:30 a.m.-5 p.m., dinner 5-10 p.m.; Sunday brunch 11:30 a.m.-3 p.m., dinner 4-8 p.m. Open Memorial Day through second week of October. Credit cards: MC, V.

hobby crest

Hobby Crest is known for its solid, home-cooked, stick-to-the-ribs chow, especially its all-you-can-eat pancake breakfast, a bargain at $1.25. The usual breakfast choices are available, but the pancakes and the American fries are the drawing cards for almost 350 people every Sunday morning. Since the dining room seats about 60, that number of people willing to drive for miles and still ready to wait in line is quite a compliment to the owners, Beverly and Virginia Collins. And it's well deserved.

The luncheon features mostly sandwiches and a good homemade soup of the day. And the baskets, available most of the day and evening, are a welcome accommodation to fishermen and others who won't put up with scheduled feedings. As for dinner, the offerings are typically American and of high quality: steaks, prime rib, fish, frog legs, shrimp, roast beef and pork, chicken, pork chops and cutlets, and ham. Most meals, including soup, salad bar, potato, and bread, are in the $7 to $8 range. Only the T-bone steak costs more than $10. Each evening a dinner special is possible, too, and the choice includes the previously listed items at a lower price (almost all about $6) as well as such earthy, humble, and always hearty main courses as Swiss steak and stuffed pork chops. On Friday several fish dinners are all you can eat; we recommend Hobby Crest's specialty, lake perch. As you can guess, the idea of this congenial restaurant and resort is, simply, good, fresh, tasty food at extremely reasonable rates.

But commonplace it certainly isn't. Hobby Crest's main lodge is the only restaurant on Hamlin Lake. The dining areas consist of the open, larger section in the center called the Pecky Cypress Room; the side porch named the Rod and Reel Room; and our own first choice for seating, the Cedar Porch, with booths and big windows. These three adjoining rooms are on the upper level of the lodge overlooking the lake and afford an exceptional view of water, woods, and sunsets. The decor is unobtrusive, the old oak and cane chairs are comfortable, and the service is cheerful and accommodating. In a way, the place is one of a vanishing breed, where food and fair prices are more important than impressive decor and pretentious ambience.

It's a pleasant drive, too. Ludington locals and tourists don't just happen upon the Hobby Crest; they must purposefully seek it out. The last two miles on Piney Ridge Road wind through beautiful dense woods to end in a secluded setting far removed from urban headaches, even the minor Ludington sort of headaches. And, remember, it's a year-round resort, too. Think about staying a few days at one of the cottages. There are 3800 acres of game fishing, boating, swimming, water sports, and miles of trails through the nearby state park and sand dunes.

A lovely lakeside near Ludington, a bargain.

HOBBY CREST RESORT AND RESTAURANT, 3264 N. Piney Ridge Rd., Ludington, MI 49431. On the west shore of Hamlin Lake; take M-116 2 miles north of Ludington city limits; then turn right and drive 2 miles on Piney Ridge. Telephone (616) 843-8838. Hours: breakfast 8 a.m.-noon, luncheon 11:30 a.m.4 p.m., dinner 4-9 p.m.; baskets (shrimp, chicken, clams, fish, burgers) 11:30 a.m.-9 p.m. Closed October 25 to Father's Day weekend and the two weeks following Labor Day. No credit cards or reservations accepted. Liquor license pending.

HERSHEY'S CHOCOLATE CAKE
From Virginia Collins, Hobby Crest

Virginia tells us that this is the recipe her

customers most often request. In a large bowl, mix together one (16-ounce) can Hershey's chocolate syrup, 4 eggs, 1 cup sugar, 1 cup flour, $\frac{1}{4}$ pound softened margarine, 1 teaspoon baking powder, 1 teaspoon salt, 1 teaspoon vanilla extract. Pour into a greased and floured 9x13-inch baking pan, and bake in a preheated 350-degree oven for 30 minutes or until cake springs back when touched lightly with fingertips.

For frosting, place 1/3 cup evaporated milk, 1 cup sugar, and $\frac{1}{4}$ pound margarine in a medium saucepan. Bring to a boil; then boil 2 minutes. Add 1 cup miniature marshmallows, $\frac{1}{2}$-1 cup chocolate chips, 1 cup coarsely chopped nuts, and 1 teaspoon vanilla extract, off heat. Stir until marshmallows and chocolate chips are melted. Frost cake when it's cool.

HOTEL FRANKFORT

The Victorian gingerbread facade of the Hotel Frankfort, sprucely painted in cream, forest green, and old gold, has been a landmark in the small city of Frankfort for more than 50 years. Actually, there's been a hotel on this site since 1867. But only recently, under the direction of the new owners, Pam and Kirk Lorenz and Pam's brother Scott, has the building offered something really special in the way of accommodations and fine food.

The imposing main dining room is decked out with floral wallpaper and carpeting and table settings of white linen, burgundy napkins, and nostalgic oil lanterns. Yet it's difficult to choose between the warm serenity of this room and the diverting ambience of the candlelit wine cellar. Reached by a spiral staircase, the low-ceiling white-washed cellar has four tables in one room and another five in a separate alcove. Walls are lined with wine bottles, and graceful arches are reminiscent of a European vintner's tasting room.

The Hotel Frankfort specializes in "always perfect prime rib" and other American favorites. But almost as popular is the steamed scrod amandine. Fish and chips, shrimp tempura, and sauteed scallops are also rewarding. There's an excellent house salad with a creamy herb dressing, and the breads are a triumph--sourdough, dill, Russian rye, and others. As at the Brookside Inn, the hotel's sister establishment in Beulah, also owned by Pam and Kirk Lorenz, the best dessert is the hot apple dumpling. (Do look at our entry for the Brookside Inn; the atmosphere there is less formal than that of the Hotel Frankfort, but the menus and dining concepts in both places are much the same.)

Here and at the Brookside, a modest selection of French and Michigan wines are available. But what is particularly noteworthy is the extensive offering of German wines, many of them prize winners and most rarely seen in Michigan restaurants and wine stores. Kabinett (special reserve) reds can be had at $13 to $16 a bottle, and there's a large number of white Rhines and Moselles, including at least a dozen rare honey-sweet beerenausleses and eight white Kabinettwein (and none of the ubiquitous Piesporter Michelsberg, which is never an estate bottling). German roses and sparkling wines complete the listing. The Lorenzes often travel to Germany to select their wines personally and import them to Michigan. They also train their staff about wine and host tastings throughout the year.

We'd heard about "the great bed and breakfast place" in Frankfort, and indeed the renovated hotel has a number of attractive rooms and provides a full breakfast to overnight guests. But in an imaginative, romantic gesture, it also rents out special "couples' rooms," each with a king-sized waterbed with mirrored canopy, a little log-burning stove, a remote-control color TV set, and a Polynesian spa. Some rooms also have saunas, steam baths, and French tanning solariums. A full dinner and breakfast are included in the price. Similar "ulti-

mate accommodations for two" may be reserved
at the Brookside Inn in Beulah.

Pamper yourself; you work too hard anyway.

THE HOTEL FRANKFORT, Main Street, Frankfort,
MI 49635. Downtown. Telephone (616) 352-9671.
Hours: 8 a.m.-closing, daily. Full bar service. Credit cards: AE, Disc, MC, V.
Nearby attractions: The Point Betsie Light Station, built in 1858, is a favorite of photographers
and artists and a great vantage point for viewing
sunsets. The national hang-gliding festival is held
every summer on Elberta Bluff south of the inlet
(Take Bye St. off M-168).

APPLE DUMPLINGS
From the Hotel Frankfort

One pastry recipe for a double-crust pie will be
sufficient for 4 to 6 apples depending on their size.
Use your favorite piecrust recipe, or see the
recipe following our Hathaway House entry. Roll
out prepared crust and cut into 4-6 squares, large
enough to enclose apples. Place 4-6 peeled and
cored apples (Jonathan, Winesap, Ida Red, etc.) in
center of each square. Combine $\frac{1}{4}$ cup brown sugar
and 1 teaspoon cinnamon and spoon into cavities.
(Use 1/3 cup sugar and $1\frac{1}{2}$ teaspoon for 6 apples.)
Dot with softened butter. Fold dough corner to
corner around the apple. Place in a lightly buttered
pan. Make syrup: In a small saucepan combine $\frac{1}{2}$
cup sugar, 1 cup water, and $\frac{1}{4}$ teaspoon cinnamon
(for 6 apples 3/4 cup sugar, $1\frac{1}{2}$ cup water, scant
teaspoon cinnamon). Bring to boil, and set aside
if making ahead. Pour syrup over apples and bake
in a preheated 375-degree oven until golden brown,
40-45 minutes. The Lorenzes serve these with ice
cream, cream, and whipped cream. Makes 4-6.

Chimney Corners

"What becomes a legend most?" Have you seen those fur ads? What most becomes Carol Channing, Mary Martin, Lena Horne, and other lovely ladies of stage and screen is a black mink coat. What most becomes Mollie Rogers of Chimney Corners fame is a black cast-iron skillet, though we wouldn't put it past her ardent admirers to chip in for a fur if they thought she wanted one. Mollie Rogers and Chimney Corners are almost synonyms. Her fans treasure her cookbook, and when they dine at the country resort outside of Frankfort, they expect, even sometimes demand, that the brioche be baked by Mollie herself and no one else.

Still, much as we revere the lady, there is more to Chimney Corners than Mollie Rogers. Set amidst hundreds of acres of forest, fields, and orchards, with a beach on Crystal Lake and distant views of Lake Michigan and the Sleeping Bear dunes, it's one of the most impressive rural hostelries in Michigan. The resort has been in business for more than 50 years and has an affectionate, devoted clientele who extol both its hospitality and its excellent American/Continental cooking.

The dark rustic main lodge, built in 1910, houses two attractive dining rooms, each with a stone fireplace, hardwood floors, traditional furnishings, and lots of good antiques. There's seating on the porch, too, and a view of Crystal Lake. Chimney Corners has a rotating dinner menu and one seating, 6:30 to 7 p.m., every evening except Sunday. All dishes are carefully chosen with consideration for the guests' pleasure, and all are completely home cooked. On our last visit the weekly entrees included rock Cornish game hens, roast leg of lamb with rosemary, roast duckling with orange sauce, prime rib, whitefish, and a special buffet on Saturday--a popular and delicious array of whitefish, chicken, roast lamb, beef Burgundy, salads, breads, and desserts.

When she's not toiling on her new cookbook, Mollie oversees the kitchen and shares in some of the cooking, but her son-in-law Rick Herman now manages the resort, and two other chefs, including Mollie's daughter, Claudia Rogers Herman, are hard at work over the pots and pans. Another change at Chimney Corners is the acquisition of a beer and wine license. The selection is appropriately small but adequate, featuring such wines as Soave, Valpolicella, white Beaujolais and Zinfandel, a Rene Junot red, and a Bereich Bingen "Kabinett" and such beers as Coors, Beck's, and Augsberger.

Vacationers staying at Chimney Corners, of course, have the best opportunity to sample the good cooking here. But it is possible to eat at the resort without being a guest by calling a day or two in advance. Ideally, however, you might think about staying in a room at the resort, even if for one night. For a longer period you can reserve a cottage (either rustic or modern) on the shore of beautiful Crystal Lake or the bluff overlooking it. Each unit has a fireplace and screened porch or deck, and the rates are quite reasonable. A variety of boats are available for rent; lawn games, tennis, and a nearby golf course offer more leisure-time activity. Nature lovers, incidentally, will be interested in seeing the American chestnut grove on the property, the largest remaining in this part of the country.

Charming countryside dining.

CHIMNEY CORNERS, 1602 Crystal Dr., Frankfort, MI 49635. Seven miles north of town on M-22, on Crystal Lake. Telephone (616) 352-7522. One seating only for dinner. Dining room closed Sunday, and from mid-October to Memorial Day. Beer and wine. No credit cards. Reservations necessary (but call ahead; there may be a cancellation).

LEMON SPONGE
From Mollie Rogers, Chimney Corners

According to Mollie, "When you need a light tangy
little dessert, it's exactly right. I often bake it in
individual custard cups, and then turn each one
upside down on a dessert place." This is a cake-
pudding that makes its own sauce.

Sift or mix together 1 cup sugar, 3 tablespoons
flour, and ½ teaspoon salt. Combine with 3 well-
beaten egg yolks. Add 1 tablespoon melted butter,
6 tablespoons lemon juice, 1 tablespoon grated lemon
rind, and 1¼ cups milk. Beat 3 egg whites until
stiff, and fold in. Pour into a 2-quart baking dish
or custard cups (set on a cookie sheet). Bake at
350 degrees till firm (about 40 minutes for the
baking dish and 20 minutes for the cups). The top
will be brown and puffy. You can serve this with
whipped cream (Mollie doesn't).

Brookside Inn
99

U.S. 31 Beulah, MI 49617 (616)882-7271

Kirk Lorenz, a second-generation Michigan
restauranteur, came by his expertise and sense of
service and community under the tutelage of his
father Ralph Lorenz, owner of the Mayflower Hotel
in Plymouth. And probably the family's Austrian
background contributed to his appreciation of fine
food and wine. Wherever his enthusiasm came from,
Michigan diners are fortunate that Kirk and his
wife Pam decided to brighten the state's restaurant
scene with two fine establishments, the Hotel
Frankfort and the Brookside Inn. Both feature
similar menus and wine lists, but each has a dis-
tinctly individual personality. And the Lorenz
philosophy of "customers first" is refreshing in that
it goes beyond typical restaurant politesse. For
example, closing hours are not posted; the dining

rooms are open "until people quit coming" (and that might be as late as 3 a.m.). According to Kirk, "We're here for their convenience, not ours." Hear, hear!

The Brookside Inn has a simple frame exterior enlivened by flower boxes and a bright green canopy over the doorway. Inside are knotty pine walls, a neutral color scheme, and 30 or 40 different collections of antiques and artifacts, among them glassware and china, beer cans and bottles, farm implements, cooking utensils, and most eye-catching, a series of life-size paper-mache figures from the 1934 Chicago World's Fair. The atmosphere is casual and relaxed. As Kirk points out, "We get everything from hip boots and waders to formal dresses." Table settings are utilitarian but boast two nice touches: Italian half-liter wine decanters filled with fresh flowers and a peppermill on every table.

The memorabilia in the main room and its extensions are fascinating, but if possible you can double your pleasure with a window seat overlooking the brook and countryside. Another choice, as at the Hotel Frankfort, is to dine in the wine cellar, a long, narrow room with the same Continental aura as in Frankfort. Still a third choice exists, and it would be our first option if the weather was right: the outdoor tables along Eden Brook, shaded by huge willows and silver maples.

Breakfast at the Brookside is a treat. The corned beef hash and the ham and cheese omelet are both excellent. And for the sweet-toothed, you can't beat the Benzie Belly Buster, a fresh strawberry or blueberry pancake with whipped cream. Eggs come with delicious dill and sourdough toast and fresh fruit preserves, and the country ham is smoked and cured right on the premises. Lunches comprise mostly sandwiches, made special by those good home-baked breads. Smaller portions of two dinner entrees are also an option--fish and chips or Icelandic scrod.

The evening menu is similar to that of the Hotel Frankfort except that sirloin steak is featured here instead of prime rib. The house specialty is that succulent steamed scrod with toasted almonds

and clarified butter. Other choices include veal
piccata, clams, spaghetti, and a combination plate
of sirloin and scrod in three portion sizes. Desserts
are old-fashioned and all-American: pies, strawberry
shortcake, brownie a la mode with fudge sauce, and
hot Michigan apple dumpling with ice cream, The
latter is downright soul-satisfying. Lawsy, is it good!
(See the recipe in this book.)

At the front entry is the bakery, which supplies
the restaurant with breads, pies, and other freshly
baked items. If you're tempted to take something
home, we recommend the huge, chewy coconut
macaroons, crunchy peanut butter cookies, and ultra-
rich, fudgy brownies. Adjacent to the bakery is a
little collectible shop that offers unusual American
and European giftware.

Enjoyable eating by the Eden.

THE BROOKSIDE INN, U.S.31, Beulah, MI 49617.
In city center. Telephone (616) 882-7271. Hours:
8 a.m.-closing, daily. Full bar service. Entertainment nightly (country fiddle playing, folk music,
or easy-listening piano). Credit cards: AE, Disc,
MC, V. Reservations accepted but usually not necessary.

PAPA KIRK'S HAM AND BROCOLI QUICHE
From the Brookside Inn

Prepare pie pastry for a single crust (use your
own favorite recipe, or see the recipe following
our review of Hathaway House in Blissfield). Roll
dough fairly thin and place in a lightly buttered
pie pan. Kirk Lorenz doesn't specify exact quantities
and, indeed, it's not really necessary to measure
out ingredients for a quiche. Just check any good
cookbook for the egg-cream ratio.

Sprinkle finely chopped onions, garlic salt, and
pepper on the pie shell. Then alternate layers of
broccoli (cut spears), ham (shaved and lightly
grilled), and grated Mozzarella cheese, preferably

ending with cheese. In mixing bowl combine eggs, whipping cream (or half-and-half), and pinch nutmeg until about the consistency of eggnog. Pour over. Bake at 350 degrees until golden brown on top and a knife inserted in center comes out clean. Let stand 10 minutes before serving.

(100) JOE'S FRIENDLY TAVERN

The name says it all. For nearly 40 years Joe's Friendly Tavern has been the social center of the small village of Empire and a recreational mecca for campers at the Sleeping Bear National Lake Shore and the D.H. Day campground, only seven miles away. It's ideal for families eating out on a small budget, for enthusiasts of local color, and for hamburger lovers. It's friendly, clean, very informal, and a bargain. Dress down for Joe's or you'll feel out of place. And don't expect "atmosphere" in the usual sense; the decor here might be labeled "fun and games." The large open dining room and connecting bar are stocked with pool tables, shuffleboard, television games, and pinball machines as well as a jukebox and popcorn machine. Some of the tables are bare, and some sport bandanna cloths. Seating for groups is unlimited--just push the tables together.

The Friendly Tavern for years had just a small bar menu offering the famous Friendly Burger, one of the best hamburgers in Michigan (the place serves up 11 tons of ground beef a year); a jumbo beef frankfurter; four dinner baskets (shrimp, fish, smelt, chicken); and unusually good homemade soup and chili. Now there's even more: nachos, wet burritos, and four very reasonable dinner plates (whitefish, an 8-ounce sirloin sizzler, 12-ounce T-bone, and catfish). There's wine by the glass and a large variety of beer; both beer and soft drinks may be ordered by the pitcher. In the summer the Friendly Tavern also serves breakfast, and we highly recommend the spicy homemade pork sausage.

The tavern's takeout service, including beer and wine, is something to consider, depending on your mood and how busy Joe's is. In the evening especially, the bar is often crowded with a wide variety of age groups and occasionally breaks the sound barrier. If this isn't your idea of fun, why not plan a picnic instead? Pack your car with Friendly Burgers, French fries, and beverages and drive west on Lake Street, following the signs to Lake Michigan. In a few hundred yards (you can walk if you prefer) is a very pleasant city park with beaches and picnic tables. Drive to the north end and enjoy a fine beach and a marvelous view of the bluffs of Sleeping Bear to the north.

Some say the best hamburger in Michigan.

JOE'S FRIENDLY TAVERN, 11015 Front St., Empire, MI 49630. Two blocks west of the traffic light at the intersection of M-72 and M-22, in the center of town. Telephone (616) 326-5506. Hours: summer 7 a.m.-2 a.m., winter 7:30 a.m.-2 a.m. Closed Christmas, Easter. Full bar service.

CHILI
From Joe's Friendly Tavern

Craig Claiborne once noted that chili con carne is conceivably America's greatest gift to world cuisine. Not a Mexican dish despite its name and once a regional dish, it's now firmly established throughout the country and varies considerably in degree of pungency and ingredients used. This is a mild version with beans. In a large saucepan or skillet, brown $1\frac{1}{2}$ large chopped onions in $1\frac{1}{2}$ tablespoons butter. Add 1 pound ground beef, and brown. Stir in 3 tablespoons flour. Add 2 teaspoons salt, $\frac{1}{4}$ teaspoon pepper, 3 teaspoons chili powder or more to taste. Mix well, then add 3 (16-ounce) cans dark red kidney beans and 24 to 30 ounces canned tomato juice. Simmer 1 hour. Serve with saltines

and side dishes of grated Cheddar and chopped green
peppers. Our hint: Like it hotter? Add chopped jalapeno peppers or dry crushed red peppers to taste.

La Bécasse
RESTAURANT

(101) French Country Cooking
Fine Wine and Spirits

There's a beguiling aura here, the soft slate-blue
shutters on the small roadside building evocative
of a sun-washed French country cottage. And the
spare white interior--white everywhere in curtains,
table linens, plates, marble wine coolers--is an
effective foil for colorful splashes of modern art
on the walls and wildflowers on the tables. The
restaurant in its more prosaic days was known as
the Woodcock, and its latest owner, Mary Ann
O'Neill, merely went with the Gallic translation,
La Becasse. Since then, it has literally and deservedly, put Burdickville, Michigan, back on the map.
Which is a story in itself. The hamlet was always
on local maps and in the big Rand McNally atlas;
but it wasn't on the official state highway map
until 1983, after John O'Neill--Mary Ann's husband,
Bloomfield Hills attorney, and professed cartophile--
convinced Michigan's Department of Transportation
of the village's historic significance as a once-
bustling little community in the late 1800s.

We probably should care more intensely about
Burdickville's history; but, to be honest, our main
concern is with its gastronomical significance. The
cooking at La Becasse is brilliantly French in both
tradition and spirit. On the changing menu are such
temptations as carrot timbales with basil sauce,
turbons of rainbow trout stuffed with scallop mousse,
escalopes of veal piquante, and tournedos Chasseur.
But the creativity is what is so disarming, yet not
surprising to anyone who's studied French cuisine,
still the most technically sophisticated in the world.
The methodology at La Becasse is grounded in the
classics, and typical dishes from various interna-

240

tional sources are atypically executed with French finesse and integrity. Last summer we ordered a velvety pheasant pate and an eggplant gratin, both immensely likable appetizers. One entree, a refined rendition of chicken mole successfully combined the best of two very disparate worlds, Mexican and French. The baked polenta, too, with morel and porcini mushrooms, was another boundary-crossing triumph. And never have we tasted such an innovative treatment of whitefish: lightly curried and paired with couscous (steamed semolina wheat), a staple entree of the Mahgreb of North Africa but presented here as a delicate accompaniment to the main dish. For dessert, though the French chocolate cake seductively beckoned, we opted for the Vacherin, a crisp mountain of meringue filled with ice cream and sauced with raspberries. Even the strong Colombian coffee was worth raving about ("It's the water," said our waitress Annie O'Neill).

All these wonders result from the imagination and labors of chef/proprietor Mary Ann, who studied at La Varenne in Paris, and her accomplished associate chef Andrew Kile, who apprenticed with Milos Cihelka at the Golden Mushroom in Southfield. All five of the O'Neill children, too, have at one time or another been involved in the business, and there's a good chance, especially during the summer and holiday seasons, that one of them might be your server, as Annie was ours. The family contribution sets La Becasse apart from the tuxedoed impersonal service you might otherwise expect of a restaurant of this quality.

Although limited to about 50 selections, the wine list represents a well-selected and -designed cellar in terms of both distinction and price. Only six cost more than $30, so there are none of the expensive "collector" items that sometimes appear primarily for show or conversation. Instead, most fall into a reasonable $15-20 range. In addition, there are six house wines offered for about $3 a glass. Wines are also available to take home at substantial discounts.

A rural revelation.

LA BECASSE, 4385 Hwy 616, Burdickville, MI (no ZIP because the U.S. Post Office doesn't recognize the place; mailing address Maple City, MI 49664). At junction of Co. Rds. 616 and 675, on the southeast shore of Glen Lake. Telephone (616) 334-3944. Hours: 5:45-9:30 p.m. Tuesday-Sunday. Closed Monday. Full bar service.Credit cards: MC, V.

NOISETTES DE PORC AUX PRUNEAUX
From Mary Ann O'Neill, La Becasse

Plan to start this dish a day in advance. First, prepare the quatre epices (meaning "four spices," which as you'll note is made up of six spices and two herbs, but how can we quibble when the results are unquestionably superior?). In a blender process 1 teaspoon ground cinnamon, 2 teaspoons ground allspice, 1/8 teaspoon ground cloves, ½ teaspoon ground cardamom, 1 teaspoon grated nutmeg, 2 teaspoons ground coriander, 2 teaspoons finely crumbled dry tarragon, and ½ teaspoon finely crumbled dry marjoram on high speed until finely powdered. You'll only need a small amount in this recipe, but keep it on hand for French pates and meat pies. (This is also available premixed from some American spice firms.)

Trim 6 loin pork chops (3/4 inch thick) around the center noisette, and remove all fat and bone. Sprinkle noisettes very sparingly with quatre epices. Put them on a plate, cover loosely with plastic wrap and let stand overnight in refrigerator. Put 24 large soft prunes in a bowl, and pour 1 bottle dry red wine over them. Add a pinch of quatre epices; mix well and let macerate 24 hours.

The next day, remove pork from the refrigerator 2 hours before cooking. Transfer prunes and wine to saucepan, bring to a boil, and simmer 5 minutes. Remove prunes to a bowl. To the wine in the saucepan, add 2 cups brown veal stock (see a good French or all-around cookbook), and reduce to 1½ cups. Pan fry the pork noisettes in unsalted butter in a large skillet; they're done as soon as a skewer goes in and comes out easily. Salt and pepper to taste and remove to a platter and keep warm. Add 1 cup heavy cream to skillet and deglaze it with a spatula, scraping to dissolve the caramelized juices of the meat. Cook over high heat until spatula is coated with cream by ¼ inch. Add wine and stock mixture, and cook until spatula is coated by 1/8 to 1/6 inch. Turn off heat. Roll noisettes and prunes in sauce to blend flavors. Add salt and pepper and lemon juice to taste if necessary. Makes 6 servings.

LEELANAU ◆ COUNTRY ◆ INN

Michigan's "thumb" may be more famous cartographically, but Michigan's "little finger," the peninsula of Leelanau County, offers a much greater variety of scenic spots, seasonal festivals, spectacular sand dunes, sunny ski slopes, flourishing vineyards, picturesque lakes, and fine dining establishments. One of the oldest and most appealing destinations for visitors to the area is the historic Leelanau Country Inn, dating back to 1891, when the Atkinson family served travelers here.

A glassed-in porch wraps around two sides of the building, affording the most desirable seating. Other dining areas are enclosed and slightly more formal. Tables are covered with pink cloths and accented with dark rose napkins, votive candles, and bud vases filled with red carnations and baby's breath.

Yet the effect is country casual. Tie-back ruffled curtains, ceiling fans, and hanging plants contribute to the warm and unpretentious decor. The soft background music is so unobtrusive that you'll hardly notice it. What you will notice is the animated talk going on around you. Good conversation over good food is a trademark of the inn, as is friendly and efficient service.

According to the owners, Linda and John Sisson, "The restaurant specializes in fresh seafood flown into Cherry Capital Airport directly from Boston's Fish Pier, fresh homemade pasta, fresh-cut steaks, and good old-fashioned home cooking." Two other phrases sum up the approach at the Leelanau Country Inn: "old-time hospitality and value." So far as we can tell, the Sissons' aims have been fulfilled. Though the county is a veritable mecca for restaurant aficionados, when you ask the locals from age 20 to 70 to name their favorite, more often than not it turns out to be the Leelanau Country Inn. The moderate prices are often cited; the efficiency is extolled (regulars tell us that they never wait for their tables when they've reserved ahead). The underlying reason for the inn's popularity seems to be a comfortable consistency.

As for the food, it's fresh, flavorful, and filling; but there are no disconcerting surprises. Steaks, prime rib, and seafood dominate the menu, along with other more homey entrees such as chicken pot pie, braised lamb shanks, and beef short ribs. But just as popular are the pastas (homemade linguine with simple, classic Italian sauces--the primaverda is a gem) and the Provencales (southern French treatments of scallops, oysters, and crabmeat). Good as all these are, we prefer the daily "signatures." On a visit last fall, these consisted of crab-stuffed shrimp, duckling with plum sauce, seafood Alfredo, and two other pasta specialties. We ordered the Alfredo--linguine tossed with crabmeat, shrimp, cream, and cheeses. It came piping hot, and the portion was very generous. On the side were perfectly cooked snow peas, buttered and with just a hint of garlic. The entire meal was splendid, and the chocolate mocha cheesecake was a fitting albeit fattening finish. Complete dinners average $8 to $10, and nothing but the lobster costs more than $15. For both quality and quantity, prices are more than fair.

The wine list is unusual, offering only Leelanau County wines, some by the glass, half-liter, and liter; others by the bottle. More than 10 selections are available from the vineyards of Good Harbor, Larry Mawby, Boskydel, and Leelanau Limited. These include two wines bottled under the inn's label and the charming Trillium in both a still white and a "champagne."

Country hospitality in the "north country."

LEELANAU COUNTRY INN, 149 E. Harbor Hwy., Maple City, MI 49664. On M-22, 8 miles south of Leland and 1½ miles south of Sugar Loaf Mt. Telephone (616) 228-5060. Hours: summer, 5-10 p.m. Monday-Saturday, 10 a.m.-2 p.m. Sunday brunch (it is "fabulous," we're told), 4:30-9 p.m. Sunday dinner; winter, closed Monday and Tuesday (but call to check off-season hours). Full bar service. Credit cards: MC, V. Note: This really is a bed-and-breakfast inn with 10 guest rooms at reasonable rates.

SWISS ONION SOUP
From the Leelanau Country Inn

First courses at the inn are generally quite traditional and expertly cooked. Our two favorites are the mussels Italiano and this soup, Swiss onion. In a large saucepan heat 2 tablespoons butter. Add 1 clove minced garlic, 3 cups thinly sliced onions, 3/4 teaspoon dry mustard, and 1½ teaspoon salt. Saute until onions are tender. Add 2 cups water. Cover, and simmer over low heat. Meanwhile, in a second saucepan melt 3 tablespoons butter. Whisk in 3 tablespoons flour, and cook 1 minute, whisking over low heat. Add 1½ cups warm milk. Cook, whisking, until smooth and thick, about 5-8 minutes Stir in ½ teaspoon prepared horseradish, 1 tablespoon dry sherry, and 1½ cups grated Swiss cheese. Add this sauce to the onion mixture, and stir thoroughly. Add ½ teaspoon pepper, ½ teaspoon soy sauce, 3 drops Tabasco, and 2 dashes Worcestershire sauce. Cook over low heat 8-10 minutes, stirring occasionally. Serves 6.

(103) A PICNIC IN LELAND

With its gray, weatherbeaten fishing shanties dating back to the late 1800s, nets drying in the sun on the docks, commercial and charter fishing boats, and those unmistakable piscatorial scents caught up by breezes over Old Mill Creek, Fishtown in Leland is considered by many to be the most charming and picturesque spot on Lake Michigan's shores. It's well worth going out of your way for--or, better yet, planning for. We suggest, to enjoy it fully, you try something different here, because what's really special about eating out in Leland is the town and its setting, not just its restaurants, acceptable as they are.

First, stop at the Manitou Farm Market (open May-October), a mile south of the intersection of M-204 and M-22 (three miles south of Leland) for the makings of a picnic. Here you'll find, under one roof, a fine bakery (great bread for sandwiches and almond bear claws that shouldn't be missed), delicatessen, farm market, and grocery store with a small selection of beer and wine. Also available are homemade fudges, jams, chutneys, and dessert toppings. Select the foods of your choice and drinks for the little ones, and then head next door to the Good Harbor Vineyards for an adult beverage (we recommend the Trillium still or sparkling white) and a tour if you have the time. Drive on to the Leland dock area parking lot, and walk over to Carlson's Fishery on the river for an additional treat of smoked fish or a delicious smoked fish sausage. The Village Cheese Shanty is another possible stop.

246

You can enjoy your lunch in Harbor Park, and there's even a small playground for the kids. Be sure to walk both the boardwalk river frontage and the pier. Along the stream are weathered buildings and pilings of the restored village, and you can watch the daily catch being cleaned at Carlson's and look into the various shops and fish-smoking establishments. On the pier are boats and launches from many Great Lakes ports. Cruises also leave here for the Manitou Islands in the summer, and yachts and fishing boats may be chartered. Leland is an artists' colony, and you'll find a number of interesting small shops and galleries along the main street.

In inclement weather or if you prefer not to picnic, you can choose from the Blue Bird, the Cove, or the Leland Lodge; each offers fairly standard American fare with a few surprises. For a lighter lunch or informal evening entertainment (at less expense), you might want to try Fischer's Happy Hour, a popular roadhouse known for its soups, chicken, hamburgers, and clientele--a cross-section of all walks of life. The tavern is located about eight miles north of town on Route 22. Eating out (that is, in) in Leland can be very pleasant, but in good weather eating out (out of doors) is better--the surroundings here seem to cry out for a picnic.

A picturesque port.

⑩④ North Country Gardens
a quaint place for homemade lunches and fresh baked goods

One of the more civilized traditions in Great Britain is a pleasant pause for afternoon tea. A little before or after four, eyes travel to wristwatches, charming little tearooms fill up with customers (frequently including charming canine companions), hotel waiters roll out the dessert

247

trolleys, and on remote highways automobiles come to a halt and motorists set up tiny linen-covered tables at the roadsides. As American tourists, we've always joined in and enjoyed it enormously.

It was, then, with great pleasure that we discovered the North Country Gardens, a quaint little bakery, tearoom, and terrace with a view of adjoining English-style gardens and an appealing luncheon and tea menu. Kris and Elizabeth "Betsy" Ernst are the latest owners of the 35-year-old greenhouse and floral shop. After a trip overseas to study British horticulture, they were inspired in 1984 to add a garden of their own along with a bakery and tearoom where people could view the annuals and perennials in an especially pleasant setting. The sunny dining area features oak tables and cane-seated bentwood chairs. French doors lead to a small patio with blue and white umbrella tables in the midst of the colorful flower beds.

On the menu are several refreshing salads, among them the deservedly popular chicken with almonds and pasta tossed with a lemon-Dijon mustard dressing, paired with warm muffins. The same chicken salad may be had in sandwiches made of freshly baked white or wheat bread or croissants. Other items worth ordering are the Gardener's Lunch (Cheddar cheese, a "hunk" of warm Italian bread, and tomato slices on lettuce seasoned with a basil dressing) and the Fisherman's Lunch (smoked whitefish from Carlson's in Leland, Cheddar, Italian bread, and fresh fruit). Soups are delicious, especially the mushroom barley and the cream of asparagus, and outstanding among the desserts is Betsy's "Super" chocolate brownie, a fudgy wonder that county residents rave about.

In the afternoon a tea time treat is featured for $1.50: a hot pot of English or herbal tea and a warm muffin with butter and strawberry jam. Even better, on Sunday there's a "high tea," actually a light buffet brought to the table and usually comprising an assortment of sweet rolls, fruit bread, shaved ham, cheeses, salad, fruit, and cookies along with tea or coffee. After your repast, feel free to browse through the garden, greenhouse, and small gift shop.

Take tea at the tip of Leelanau.

NORTH COUNTRY GARDENS BAKERY AND TEA ROOM, 950 Mill St., Northport, MI 49670. A half mile north of town on M-201. Telephone (616) 386-5031. Hours: in the summer 7:30 a.m.-5 p.m. Monday-Saturday, 9 a.m.-3 p.m. Sunday; in the fall 9 a.m.-3 p.m. Thursday-Saturday, 9 a.m.-5 p.m. on Sunday. No alcoholic beverages; no smoking. Credit cards: MC, V.

BUTTERMILK BRAN MUFFINS
From Elizabeth Ernst, North Country Gardens

This is an old family recipe, according to Betsy Ernst, and one of the top sellers in the bakery. In a large bowl, mix together one (15-ounce) box raisin-bran cereal, 5 cups flour, 3 cups sugar, 5 teaspoons baking soda, 2 teaspoons salt. Preheat oven to 350 degrees. In a second bowl beat 4 eggs; add 1 cup melted margarine and 1 quart buttermilk and mix together. Stir this into dry ingredients. At this point, the batter can be refrigerated up to 6 weeks in a closed glass or plastic container. Fill muffin tins with paper liners; then fill 3/4 full with batter. Bake 20-25 minutes until tops are golden and spring back when lightly touched with fingertips. Makes about 24 muffins.

The store-front restaurant has the look of a European cafe about it with its lace curtains, floral awnings, and simple brown tile floor. Krys Dahlberg, who opened Epicure Art in Eating in 1979, calls it "vaguely Continental." And indeed the aura here is somewhat Breton, more simple than rustic. On the walls some black and white photos taken by a customer join the four large chalkboards that serve in lieu of a menu, and a huge oak breakfront separates the small dining room from the kitchen. Nothing much detracts from the food, which is as it should be here. Even the background music is soothing and soft and classical. And smokers will need to call on all their will power; there's not even a smoking section.

The cooking style is wide-ranging and eclectic. You'll find French and Italian classics like creme caramel, pots de creme, veal scallopini with porcini mushrooms and Marsala wine, and pasta primaverda. And you'll also be tempted by things like roast quail with orange-Bourbon-cherry sauce, sauteed chicken breast with basil cream, curried rice and shrimp, and jalapeno rice casserole. But there's no food snobbery at the restaurant; it caters to homey American tastes, too, with such solid fare as "Clancy's chicken wings," New England clam chowder, "hog heaven" and "gobbler" sandwiches, peach cobbler, and carrot cake.

One slate lists wines by the glass, and the choice is more than adequate--on our last visit 14 Michigan, Californian, and German wines. But the printed list is much more interesting with more than 50 well-chosen French, German, Californian, German, assorted sparkling, and fortified wines. About half are French, and prices range from $11 to $100 (for a '78 Mouton-Rothschild).

The menus rotate frequently, allowing Krys and her able assistant Paddy Brown to take the best advantage of fresh Michigan products. According to Andre Simon's Dictionary of Gastronomy, an epicure is one "who indulges systematically and critically in the luxuries of the table. The name is derived from a celebrated Athenian teacher [who] held that human happiness was the ultimate end of all philosophy, and that pleasure constituted the

250

highest happiness....In today's sense, the epicure is a gourmet, one who is fastidious about his food and a connoisseur of food and wine." Larousse Gastronomique, on the other hand, doesn't even list "epicure" but does mention the word "gourmet" as being used "in the inexact sense" of a "gourmand" or "connoisseur of good things." Note, too, that no matter what this abused word means, "gourmet" is a noun, not an adjective, as in "gourmet cooking." And "epicure" is a noun, so there's been some understandable confusion as to the correct name of Epicure Art in Eating, some grammatical food writers calling it The Epicure. We promised Krys we'd use HER name for her restaurant.

Culinarily correct!

EPICURE ART IN EATING, 111 Saint Joseph St., Suttons Bay, MI 49682. In village center on M-22. Telephone (616) 271-6100. Hours: summer 11:30 a.m.-4 p.m. luncheon, 5:30-10 p.m. dinner; winter 11:30 a.m.-3 p.m. luncheon, 5:30-9 p.m. dinner (till 10 p.m. Saturday). Closed Sunday, Monday. Beer, wine, and after-dinner drinks only. Credit cards: MC, V.

On Old Mission Peninsula overlooking Bowers Harbor and the west arm of Grand Traverse Bay, the blue and white, two-story frame inn nestled in tall pines has been a landmark for a century. It was built as a private home and converted into a restaurant in 1960. In the 1970s a new and more casual dining area, the Bowery, was added to what was once the servants' quarters.

The decor, including the table settings with crisp linens and pewter service plates, is charming. The old, original curving stairway still greets visitors at the front entrance. In the bayside dining area there are four rooms on one level and another upstairs. The Harbor Dining Room, decorated in black, gold, and neutrals, has a marvelous table for eight by the bay window (reserve Harbor 3, but do it well ahead; it's usually booked a month or so in advance). The only tables to avoid are 10,11, and 12 near the exit to the kitchen; all the others are fine. Adjoining this room is the Patio, primarily used for larger groups. The Bay Dining Room nearby overlooks the terrace and bay, and its cheerful yellows and golds are enhanced by plants and latticework. Bay 5 and 6 are the choice tables here. The Alcove, off the Bay Room, is especially appealing for those wishing privacy: only four little tables for four (our favorite is Bay 11, under a Tiffany lamp). Our least favorite room is the Study on the upper floor.

The menu at first glance appears limited--mainly steak, prime rib, and seafood. But there's more here than meets the eye. Chef Greg Nicolaou, a graduate of the Culinary Institute of America, offers a creative specialty each evening, on the order of salmon en croute or cherry duck. And on the regular bill of fare are some appetizing dishes: veal Normande (sauteed escalopes with Calvados sauce), medallions of lamb baked in pastry with Feta and spinach, seafood fettuccine, shrimp Cantonese, and what most newcomers here seem to end up with, the highly acclaimed and truly delicious "fish in a bag," a specialty of the restaurant since its beginnings.

The wine list, much improved since our first edition, numbers about 100 entries with a wide price range. On the lower end of the scale are a 1984 Mondavi red, Mouton-Cadet, Chateau Ste. Michelle '84 (from Washington state), '83 Chateauneuf-de-Pape, some Michigan wines, and good German whites. For connoisseurs with cash, consider the '75 Mondavi Reserve Cabernet ($65), Chateaux Latour and Lafite-Rothschild ($120,$130), or Dom Perignon

($95). The Brunello '77 (8 on a scale of 10) at $35 is, though a bit young, a good choice. House wines are Inglenook generics and Dourthe French red and white.

A much less expensive alternative to Bowers Harbor Inn is the Old Mission Tavern, open noon to midnight Thursday through Sunday and located at 17015 Center Road (about 4 miles north of the Bowers Harbor Access Road, on M-37). It's a rustic cabin that offers soups, sandwiches, pierogy (Polish dumplings), burritos, and locally popular steaks. It's also an artists' co-op and, as far as we know, may be the only place in Michigan where you can get a beer, a bowl of soup, a banana split, and a watercolor to go. Stop in for a drink if nothing else; the tavern is a showcase for people-watching. But for fine dining in a lovely setting, Bowers Harbor Inn is our first choice.

The west bay's best.

BOWERS HARBOR INN, 13512 Peninsula Dr., Traverse City, MI 49684. Three-quarters mile north of Traverse City on M-37, then 8 miles northwest on Peninsula Dr. Telephone (616) 223-4222. Hours: 5-9:30 p.m. all year. Closed Sunday, Monday. Full bar service. Dancing and entertainment in the Bowery. Credit cards: AE, MC, V. Reservations not taken in the Bowery.

Nearby attraction: Chateau Grand Travers , 45 acres of vineyards that overlook Grand Traverse Bay, is located at 12239 Center Rd. (M-37), north of the inn.

TROUT EN CROUTE
From Chef Greg Nicolaou, Bowers Harbor Inn

Remove heads, tails, and fins from 4 (10-ounce) boneless rainbow trout. Wash and dry the fish. Soften 8 ounces butter and blend in 1 tablespoon dill weed, 4 dashes Tabasco, and a pinch white pepper. Place 2 ounces of the seasoned butter in the body cavity of each fish. Mix 2 pounds flaky pie dough, and roll out ¼-inch thick. Wrap each fish in dough, sealing all edges and trimming off excess dough. Bake in 400-degree oven about 25 minutes or until golden brown.

Meanwhile, make Hollandaise sauce. In double boiler over simmering water, put 4 egg yolks and whip them constantly until they thicken. Remove from heat and slowly add 1½ cups warm, not hot, clarified butter, whipping constantly. Whip in the juice of 1 lemon, a dash cayenne pepper, and a dash salt. Serve with the baked fish. Serves 4.

Our hints: See pie pastry recipes in our index. To clarify butter, melt over very low heat; remove from heat and let stand a few minutes so the solids settle. Carefully skim or pour the clear butter fat off. Use the curds to flavor vegetables.

Dan and Jan Kelly's trig new restaurant in the shadow of the old Park Place Hotel was a roaring success from the day it opened, and deservedly so. The Kellys, both Traverse City natives, had the sense and savvy to offer things that no one else offers around here. Things like cheese and chocolate fondues, steamed artichokes, pasta salad, veal forestier (see the recipe below), and chicken breast stuffed with Brie and prosciutto. Still, in keeping up to the minute with restaurant trends, simpler tastes haven't been ignored. The Kellys serve up one of the best hamburgers in the city, several delectable pasta entrees, and the inevitable but always popular steaks and prime rib. Prices are moderate.

The dining room is a stylish melange of natural oak furnishings and rich green (Kelly green, of course) carpeting and upholstery. Skylights, hanging plants, and Ansel Adams photos round out the California theme the Kellys are aiming for. Adjacent to the room in front is a separate bar with a modern pub-like atmosphere and the same striking color scheme. At the rear of the building is a canvas-enclosed patio complete with trees and shrubbery, a delightful spot for summer lunching and dining. In the main dining room, we like the three front window booths, especially during the daytime.

Dan Kelly has worked in the restaurant business since he was 14 years old. That experience plus his training at Michigan State University's hotel and restaurant management school plus downright talent explain why it's not so surprising that D.J. Kelly's hasn't seemed to have gone through the growing pains typical of so many new enterprises.

Aside from a good selection of sandwiches, pastas, and a few heavier items, the fondues (in two portion sizes and prices) are a noteworthy inclusion on the luncheon menu. Offered are the classic Swiss fondue of Emmenthaler and Gruyere cheeses and a tangy Monterey Jack and green chili mixture, both accompanied by bread cubes and apple wedges. Fondues also appear on the dinner menu, and we can imagine enjoying a meal of one or two of the fine appetizers followed by a fondue and finally by a seductive something from the dessert tray. Cooking it yourself in D.J. Kelly's sturdy pewter fondue pot makes for a romantic, unhurried evening (but leave your marshmallows at home).

Of the appetizers, which are large enough to share, we have trouble choosing among the escargots de Jonghe, the oysters Florentine, the smoked fish sampler, and the steamed mussels. On grossly self-indulgent nights, we'll order two. Among Dan's better dinner entrees are the veal Oscar, roast duck with cherry or Bordelaise sauce, and the "green peppercorn New York"--a strip steak served with sauce Daniel, Chef Dan's own rich brown sauce enhanced by Dijon mustard, scallions, and green peppercorns. The price of entrees generously includes a tureen of soup, spinach or tossed salad, pilaf or

255

potato or vegetable, and a crusty French bread.

D.J.'s wine cellar has more than 30 selections, most falling below $15; and nine of these can be purchased by the glass. Nothing really great but all reasonably priced and some real bargains.

A voguish setting and menu.

D.J. KELLY'S, 120 Park St., Traverse City, MI 496 84. Downtown. Telephone (616) 941-4550. Hours: luncheon 11 a.m.-3 p.m., Monday-Saturday, country brunch on Sunday; dinner 5-10 p.m. Monday-Thursday, 5-11 p.m. Friday-Saturday, 5-9 p.m. Sunday. Full bar service. Credit cards: AE, MC, V.

VEAL FORESTIER
From Chef Dan Kelly, D.J. Kelly's

First make a rich brown sauce, using beef and veal bones. Use any technique for making a standard brown sauce. For each portion, pound a 6-8-ounce slice of top round of veal until very thin, 1/8 to ¼ inch thick. Dust with flour seasoned with salt and white pepper. Saute over high heat in 2 tablespoons clarified butter. When almost done, add ¼ teaspoon minced garlic and 2 tablespoons Madeira wine. Set veal aside, and keep warm.

In the same pan, add ½ cup of the brown sauce. Heat to a boil; then add 1 ounce fresh morel mushrooms and 1 ounce fresh chanterelle mushrooms. Immediately pour over the veal. Serve with wild rice. Makes 1 serving.

(108) **Pasties** by Jean Kay
& TC CHEESECAKE

Pasties in the L.P.? We looked askance at first, but after one bite, we knew we were tasting the Right Stuff. But the Right Stuff with a difference. This tiny Traverse City bakery takes an authentic

Cornish approach to the pasty, varying its crusts and fillings according to the creative choice of owner and baker Jerilyn DeBoer. Admittedly, the Cornish miners' wives probably varied pasties out of necessity rather than creativity, but vary them they did with rabbit, game, jam, almost anything that happened to be on hand--which usually meant potatoes and rutabaga.

Jerilyn's "original" pasty with chopped steak, potato, and rutabaga filling is the most popular and is comparable to our favorite from Lawry's, outside of Ishpeming in the Upper Peninsula. But she also sells five other varieties: vegetarian, steak and Cheddar, quiche (ham, Swiss cheese, eggs, and vegetables), chicken with vegetables and cheese, and German (ham, Swiss, and sauerkraut). The crust is thinnish and flaky, and pasties may be purchased in two sizes (10 or 16 ounce) with either a white or whole wheat crust (or rye for the German version). In peak season 300 pasties will be sold each day (more than 500 between two locations).

Jerilyn's business is an outgrowth of Pasties by Jean Kay, established in Iron Mountain by her parents, Jerry and Jean Kay Harsh. Her Front Street enterprise opened in 1979, and a second shop on 14th Street was established five years later. But Jerilyn doesn't limit herself to what she calls "the science of pastyology." She offers fresh deli salads, breakfast pastries (including a cream cheese Danish that rivals Copenhagen's finest), and some 17 varieties of melt-in-your-mouth cheesecake. We love the pralines and cream and the chocolate almond, but the new "turtle" with pecans, fudge topping, and caramel sauce is to die for.

All of these treasures may be taken out (think about a picnic at Clinch Park by the marina) or eaten on the premises. A bright green counter affords a view of the landmark Old Kent Bank and the endless stream of tourists on Traverse City's main street. It's a cubbyhole of a place, but you can't miss it--look for the British flag flying over a parking meter in the front.

Tasty turnovers and champion cheesecakes.

PASTIES BY JEAN KAY, 111 W. Front Street (at Union), Traverse City, MI 49684. Telephone (616) 941-7821. (Also at 510 W. 14th St.). Hours: 8:30 a.m.-6:30 p.m. Monday-Friday (till 6 p.m. on Saturday). Closed Sunday. No alcoholic beverages. Credit cards and reservations not accepted. Will ship air express or UPS; call for rates.

(109) SLEDER'S FAMILY TAVERN

Bob Classens, who has owned Sleder's since 1974, was once a barber and antique dealer. He gave up barbering but still retains an active interest in antiques, as the tavern well illustrates. In four years he restored the interior of an old building to what it was some 90 years ago. It is now a veritable mecca for the antique enthusiast. Look at the authentic, ornate old embossed metal ceiling; the cash register and jukebox; the ice-cream-parlor chairs; game trophies; and great old beer signs. You might not notice it at first amid all this fascinating clutter, but even the floor is an antique-- with marks from the hobnailed boots of loggers, made years ago when the "Slabtown" mill was nearby.

The place has been in the hands of the Sleder family for about 100 years. Originally there was a theater and dance hall upstairs. Since the building was constructed, there has ALWAYS been a tavern here, even during Prohibition years, when the chief of police was known to come in for a drink. Most of the stuffed animals and birds on the walls were raised and/or shot at some time or another by the Sleders; today they're collectors' items. The buffalo head is new, purchased for an outrageously low price at--would you guess?--a garage sale.

There are three dining rooms now. We prefer the large one that houses the long old oak and ash bar and that offers more things and people to gawk at. But if Sleder's is busy (and it often is), you may have to sit in the back room (once called the Indian Room and later the College Room--ask Bob about that) or in the dining room once known as the Ladies' Room. Those were discriminating days. But wherever you sit, it's noisy and bustling. And there's no background music to detract from the talk. The joviality and cheerful service here make Sleder's the closest thing we've seen to an Americanized version of a friendly English pub.

In the summer you might prefer to sit in the new addition, called Slavka's, Bohemian for "Sylvia's," after Bob's wife. This is a 120-seat white Victorian-style porch with its own bar. The tables, by the way, are all on old sewing-machine bases, the result of more antique collecting.

The menu is simple and American: mostly soups, sandwiches, "baskets," burritos and nachos, a good vaiety of salads, and two extremely popular items: the "famous" buffalo burgers (with Swiss cheese and grilled onion on a grilled onion bun) and the burger bar. The latter is a help-yourself selection of about 24 hamburger toppings. Check the hanging slate and the small chalkboard over the bar, too, for daily specials. On Sundays Sleder's features a family-style chicken dinner (baked or deep-fried with dressing, potato, roll and butter for $5.95). And we certainly mustn't neglect to mention a special treat at Sleder's: the freshly roasted unsalted peanuts. At least 300 pounds are dished out each week, and they're kept warm in an old-fashioned popcorn machine.

Charming, festive, a bargain--don't miss it.

SLEDER'S FAMILY TAVERN, 717 Randolph St., Traverse City, MI 49684. One block west of Division St. (U.S. 31 at M-37). Telephone (616) 947-9213. Hours: 10 a.m.-midnight Monday-Saturday, noon-

10 p.m. Sunday. Closed holidays. Open Memorial Day to Labor Day. Full bar service. Credit cards: MC, V.

CLAM CHOWDER
From Marty Clement, Sleder's Family Tavern

According to Metropolitan Detroit magazine's brief review of Sleder's, "Don't miss the creamy clam chowder on Fridays--Michigan's finest." Well, you won't need to miss it; you can make it at home. Marty gave us recipe that makes 5 gallons. We've decreased it to more manageable proportions.

In a stockpot or large saucepan, combine 1 pound cubed potatoes, $\frac{1}{4}$ pound cubed carrots, $\frac{1}{4}$ cup diced onions, $1\frac{1}{4}$ ounce white wine, a rounded $\frac{1}{2}$ teaspoon garlic, $\frac{1}{4}$ teaspoon white pepper, $\frac{1}{4}$ teaspoon salt, 2 (6.5 ounce) cans minced clams, and 2 (8 ounce) bottles clam juice. After vegetables are tender, thicken hot soup with roux (equal parts flour and butter or margarine mixed to a paste); add in small bits and stir till blended. When thickened to desired consistency, stir in $2\frac{1}{2}$ cups heavy cream. Heat just to serving temperature. Makes 2 quarts, serving 8-12.

(110) **⊃SYDNEY'S**

PASTA BAR • DELICATESSEN • SODA FOUNTAIN

Well, golly, how do you describe a real super spot like Sydney's? We mean, wow, there's not many places these days where you can slouch over a bright red counter, power down a chocolate malt and listen to Doris Day singing "It's Magic." Gee, whiz, it's the kind of fab place that makes you want to smoke in the washroom and neck in the back booth with James Dean or Natalie Wood.

Sydney's is a time capsule dating back to the

1950s and even before. It has a fresh, clean, Art Deco atmosphere complete with white tile walls, black booths, and frosted etchings on the mirrors. At first glance one might think that a slick interior decorator was called into the old building and told to spruce it up. Yet, in fact, the interior has changed very little from its earlier days as a downtown diner with a 50-year history. The hard black and white checkerboard floors and high ceiling tend to make the place a trifle noisy--but do you want to listen or eat? (Actually, a lot of people do like to listen to the old records of 1940s swing and 1950s boogie). But even if the cafe decor is characterized by practical, durable synthetics, there's nothing synthetic about the food.

Sydney's, named after Sydney Marie, the baby daughter of owners Forrest and Annette Nelson, opened in November 1985 and doesn't even call itself a restaurant. Instead, it is a "pasta bar, delicatessen, and authentic soda fountain."Everything served here is freshly prepared and cooked, including the pasta (see the machine at work in the window) and the breads. The breezy, chatty menu offers a full range of deli sandwiches, including a "create your own triple decker." Linguine is touted as the "star of the show" and appears in seven basically traditional renditions. On the trendy side are the "extraordinary pizzas" topped with such wayward items as fruit and Brie, spinach and Feta. You can even "create your pizza," choosing from cappicola ham, artichoke hearts, pesto, fresh tomatoes, and lox, among other more commonly listed ingredients. Sydney's is also proud of its half-pound hamburger and cheeseburger ("not just one skinny slice, we're talkin' cheese!") and its "build your own burger." Two especially palatable options are the Traverse City Blintz ("not a football team") with sour cream and cherry sauce and the pan-fried potato latkes (pancakes). A full range of fountain ice cream specialties goes without mention. But what really cries out for mention is the appetizer listing: chopped liver, smoked whitefish, cold cherry soup, escargots, gazpacho, baked Brie, and lox among others (Traverse City teens must be the most sophisticated in the state). All price are low to moderate.

To sum up, this new and relentlessly perky establishment bids fair to becoming the area's swingingest night spot for young people and non-drinkers. (For passive drinkers who want entertainment, it's Dill's Olde Towne Saloon; for dancing drinkers it's the Trillium; and for nondancing, talkative drinkers, it's Sleder's Tavern.) But at any time of day it's well worth stopping in at Sydney's for a snack of your choice and

a sentimental journey.

SYDNEY'S, 128 E. Front St., Traverse City, MI 49 684. Downtown. Telephone (616) 947-6770. Hours: Monday-Saturday 11 a.m.-11 p.m., Sunday 9 a.m.-11 p.m. (Sunday brunch 9 a.m.-2 p.m.). Street parking (a bother) or use lot one block away towards the lake. No alcoholic beverages. Credit cards: V, MC. Reservations taken only for the big "conference" table in the rear, which seats 12 or so.

SYDNEY'S BROTHER'S MOTHER'S CHOCOLATE CHIP COOKIES
From Forrest Nelson, Sydney's

You'll find these supersized cookies at the front counter of Sydney's, and once you taste them, you won't want to wait till you get back to Traverse City to eat them again. So, lucky you, here's the recipe. Cream 1 pound butter until soft. Add 1 pound granulated sugar and 1 pound brown sugar and blend until smooth. Add 4 eggs and 2 teaspoons vanilla; blend well. Sift together 15 ounces oatmeal (ground in blender to a flour), 1 pound 4 ounces flour, 2 teaspoons baking powder, and 2 teaspoons baking soda. Mix only 1 minute. Add 12 ounces chopped pecans and 2 pounds Leelanau

Chocolat Chocolate Chips (or another lesser brand
of your choice). Mix until just blended. Drop heaping spoonsful of dough onto greased cookie sheet.
Bake for about 8 minutes at 350 degrees. Cookies
will be soft when removed but will firm up as they
cool. Yields approximately 2 dozen 4-ounce cookies.

Trillium

Located in one of the state's loveliest natural
areas, situated in the uppermost two floors of the
spectacular Tower at Grand Traverse Resort,
dedicated to regional American cooking, and named
after our most endearing wildflower, the Trillium
is surely the most dramatic new restaurant in
northern Michigan, including the Upper Peninsula.
Day or evening, the glass-enclosed elevators rising
to the top of the 16-story building offer an initial
glimpse of the marvelous view yet to come. The
$27 million structure, which opened in June 1986,
overlooks east Grand Traverse Bay, a golf course
designed by Jack Nicklaus called the Bear (after
Nicklaus' nickname "Golden Bear"), and miles and
miles of verdant, scenic countryside. Almost all
tables at the Trillium have a view, but those right
at the windows are in greatest demand (reserve
several days ahead).

But even without a view, the Trillium is outstanding. Table settings reflect the restaurant's theme:
dark green and white linens and gilt-edged, green-
banded service plates with the Trillium motif.
Seating consists of lily-patterned banquettes and
comfortable rattan chairs, most of them oriented
to the glass window walls. But the architectural
treatment of the trilevel restaurant and lounge is
what defines the sparkling persona of the place.
The high glass ceiling at night becomes an enormous
grid of white lights against the dark sky, and the
incandescence is reflected in ricochets up and down

and across the room. Other sensory pleasures contribute to the effect. During the dinner hours,
Torch, a talented nine-piece ensemble from nearby
Torch Lake, plays soft, listenable jazz and then
later show tunes and popular music of the 40s
through the 80s. A small dance floor adjoins the
bandstand.

All of this might suggest that the cuisine couldn't
possibly keep pace with the dazzling surroundings.
But luckily the Trillium boasts a most accomplished
chef, Lisa Young. On the menu are a number of
old standbys, such as oysters on the half shell, lamb
chops, barbequed ribs, shrimp scampi, steaks, and
prime rib. But the latter, unlike in most restaurants, is dry-aged certified Black Angus beef, cut
to your specifications and priced by the ounce.
Other entrees are more inventively handled, among
them walleyed pike with sorrel herb butter and
toasted pine nuts, marinated and broiled swordfish
with stir-fried vegetables, and the Trillium veal
chop with chanterelle mushroom sauce. Two or three
specials also appear; for example, in the fall there
might be roast pork loin stuffed with dried fruits
and walnuts and paired with Port wine sauce. On
our visit, we ordered the roasted chicken breast
enclosing a spinach and sage mousseline stuffing
and served with fresh shiitake and enoki mushroom
sauce (see the recipe below). It was presented
beautifully and accompanied by a small browned
new potato and perfectly cooked cauliflower with
a dill-sage sauce that complemented the mousseline.
We highly recommend it. As we do two of the
appetizers: the country pate and the seafood vegetable stew, a melange of shellfish, swordfish, and
fresh vegetables much like a bouillabaise. This dish,
like the veal chop, is labeled a "signature item,"
meaning that Chef Lisa is especially proud of this
offering. Salad greens seem only minutes old, and
the creamy cucumber house dressing is much zestier
than it sounds. The bread basket includes chewy
sourdough rolls and so-so pizza bread. Entree prices
range from $15 to $20, reasonable for the quality.

The emphasis here is on California wines, which fill four pages in the long list. But you can also select French, German, and Michigan varieties, including, of course, Good Harbor's Trillium. Prices are in keeping with the ambience. If you'd like to taste some better wines by the glass, the Trillium has a Cruvinet, a French device that stores and dispenses opened bottles of wine.

Of the other dining rooms at Grand Traverse Resort, only the Trillium's more sedate sister restaurant, the Hannah Lay Room on the first floor, offers the same sort of glamor. This room was named after Perry Hannah, an early lumber baron of Traverse City ("lay" refers to "the lay of the land," owned by Hannah, on which the resort now stands). Here you'll find more French fare, more tableside cooking and salad tossing, and more intimate seating. Expect such traditional items as coquilles St. Jacques, tournedos, rack of lamb, roast duckling (the specialty), souffles, and flambeed desserts. The Hannah Lay is certainly worth a visit if you'll be in the area for a time. But our first choice is the more extravagant mood and merry-making of the Trillium. We should note that, though there are fresh flowers on the tables, you won't see any trilliums. They're protected by law since, if a blossom is picked improperly, the entire plant cannot reproduce itself and will die. Fortunately, we don't see any indication that its namesake, the Trillium Restaurant, is an endangered species.

The acme of Acme.

THE TRILLIUM RESTAURANT AND LOUNGE, at the Grand Traverse Resort, U.S.31 north, Acme, MI 49610. At intersection of U.S.31 and M-72, 6 miles northeast of Traverse City. Telephone (616) 938-2100. Hours: breakfast 6:30-11 a.m. every day, luncheon 11:30 a.m.-2:30 p.m. Monday-Saturday, dinner 6-10 p.m. Sunday-Thursday (till 11 p.m. Friday-Saturday). Full bar service. Credit cards: AE, DC, MC, V.

ROAST CHICKEN WITH SAGE MOUSSELINE
From Chef Lisa Young, the Trillium

This is delicious and spectacular-looking--and much easier than you'd guess, especially if you have a food processor. First, prepare the chicken mousseline. Trim all fat from 1 pound chicken breast (skin removed), and cut into cubes. Place in work bowl of processor, and process until smooth. Add 1 egg white, 2/3 cup heavy cream, 1 tablespoon Port wine, 1 teaspoon quatre epices, 1 teaspoon dried sage, 1/8 teaspoon cayenne pepper, and 1 slice white bread (crust removed). Process again. Fold in 2 tablespoons finely diced carrots.

With skin side down, lightly salt and pepper 4 whole boneless chicken breasts (skin on). Cover each with spinach leaves (6 ounces blanched spinach in all). Divide the mousseline into 4 equal portions, and spread on top of the spinach. Roll breasts up, from right to left. Lay each on a piece of caul fat (ask your butcher for 4 pieces) and envelop each one, with seams on the bottom. Dredge each in flour and brown in 3 tablespoons butter. Transfer to baking sheet, and roast 20-25 minutes at 400 degrees. Serve on top a wild mushroom or champagne sauce. Serves 4.

Our hint: See the recipe for Noisettes de Porc, which includes directions for making quatre epices; the recipe follows our review of La Becasse, number 101 on our map.

(113) Spencer Creek Landing

Once upon a time, way back in 1854, Alden, Michigan, was a lumber camp known as Spencer Creek. That was before native son William Alden Smith made his name in banking and railroading. Today it's still a blink-or-you'll-miss-it village, not much bigger than when it was called Spencer Creek. But lumbering is no more, William Alden Smith is a mere memory, and this little whistlestop means only one thing to a creature with any culinary intelligence: Spencer Creek Landing. And it is truly a landing with 16 boat slips. You can reach the place either by road or by boat, depending on how rich you are. Actually, at least half of the lunch trade comes by water.

The two-story white house with dark green awnings was the private home of an Oldsmobile dealer until 1981, when it was acquired by Jeff and Laura Kohl. The three oak-trimmed dining areas are small and homey; the decor is attractive and traditional; and there's a timeless quality here. New customers sometimes call and plead for a "lake view," but they're really wasting their time-- every table has a view of beautiful Torch Lake, which occupies a giant trough eroded by glaciers in the same fashion as at the Finger Lakes in New York state.

"Regionally fresh cuisine" is the concept at Spencer Creek Landing, and it's a concept that's working well for many of Michigan's most dedicated and creative restauranteurs. The Kohls offer a limited but most engaging list of entrees, a catalogue that changes periodically according to customer preference. On our last visit, eight main courses appeared on the menu: among them, sauteed whitefish with watercress sauce, veal scallops with Gorgonzola sauce, and beef tenderloin accompanied by goose-liver pate and red-wine-shallot sauce. The prices are somewhat high but certainly fair for a fine dining experience. Entrees come with a complimentary appetizer, soup, salad, and fresh cracked wheat bread. For the same courses in a restaurant with an a la carte menu, you'd probably pay more and enjoy it less.

In addition to four bubbling wines, including a '76 Dom Perignon, the Kohls offer 38 still wines. Twenty of them are whites in the $15 to $25 range from France, California, and Germany. Here you'll find a Chateau Carbonnieux, a Latour-shipped Char-

donnay, and a Chablis Premier Cru "Vaillons." Reds
are divided between French and Californian with
enough variety to draw your attention and please
your palate. Prices are similar to those of whites,
topped by a Monterey Chalone (California) and a
1976 (except for the Champagne, the only vintage
given on the current list) Chateau Cos d'Estournel,
the highest-ranking wine (a second growth) of St.
Estephe. If you prefer a St. Julian, the Gruaud
LaRose might interest you.

We prefer to have dinner at Spencer Creek
Landing, but luncheon is available in the adjoining
Cafe, which was once part of the original property,
a 1930 automobile showroom (for just two cars).
It's now an airy dining room serving up salads and
sandwiches and perhaps more, depending on the re-
ception it gets in the next couple of summers.
Interestingly from a health standpoint, the Kohls
don't even own a deep fryer. You can expect a
meatloaf sandwich here, but not a hamburger.

Sometimes it's good to be up a creek.

SPENCER CREEK LANDING, 5166 Helena Street,
Alden, MI 49612. Village center; if you miss it, go
to the nearest optometrist. Telephone (616) 331-
6147. Hours: 5 p.m.-? (depends on reservations)
Monday-Saturday. Closed Sunday; in fall and winter closed Sunday and Monday. Closed months of
November and March. Cafe open for lunch and
snacks (call for hours). Wine and beer. Reservations necessary for dinner, not taken in the Cafe.
Credit cards: MC, V.

BAKED STUFFED RAINBOW TROUT
From Jeff Kohl, Spencer Creek Landing

Roast 1 cup almonds in 300-degree oven until
lightly browned. In food processor coarsely chop
3 slices bread. Saute 1 chopped onion and 1 clove
minced garlic in 3/4 stick butter until soft. Mix

268

together the almonds, bread crumbs, sauteed onion
and garlic, 1 cup chopped parsley, and 2 ounces
fresh-grated Parmesan cheese. Salt and pepper to
taste. Fill each boned trout with ½ cup of the mixture. Skewer closed and brush with oil. Bake 20-
25 minutes at 450 degrees. (Optional: wrap trout
in oiled parchment paper and bake as above.) Serve
with lemon butter. Jeff notes that baking time
depends on the size of the fish. We should add that
the amount of stuffing here will be sufficient for
4-6 trout. Try the stuffing with another kind of fish,
too, if you like.

One of the things about restaurant listings that
drives the management crazy is a reference to who
once owned the restaurant or what it once was.
Well, here we go again. Shanty Creek, built as a
private club in 1962, has had a long and checkered
history. Over the years it's changed hands several
times; and in 1978, when it became a Hilton
franchise, we assumed it had finally found its
niche. But, no, there's now a new custodian, the
Club Corporation of America, and we also find
that Shanty Creek has merged with Schuss Mountain Resort; a shuttle service connects the two. A
third golf course, the "Legend," designed by Arnold
Palmer, has been added, and between the two sport
centers there are now 34 ski slopes. These changes
have surely affected the dining room at Shanty
Creek, and we can't vouch for its consistency.
    So why do we include the resort in our guide-
book? Because the lodge is structurally perhaps the
most dramatic building for its purpose outside of
Detroit. Few places in Michigan can boast such

overall attractiveness of entrance grounds, architecture, and interior design in the dining room and lounge. These rooms are are beautiful--large, open, contemporary, even with full-grown trees--and the view is outstanding. Lunchtime or daylight is best, but the evening view to the west from high on the 13,000-year-old glacially formed Inner Port Huron Moraine can be spectacular. Shanty Creek is one of the very few ski lodges located on top rather than at the bottom of the slope, affording an exceptional view unlike most others in Michigan.

You can see not only Lake Bellaire and Torch Lake, but on a clear day you can see the gulls sharpening their beaks on Grand Traverse Bay. While here, you might also want to tour the facilities, including an indoor and outdoor pool, game room, several shops, recreational possibilities, and lodging (some nice condominiums).

The cuisine is not nearly as splendid or creative as the architecture. But the food is well prepared, and the setting is so delightful that we don't think you'll be disappointed. The breakfast and luncheon menus are fairly imaginative and appeal to a variety of tastes. In the evening the lodge offers tried and true, substantial American restaurant fare: the customary steaks, ribs, chops, along with several seafood and Great Lakes fish entrees and a few other standards. Somewhat more inventive are the sauteed scallops, shrimp brochette, and veal chops with morel sauce.

To finish, there are some seductive desserts; we especially like the baked Alaska and the hot Viennese apple pie. Or you can opt for razzmatazz--flambeed desserts and flaming coffees to make you oooh and aaah. Though there's no dress code, you might want to put on a bit of the dog; you'll see lots of coats and ties here as you would at any convention center.

A best view from a beautiful building.

SHANTY CREEK, Bellaire, MI 49615. Two miles southeast of Bellaire, 1 mile east of M-88. Tele-

phone (616) 533-8621. Hours: breakfast 7:30-11 a.
m., luncheon noon-2:30 p.m., dinner 5-9 p.m. Open
year round. Full bar service. Entertainment nightly
except Sunday, 5 p.m.-2 a.m. (off season 3 nights
a week). All major credit cards.

IDAHO PIE
From Shanty Creek

Fit pie pastry into a 5x10-inch casserole dish (or
other 1-quart baking dish). Mix together gently 2
cups cooked cubed potatoes (about 2 large Idahos),
1 cup cubed smoked ham, 1 cup small-curd cottage
cheese, 1 cup sour cream, ½ cup (or more) grated
Cheddar cheese, 2-4 tablespoons grated Parmesan
cheese (or to taste), and 2-4 tablespoons chopped
parsley. Fill the pastry-lined casserole. S prinkle
with paprika. Bake about 1½ hours in a preheated
350-degree oven until browned and bubbly. Makes
4-6 servings.

(114)

Alas, one of the most fanciful fringe benefits
of eating out in Michigan is no more. For years
the Brownwood Farm House was the only place in
the state (in the world?) where you could enjoy
your cocktails on a stagecoach drawn by a team
of four black horses. Sadly, the barn burned down,
along with the irreplaceable antique carriage. (The
horses were saved and now, at pasture, probably
miss those joyous daily outings from Brownwood
Acres to Central Lake.) But there are still lots of
reasons to head for Torch Lake, one of Michigan's
most beautiful.
Brownwood Acres has been the Brown family's
farm since 1939. In 1947 they built a roadside
stand to sell honey and home-grown vegetables, and

from that modest beginning has evolved an impressive complex of commercial enterprises, including
the Honey House gift shop, the Schoolhouse (Antrim
County's oldest log school, now an ice cream parlor), the Country Store (a rebuilt stagecoach inn),
the Barn Boutique and Brownwood Squire (clothing
shops), and of special interest to diners, the Farm
House and Barn, a large and lively restaurant and
entertainment center seating 240 people and amiably
decorated in early American with wagon-wheel
chandeliers and red-checked tablecloths.

The menu is American and blatantly appeals to
the hungry and the greedy: all-you-can-eat steamed
and fried shrimp, crab, steak, combination dinners,
and the Country Dinner--chicken and pork chops
accompanied by stuffing and slaw, cornbread and
biscuits, vegetable and potato. On a less monumental
scale, there's even an all-you-can-eat soup; "help
yourself to the steaming kettle" served at your
table, for a mere $1.50. More prudent or less
ambitious diners can avoid all this extravagance
and order steaks, ribs, chicken, and fish (the most
exotic offerings are teriyaki chicken and crabmeat-
stuffed trout). But even this won't save you; dinners
include your own "personalized salad bar," homemade biscuits and cornbread with Brownwood's own
cherry butter, and your choice of potato. Plan on
jogging the next day.

There are three seating areas under high, open-
beamed ceilings: the Farm House, the Harvest Room,
and the Barn--in which a seven-piece ensemble,
Barnstorm, entertains on weekends in season (vocal-
ist Becky is the wife of Brownwood's manager). In
warm weather one wall opens, and there's dancing
outside, too. This is a cheerful, informal, gregarious
place, and you won't find any secluded, quiet little
spots. But you can have a good time, especially
with a group or the family. The prices, for what
you get, are moderate and fair, and the portions
most generous.

Lively doings down on the farm.

BROWNWOOD FARM HOUSE, E. Torch Lake Dr., Central Lake, MI 49622. Three miles west of town (take W. State St. to the end, turn right at the Chatterbox Party Store, and drive 1000 feet) or 3 miles south of Eastport. Telephone (616) 544-58 11. Hours: noon-3 p.m. luncheon, 5-10 p.m. dinner (till 11 p.m. Friday-Saturday). Call to confirm off-season hours. Full bar service. Entertainment and dancing on weekends. Credit cards: AE, MC, V.

CREAM OF CHICKEN SOUP
From the Brownwood Farm House

Simmer 5 pounds stewing chicken in 1 gallon (16 cups) water until tender, about 2½ hours. Remove chicken from stock; discard skin and bones, and return the meat to the stock. In a saucepan saute ¼ cup corn, ¼ cup green peas, ¼ cup chopped onions, ¼ cup chopped carrots, and ¼ cup chopped celery in 2 tablespoons butter. Add vegetables to the stock along with 1 quart (4 cups) cream. In the same saucepan heat ½ cup oil and ½ cup butter until warm. Add 1 cup flour, whisking continuously until a medium paste (roux) is prepared. Add roux to the soup while stirring continuously until desired thickness is obtained. Salt and pepper to taste. Garnish with chopped parsley. Serves 12.

(115) **Busia's**
a Polish kitchen

"Busia's" is country Polish for "grandmother's," but chances are that your grandmother wasn't Polish. And she certainly wasn't anything like this grandmother, Barbara Mackowiak, who has single-handedly challenged the bogus Alpine-village eateries on Main Street in Gaylord to a duel of the culinarily dexterous. This is a city that has lost its identity to tourism; Gaylord, once 80 percent Polish,

273

is still more than 50 percent Polish no matter how many cute little cuckoo clocks are ticking above the cash registers. If you can find a single Swiss soul in town, let us know.

Busia's (pronounced "Boo-sha's") is a simple cafe with booths in the back and utilitarian tables in front, family photos, and pictures of Old Gaylord on the wall along with a few Polish hangings and some plants to soften the generally stark effect. But we came to eat, remember? "Polish and other ethnic food has so much to offer," says Mrs. Mackowiak, our affable hostess. And we certainly agree. The menu here includes such Eastern European delights as "czarnina" (a sweet-sour duck soup with prunes and raisins that's a billion times better than it sounds), "nalesniki" (pan-fried crepes filled with cottage cheese and onion), "golabki" (cabbage "blanket" around meatball "pigs"), and "barszcz" (don't even try to pronounce it--a beet and mushroom soup served with hearty kluski noodles).

If these aren't ethnic enough, we urge you to try the house specialty in whatever form it appears on the menu: Busia's homemade kielbasa, flavored with marjoram and allspice. The kielbasa platter is an absolute winner, combining the toothsome sausage with kluski noodles, potatoes, sauerkraut, and sausage pierogi (dumplings). The kielbasa is made right here in Gaylord; the lard-rendering press used in its production is even pictured in the restaurant's logo. According to Barbara, "We're into our third ton of kielbasa." Now, that's what we call popularity.

On Sunday you might want to try the special boiled dinner of pork, potatoes, carrots, cabbage, kluski, and broth. And don't ignore the salads; these are well-considered niceties: the house specialty combines creamy cucumbers and onions lightly flavored with dill, and almost as good is the sauerkraut salad. As for desserts, the peanut butter pie is famous in the county, and the bread pudding is an old-fashioned "grandmotherly" treat. Busia's bills itself as "the next best thing to home," a sentiment to be applauded, but in these days of freezer dinners, sometimes meaningless. We'd venture to guess that a good many homes are the next best thing to Busia's.

Moderate prices, marvelous food.

BUSIA'S, 324 W. Main St., Gaylord, MI 49735. In city center. Telephone (517) 732-2790. Hours: Monday-Thursday 7 a.m.-9 p.m. (till 10 p.m. Friday-Saturday, till 3 p.m. Sunday) in the summer; Monday-Thursday 7 a.m.-8 p.m. (till 9 p.m. Friday-Saturday) in winter. Closed Christmas, Easter, and Thanksgiving. Free parking in rear. No alcoholic beverages. No credit cards. Reservations taken for large groups only.

PIEROGI
From Barbara Mackowiak, Busia's

Barbara notes that this dough is basic for any noodle (kluski) or pierogi. Busia's offers a choice of fillings for the dumplings: potato and Cheddar, sauerkraut and sausage, chicken and dressing, ham and Cheddar, and others. In the Polish home, leftovers would be used, and mixtures would be combined according to personal taste. We include a couple of examples at the end of this recipe.

Place 2 cups flour on a board or in mixing bowl. Form a well; crack 2 eggs into it. Add ½ teaspoon salt and 1/3 cup water. Work flour toward the center of the well, blending ingredients thoroughly. Work dough until it's smooth and pliable and rolls easily. Roll out on floured surface. Spoon filling onto ½ of the dough. Fold other half over filling. Using a 3-inch biscuit cutter, press firmly over the mounds of dough and filling so that rounds are sealed well. It's helpful to moisten dough around filling before sealing. Cook pierogi in boiling, salted water 3-5 minutes. Drain and serve hot with butter and sour cream. They're also delicious pan fried.

275

Any leftover dough can be cut in strips for noodles. Cook these the same way and serve with butter or gravy.

Fillings: (1) Potato-cheese: boil 1 large potato and mash. Add 1 small onion that's been sauteed in 2 tablespoons butter. Add ¼ cup cheese of your choice and salt to taste. (2) Cheese filling: mix crumbled dry-curd cottage cheese with beaten egg.

THE ROWE
116 Michigan's Country Inn

The Rowe reminds us of one of those marvelous little French restaurants trying to earn another star in the Michelin guide. For efficiency and cuisine, it can hardly be topped. The dining room is modest, unpretentious, and somewhat crowded; and the general atmosphere is convivial--the clientele are clearly among the most enthusiastic diners we've seen in Michigan. There are very few tables, and the best are toward the west side away from the doors. On our first visit years ago, we were fortunate to be seated at the splendid table for two in front of the window and were able to enjoy a full moon along with a lovely five-course dinner. The service was exceptional; the timing between courses nearly perfect; and our waitress Ann Hines was genuinely friendly and interested in pleasing us.

The Rowe was built as a hamburger and chicken spot in 1947, and in 1972 Wes and Arlene Westhoven turned it into one of the most appealing country inns in Michigan. Prices are high, but the value is even higher. The cuisine, once European, gradually evolved into Michigan regional cooking and is the forerunner and still one of the leaders in that approach, so well entrenched now. The menu, posted on a blackboard, changes by degrees so that within a week or two all items on the list are new. (Some 250 to 300 entrees are served during a year's time.)

There are four courses at dinner, priced according to the entree; dessert is extra, and there may be a surcharge for more extravagant dishes.

Chef Jim Milliman is as creative as his predecessor, Harlan "Pete" Peterson, a long-time chef at the Rowe who opened his own restaurant, Tapawingo, just a stone's throw away in Ellsworth. Jim may have graduated from the University of Hard Knocks, as he puts it, but he has better taste and greater skill than many of the more formally trained chefs in the country. Let's just take a look at a few of the unparalleled offerings that have appeared recently on the blackboard menu at the Rowe: plum and Beaujolais soup, wild rice and bacon chowder, pheasant and black walnut terrine, spinach and Gruyere cheese in brioche, pecan chicken breast with watercress sauce, and char-grilled lamb chops with rhubarb chutney. Even salads are given meticulous attention; imagine wild leeks with watercress and Creole vinaigrette or spinach with smoked chicken, cashews, and honey-lemon vinaigrette. Desserts are always wonderful. Country-style cobblers, dumplings, and strudels appear side by side with such luxurious sweets as white chocolate mousse with sour cherry sauce and marquis au chocolat, a rich French confection. For a less filling finish, there's Chef Jim's own ice cream; we tried a phenomenal plum-hazelnut last summer. And all these splendrous works come out of a kitchen no bigger (possibly smaller) than your own.

More than 150 wines are offered, including 34 chateau-bottled Bordeaux ranging from the famous '73 Mouton with its Picasso label down to a modest Laurentan for less than $15. The '80 Gloria is a super buy at $20. And if money is no object, there are one '55, one '59, and two '61s on this impressive list. Good selections from Burgundy and California are also available. Finally, believe it or not, you'll see a 1923 Santo Brolio, Chiantis from 1940 and 1947, and a 1955 Brunello di Montalcino Reserva, which might be one of the best bottles of wine available in the world. All in all, the five-page list is a great tribute to the highest level of professionalism and good taste.

Inexperienced diners-out will adore the Rowe. Here you needn't fear misunderstanding or mispronouncing "feuilletage" or mishanding a Baccarat goblet or losing your aplomb with a haughty tuxedoed waiter. Here the combination of informal atmosphere and superior cuisine gives an overall feeling of dining with, say, Julia Child in her famous kitchen. And if you're fortunate, you'll be served by Ann, the best waitress in the county-- no, make that the state.

Extraordinary country inn, one of the best in the country.

THE ROWE, MICHIGAN'S COUNTRY INN, Ellsworth, MI 49729. On C-48, 12 miles south of Charlevoix; 6 miles east of M-31; 1 mile east of Ellsworth. Telephone (616) 588-7351. Hours: 6-10 p.m. daily in July and August. Closed Monday in September, October, May, and June; closed Monday through Wednesday November through April; and closed entirely for 2 weeks in December. Full bar service. Credit cards: MC, V. Reservations necessary (but do call, and they may fit you in; they did for us).

SAUTEED VEAL WITH MICHIGAN
MOREL MUSHROOM CREAM SAUCE
From Chef Jim Milliman, the Rowe

Chef Jim notes that pheasant or chicken would be a good substitute for veal in this recipe. Saute $\frac{1}{4}$ cup diced shallots in $\frac{1}{4}$ cup butter until soft. Stir in $\frac{1}{4}$ cup flour. Gradually add 3 cups chicken stock. Add 1 cup heavy cream. Stir in 1 cup morel mushrooms and 2 teaspoons finely minced ginger. Cook over low heat about 5 minutes. Dust the desired amount of veal medallions with flour, and saute. When cooked, remove from pan and keep warm. Deglaze the pan with 2 tablespoons brandy. Add the desired amount of the morel sauce to the veal. Heat, salt and pepper to taste, and serve at once. Our hints: This amount of sauce will suffice for 3-4 pounds veal, depending on your tastes. In sauteeing the veal, treat it like fish; it cooks very, very quickly and shouldn't be overdone.

⑪ *Tapawingo*

Tapawingo is the quintessential contemporary restaurant, stylishly and tastefully meeting almost every criterion for fine dining. All the components are here: an erstwhile summer home, the color of twilight and just a few feet from a sparkling little lake; a cool, sleek, uncluttered elegance in decor with classic cantilevered Marcel Breuer chairs and a spare gallery interior; a white and yellow color scheme derived from the trillium, the restaurant's wildflower motif; friendly and knowledgeable service; and low-keyed jazz and classical music (live in summer, tapes off season). Rarely have we seen such meticulous attention paid to every aspect of the gastronomic experience. Even the table settings are faultless: trillium-patterned service plates, nostalgic bouquets of garden flowers in tiny porcelain vases, and a superlative Peugeot peppermill on every table.

Reigning in the kitchen is the propietor, Harlan "Pete" Peterson, a gifted chef who charmed customers for about eight years at the nearby Rowe Inn, after a previous career as a design engineer at Ford Motor Company. His cooking style is regional American cuisine, focusing on fresh local produce, fish, and other primarily Michigan ingredients. This is a concept that has taken the state by storm, but Pete Peterson and Wes Westhoven of the Rowe were in the forefront.

The size of the menu at Tapawingo is perfectly suited to both clientele and chef: large enough to afford diners an exciting variety and small enough to assure personal attention in the kitchen. Fewer than a half-dozen appetizers, principal dishes, and desserts are offered each evening. For starters there might be mushroom-clam bisque or Michigan turtle soup; curried chutney chicken with water chestnuts, almonds, and grapes; smoked whitefish mousse; and veal, pork, and garlic sausage. We fell in love with the Montrachet cheesecake in a rich sesame-crumb crust; the sweetness of the sun-dried tomato garnish provided a perfect contrast to the tangy goat cheese.

Featured entrees might be whitefish baked in parchment; medallions of beef tenderloin with brown sauce enhanced by Roquefort and Port wine; or breast of pheasant with fettuccine tossed with creamy morel sauce and garnished with buttered fiddlehead ferns. On our visit last fall we opted for the veal scallop with basil cream sauce, julienned prosciutto ham, and toasted pine nuts. This glorious creation came with succulent miniature vegetables and a fresh herb garnish. Like everything served here, it was something of an artist's inspiration, translated into highly edible form. Even the baguettes and butter curls were irreproachable.

The tariff runs about $21 to $26 for four courses and is worth every penny. If you're feeling expansive, desserts here are splendid. For $4 more, there might be a choice of such delights as apple cobbler, Belgian chocolate terrine with Grand Marnier sauce, frozen white chocolate mousse with raspberry sauce, and caramelized walnut tart. The menu is constantly evolving, and Chef Peterson's repertoire seems infinite. But, we assure you, whatever you order at Tapawingo will be freshly prepared with uncommon finesse.

The restaurant has six low-priced house wines and a long list of selections mainly from France and California, augmented by a few from Italy, Germany, and Michigan. A good number cost less than $15, all are fairly priced, and there are some excellent possibilities, for example, a very highly rated '76 Malartic-Lagraviere for $28, a fine '78 Meyney for $24, and a superb '78 Brunello for $29. In all, the cellar here is both carefully chosen and appealing.

No one just "happens to be" in Ellsworth, Michigan (population about 400). One makes a specific point of coming here, usually for dinner at the Rowe or Tapawingo, and you can't go wrong with either one. As for the latter, Indian folklore has it that the name means "resting place." And what a wonderfully descriptive name it is. This is the kind of restaurant where you'll want to spend the entire evening. And we can't think of a nicer way to while away two or three hours than at Tapawingo.

Incomparable innovations, one of Michigan's best.

TAPAWINGO, 9502 Lake St., Ellsworth, MI 49729. Telephone (616) 588-7971. Hours: summer 6-10 p. m. Tuesday-Saturday; winter 6-9 p.m. Thursday-Saturday. Closed November. Full bar service. Credit cards: MC, V.

CARAMELIZED WALNUT TART
From Chef Pete Peterson, Tapawingo

For tart shell, with mixer or food processor combine 1/3 cup butter with ¼ cup sugar until light and fluffy. Add 1 egg yolk, and beat well. Gradually add 1 cup flour just until blended. Press (crumbly) dough into 9-inch tart pan with removable bottom. Bake in center of preheated 375-degree oven 12 minutes, until lightly browned. Cool.

Prepare filling. Spread 2 cups coarsely chopped walnuts on cookie sheet and bake in 375-degree oven for 5 minutes. Sprinkle nuts in bottom of tart shell. In heavy 2-quart saucepan, stir 2/3 cup packed light brown sugar with ¼ cup butter, ¼ cup dark corn syrup, and 2 tablespoons heavy cream. Stirring constantly, bring to boiling over medium heat; boil 1 minute. Pour over walnuts. Bake in center of 375-degree oven for 10 minutes, or just until mixture is bubbly. Place on wire rack to cool. Serve at room temperature with the remaining cream, whipped (in all, ½ cup cream in recipe).

SMOKED MICHIGAN WHITEFISH MOUSSE
From Chef Pete Peterson, Tapawingo

This is wonderful and wonderfully easy; Pete notes that the mixture may be piped into small gougere (cream puffs) or served as is for an hors d'oeuvre. Saute 1 cup chopped onion slowly in 8 ounces unsalted butter, until transparent. Cool to room temperature. Process in food processor along with 1 pound cleaned, defatted smoked whitefish, 8 ounces room-temperature cream cheese, juice of ½ lemon, and white pepper and cayenne to taste. When mixture is smooth and fluffy, turn into individual ramekins, chill, and garnish with fresh dill. Makes about 3 cups. Pete notes that, after processing, the mixture can be put through a fine sieve for a smoother mousse.

(118) The Argonne

There are few places these days where you can order for a single price all the jumbo shrimp you can eat. This has been the specialty at the Argonne for more than 30 years, and though the price isn't nearly as low as it once was, it's still an acceptable value for the shrimp lover. And they are jumbo. The only condition the restaurant makes is that shrimp "boats" (plates of six or ten shrimp) will not be served with the family-style dinner at the same table. The shrimp is either steamed or deep

282

fried in a specially seasoned beer batter. And we're pleased with the choice of butter for the steamed shrimp: lemon, garlic, or drawn.

We can't imagine why anyone would even look at anything else on the menu, but there are some other agreeable offerings: fresh broiled whitefish, Alaskan King crab, steamed lobster tails, prime rib, New York strip steak, and Southern fried chicken. All dinners are served with either French fries or baked potato, cole slaw or tossed salad, and homemade bread. The wine list is unimpressive; unless you want to splurge on champagne, probably your best bet is the California chablis by the carafe.

The Argonne, still family owned and operated, was built in 1929 and named for the original owner's brother, who was killed in "that battle" of World War I. The large old stone building on spacious grounds houses a single dining room that can seat more than 150. With gold-colored carpeting and tablecloths, it's a pleasant, comfortable place. The supper club is tremendously popular, so it's wise to arrive early.

For the shrimpomaniac.

THE ARGONNE SUPPER CLUB, Boyne City Rd., Charlevoix, MI 49720. Just east of the city; turn right off U.S.31 on Boyne City Rd., then drive about 2000 feet. Telephone (616) 547-9331. Hours: 5-10:30 p.m. daily. Closed November 1 to May 1. Full bar service. Credit cards: MC, V. Reservations not accepted.

Charlevoix dining note: Tom's Cafe, 307 Bridge St., downtown, is famous for its chocolate chunk ("Tom's Mom's") cookies and other treats; on the menu are wild game soup, Greek and Italian things and grilled swordfish. More intriguing is the cubbyhole storefront bistro, Terry's Place, on Antrim St. around the corner from its sister establishment Great Lakes Whitefish and Chips. We discovered it too late but have heard that both of these eateries are run by Terry Left, executive chef of the

Cafe Chauveron in Bay Harbor, Florida. That tells us something very provocative since that fashionable Florida restaurant served us one of the most memorable meals we've had in this country (we can still taste the Grand Marnier souffle with chestnuts). Terry's is open June through Labor Day.

BEER BATTER
From our files

Sometimes the simplest is best. This is an incredibly easy recipe that we've used for years and reminds us of the Argonne's batter. Try it on fish, onion rings, vegetables, or anything else you deep fry. The recipe? Mix 1 cup of beer with 1 cup of flour. That's it. Depending on your tastes and what you're cooking, you might want to add more beer for a lighter batter. Dip food into the batter, let excess run off, and deep fry in oil heated to about 375 degrees. Drain food on paper toweling or brown paper bag. (A French whisk most easily blends the batter.)

At One Water Street, the location, the building, and the menu are all equally worthy of attention. (The Stafford hospitality is a given.) We have for years been fond of the venerable Bay View Inn, celebrating its 100th year in 1987, and the sophisticated dockside Pier in Harbor Springs. And now Mr. Smith has done it again. The site of One Water Street at the mouth of the Boyne River is the "original place used for centuries by the area's native Americans, trappers, and missionaries and by the early pioneers looking for fulfillment of their dreams," according to a historical note on the menu. And that setting is something to behold--

windows on three sides of the structure offer a panoramic vista of crystalline Lake Charlevoix and the Boyne River, with a glorious sunset as an encore.

The building itself is modern with touches of the past and has been designed so that the dining rooms and lounge, each with their own decor, represent shops off One Water Street--the tiled foyer with plantings, street signs, and lamp posts. To one side is a trellised gazebo, the hostess' station. Not only every room but every table has a view, though some (those closest to the lake) are better than others. The Harborage is the more formal dining area with floral carpeting, rosy linens, and petal-shaped light fixtures. Across the "street" is the Marina-side Room, sleeker and more modern with light wood and Venetian blinds. If you like to sink into spacious, comfortable booths, this is your room. The lounge, with gray flannel and pinstripe upholstery and walls, hunting trophies, and a fireplace, has the masculine atmosphere of an English club. The entire decor is characterized by soft, muted colors and a stylized elegance. Take a good look--it cost $2 or $3 million, according to which newspaper you read.

The cooking style is regional American, in keeping with the aim of preserving Boyne City's Great Lakes' heritage. It's an eye-catching, taste-tempting menu. Standouts among the starters are the oysters Louisiana, the soup sampler, and the pasta roll (filled with vegetables and ricotta cheese). Soups include Michigan black cherry, baked mushroom and onion, and Great Lakes chowder. As for main courses, diners have such options as veal Lafayette (with a Tawny Port sauce), stuffed trout Hemingway with dill sauce, breast of Michigan pheasant Normandy, as well as the obligatory stir-fry (ginger pork), pasta (fettuccine Americana), and Cajun dish (shrimp jambalaya). And, of course, there are the solid, savory standbys: broiled white-fish and lake trout, rack of lamb, roast duckling, chicken, and steaks. Many of the same items are on the luncheon menu on a smaller scale.

Though not overly large, the wine list here is interesting. There's a low-priced carafe and eight "featured house wines" under $10 per bottle. Add to that more than ten sparkling choices and more than 30 still whites, the latter from France, Germany, California, and Michigan. Twenty reds are available at appropriate prices; these are from either California or France. The one weak spot is in the red Bordeaux, where of six offerings four are expensive Premier Grand Crus (two vintages each of Lafite and Mouton) and only two under $20. Even so, you'll likely find something nice on a list that is clearly designed to make wine affordable for those on a limited budget.

A precocious new addition to the
Stafford Smith family.

STAFFORD'S ONE WATER STREET, Boyne City, MI 49712. One block off Main Street on the waterfront. Telephone (616) 582-3434. Hours: 11:30 a.m.- 11 p.m. Monday-Saturday, till 10 p.m. on Sunday. Closed Christmas. Full bar service. Credit cards: AE, MC, V.

CHAR-BROILED BREAST OF PHEASANT
WITH MOREL MUSHROOMS
From Chef Dennis Crissman, One Water Street

We tried this wonderful recipe on our charcoal grill with a handful of moistened mesquite chips (soaked a few minutes in warm water). You can substitute fresh mushrooms of any variety if dried morels are unavailable. We served this dish with wild rice and Chef Bill Wolf's pear and parsnip puree (see Darby's)--fantastic!
Prepare herb marinade: Mix together 4 cups salad oil, 3 ounces country Dijon mustard (we used Pommery Moutarde de Meaux), 1/3 cup Worcestershire sauce, 1 tablespoon dried chervil, 1 tablespoon fresh chopped chives, 1 tablespoon fresh chopped parsley, 1 teaspoon salt, and 1 teaspoon ground

286

black pepper. Add 4 boneless breasts of pheasant
(wing bone left on). Marinate for at least 12 hours
in the refrigerator.

Preheat a grill or char-broiler, using mesquite
if available. Grill the pheasant skin side up until
charred outside, about 7 minutes; turn and cook
another 7-8 minutes. Should be charred outside, but
juicy inside. Set the pheasant to one side of the
grill to keep it warm.

In a saute pan, melt 2 tablespoons unsalted butter. Add 2 ounces reconstituted dried morel mushrooms (soak dry mushrooms about 30 minutes in
warm water) and 1 clove minced garlic. Saute
lightly. Add 3-4 tablespoons dry Sherry wine, stir,
let boil a moment or so.

Have four servings wild rice prepared. Place on
four serving plates. Place pheasant breasts on top
of rice. Garnish with morel mushroom sauce.
Serves 4.

"What's a walloon, Mommy?" your little one
might ask.

"A walloon, my dear," you'll answer if you
happen to know, "is a person of Celtic origin who
lives in southern Belgium, and the Walloon language
is Belgian French."

"Do people speak Walloon at Walloon Lake?" your
tot might persist.

"No, but the language at the Walloon Lake Inn
is also a hybrid: Michigan French," you might
answer if you happen to know.

And more and more people are getting to know
that. Chef/owner David Beier has successfully combined classic French cooking techniques with the
use of Michigan food products at his restaurant
on one of Ernest Hemingway's favorite fishing

lakes. We have a feeling Papa might have preferred a blood-red steak to one of Chef David's exquisite trout coulibiacs. Nevertheless, a lot of tradition, both French and American, converges in this nearly 100-year-old inn in the tiny village of Walloon Lake. Look for the rambling white cottage with red gabled roof and green awnings.

The dining room's color scheme is a fresh green and white. A few knotty pine wall panels add a country touch, and large windows overlook the lake. A small porch provides a pleasant waiting area where you can enjoy cocktails before dinner. Service here, you'll find, is highly professional. The wait staff are required to learn about food and wine, and most are more experienced than the help in nearby seasonal places.

Menus change yearly and are always exciting. Classic French exciting? Yes, because you don't see it that much outside big cities. Also, some chefs have become so inventive that many of the finest traditional dishes are no longer available to connoisseurs. (We'll take perfect escargots Bourguignonne any day over snails bathed in raspberry vinaigrette served on a leaf of radicchio.) And at the Walloon Lake Inn meticulous attention is paid to every aspect of cooking and presentation. Chef David and his sous-chef Daniel Vernia, with a background in American cooking, smoke their own trout and grow their own herbs and baby vegetables. In fact, in fall 1986 they began to offer an annual four-week session of hands-on cooking classes at the inn (including lodging and breakfasts, limited to six persons).

The appetizers are French and flavorsome: pate, bouchees de mer (puff pastry cases filled with sauced shellfish), stuffed mushrooms, onion soup. Of the entrees the rainbow trout Hemingway is a house favorite. Also available are that superb coulibiac (trout in pastry with Hollandaise); nested quail with walnuts, wild rice, and Madeira; and strawberry almond duck, among other tempting choices. A daily specialty worth trying is the veal du jour, on the order of sweetbreads or medallions of veal with foie gras. Other specials appear, too, sometimes venison, salmon, or our favorite fresh-water fish, walleyed pike. Desserts are enticing: chocolate mousse, creme caramel, citrons givrel (lemon sherbet in lemon cups with Triple Sec), and a pastry du jour, possibly chocolate mousse torte or apple spice cake. Dinners average about $30 per person; memorable meals do not come cheap.

The wine list is modest and includes both house selections and a sprinkling of reds and whites from California and France plus a few bubbling wines. But all are priced quite fairly, and some are sur-prisingly reasonable, making up in affordability what is lacking in volume. And if a regular bottle is more than you want, smaller sized offerings are available (down to the glass).

Felicitous francophone feasts.

WALLOON LAKE INN, Walloon Lake Village, MI 49796. In village center. Telephone (616) 535-2999. Hours: 6-10 p.m. daily, luncheon by private arran-gement. Full bar service. Credit cards: MC, V. Ar-rive at 6 if you want a window seat. Dress code: no shorts. Call for information on cooking school and bed and breakfast accommodations.

DRESSING ALLEGRO
From Chef David Beier, Walloon Lake Inn

At the inn this dressing is tossed with Boston lettuce immediately prior to serving. "Allegro" means "happy," and we hope you'll be happy with this recipe. Combine in food processor or blender 14 ounces salad oil (about 1 1/3 cup), 1 cup vinegar, 3/8 cup balsamic vinegar (about 3 tablespoons), $\frac{1}{4}$ cup lemon juice, 2 anchovies, 1 egg, $1\frac{1}{2}$ tablespoon salt, $1\frac{1}{2}$ teaspoon mustard, 1 teaspoon minced garlic, $\frac{1}{2}$ teaspoon capers, $\frac{1}{2}$ teaspoon freshly ground black pepper, $\frac{1}{4}$ teaspoon rosemary. Blend until smooth. Yields about 3 cups, enough for 24 salads.

Founded in 1886, the Bay View Inn has had a long
history as one of the oldest continuously operating
hotels in the area. This is a place that takes you
back--way back to the Victorian days of northern
Michigan, when the train ran every 15 minutes
between Petoskey and Walloon Lake and later stopped
at Bay View itself, only a few steps away from
the inn's front porch. By 1911, 116 passenger trains
whistled through or stopped daily outside the the
Bay View Inn each summer, and on some Sundays
there were more than 3000 passengers.

But we are more concerned with its years since
1961, when Stafford Smith, only three years out
of our alma mater Northwestern University (he left
when we did), married Janice Johnson of Flint,
purchased the financially struggling inn, and set a
about restoring it to its previous grandeur. Take
a look at the front porch as you enter--and the
no less than a dozen rocking chairs. The lobby, too,
has the aura of a Victorian parlor, complete with
large, randomly mixed floral arrangements. Just a
few feet away is the Sun Room, a front lounge
with white wicker furniture in the Southhampton
tradition. The rest of the first floor contains four
dining rooms, each a stunning evocation of the
19th century. We like the trellised garden effect
of the Rose Lawn Porch for breakfast and the
Staffordshire Room, decorated with opulent gilt-
framed mirrors and crystal chandeliers, for dinner.

Breakfasts at the Bay View Inn are special. The
French toast is a thick slice of raisin bread dipped
in a buttermilk batter, grilled, and served with
Michigan maple syrup. Biscuits and gravy, omelets,
eggs Benedict, and whole wheat pancakes are other
options. And a local rumor says that there are no
better waffles in the state. We ordered an omelet,

which came with sauteed potatoes, a slice of melon, and an English muffin--plus a basket brimming with pecan rolls and blueberry muffins. Surely the biggest and best breakfast in the Petoskey area (but at about $5 per person, it's high for families).

Luncheons and dinners feature "regional recipes as well as traditional cuisine." Choose from such customary entrees as rack of lamb, broiled whitefish, roast duckling, and broiled scallops or from such tantalizing possibilities as curried pork tenderloin, veal Louisiana with tomato concasse and Creole mustard sauce, or shrimp stir fried with vegetables and served on rice with a honey-mustard sauce. For lunch the choices are less interesting but perfectly adequate. We like all the salads and the chicken jardiniere (boneless breast sauteed with vegetables and topped with Hollandaise). Good homemade breads accompany all entrees.

Country comfort and century-old charm.

STAFFORD'S BAY VIEW INN, U.S.31, Petoskey, MI 49770. Telephone (616) 347-2771. Hours: breakfast 8-10 a.m., luncheon 11:30 a.m.-2 p.m., dinner 6-9 p.m., Sunday brunch 10 a.m.-2 p.m. Call about off-season hours. No liquor license by local law. Credit cards: AE, MC, V.

CHICKEN DIJON
From Stafford's Bay View Inn

In large heavy skillet heat $\frac{1}{4}$ cup unsalted butter over moderately high heat; in it saute 8 large shelled, deveined, and butterflied shrimp for 3 minutes or until just cooked. With a slotted spoon, transfer to a plate. Skin, bone, and halve 2 (1-pound) chicken breasts, and flatten slightly between sheets of dampened waxed paper. Dredge in flour, and shake off excess. Salt and pepper, and brown in the skillet on both sides over moderately high heat. Transfer to a plate.

In the same skillet cook 2 tablespoons minced shallots over moderate heat, stirring, for 1 minute. Add ¼ pound minced mushrooms and cook, stirring, for 2 minutes. Add ¼ cup medium-dry sherry wine, and boil the liquid until reduced by half. Add 2 cups heavy cream, the chicken, and any juices that have accumulated on the plate. Simmer, turning the chicken to coat with sauce, for 5 minutes or until the chicken is springy to the touch. Stir in 2 tablespoons Dijon mustard, the shrimp, and salt and pepper to taste. Simmer until heated through. Transfer chicken to heated platter; top it with shrimp and sauce. Garnish with minced parsley. Serves 4.

BILL'S FARM MARKET

Why a farm market in a book about Michigan eateries? Because it's a very special place, where some of the best chefs in the area buy their vegetables. This is not a "farmers' market," as urbanites think of it, with growers from miles around bringing in truckloads of produce to a central clearinghouse. This is Bill's Farm Market, located right on the farm, meaning that almost everything you buy here is sown, grown, reaped, and heaped by Bill himself!

"I started selling vegetables on a small card table in front of the house. Mostly I grew beets, carrots, a few tomatoes," says Bill McMaster, not yet 30 years old and now a pro in the produce field. In 1982 the present farm market building was built next door to the farmhouse, where Bill lives with his parents and brother. The sales area is limited, 15 by 26 feet, but as Bill notes, "We cram a lot of stuff into that small space."

And what good stuff it is. Sweet corn is his major crop, taking up 15 acres, but more than 25 vegetables, including five varieties of lettuce ad 12 varieties of squash, are also grown on the farm (we love the tiny Gold Nuggets and "sweet potato" squashes). Bill's is known, too, for miniature and unusual vegetables--tiny carrots and corn, yellow scallions, golden beets, Oriental pak choi, kohlrabi, and kale--which are served in area restaurants and in dining spots as far away as in New York. Fresh herbs are also available and lend a tantalizing aroma to the marketplace.

In the spring Bill's greenhouse nearly bursts at the seams with more than 40,000 plants: cabbage, cauliflower, green pepper, broccoli, tomatoes of different varieties, and flowers that are sold fresh-cut or dried. In the fall the lawn in front of the farmhouse and market becomes a huge pumpkin patch, and customers come from miles around for the apples, squash, Sebago potatoes (some people buy bushels at a time and store them all winter), Michigan popcorn, and cider. Later still, Bill does a bustling business in Christmas wreaths.

In addition to his own produce, Bill's little market houses Michigan honey, maple syrup, local jams and preserves, a small selection of cookbooks, and occasionally wild berries and mushrooms that the neighbors bring in. If you're vacationing up north, we can't think of better souvenirs than the homemade and home-grown items from this delight-ful country market.

Thumbs up for the greenest thumb in Michigan.

BILL'S FARM MARKET, 4450 Mitchell Rd., Petos-key, MI 49770. East of Petoskey city center, 3½ miles. Telephone (616) 347-6735. Hours: 10 a.m.-7 p.m.

BETH AND KATE'S PUMPKIN BREAD
From Ellen Wilkerson, Holt, Michigan

Each year just before Christmas Kate and Beth

bring us this wonderfully aromatic treat. The bread is great, the girls are charming, and we don't know which we like best.

Beat together 3 cups sugar, 1 cup vegetable oil, and 4 eggs. Add 2/3 cup water and 2 cups canned or cooked and mashed pumpkin. Sift together 3 1/3 cups flour, 2 teaspoons baking soda, 1¼ teaspoon cinnamon, ½ teaspoon ground cloves, ¼ teaspoon ground allspice. Stir into pumpkin mixture along with 1 cup chopped pecans. Bake in 2 ungreased loaf pans at 350 degrees for 1 hour. Allow to cool in pans. Makes 2 loaves.

(123) STAFFORD'S

Pier

RESTAURANT

Harbor Springs, one of the most easily accessible yet naturally protected deep water harbors in the Great Lakes, was a popular stop for passenger boats at the turn of the century. And for those today driving on Route 31 through Petoskey, we suggest a short, picturesque seven-mile excursion to this exclusive coastal village for a visit to the Pier. The main dining area, the Pointer Room, probably affords the finest view of Little Traverse Bay with the city of Petoskey visible on the other side. A veritable extension of the restaurant (hence its name) is the wide steel pier reaching out about 200 feet into the harbor and flanked by an incredible array of motor launches and sailing ships. Within walking distance is the small shopping district of Harbor Springs, catering to well-heeled tourists and boasting expensive little boutiques, art galleries, craft and gift shops.

The room is named after the "Pointer," which was once moored here and from 1930 to 1949 carried passengers across a small bay to Harbor Point, where automobiles were then prohibited. Harbor Point itself was founded as a resort area in 1878 and still retains some of the exclusive flavor of its early days. But all that is now left of the Pointer is its mooring place. And it's still a welcome mooring place for both waterfarers and landlubbers.

The place has evolved over the past decade. The former nautical touches are no more, and in some ways we miss the bright blue linens on the tables. But there are compensations. A delightful patio has been added for luncheon in the summer or cocktails before dinner; and the new, more feminine decor with a rich color scheme of rose, cerise, and burgundy is effective, along with the hanging bouquets of silk flowers in porcelain bowls. Table settings conform to the pretty theme: rose and dark red semi-Oriental service plates, pink napkins, and brass candlesticks. Only the captain's chairs are holdovers from the past.

The dinner menu is much more imaginative than it was years ago. Among the appetizers are frog legs in garlic butter, veal and apple terrine, baked Brie in phyllo, and a good choice for a group: "A Taste of Stafford's," a combination plate of several hors d'oeuvre to share. The soup sampler offers the same convenience. A salad bar is included with your entree, but we recommend instead any of the specialty salads available at no extra charge: a classic Caesar, a bibb and walnut-mushroom concoction with raspberry vinaigrette, pasta primaverda with pesto, or the trendy bibb and radicchio with all sorts of tasty and unusual things including tomato concasse, pancetta ham, balsamic vinaigrette, and warm goat cheese.

All the conventional main courses are on the menu, as well as lake trout with dill Hollandaise and whitefish sauteed with lemon, shallots, and capers. But you must also check the specialties: duckling with raspberry sauce, stir-fried ginger pork, veal with seafood-stuffed morels, chicken Dijon, and several others. Prices are in the $13-$16 range.

Desserts are appealing, too, and we'll mention just two to set your mouth watering: white and dark chocolate mousse topped with pistachios and mocha-toffee pie. The wine list is limited but adequate. Glasses and carafes (none over $10) can be ordered, and for house wines these are better than average: Chardonnays, Dourthe vin blanc, Rhone, Cabernet Sauvignon, Partager vin blanc, and others. Also nice are the splits of champagne and other sparkling wines at $2.50.

For the budget-minded and families, the Pier has another dining room downstairs, the Chart Room, offering sandwiches and lighter dinners (the ribs are legendary) at lower prices than in the Pointer Room but lacking that excellent view.

A fashionable harborside gathering place.

THE PIER, 102 Bay St., Harbor Springs, MI 49740. On the harbor. Telephone (616) 526-6201. Hours: in the Pointer Room, luncheon 11:30 a.m.-3 p.m., dinner 5-11 p.m.; in the Chart Room, luncheon 11: 30 a.m.-5 p.m., dinner 5-11 p.m.; Sunday, brunch menu noon-3 p.m., dinner 3-10 p.m. Closed Christmas Day. Full bar service. Credit cards: MC, V. Reservations not accepted in the Chart Room.

A note for "gourmets": There's a new kid on the block in Harbor Springs, Benno's, who doesn't even have a sign out in front (he has only a miniscule sign at his Detroit restaurant). You can find the place behind the Northern Title Company, a beige and brown box of a building with no charm but with an address, 151 Bay St. We arrived here out of season and were only able to poll some of the locals, who looked askance ("he's never open," "it only serves about 8 people," "I don't know how he stays in business"). Still, everyone agrees that, if you can get an appointment, the food is excellent. We plan to check it out next summer.

PEANUT BUTTER PIE
From the Pier

This is still a top seller at the restaurant. It's

easy, can be prepared in advance, and is a guaranteed hit with children of all ages. Blend together until well mixed 2/3 cup peanut butter, ¼ cup Karo syrup, ¼ cup water, and 1 quart vanilla ice cream. Pour into a 9-inch prepared graham cracker pie shell. Freeze. To serve, top with a mixture of 2/3 cup peanut butter and ¼ cup Karo syrup. Sprinkle liberally with Spanish peanuts. Serves 6-8.

Vivio's ⑫④

Vivio's has been a long-time favorite of ours, a perfect spot to visit after a long day of morel hunting in May. You can expect efficient service, good food, fair prices, and, if you order the right thing, it's also a bargain. And it's unquestionably unpretentious and a delightful place for families; there are seven high chairs, but it seems that these are never enough. Northern Italian cooking has been the specialty here since the restaurant opened in 1938. The pasta is homemade and al dente, and the sauce is superb--we've seen and been duly impressed by the enormous vat in the kitchen, where it simmers constantly and, we like to think, ages beautifully like vintage port.

The loyal clientele generally order the pizza, veal Parmigiana, baked mostiaccioli, spaghetti, and ravioli. Our own first choice is the splendid combination pasta plate, half spaghetti and half ravioli. But the Sicilian shrimp, cannelloni crepe (see the recipe below), and linguine with clam sauce are just as tempting. Assorted steaks, chicken, seafood, and sandwiches are available at reasonable prices.

But we think that once you breathe in the pervasive aromas emanating from that bubbling sauce in the kitchen, you'll stick with the Italian specialties.

Vivio's has two dining rooms, but we prefer the large original room with the huge stone fireplace and open-beamed ceiling. The building, an authentic log cabin, is decorated in Northwoods Rustic with checked tablecloths and with stuffed game and birds on the walls and overhead.

Italian and inexpensive, a bargain.

VIVIO'S NORTHWOOD INN, U.S.27 and M-68, Indian River, MI 49749. One mile southwest of town on M-68. Hours: 5 p.m.-midnight Monday-Saturday, 4-11 p.m. Sunday. Closed Thanksgiving, Christmas. Full bar service. No credit cards or reservations (except for large groups) accepted.

CANNELLONI CREPES
From Vivio's

First, mix the crepe batter. Combine 4 eggs, a pinch salt, 2 cups flour, 2¼ cups milk, and ¼ cup melted margarine. Beat until smooth. Refrigerate 1 hour. Cook crepes in a lightly buttered or oiled crepe pan or small skillet and set aside.

For the filling, mix together by hand 2 cups small-curd cottage cheese, one (8-ounce) package cream cheese, and 4 tablespoons butter. Add 4 tablespoons chopped parsley, 2 eggs, 2 chopped scallions, and a dash salt. Spoon 3 tablespoons of filling onto each crepe. Roll up, and place in a greased baking dish, seam sides down. Cover lightly with your favorite spaghetti sauce (see Lapeer Family Inn's recipe in this volume). Sprinkle grated Romano cheese on top. Bake until hot in a preheated 350-degree oven, about 20 minutes.

Located on the east bank of the fast-flowing Cheboygan River and in a wooded country setting, the Hack-ma-Tack Inn is clearly the best

298

restaurant in the Cheboygan area. The site, at one of the northern openings into the Southern Peninsula's largest wilderness areas, drained by the Black and Pigeon Rivers, encourages the imaginative to recall the Ojibwa, the French trappers, and Michigan's spectacular era of river logging. Today, however, you'll find a rambling, well-worn building with a large, airy dining room decorated in early American. The tables are spruce and cheerful with vibrant blue tablecloths and glistening glassware. The open-hearth grill adds to the interest of the place, but most attention is drawn to the pleasant view of the woods and river through the sparkling facade of windows. Adjacent to the dining room is a small bar and lounge with glass doors opening to within a few feet of a 400-foot docking area along the river bank. On nice days some guests arrive by boat, and many prefer to enjoy their refreshments outdoors rather than in the lounge.

The menu appeals to basic American tastes for charcoal-grilled steaks (including Michigan buffalo steaks), prime rib, lobster tails, and whitefish amandine. Numerous other offerings are in the same vein. The menu is not particularly innovative, but what this restaurant has is fine quality and adequate servings. These are enhanced by several appetizers (the smoked whitefish vinaigrette is the most unusual); yet another salad bar; and a decent, though not distinguished, dessert selection. The combination of food and setting makes the Hack-ma-Tack rather special for this part of the state, and if you're heading southeast on Route 23 toward Alpena, it's a long, long way before you'll find anything as good.

A serene riverside setting.

THE HACK-MA-TACK INN, 8131 Beebe Rd. (Rural Route 4), Cheboygan, MI 49721. Five miles south, 2 miles southeast of the junction of M-27 and 33. Telephone (616) 625-2919. Hours: luncheon noon-3 p.m., dinner 5-10 p.m., Sunday 4-9 p.m., mid-June to Labor Day. Closed November-April. Full bar service. Credit cards: DC, MC, V. Reservations not taken.

(126) THE DAM SITE INN

From the entryway, furnished with handmade cherrywood tables and hutches, to any one of the five dining rooms, decorated attractively in modern but not avant-garde style with a few country touches, the Dam Site Inn is very well maintained and pleasing to the eye. We especially like the Coral Room (try to get table C6); unfortunately reservations aren't taken, so only early and late comers are likely to have much choice. But the restaurant seats about 240, and many of the tables have views--of the surrounding countryside or the dammed Maple River, giving the illusion of a small lake. If it's necessary to wait, you'll enjoy the lounge with its white Saarinen chairs and roomy bar.

The specialty of the house (and by far the most frequently ordered item) is the exemplary pan-fried chicken dinner, family style, all you can eat, served with excellent homemade noodles cooked in broth, gravy, potatoes, peas, and beverage. You may call ahead if you prefer your chicken stewed. (Call, too, if you want the livers and gizzards saved for you.) The steaks and seafood are also well received, particularly the butter-broiled scallops. Dinners are served with a generous relish plate, salad, vegetable, potato, and hot buttermilk biscuits. Prices are moderate. There are a few additional side orders such as soup (a special chowder on Friday only) and onion rings. If you can make room for it, try the chocolate angel food cake.

The Dam Site Inn on our last visit had a better than average wine list with a few exceptional offerings (such as Chateaux Lafite, Mouton, Haut Brion, and Latour)--at substantial prices, however. You may visit the cellar if you wish, but the setup isn't especially impressive. The kitchen, too, is always open for your inspection, and we found it to be immaculate.

Comfortable country dining.

THE DAM SITE INN, Woodland Rd., Pellston, MI 49769. About 7 miles west of I-75, 1½ miles south of Pellston off U.S.31. Telephone (616) 539-8851. Hours: 5-10 p.m. Monday-Saturday, 3-9 p.m. Sunday. Closed about six months of the year, from the end of trout season (the third Saturday in October) to the end of April. Full bar service. Credit cards: MC, V. Reservations taken only for groups of six or more.

(127) *Legs Inn*

According to our Emmet County informer (none other than Doug Weaver, who is also the undercover Athletic Director at Michigan State), the Legs Inn is still drawing the crowds every summer. One word for this place, and normally we hesitate to use it, is "unique." Our aim in this book is to describe, but how do you describe the indescribable? The Legs Inn must be seen to be believed. The building is extraordinary--both the exterior and interior are unlike those of any other restaurant we've seen.

Stanley Smolak, the uncle of the present owner, made the Legs Inn a lifetime project, starting in 1932, and he was still working on it almost 20 years ago before he died at the age of 81. He laid all the field stones by hand and constructed and carved nearly everything within the large masonry building, from the chairs and doors to the bars and window carvings. His sculptures are contortions in wood, protean, imaginative, grotesque, wonderful. A colorful local figure in his day, Mr. Smolak was even made Honorary Chief White Cloud by the

Ottawa in this Native American village (see the museum across the street). The "legs," by the way, refer to the line of stove legs that are perched atop the front of the structure, giving it the appearance of a fort as seen by, say, Salvador Dali.

But what is most important about the Legs Inn is that the eastern European food here is as good as any you'll find in the state. And, on top of that, it's a bargain. Eating out in Michigan has certainly been enhanced since Helen Smolak, the owner's attractive wife, assistant manager, sometime bartender, and chef, came here from Poland in 1974. She's already built up quite a following. Customers sometimes call ahead to see if she's baked one of her superb tortes that day and, if not, might change their minds about coming. The breads and soups, too, are always freshly made; and Helen is in charge of the marvelous European specialties: homemade Kielbasa with sauerkraut, golombki (stuffed cabbage rolls), pierogi (dumplings filled with potato and cheese or meat and sauerkraut), and bigos (the hearty national stew of Poland). If you're fortunate, you might be able to try some of Helen's borscht or sauerkraut soup before your main course. On Friday and Saturday the Legs Inn features a 12-ounce pan-fried whitefish fillet at a lower price than in any restaurant we've found in Michigan.

To get to Cross Village, either go due west from U.S.31 at Levering or take one of the state's most pleasant drives by going north from Harbor Springs on M-119. You might even catch a glimpse of a maneuvering B-52 bomber traveling hundreds of miles per hour only a few hundred feet above the lake. But, however you get to the Legs Inn, get there. There's nothing like it in Michigan.

Bohemian, bizarre, beguiling, and a bargain.

THE LEGS INN, Lake Shore Dr., Cross Village, MI 49723. In village center. Telephone (616) 526-5087. Hours: 10 a.m.-10 p.m. from May 1 to November 15; rest of year open only Friday, Saturday, Sunday. Full bar service. Band and dancing weekend evenings. No credit cards.

KENVILLE'S

Here is food just like Grandma used to make-- Grandma Kenville, to be exact. This bright, bustling, but plain family-style restaurant is across from the docks in downtown Mackinaw City. Kenville's forte is traditional American cooking, and we like it for several reasons: the efficiency and cleanliness, the large servings, the flavorful and hearty fare at low prices, and the convenience to the docks if we're waiting for or returning from a ferry to Mackinac Island.

The best seats are in the booths by the windows (better for two persons than four), but avoid the first two or any of the tables near the entry. There's no waiting room, and the place is packed daily with what appears to be half the population of Mackinaw City. In fact, we've been told that people stand in line outdoors, even in the rain, for a meal at Kenville's.

The restaurant offers a la carte or plate dinners (with potatoes, muffins, and wonderful buttery rolls) at very reasonable prices. Full dinners are further accompanied by soup or juice, choice of salad, and dessert. Entrees include such simple and savory possibilities as roast beef, meatloaf, beef stew, succulently tender liver with onions or bacon, and the perennial favorite--baked, crispy chicken with really unusual and delicious biscuits (is it necessary to mention gravy?). Or choose from the sandwich list; the Glorified Hamburger is a winner. Your plump friends might wish to take on the regionally famous lemon meringue pie. If such homey food in a Midwestern cafe setting doesn't at first appeal to your adventurous instincts, we urge you to give it a second thought. It's surprising how many times in gastronomic conversations hundreds of miles from Mackinaw City we've listened to the words "You've probably never heard of it, but there's a great little place called Kenville's...."

The American cooking here is not prosaic or prototypical. The recipes have been passed down through three generations of Kenvilles. You won't find them in a cookbook; they're not even written down for the cooks. Any family member who wishes to be part of the restaurant must commit them to memory and learn every phase of the business as well. (Curiously, with all that dedication in the kitchen, the service is somewhat hurried and frantic under the watchful and intimidating eye of the manager.)

Fine family fare, a bargain.

KENVILLE'S, 112 S. Huron Ave., Mackinaw City, MI 49701. Across from the docks, at the railroad tracks. Telephone (616) 436-7131. Hours: 8 a.m.-10 p.m. daily. Open April 1 to October 20. No alcoholic beverages. Reservations not accepted.

Nearby attractions: Do visit Fort Michilimackinac, founded by the French in 1714, and watch the MSU archaeological dig in the summer as well as some historical pageantry. And, of course, aim your camera at Big Mac (no relation to Mc-you-know-who), which arches 5 miles over the Straits of Mackinac, where Lake Michigan and Lake Huron meet, to connect the Upper and Lower Peninsulas.

GRANDMA'S PIE CRUST
From Kenville's

Since we were unable to wheedle a new recipe out of the Kenvilles, we're repeating this one, a sought-after and very good version of old-fashioned flaky pie pastry. Plan on making this a day ahead.

304

Mix until smooth and creamy 5 ounces lard, 6
ounces Crisco, 3 ounces butter, and 3/4 teaspoon
salt. Add 2¼ cups flour, and mix to a paste. Stir
in 1¼ cup water. Cover and refrigerate dough 24
hours. Makes enough for 1 double-crusted pie.

(129) Grand Hotel
— MACKINAC ISLAND

Graciousness, serenity, nostalgia, the Good Life--
no one word or phrase can capture the personality
of the aging but still lovely queen of Michigan's
resort hotels. Certainly the best-known structure
on Mackinac Island, it has an honorable history,
dating from 1887, as the summer stopping place
of presidents, ambassadors, generals, and kings.
Once the social scene of the elite--Mrs. Potter
Palmer, the Cudahys, and other tycoons of the
Chicago business world--it now hosts a steady stream
of conventions, booked at least two years in
advance, and visitors from all walks of life who
want to luxuriate in the unhurried quality and
niceties of a bygone era.

The Grand Hotel, an imposing Classical Georgian
building set on 500 acres, advertises itself as the
"world's largest summer hotel." The surroundings
are geared to leisure, like a cruise ship on the
Caribbean; a stay at the hotel lends itself to lazy
and self-indulgent pleasures: walks through the
beautiful sunken gardens, carriage tours, riding
instruction, bicycling through the 2000-acre state
park nearby, or just sitting on the veranda and
looking out on the rest of Michigan. And, of course,
savoring some fine meals.

The main dining room seats 600 to 1000 people.
Appropriately the decor is 1930s "summer style,"
and the colors--green, white, yellow--are fresh and
summery, too. There is something reassuring and
uncomplicated in both decor and menu. The food,

by design, is traditionally American. Meals are price fixed, table d'hote, and, not surprisingly, expensive (as of our last information, breakfast $9, luncheon $19.50, and dinner $35 per person). The menus change daily. In the evening prime rib and broiled trout or whitefish are regularly served (and regularly ordered), but the other entrees vary: seafood Madagascar, osso buco, lamb and linguine casserole, veal chop Orloff, braised roulade of beef, and rainbow trout meuniere.

On any one menu, the choices are generally roasts, chops, and broiled fish plus one or two "gourmet" offerings. Usually three soups are available, on the order of gazpacho, seafood bisque, chicken minestra, or chilled cucumber. First-course options might include smoked Nova Scotia salmon, marinated mushrooms, ham timbale, or avocado mousse. On the wine list are Dom Perignon, Le Montrachet (1973), and a 1964 Lafite at prices appropriate to their distinction. Most of the remaining offerings cost less than $20, and many of these less than $10. The breakdown is expectable: one rose, six sparkling, nine whites, and eight reds.

New to the Grand Hotel since our first edition is the Geranium Bar, a gourmet luncheon place seating about 40 people and with a light, summery color scheme--lots of white, greens, and of course the bright red of geraniums. It, too, is open to the public, but reservations aren't necessary. There's a fresh pasta daily, some salads and cold plates, and a few more elaborate dishes, such as sauteed veal Zurichoise (in a Chablis-cream sauce), scampi Portofino (sauteed with tomatoes and spinach, in a white wine and herb sauce), curried lamb chops, terrine of scallops with dill sauce. Of the desserts we favor the apple sour cream pie and the praline mousse.

Mackinac Island is formed of 350 million-year-old Devonian rock. The topography, however, evolved late in earth's history, and wave-eroded notches from higher levels of Lake Huron thousands of years ago are apparent in many places--in fact, the

Grand Hotel is nestled into one of these. With European settlement, the island and its nearby areas became commercially and strategically important to the French, then the British, and finally the Americans. Remember, St. Ignace, the closest mainland village, was established more than 300 years ago! Now, of course, the island's main function is recreational. And the combination of history; setting; scenery; transportation only by foot, bicycle, or horse and carriage; and this grand old hotel makes a visit to Mackinac Island one of the most adventurous experiences in Michigan.

Grand in every respect.

THE GRAND HOTEL, Mackinac Island, MI 49757. Telephone (906) 847-3331. Hours: breakfast 7:30-9:30 a.m., luncheon noon-2 p.m., high tea 4 p.m., dinner 6:30-8:45 p.m. Open mid-May to November. Full bar service. Entertainment, dancing. Gentlemen, coats and ties requested after 6 p.m.; ladies, wear dresses or your better pantsuits. No credit cards or reservations for meals.

WHITEFISH WITH WALNUT BUTTER
From the Grand Hotel

Whitefish, a Great Lakes specialty, is popular in all northern Michigan restaurants. The walnut butter in this recipe would also be good with baked trout or bass. Rub vegetable oil on both sides of a 2-2½-pound whitefish. Place on a lightly greased baking sheet, and sprinkle with ½ teaspoon salt, ½ teaspoon paprika, and ¼ teaspoon pepper. Combine ½ cup dry white wine and ½ cup water. Pour over fish. Bake 20-30 minutes in preheated 350-degree oven. In a small skillet melt ¼ cup butter, and stir in ¼ cup chopped walnuts. Cook until lightly browned. Serve over fish. For 4 people.

A snug little hideaway, the Hungarian Kitchen
has been here for years and has been gently doing
its job of converting heathen Michiganians to good
Magyar food. Half-hidden in Lake Michigan's shoreline dunes, it's one of the most agreeably evocative
eating places in the Upper Peninsula. Once a beach
house, it now contains a small dining room with
latticed windows, knotty pine walls, and just eight
tables, each seating up to six people. The three
in the front alcove facing the lake are especially
appealing. Much of the charm here is that small,
intimate, homepun setting and an elusive eastern
European aura that affords a wistful glimpse into
an all-but-forgotten past.

As for the food, even though the offerings are
limited, we give it top billing--but only if you order
the authentic Hungarian dishes. The dedicated chef
regularly serves two soups, bean and chicken, both
virtuoso performances. Entrees include genuine food:
a marvelous chicken paprikash--large pieces of
meltingly tender chicken and tiny, succulent dumplings in gravy; stuffed cabbage rolls with a pungent
home-pickled sauerkraut; and an exceptionally savory
goulash, made with braised sirloin tips. Each of
these is served with a small loaf of homemade
bread, fresh vegetables, and your choice of potatoes
or dumplings (we definitely prefer the superb
fingertip-sized "nokedli" dumplings). Three desserts
are offered on the standard menu: a wonderful
torte with either an apple or cherry filling and
"modarte, " an unalloyed delight of creamy custard
with a fluffy meringue topping.

U.S.2 is one of Michigan's smoothest and most
scenic highways, with numerous pulloffs for picnics,
beaches, and a continuous view of the lake. There
are several other small, similar restaurants in the
area; but if you want to sample some of those

Kovacickian, Transylvanian treasures, be sure to stop at the Hungarian Kitchen, located on the north side of the highway across the road from Lake Michigan. And be prepared to park in the sand dunes. If the restaurant is full, you may need to walk a short distance and end up with grit in your shoes-- but this is a small price to pay when you think of what awaits you.

The best of Budapest, and a bargain.

THE HUNGARIAN KITCHEN, Rte. 2, St. Ignace, MI 49781. Twelve miles west of St. Ignace; 8 mi. south of Brevort. Telephone (906) 643-7693. Hours: after Labor Day until September 15, open daily 12 noon-10 p.m.; closed September 16-June 15; open daily June 16-30 noon-10 p.m.; open daily July 1-Labor Day 8 a.m.-10 p.m. No alcoholic beverages. No credit cards.

HUNGARIAN PINCHED NOODLES
From our files

They're called "pinched" after the method of forming them. These are served in soup or cooked and tossed in butter and presented as a side dish. Sift 1 cup flour and ½ teaspoon salt into a mixing bowl. Make a well, and break in 1 large egg. Add a little water, enough to make a soft dough. Mix well, and then knead until smooth. On a lightly floured pastry board, roll out until 1/8 inch thick.
Bring a large pot of salted water to a full, rolling boil (true also of soup stock). Pinch off little pieces of the dough with fingertips and add to water or soup. Cook until dumplings rise to the top. Serves 8.

The Antler's bills itself as "a little bit o' Ireland,"

but the atmosphere and food are a lot more American than Erin. The history of the place dates back more than four generations and three family ownerships to the era when it was known as the Bucket of Blood and Ice Cream Parlour (the latter providing a "front" during Prohibition). It was closed down, however, when internal revenue agents found that it sold only one quart of ice cream a month and yet took in a profit of $900. It has been said that since that time the Bucket of Blood became the first lemonade stand in history that refused to serve minors.

The decor is probably best described as "a chaotic assemblage of artifacts" (junk?), primarily hung from the ceiling and attached to the walls, including bear traps, old flags, mounted fauna and fish, swords, hardhats, a stuffed black bear and assorted other animals, street signs, and an enormous collection of bells (do ask the bar man to "ring the bells"). None of this is apparent from the unimposing exterior, done in American roadhouse style.

Sit anywhere at the Antler's. There's no "best" table; no matter where you are, you'll be surrounded by noisy, happy eaters and the clanging of bells or the sizzling of steaks. If you happen to find yourself at the windowside table near the bar, don't be startled to look up and see a stuffed python peering down at you. And don't look for intimacy; small parties may find themselves sitting at long tables with other groups. Obviously there's no elegance or delicacy here, but it's lots of fun.

The menu should be registered with the Library of Congress (in the humor section) and possibly used as an "example" by a diligent English teacher (misspellings abound). As for what's offered on the menu, there's something for everyone, from grilled cheese sandwiches to a 28-ounce porterhouse steak. There's an Irish onion soup, fresh lake trout, barbequed ribs, assorted steaks, seafood platter, fried chicken, crab legs, shrimp, and scallops. Dinners include "choice of potatoe [sic], salad, tea or coffee, placemat, napkin, knife, fork, plate, and table-n-chair." If you're in the mood for something simpler, say a hamburger, you can order the Family Burger--five pounds of ground beef on a 16-inch bun (we defy you to find a bigger burger in Michigan). You can even get a peanut butter sandwich (for $5.95; jelly is extra). Undistinguished wines are served by the glass, half-liter, liter, and bottle; but beer seems to be the beverage of choice.

The Antler's is a fine place for the whole family from Grandma to the babies. Furthermore, the food is good and the prices low. But be sure to dress down unless you want to be conspicuous. Noise and all, as far as we're concerned, when we're in Sault Ste. Marie, it's our favorite place. In fact, we like it better than the locks.

A boisterous, bell-ringing bargain.

THE ANTLER'S, Portage Ave., Sault Ste. Marie, MI 49783. At the east end of Portage Ave., paralleling the east approach to the "Soo" locks. Telephone (906) 632-3571. Hours: 10:30 a.m.-midnight. Closed Christmas. Full bar service. All major credit cards. Reservations not accepted.

Nearby attractions: In the daytime there are numerous soo-lock-related tours and lookouts. Nightlife includes Vegas Kewadin, a $1 million casino operated by the Sault Chippewas. Nevada it's not.

VEGETABLE SOUP
From the Antler's

Cut up one 900-pound steer into very small pieces. Finely chop 1 truckload of mixed carrots, corn, and potatoes, and combine with contents of 1 tanker of crushed tomatoes. Place all ingredients into a very large vat; then, with the vat, get into 1 very old birch-bark canoe, preferably one that's been hanging from the rafters for quite some time (this adds to the taste), and paddle rapidly to make sure everything is well mixed. Finally, simmer for 3 weeks, or until soup is just ready to boil. Shut off heat and allow to cool. (If cooking in February, it cools much faster.) After mixture is cool, pour into 47,000 soup bowls and hope for the busiest winter you've ever had.

Our hint: The birch-bark canoe is essential for an authentic flavor, but an aluminum canoe, paddled at top speed, is an excellent substitute.

(132) Eagle's Nest Inn

Ha, the name fooled you, admit it. You were expecting perhaps a revolving restaurant on an upper story of a skyscraper or a clever adaptation of a forest ranger's lookout tower. Instead, the Eagle's Nest is a tidy little Cape Cod cottage adjacent to Highway M-77. Still, there's a point to the name: the entire building, some 50 years old, was originally a homestead on the Seney National Wildlife Refuge not far north of here (of which more later). It was moved part and parcel to its present location and converted into one of the homiest restaurants we've visited, with only three dining areas--the porch, what was once a bedroom, and the former living room with fireplace, our favorite. The rooms have hardwood floors, are simply decorated, and boast many rare photos of wildlife and waterfowl. A kitchen about half the size of your own and a single generic restroom take up the remaining area on the first floor.

Carma and Tom Gronback offer good, solid home cooking at just as good prices, and the inn is gaining a reputation in these parts for its specialties, freshly caught Great Lakes whitefish, lake trout, and perch. The approach is exemplary; the less is more insofar as most fish preparations are concerned. Recently a chef with 30 years at the Marriott Corporation in Milwaukee proclaimed that the Eagle's Nest had the best broiled fish he'd eaten anywhere. The customary steak, roast beef, chicken, and combination steak and fish dinners are more than acceptable, but we heartily recommend the Great Lakes fish. Included with the entree are an excellent soup, salad, choice of potato, and warm loaf of bread. No sweets appear on the menu, but do ask; usually there are seasonal fresh fruit desserts or a creamy cheesecake (see the recipe below). We also like the luncheon offering of a whitefish sandwich or plate, as well as other nicely prepared hot and cold sandwiches; only the steak sandwich costs more than $4.

Your visit to the Eagle's Nest wouldn't be complete without a stroll around the attractively landscaped grounds behind the restaurant. Here you'll find a trout pool and two large duck ponds with several families of mallards that customers enjoy feeding and photographing. The Manistique River also winds through the property, and the Gronbacks rent out canoes for trips through the Seney Wildlife Refuge, a 96,000-acre land and water conservation area that's one of the largest east of the Mississippi. Here you may see many of the over 250 species of birds that have taken refuge, including the bald eagle and the sandhill crane, as well as deer, black bear, beaver, and coyote. The couple also operate a riverside campground with a hot tub/ spa and other outpost campgrounds at several locations. You might consider letting Tom and Carma help you plan an overnight canoe trip on the Manistique or a trout-fishing adventure on the famous Fox River.

Home-style cooking in a real home--
a Germfask gem.

EAGLE'S NEST INN, Hwy M-77, Germfask, MI 498 36. At the north end of town. Telephone (906) 586-9801. Hours: 11:30 a.m.-8 p.m. for lunch and dinner. Closed Monday. Season runs May 1 through mid-October, but inn is open a short period during off-season hunting (call). No alcoholic beverages. No credit cards. Reservations not necessary.

CREAMY CHEESECAKE
From Carma Gronback, Eagle's Nest Inn

Prepare 1 graham-cracker pie crust (use your favorite recipe or a purchased shell). In mixing bowl beat 8 ounces softened cream cheese until fluffy. Gradually blend in ½ cup sugar, 1 tablespoon lemon juice, ½ teaspoon vanilla extract, and a dash salt.

Add 2 eggs, one at a time, beating well after each. Pour into crust. Bake 25-30 minutes in preheated 325-degree oven. Combine 1 cup sour cream, 2 tablespoons sugar, and ½ teaspoon vanilla. Spoon over top of pie and bake 10 minutes longer. Cool. Serve chilled.

Munising, for us, always meant a boat tour to the Pictured Rocks, a 37-mile and three-hour trip that shouldn't be missed if you can afford it and you're in the area. But the Dogpatch was something new to us when we worked on the first edition of this book in 1979--and, at certain times in the evening, as colorful in its own way as Pictured Rocks. It's an ultra-casual, American-style restaurant and bar with some exceptional bargains in food.

The frame building was erected by the owner in 1966, and over the years there've been changes and additions, most recently the cozy Sugarbush Bar (with its own finger-food menu) and a gift shop. The decor is, of course, rustic, and the walls are profusely decorated with country-humorous signs and colorfully painted figures from Al Capp's famous cartoon, "Lil Abner."

But back to those bargains. The Dogpatch now serves "Pork Avenue" breakfasts, and the menu is as fun to read as the food is to eat. We admit a bias for the "delishus porkluv sausages from the wildly romantic boar" and the buttermilk pancakes ("gollee, ther good eatin"). And, yes, grits are available. Two steak dinners, Senator Angus Critterman Filet Mignon and Colonel W.C. Cornfield Ribeye, as well as a charbroiled ground round and New York strip steak sandwich, include soup, salad (from the "super fixins" at the salad bar), baked or French-fried potatoes, and rolls. Those soups are special--"back to basic, hand prepared" (see the recipe following).

The "world-renowned" Lake Superior trout dinner can be had for a lower price than any we've seen in this area and is one of the most popular menu items, along with the Abner, a "whompin" charbroiled hamburger on a toasted bun. Other closed and open sandwiches are on the agenda: the Great Smoky Mountain (ham, bacon, and Swiss cheese on a toasted English muffin with Thousand Island dressing), Pappy's Foggy Mountain Breakdown (beef and gravy--"it'll turn you loose!"), and Ari Saari ("ain't nuthin this side of the Acropolis"), an Athenian gyro, surely the only gyro in the Upper Peninsula. For dessert, our own preferences waver between the apple pie and cheesecake. Sundaes and malts are also offered "cuz they luv ya."

Whimsical and lively, a bargain.

THE DOGPATCH, 325 E. Superior St., Munising, MI, 49862. In the city center. Telephone (906) 387-9948. Hours: 7 a.m.-11 p.m. Monday-Saturday, 12 noon-12 midnight Sunday. Closed Christmas, New Year's Day, Easter, and Thanksgiving. Full bar service. No credit cards.

Nearby attractions: For those who'll have time in this area, see the Pictured Rocks by either driving to the cliffs' overlook well east of town or taking the more expensive but more revealing boat trip from the downtown docks in Munising. If you don't have much time, at least see Munising Falls, at the end of a charming, scenic $\frac{1}{4}$-mile trail--you can actually walk behind the falling water; this is something kids will adore. For the most adventuresome of all (who also own the right equipment and are adequately trained), boats may be chartered at Munising to transport you to the Alger underwater preserve, where ten shipwrecks are protected for your diving enjoyment. There's nothing like it elsewhere in Michigan.

CHEESE CHOWDER
From Karin Ramsay, the Dogpatch

In a small skillet saute ½ cup chopped green pepper and ½ cup chopped carrots in 1 stick butter. Place 2 cups peeled, chopped potatoes and 1 medium chopped onion in a stock pot with chicken broth to cover (may use chicken base and water or canned broth). Add sauteed peppers and carrots.

In a small saucepan make cheese sauce. Melt 2 tablespoons butter, and add 2 tablespoons flour. Cook over low heat about 2 minutes, without browning flour. Gradually whisk in enough milk or half-and-half to make a creamy sauce (1½ to 2 cups). Off heat, add 1 cup shredded Cheddar cheese, and stir until melted. Add cheese sauce to soup, and mix until blended (a little beer may be added if desired). Add 1 teaspoon chopped parsley. Serves 8 to 10.

THE CAMEL
(134) RIDER'S

If southern Michiganians think that the Upper Peninsula is off the beaten track (a recent estimate has it that no more than 20 percent of Detroiters have ever even crossed the Mackinac Bridge), well, then, you should see THIS track, remote by U.P. standards. The Camel Rider's, referring to the irreverent nickname of the Lebanese who once owned this place, was built in

1938 and is not only a restaurant but a year-round resort for canoeists, fishing enthusiasts, skiers, hunters, and snowmobilers. The cottages and outbuildings are located deep in the heart of Hiawatha National Forest, and the quaint log cabin housing the dining room overlooks Deep Lake, one in the beautiful Chain of Lakes.

The owners, Harvey and Dolores Krajcik, have created an atmosphere of rustic warmth as inviting as any we've seen. The tables are set with red-checked quilted mats over cobalt blue tablecloths, and in the evenings when the candles are lit in the wooden chandeliers, the heavy beams and timbers take on a comfortable glow. The two round tables in the corners next to the windows facing the water are our favorites; and the table for eight between them, also with that great view, is our first choice for a larger group.

The Camel Rider's has a full menu daily in the winter, dinners only in the summer. The food is simple and homey, on the order of steak, whitefish, and a tremendously popular fish fry (whitefish and trout) every Friday evening. The house specialty is sirloin for two. All entrees and accompaniments are cooked from "scratch," and you can tell the difference. Prices are exceptionally low for the quality: $3 and up at lunchtime, $6 and up for dinner.

The closest large town is Munising, about 20 miles north and probably where you'll be staying unless you've rented a cottage at the resort. But you'll enjoy the drive to the Camel Rider's, especially the last several miles of winding unpaved roadway through the dense forest. But because it isn't a short trip, we advise you to phone ahead of time to be sure you can be accommodated.

A northwoods oasis, and a bargain.

THE CAMEL RIDER'S RESTAURANT AND RESORT Wetmore, MI 49895. Eighteen miles south of Wetmore on Forest Highway 13 (designated "H-13" on the map). Telephone (906) 573-2319. Hours: Tuesday-Saturday in summer, 5-9 p.m.; Sunday 4-9 p.m. in summer; Tuesday-Sunday , 9 a.m.-9 p.m. in winter. Closed Monday. (Call if in doubt; it's a long drive!) No alcoholic beverages. No credit cards as of this writing.

Visit the HISTORIC (135)

House of Ludington

What do we have in common with John Philip Sousa, Jascha Heifetz, Al Capone, Price Bertil of Sweden, Jimmy Hoffa, Willie Nelson, and Governor James Blanchard? You guessed it; we've all enjoyed the food and services of the House of Ludington in Escanaba. As you can imagine, the place is steeped in history, not surprising since it dates back to 1865. Originally made of wood, in 1883 the hotel was torn down and rebuilt in brick. By 1910 it had expanded to 100 rooms. And in 1939 it was sold to Pat Hayes, a colorful Chicago entrepreneur who implemented many renovations, most notably the glass-walled elevator installed in 1959, in those days and in the U.P. quite an original device. With Hayes' death in 1971, the House of Ludington fell into a state of decline.

When Jerry and Vernice Lancours bought the hotel in 1982, years of neglect had taken their toll. They deserve credit and thanks for restoring the rich flavor of tradition that characterizes this inn. The exterior of the cupola-crowned white building with green-striped awnings looks much as it always did, but the Lancours had to start nearly from scratch to renovate the rooms inside. Today there are 23 guest rooms, each done in an individual style, along with posh hair salons, a gift and antique shop, and a cake decorating outlet specializing in "portrait" cakes (Gov. Blanchard ordered an Iococca cake for the Chrysler chairman's birthday). The

318

dining rooms have been decorated in the Grand Old Tradition and, quite simply, transport you to the Victorian era, the plush and bittersweet times of girls in red velvet swings and birds in gilded cages. What anachronisms exist are unobtrusive and only make you more comfortable.

The two dining areas recall the quieter pace of the 19th century. The Emerald Room, with a soft green and coral color scheme, has walls adorned with faded photographs of early Escanaba residents. Yet attractive as it is, our favorite is the stately King George Room at the front of the hotel. Here window tables afford a view of Ludington Park and the waters of Little Bay de Noc. Other tables hug the cheerful stone fireplace or are positioned near the hand-carved cherrywood cabinets that once belonged to Lewis Cass, Michigan's first governor.

Cooking in the Upper Peninsula is less experimental than in large urban areas and heavily trod tourist areas. And for fine dining, beyond a few scattered roadhouses specializing in prime rib and more often steak, we can count the best on the fingers of one hand. One of them certainly is the House of Ludington. Classic dishes such as duckling a l'orange, veal Marsala, and Chateaubriand appear on the menu. But several more homespun entrees, some of them Bavarian, are also offered by Chef Toren Utke, for example, braised lamb shanks jardiniere and Alpine schnitzel. Portions are generous, and prices moderate.

The luncheon menu, too, attends to hearty appetites and varied tastes. The casserole of ham, turkey, mushrooms, and water chestnuts and the quiche are both popular. But we opt for Chef Utke's Wagnerian specialties: beef rouladen and veal bratwurst with red cabbage, dumplings, and kraut. On Sundays the House of Ludington prides itself on its brunch. We haven't tried it, but we've been told it's worth driving 50 miles for. Brunch here means table service, and it also amounts to a midday dinner: cheese, fruits, and breads; egg courses; meat entrees such as barbequed ribs and chicken livers; and a dessert tray. The hotel serves about 300, and turns away another 150; on our last visit brunch cost $8. Service by young, earnest waiters is splendid. We were tended to royally by Pete, an ex-football player now attending Northern Michigan University. The wine list is modest, but you'll find something enjoyable at a good price (most bottles cost less than $15).

Plan on an evening at the House of Ludington. The lounge provides exceptional entertainment; on one visit we enjoyed the music of young violinist Paul Lundin during dinner and later the musical comedy duets of Mike and Dorien McFarlane, who've sung at the Waldorf in New York and on several cruise ships. At another time we were impressed with the selections of house pianist Mary Snyder. The stage is tiny, and there's a friendly camaraderie in the lounge. Romanticists might prefer one of the curtained private booths.

A historic hostelry, the U.P.'s finest.

HOUSE OF LUDINGTON, 223 Ludington St., Escanaba, MI 49829. At the east end of the street, on the shore of Little Bay de Noc, Telephone (906) 786-4000. Hours: breakfast 7-9:30 a.m. daily; Continental breakfast 9:30-11 a.m. daily; luncheon 11 a.m.-2 p.m. Monday-Saturday; dinner 5-10 p.m. Monday-Saturday; Sunday brunch 11 a.m.-2 p.m. Not open Sunday evening. Full bar service. Entertainment Monday-Saturday. Credit cards: DC, MC, V.

Nearby attractions: On the garden peninsula across the bay is historic Fayette, Michigan's most interesting ghost town with 19 remaining buildings and a natural harbor; open May 15-October 15. If you're here in August, keep in mind that the Upper Peninsula State Fair is held in Escanaba each year and did you know that Michigan is the only state in the country to have two state fairs?

Dining notes: If you intend to be in town for more than a day and want to sample some other eateries, we suggest that you try the Swedish Pantry just a block away from the hotel; specialties are ethnic, wholesome, and tasty (try the potato sausage and limpa bread). Also, for unbelievably low-priced Mexican food and steaks (and in season all-you-can-eat smelt for $2) and for a tavern atmosphere with a capital "A," stop in at the Station Bar at 1837 3rd Ave. North. Owner John Anderson's father was a conductor on the Chicago & North Western Railroad, and the bar boasts some great old depot murals. Good vibrations here.

Last, and this is only if you have time to plan ahead, consider making reservations at the Prophet, a place even more mysterious than Benno's little no-see-um eatery in Harbor Springs. There are no ads, no posted hours of business, no listed phone number. But lots of Escanaba underground eaters swear by it. Call Don Syklli one or two days in advance (786-1208) and arrange for a Middle Eastern feast, including a belly dancer if you wish. Open May-September; a word-of-mouth marvel.

STUFFED BEEF TENDERLOIN FILET
From Chef Toren Utke, House of Ludington

For each serving, pound out an 8-ounce filet of beef tenderloin until flat. Sprinkle with a pinch each of garlic salt, oregano, and basil and 1 teaspoon grated Parmesan cheese. Place a 3-4-ounce slice ham and a 3-ounce slice Swiss cheese on the meat; then place 2 slices tomato on top, and roll up the meat, enclosing the filling as for an egg roll. Secure with toothpicks or string if necessary. Dredge rolls in flour, dip in egg wash (1 egg mixed with 1 cup milk). Coat with dried bread crumbs. Deep fry in oil at 375 degrees until brown. Then bake in a preheated 350-degree oven 30 minutes.

(136) **SOLBERG'S BAR**

Felch? Now, 'fess up, how many of you trolls have ever heard of Felch? "Trolls," for the uninformed, is the U.P. term for all of us creatures who live under (south of) the bridge--in this case, the Mackinac Bridge. And Felch, for the uninformed, is the baseball capital of Michigan. And not only the baseball capital but the basketball capital and the hockey capital and the beer capital--according to the enthusiastic patrons of Solberg's Bar. And even more, this is a real-life rural version of TV's "Cheers"--everybody knows everybody's name here, or so it seems.

The tavern and restaurant have been in the Solberg family for three generations since the late 1800s, and for the life of us, we cannot figure out why we never heard of it long before now. Well, actually we can. Downtown Felch doesn't exactly etch itself onto one's attention or memory. A single small sign on the highway is followed by a wide spot in the road and three buildings: a whitewashed concrete box that houses a generic restaurant ("Food" says the sign) and gas station (nameless pumps), an abandoned general store, and Solberg's Bar. If there's more, it's unobtrusive. Yet because nothing else is nearby, customers flock from many miles around to this out-of-the-way tavern--in the winter skiers and snowmobilers, in the spring and fall fisherman, and all year round servicemen from Sawyer Air Force Base and knowledgeable locals.

They come for "the best food in the county," for "filets out of this world," for "really special French fries," and for a friendly atmosphere unexcelled in the state. In the front of the long bar area is displayed the baseball trophies won by John Hiller, Detroit Tiger pitcher for 14 years, who lives in the area and is revered locally; it's a veritable little Hiller museum. Numerous other sporting cups and trophies adorn the wall in the back of the bar. For historical details, ask one of the regulars or Dewey Solberg himself, who's probably presiding at the bar.

The dining room seats about 60 and is decorated with simple, utilitarian furniture in a light and dark blue color scheme. Solberg's reputation is built on

322

the filet mignon, a 14-ounce cut from the center of the tenderloin, and the primest of prime rib. Also on the menu, at moderate prices, are barbequed baby back ribs, a number of Italian entrees (veal Parmesan, ravioli, spaghetti), deep-fried lake perch and walleyed pike, and several other fairly traditional offerings. For those who can't make up their minds, there are combination plates.

We are especially fond of Solberg's Bar. It's been sitting out there for decades, seemingly in the middle of nowhere (forgive us, Dewey and all of you good U.P. folks), doing just great. Yet a lot of big, elaborately decorated restaurants sitting in the middle of somewhere fall flat on their fancy faces.

Solberg's for the Hall of Fame.

SOLBERG'S BAR AND SUPPER CLUB, Felch, MI 49831. On county road 569; about 25 miles from Iron Mountain. Telephone (906) 246-3227. Hours: 5-9 p.m. Wednesday, Friday, Saturday, Sunday (bar open 7 days a week). Full bar service. No credit cards accepted.

HOUSE SPECIALTY SALAD DRESSING
From Dewey Solberg, Solberg's Bar

In a large mixing bowl combine 2 cups sugar, 1 cup vinegar, 1 cup catsup, 2 chopped onions, 2 cups salad oil, 2 tablespoons celery seed, and 1/8 teaspoon salt. Makes about 1 quart. Halve or quarter the recipe if you wish.

The Stables
"YOUR WELCOMED AT OUR TABLES" (137)

You'll notice a profusion of Italian names on business sites in Iron Mountain, the legacy of a

323

large number of Italians attracted to mining in these parts years ago. So it should tell you something about the Stables to learn that this is where the local paesanos come to eat. For the food, of course--because it's authentic, freshly prepared, and delicious--but also for the friendly and happy atmosphere. What a pleasure to discover this neat, slate blue and white building, surprisingly on a quiet residential street. No, it wasn't once a home. And the Stables has never seen a horse, unless it was one that pulled a carriage out in front at the turn of the century. Constructed in about 1890, it has been owned by the same family of Italian descent for over 80 years and operated as a neighborhood bar, famous in the past for Saturday night pig roasts.

Carol and Butch Hoyum, who've managed the place for the last five years, no longer offer roast pork sandwiches, but there's certainly something for everyone in what they do provide. And the Stables cook has had 40 years of experience. The steaks are well known regionally, and the Italian entrees (served nightly except Friday) are wonderful: spaghetti, gnocchi, meat- or cheese-filled ravioli, and polenta, each of which can be ordered with sauce, with meatballs, or with Italian baked chicken. There are also lasagne and a few other non-Italian items (crabmeat, shrimp, lobster, and fried chicken). An unusual appetizer is the deep-fried, beef-filled ravioli with a hot sauce; one order is enough to share.

On Friday the Stables is known for Mother Mae's old-fashioned fish fry. The Friday evening special, a U.P. tradition, is so popular that reservations are essential. This is by far the busiest night at the Stables. You have a choice of perch, cod, shrimp, walleyed pike, "sea legs" (part pollack and part crabmeat imitation crab legs), or a combination. Dinner includes slaw, potato "logs" ("hand hewn, bronzed, and seasoned") or potato salad, bread and butter. It's a bargain--on our visit last summer, $4.50 to $5.95.

The interior decor is meant to be "quaint," according to Carol Hoyum. We like the rustic barroom, where the roomy, nearly private booths are walled in dark barnwood, each with its own picture, and the seats are upholstered with thick carpeting. Notice, too, the mirrored, painted, and gilded backbar, one of the oldest in the Upper Peninsula. The Hoyums plan to restore it to its natural wood finish. Adjoining the bar is a more modern dining room paneled in knotty pine and with a few antiques; larger groups dine here.

The wine list includes several varietals from Inglenook and the ubiquitous Piesporter Michelsberg, a Valpolicella and Soave from Bolla, three acceptable sparkling wines, and the Stables' most popular wine, Mamartino, a semidry white available by the bottle or glass. You can also order glasses of Inglenook Chablis and Rhine, Lambrusco, rose, and Mondavi's Fortissimo. All wines are fairly priced.

Great staples in the Stables.

THE STABLES, 416 Fourth St., Iron Mountain, MI 49801. Five short blocks off U.S.2 (large sign on highway; opposite a Hardee's on 4th St.). Hours: 11 a.m.-10 p.m. Monday-Saturday. Closed Sunday. Full bar service. All major credit cards.

(138) THE BLIND DUCK INN

A low, rustic building constructed of vertical dark logs and affording a pleasant view of a small lake, the Blind Duck Inn is one of the most popular dining places near Iron Mountain. The owners are duck hunters, hence the name; but the cuisine is, interestingly, Mexican-American. The inn houses a large, roomy bar and lounge with a handsome fireplace; a porch for drinks and appetizers in the summer; and an informal, comfortable dining room enhanced by four mirrors that reflect the view of woods and lake and contribute to a feeling of spaciousness. Sit by the window if you can. (Reserve tables 15,16, and 20--for four persons-- or 17, 18, 19 for larger groups.)

The fairly limited menu offers steaks, hamburgers, fish, spaghetti, and ravioli; but we recommend the "famous wet burrito," an unusual version of chiles rellenos (somewhat like a strata), Mexican baked chicken, turkey chimichanga, and the "Mexican lasagne." The mountainous servings are reasonably priced, and the budget-minded can eat here comfortably. At lunch you might even ask for smaller portions unless you're really hungry. We found two enchiladas instead of the three on the menu quite adequate. On Mondays, the Blind Duck Inn features a sensational Mexican buffet at 5:30-8:30 p.m.--all you can eat for $5.95, a bargain.

If you like cocktails before dinner, you might consider the Blind Duck's Margarita, an enormous, frothy version blended with ice and large enough for two. And, after dinner, there's a choice of mud duck pie, deep-fried ice cream, cinnamon tortilla chips, and empanadas (apple- or cherry-filled tortillas). And, yes, you'll see ducks. On our last visit at least a dozen quacked their little heads off right outside our window.

Fiesta in the firs.

THE BLIND DUCK INN, Cowboy Lake, Kingsford, MI 49801. Across from the Iron Mountain airport terminal. Telephone (906) 774-0037. Hours: 11 a.m.-10 p.m. Monday-Thursday, 11 a.m.-11 p.m. Friday and Saturday, 4-10 p.m. Sunday. Closed New Years Day, Easter, Thanksgiving, and Christmas. Full bar service. Credit cards: MC, V.

MUD DUCK PIE
From the Blind Duck Inn

We tested this recipe for mud pie in 1980; suddenly, in 1987, it's appearing in all the trendiest restaurants in Detroit and other urban areas. Here it is again in all its simplicity and goodness.

Make a piecrust of 5 ounces Nabisco Chocolate Wafers (crushed) and 4 ounces melted butter or margarine. Press into a pie tin. Chill 30 minutes or more. Fill with coffee ice cream. Freeze until firm. To serve, top with hot fudge sauce.

Our hints: Substitute Oreos for the wafers, since the latter are sometimes hard to find. The crust will be sweeter but perfectly acceptable. You can buy the fudge sauce, and if you do, why not go with Michigan's own Sander's Hot Fudge? Or, if you're a purist, here's our recipe. Mix 2 cups sugar, 2/3 cup cocoa, ¼ cup flour, and ¼ teaspoon salt in a saucepan. Add 2 cups water and 2 tablespoons butter. Cook to the boiling point. Lower heat and cook about 8 minutes, stirring. Cool. Stir in 1 teaspoon vanilla extract. Serves 6-8.

(139) ALICE'S

Warm, winsome, wonderful--that's Alice's in the heart of the U.P.'s iron country. We're hard put to think of another restaurant that offers such charm and intimacy as this one and such a welcome from the attractive owner, Alice Tarsi, who with two sisters and a niece has operated this extremely successful Italian eatery since June 1973. Don't let the location near a motel or the unimposing exterior fool you (it's not Alice's fault, because it's not Alice's building).

You'll be delighted with the snugness of the interior--varying shades of red, including velvet chandeliers, and an especially pleasing, cozy atmosphere. Since our first guide came out, there's been but one addition to the decor: more of those multicolored minilights, an Italian conceit we've come across frequently but never found so effective as here. All the tables are inviting, but smaller groups might prefer the alcove off the main dining room for a bit more seclusion. The window air conditioner still takes a bit of getting used to, but the food and cheerfulness in setting and service compensate for that minor fault.

The menu offers such specialties in the finest Capeccian tradition as chicken cacciatore, lasagne, mostiaccioli, fettuccine alla carbonara or alla Armando, and the popular gnocchi. Accompanying the pasta dishes is a choice of meatballs, beef rolls, Italian sausage, or chicken. The Saturday special is a captivating breast of chicken Valdostana, Everything is homemade, even the bread sticks and an absolutely delicious onion bread. We strongly recommend that you try the soup with cappelletti ("little hats" filled with chicken), well worth the extra. As for quality and price, we urge you to order from the right (Italian) side of the menu. Or, if you must order an American meat course, consider the pork chops, which we're told are very good. To finish, one of the best of all possible Italian desserts, "zuppa inglese," for which we include Alice's recipe, may be specially ordered. Call a day ahead for this beautiful "crema" (custard and sponge cake with rum and Rosolio, a relative of the English trifle).

Wine (American) is available by the carafe, but for a little more money, we suggest that you enjoy a bottle of one of the Italian wines with this fine, authentic Italian food. It's a small but acceptable wine list with four Italian whites and six reds at very modest prices. In fact, there are some real bargains here, both in wine and food. Iron mining is now inactive at Iron River, but the legacy of earlier days--and of the Italian immigrants who came here originally as miners--is this marvelous little restaurant.

328

Priceless, a little gem.

ALICE'S SUPPER CLUB, West U.S.2, Iron River, MI 49935. Next to the Trav-Lures Motel, 2 miles west of the city center on U.S.2. Telephone (906) 265-4764. Hours: dinner only, 5-10 p.m. daily, year round. Full bar service. No credit cards.

Other options: If you're faced with constraints of time and distance (common as one travels in the U.P.'s vast open spaces), you may unfortunately find yourself in Iron River before Alice's opens, in which case you should head for town and get a table at the Happy Italians. Or you might arrive at Alice's without a reservation and find that the entire Iron River police force is occupying all the tables for the evening, in which case you should ask the locals how to find County Road 424 and drive east to Losey's Landing (on the south side of Chicaugoan Lake), where the food's less interesting than at Alice's but where you'll enjoy the view and, on weekends, a chance to boogie.

NONA'S ZUPPA INGLESE
From Alice's Supper Club

Alice wants us to give credit to Nona, her mother, for the creation of this recipe. If quantities seem peculiar to American cooks, it's because the recipe was originally written European style with metric weights and measures.

First, make the sponge cake. Beat 12 egg yolks until thick, at least 5 minutes. Gradually beat in 12 tablespoons sugar. Sift together 14 tablespoons flour and 4 teaspoons baking powder. Beat this into the egg mixture. In a second bowl beat 12 egg whites until stiff, and fold them into the first mixture. Grease the bottom of a 9x13-inch pan. Pour in the batter, and bake in a preheated oven (325 degrees) for 35 to 40 minutes until the cake is done when tested with a toothpick or cake tester.

For the custard, beat 15 egg yolks until thick. Add 15 tablespoons sugar and 8 tablespoons flour. Stir in 1 quart milk. Add the grated rind of 1 lemon and 1 cinnamon stick. Place mixture in the top of a double boiler over hot water. Cook over low heat until it thickens or coats a spoon (don't overcook or let it boil). The custard should not be as thick as pudding.

When the cake is cool, slice it about $\frac{1}{4}$ inch thick. Line a platter or individual serving dishes with cake. In a small bowl mix together equal parts of rum and Rosolio (an Italian liqueur, or substitute maraschino cherry juice). Sprinkle this over the cake; it should be fairly well soaked. Then spread the custard over the cake. Repeat layers. Refrigerate until ready to serve. Makes 20-24 servings.

(140) LAWRY'S PASTY & PIZZA

The Cornish pasty is, literally, a taste of Michigan history. Pasties (pronounced "pass-tees") were first prepared for miners in Cornwall, England, as portable meat pies for their workday lunch. As the miners emigrated to other parts of the world, the pasty went with them. Pasties vary tremendously in quality, flavor, and texture. The best we've eaten are those indigenous to the metal-mining areas of the Upper Peninsula: one in the copper range at Laurium (see Toni's Country Kitchen in this book) and the other in the iron-mining district west of Marquette, Lawry's (formerly Madelyne's). Lawry's creation has been awarded a Culinary Hall of Fame medal.

Any visitor to the Upper Peninsula should try an authentic Cornish pasty--a flavorful but simple blend of beef, potato, onion, and "bagies" (big yellow turnips called "Swedes" in Cornwall and rutabagas here), encased in a pastry so that it can be easily eaten by hand or with a knife and fork. This sounds pretty uncomplicated, but in fact there are as many versions of pasties as there are cooks who put them together. In Cornwall they're likely to be filled with anything from eel to rabbit, herring to chicken, apples to jam. But the more familiar beef and potato variety is what you'll get in most of Michigan.

Lawry's mixes suet and parsley into the meat filling and uses a short lard pastry dough, slightly less tender than piecrust. Accompaniments vary to suit individual tastes. The pasties can be eaten as is, but more often the customers add catsup. A few even top them with mustard, hot sauce, or vinegar. Consider ordering one or two at a time and sharing, because they're quite substantial.

Madelyne, Nancy Lawry's mother-in-law, started preparing pasties and selling them from a roadside stand more than 30 years ago for the lunch pails of construction workers on the highway on which the restaurant is now located. About six years ago Nancy and her son Pete, the manager, took over the operation. Though pasties are still the most popular offering, Lawry's also does a brisk business in pizza, especially in the evening. You might try the Large Works--pepperoni, sausage, mushroom, onion, green and black olives, green pepper, and extra cheese on a medium-thick crust--or check out the daily pizza special. Also available are home-baked goods (cookies, cinnamon rolls, tea rings) and ice cream (the peanut butter fudge is the top seller). Inveterate souvenir collectors can even purchase a tiny magnetic pasty for a dollar. We prefer the real thing!

The place is easy to miss, so be alert when seeking it out. Look for the Green Acres Motel on the south side of the highway; Lawry's is adjacent, a cream-colored concrete-block cabin with rust trim and an American flag at the doorway. You can eat here at one of the three small tables or at the counter, but most of the business is carry-out (including frozen pasties to bake at home). If you're driving through or camping at the large and popular Van Riper State Park a few miles west, you might stop at Lawry's and pick up a few pasties--they were created to travel well--and warm them up in camp, if you'd like. For a very reasonable price you can treat the family to a nutritious and filling meal, and like the miners you won't need to worry about who does the dishes.

For a hearty Cornish treat.

LAWRY'S PASTY AND PIZZA, U.S.41, Ishpeming, MI 49849. Four miles west of Ishpeming on U.S. 41. Telephone (906) 485-5589. Hours: 8 a.m. to 12 midnight, year round. Closed Christmas Day, New Year's Day, Thanksgiving, Easter. No alcoholic beverages. Credit cards and reservations not accepted.

CORNISH PASTIES
From our files

First, mix pastry. Sift 1 1/3 cups flour with a large pinch salt. Blend in ½ cup lard till crumbly. Add 2-4 tablespoons cold water, and stir with a fork until dough leaves the sides of the bowl and holds together. For a flakier crust, roll out the dough, dot the surface with small pieces of butter, fold both sides toward the center, and chill. After 20 minutes or so, roll out again. Cut out 6 rounds.
Mix the filling. Toss together until moist 3/4 to 1 pound stewing meat or steak cut in ½-inch cubes, ½ cup finely diced potato, ½ cup finely diced rutabaga, ½ cup finely diced onion, 1 teaspoon salt, ¼ teaspoon pepper, 2 tablespoons chopped parsley (optional), 1 dash thyme, 1 teaspoon Worcestershire sauce, 2 tablespoons water. Place the filling on the rounds of dough. Fold pastry over and seal edges with fingers or fork. Bake 45 minutes on an ungreased cookie sheet in a preheated 400-degree oven. Makes 6 pasties.

amigos

"Entre Amigos" means "among friends" in Spanish, and we had a fine dinner there last summer among friends, including the writer David Goldsmith, and can vouch for the appropriateness of the restaurant's name. Here in what was once Marquette's Opera Building (circa 1890) and later the town soda parlor is now one of the most popular eateries in the city. With dark brick facing, it's clearly more modern than many other downtown buildings, yet it manages to blend in effectively with the red sandstone that predominates. (And, yes, those celebrity signatures on the sidewalk out front are authentic.)

The owner Joe Constance is a "sweetheart," according to ex-employee Kit St. Germaine, who worked here for four years and who was also a sweetheart to show us around. Joe's already made two trips to Mexico with U-Hauls to bring back the wealth of paraphernalia that now adorns his restaurant: pinatas of every size and color, hats and hangings, and hundreds of glazed tiles used on the risers of stairs and elsewhere. The resulting atmosphere has an authentic south-of-the-border feel to it. The main dining room is separated into two parts by a wishing well; we much prefer the seats in the front section, with its comfortable booths and pinata-decorated chandeliers. And if you want privacy for a dinner with close friends, ask for the "front room," a bricked-in niche just big enough for four to six people.

But, although the decor is calculated to make you feel like Don Alfonso, proprietor of El Rancho Grande, the food is definitely "del pueblo" (of the people). Entre Amigos bills itself as the "home of the awesome wet burrito." In too many Michigan restaurants we've come across the "original wet burrito," but this was indeed the first truly awesome one we've seen: a 13-inch tortilla bulging at its seams with beef, lettuce, tomato and topped with sauce and more than a quarter of a pound of cheese. Other options for less gargantuan appetites include the usual assortment of nachos, tacos, tostadas et infinitum. But one touch we like, and you will, too, is the chance to customize orders with your choice of fillings and toppings. For example, last time we chose the shredded beef instead of the ground in our enchiladas. Other less typical items are the superb chicken relleno (breast of chicken topped with a chile relleno and cheesy sauce) and the tasty Mexagna, a lasagne-like casserole with Mexican ingredients. We can also recommend the crispy, delicious "super quesadilla" and the black bean soup, redolent of cumin and Cuba. Most dinners are priced under $5, and those costing more generally are, again, awesome and should be shared.

Don't pass up at least a visit to the second-floor lounge, Margaritaville, doubtless named after the million-seller hit by Jimmy Buffett (terrific to dance to, by the way). It's cleverly decorated like a small "village" of booths, each representing a particular building. Opposite the bar are three booths, two of them jails with iron bars on their "windows" and one the "policia carcel" (police station). An amusing facet is that each booth has its own distinctive method for summoning the server, for example, tin cups for the "prisoners" to rattle and a flashing blue light above the police booth. You get the idea. Other booths depict bank, church, auto shop, curio store, barbershop, and movie theater. In the middle of the room is a park complete with fountain and off to one side even a red-light district. Up here a luncheon buffet is served Monday through Friday at 11 a.m. to 3 p.m., and it's a bargain for trenchermen--all you can eat of assorted Mexican dishes.

For gringo gourmands, a bargain.

ENTRE AMIGOS, 142 W. Washington, Marquette,

MI 49551. Downtown. Telephone (906) 228-4531. Hours: 11 a.m.-midnight, daily. Wonderful free covered parking in back. Full bar service. Reservations taken except for Friday and Saturday; be prepared to join a line outside, but the wait's usually less than 20 minutes. Credit cards: MC, V.

Nearby attractions: Drive by the iron ore loading docks and go on to Presque Isle City Park, a 320-acre peninsula almost surrounded by Lake Superior. For spectacular views, there's Mount Marquette Scenic Lookout off U.S.41 on County Rd. 553 and the tower of the Coast Guard Lighthouse downtown. Kids will enjoy riding on the Iron Horse steam railroad for a 1½-hour trip through a wilderness area (call 228-8785).

(142) Welcome to the FIRESIDE ROOM at

THE **Northwoods** 53Rd Year Of Excellence

Our own memories of the Northwoods go back almost 20 years ago to one of the best lake trout dinners we've had in Michigan. And though the place has had its ups and downs, its many regular customers and gradual expansion attest to its efforts to please. Established in 1934 by Fred Klumb and now owned and operated by his son Ron, it first became known for its chicken dinners; and later, as in many restaurants in this part of the state, whitefish and lake trout became specialties.

The Northwoods has a standard American dinner menu (steaks, seafood, turkey, roast duckling) with the addition of evening specials and a few "gourmet" offerings, among them chicken Oscar, stuffed shrimp, and veal parmigiana. Nothing is frozen, and the restaurant takes pride in its butcher shop, where it ages and cuts all its own meats. A pleasing addition to the menu since our first edition is the "heritage specialties" section, featuring sauerbraten, veal schnitzel with mushrooms and sour cream

335

sauce, and "kassler rippchen" (German pork sausages served with sauerkraut). Another new idea Ron Klumb has introduced is the "5-4-7" dinners: five different dinners served from 4 to 7 p.m. for $5. Early birds have a choice of poultry, pork, beef, seafood, or pasta entrees. Along with the main course, diners can select three of eight accompaniments. It's a bargain if you don't mind eating early.

The baked goods are irresistible. Shirley Duvall has been baking for the Northwoods for more than 20 years and is locally (perhaps regionally) known for her banana pie. The pecan pie is also well worth trying. And ask about the fresh fruit sorbets, as good for dessert as for palate refreshers (and a lot less fattening).

As for wine, the list now numbers about 70 selections and is much improved over previous years. There's a good range of quality and prices with French, Italian, German, and Michigan wines well represented and with an especially nice assemblage of sparkling wines at $9 to $95. Wines by the glass and carafe are also available.

In regular use are two dining rooms, the original Cedar Room, cozy and cheerful and seating about 40, and the much larger Fireside Room, facing the woods in back (ask for tables 11-14 by the windows). The decor pays tribute to the colorful part of Michigan's lumber industry. Both rooms are pleasantly woodsy with fireplaces and rustic logs and stone. A third, more formal room, generally used for private groups, is a recent addition, along with an enlarged entryway. The cocktail lounge has recently been expanded, too; it's now on four open levels separated by heavy log stairways and beams and decorated with rare hunting trophies, Indian artifacts (take a look at the snowshoe divider in the Cedar Room), and unusual chainsaw carvings. The lounge has a small menu with such items as pizza salad and venisonburgers. And there's a dance floor and entertainment five nights a week.

Woodsy and well established.

THE NORTHWOODS SUPPER CLUB, Box 97, Marquette, MI 49855. Four miles west on U.S. 41, ½ mile south on M-28. Telephone (906) 228-4343. Hours: 11:30 a.m.-1:30 p.m. year round; Sunday brunch 10:30 a.m.-2 p.m. and breakfast buffet 9 a.m.-1 p.m. Closed December 24, 25, 26. Full bar service. Credit cards: AE, MC, V. See Entre Amigos for nearby attractions.

POPPY SEED CAKE
From the Northwoods

Blend together 1½ cups sugar, ½ cup shortening, 3/4 cup milk, ½ cup poppy seeds, 2 teaspoons baking powder, 2 cups flour, ½ teaspoon salt, and 4 beaten egg whites. Pour into a greased and floured 8-9-inch springform pan. Bake in a preheated 350-degree oven 30-35 minutes, or till springs back when lightly touched in center. Remove from pan, and let cool. Mix the filling. Combine 3/4 cup sugar, 2 cups milk, 1 teaspoon vanilla, 1 tablespoon butter, ½ cup chopped walnuts, 2 tablespoons cornstarch, and 4 lightly beaten egg yolks in saucepan. Cook over medium heat until thickened. Let cool. Spread on top of cake. Top with whipped cream, and sprinkle with chopped walnuts.

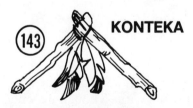

KONTEKA

Konteka, named for a leader of the Chippewa, is arguably the best restaurant and meeting place in the far western Upper Peninsula. We could go so far as to label it a veritable oasis in an area so limited in facilities (other than for campers and sportsmen) that it's worthwhile to drive a little farther to get there. We haven't found anything open to the general public that matches Konteka in this remote part of the state.

The comfortable dining room has a number of large windows that provide a pleasant view of the woods. At the entryway you can see a big piece of native copper; and all the available wine selections, about 20, are effectively displayed near the salad bar. An adjacent oval bar and lounge overlooks an automated eight-lane bowling alley and is well insulated for sound. There's also a small, utilitarian coffee shop that serves breakfast and delicious freshly baked cinnamon and pecan rolls and donuts.

On the dinner menu, aside from a notable assortment of steaks and seafood, are meltingly tender grilled lamb chops; scallops in a creamy sauce, served over broccoli; and Konteka's Trio, a fortuitous combination of barbequed ribs, pork chop, and lamb chop. Soups are well made, with one or two available each day; favorites include the cream of cabbage, minestrone, chicken with dumplings, and corn chowder. The bread is baked fresh, and for dessert a peanut butter ice cream pie and several ice cream drinks are offered. One item that really impressed us was the Lithuanian dumplings available as an appetizer. These represent home-style Eastern European cooking at its best. Some customers are so enamored of them that they order only dumplings and salad for dinner. We think that's not a bad idea at all except that it's hard to pass up the lamb chops or Trio.

The restaurant is within view of the White Pine mine's smokestack that towers over 500 feet and is the tallest in Michigan. The U.P.'s last operational copper mine, it had shut down in 1982 but reopened as the Copper Range Company and is now majority-owned by the mine workers. Though it once employed as many as 3000 men, it now uses only about 910 who work at two levels, 500 feet and 1800 feet, in a maze of corridors under five square miles of land. Konteka is also in close proximity to the Porcupine Mountains State Park, one of the most popular backpacking areas in the Great Lakes region and famous for the easily accessible and spectacular view of Lake of the Clouds.

The best in the west.

KONTEKA, Mineral River Plaza, White Pine, MI 49971. Off M-64, 13 miles west of Ontanagon, then 6 miles south. Telephone (906) 885-5215. Hours: 6 a.m.-9 p.m. Closed Christmas. Full bar service. Credit cards: MC, V.

RAW VEGETABLE SALAD
From Marge Razmus, Konteka

This is certainly the most popular dish on Konteka's salad bar. Mix together in a large bowl 1 head broccoli (in flowerets), 1 head cauliflower (in flowerets), 1 bunch sliced green onions, 1 can halved water chestnuts, 1 can pitted ripe olives, 6 tomatoes in wedges, 1 pound sliced fresh mushrooms, 1 package Good Seasons cheese-garlic dressing mix (sprinkled on dry), 2 teaspoons Italian seasoning, and 2 teaspoons garlic salt. Marinate several hours or overnight; it'll stay nice several days. Serves 8-12.

KEWEENAW BERRY FARMS

A bakery, a produce market, an ice cream stand, a doughnut shop, a gift boutique, a bookstore--all of these along with a small Early American dining room are housed in a large, old-style but modern barn just off the highway. On your way to or from Houghton, this is pleasant stop for snacking and browsing, and if you're satisfied with hot dogs or pasties,it'll do for lunch. Much more appealing, though, are the baked goods--such treats as zucchini nut bread,cinnamon loaf, muffins, and Nisu braid, a cardamom-scented Finnish bread.

The muffins and desserts depend on the berries

available. In season you might be lucky enough to try the exceptional strawberry muffins or the strawberry ice cream or shortcake. Blueberries were the star of the show on our visit in August, and we had our choice of fresh blueberry ice cream (soft or hard), pie, or muffins. We could even have bought some blueberry soap and a blueberry cookbook as souvenirs. (If you care, Michigan ranks number one in the United States in blueberries; we produce nearly half of the entire country's crop.) The little gift shop, by the way, is not as plastic-oriented as some. Take a moment to look around. Some unusual preserves and spice mixtures are for sale as well as several local cookbooks and a good selection of volumes about the Upper Peninsula.

Keweenaw Berry Farm opened in mid-1985. About 100 acres are devoted primarily to berry growing of all kinds, but plans are under way to open a cider mill. Whether or not you have children, don't confine yourself to the niceties of the barn. Out in back is a petting area with cows, chickens, ducks, pigs, buffaloes, and the most petted of all, rabbits.

It's the berries!

KEWEENAW BERRY FARM, U.S.41, Chassell, MI 49916. Three miles south of town. Telephone (906) 523-6181. Hours: 8 a.m.-9 p.m. Monday-Saturday, 10 a.m.-9 p.m. Sunday. Open May 1 until January 1. No wine or liquor. If you call for a reservation, they'll think you've gone off your rocker. NOTE: In our first edition, we included an entry for the Summer Place, a lovely restaurant just north of Chassell. There's been a recent change of ownership, and we were unable either to try the place again or to determine the direction of its future. The attractive old summer house with a gracious lawn and lake view might still be worth visiting, but we can't honestly vouch for it at this time.

Anyone who can encourage so many young people to eat escargots and steak tartare surely has reached the apex of restauranteurship. And that's exactly what Big Jon Davis appears to have done at the Library. The eatery is housed in an old building that dates to 1863 on what was once the main street of Houghton at the turn of the century. It was then called the Palm Gardens Cafe and was an elegant dining place during the heady mining days, replete with potted palms and brass spittoons. Later it became the Board of Trade, an eating establishment and historic bordello. Now, as the Library, with attractive stained glass windows and carpeting even on walls and doors, it caters to Michigan Tech students and others of any age who are young at heart. (Wear your jeans.)

The Library has dining areas on two floors, each with its own bar and the same menu. The atmosphere in both is relaxed but there are some differences. We prefer the upper level, known as the Homonym. The enormous bar stools are downright bizarre but surprisingly comfortable.

The garrulous menu is fun to ponder over. Appropriately, it reads like a library book, complete with title page ("Big Jon's Encyclopedia of Damn Fine Victuals"), table of contents, and a wealth of offbeat or humorous inclusions other than food listings. We especially enjoy the five "chapters" in the life of the Earl of Sandwich and the sprinkling of Big Jon's adages--for example, "If your bar bill is not as large as your food bill, you are not eating a balanced diet." On the last page is a brief story with blanks for customers to fill in; we can imagine some of the bawdy lines students come up with.

Most items are priced less than $5, putting the Library in the bargain category; but the offerings are primarily "nibbles and bickes," pizza, sandwiches, salads, soup, and chili. Of the extensive selection of sandwiches, the R.B.2 is most popular--hot beef with cheese and mushrooms on pumpernickel or rye-- as is the Epicurean, devised by the help (roast beef, bacon, cheese, lettuce, tomatoes, and mayonnaise). The BTO (mushroom, Swiss cheese, and onions) is apparently a sleeper; it's described on the menu as "the best tasting sandwich nobody orders." There's a reasonably priced tenderloin steak as well as deep-fried seafood, lasagna, and a daily special, such as linguine carbonara, cashew chicken, gingered shrimp, and sole with mousseline sauce. Saturday features prime rib for lunch and dinner, and Sunday evening is the pizza buffet--all you can eat of pizza and salad for $4.99. A modest selection of wines and low-priced liters of house wines are available, though beer seems to be the favorite.

After eating, you might enjoy a brief walk, either out the main door to the left to look at the relic depot and the wharfs or to the right uphill to see reconstructed Douglass House Hotel, named in honor of Douglass Houghton, the state's first geologist, who perished in a storm off the coast of the penin- sula and after who the town was named.

A library of fun and flavors, a bargain.

THE LIBRARY, 62 N. Isle Royale St., Houghton, MI 49931. A half-block off north U.S.41 downtown. Telephone (906) 482-6211. Hours: 11:30 a.m.-1 a.m. Monday-Saturday, 5 p.m.-1 a.m. Sunday. Closed on Christmas (check on other holidays). Full bar ser- vice. Street parking or city lot. A small lot at the side of the Library carries this sign: "If you are not dining or drinking at the Library, get your car out of here." No credit cards.

Nearby attraction: On M-26 in Ripley is a sub- teranean adventure, a guided tour of the Arcadian Copper Mine. Close by is the Quincy Hoist on U. S.41 in Hancock, once used by the copper mines to bring the mineral to the surface; it's worth a stop.

ORANGE-BRANDIED ROCK CORNISH HEN
From Big Jon Davis, the Library

Though not on the menu, this was featured at one of the restaurant's periodic wine tastings. For the sauce, combine in a saucepan one 6-ounce can frozen orange juice concentrate, 8-16 ounces brandy (to taste), and juice from a 3-ounce jar maraschino cherries (reserve cherries). Heat to simmering. Add 3 tablespoons honey and 1 tablespoon grated orange peel. Thicken with mixture of 2 teaspoons cornstarch and 2 teaspoons water.

For the stuffing, combine 3 cups long-grain rice (or long grain and wild rice) that has been cooked in chicken broth, 3 cups salted croutons made from Jewish rye or pumpernickel, ½-1 cup slivered almonds, and 1 large orange (peeled and diced). Chop the reserved cherries and add. Add enough of the sauce to moisten stuffing, saving about half of it for basting.

Stuff 6 Rock Cornish game hens with this. Garnish the breast of each bird with an orange slice and cherry. Bake at 275 degrees until brown and tender, basting every 15 minutes with the sauce. Serve each bird on a base of chopped raw spinach and chopped almonds over a bed of romaine lettuce. Serves 6.

⑭⑥ Toni's Country Kitchen

For the past 20 years Toni's has become better and better known throughout the state among discriminating fanciers of Cornish pasties and other baked goods. The original owner Toni Coppo is now retired and spends her winters in Arizona, a far cry from winters in Laurium. But the new owner, Eric Frimodig, who has been in the restaurant business since he was 15, continues to meet the exacting requirements of his clientele and is a more-than-worthy successor to the redoubtable Toni.

The small bakery-restaurant, decorated in Early American style, seats 24 if you want to eat your pasties still steaming from the oven. The kitchen is spotless, the aromas are tantalizing, and in the morning the glass showcase is laden with delicacies (and sadly depleted each afternoon). The pasties sell quickly, so avid customers usually call ahead, and we advise you to do the same. However, if you've had your fill of U.P. pasties, you might instead try one of Eric's other lunch or snack offerings: a sandwich (including an unusual pizzaburger), homemade soup (we like the cheese broccoli and tomato vegetable), saffron or cinnamon toast, bratwurst, or cudighi--a spicy Italian pork sausage seasoned with cinnamon, cloves, mace, and red pepper and simmered in Lambrusco.

The sweets are just about irresistible. One of us is enamored of the fruit tarts, and the other adores the ginger cremes. Yet nearly as good as these are the Cousin Jacks--soft, biscuit-like raisin cookies--and the date sandwich cookies (see Eric's recipe below). Four or five different breads are also baked daily, including our favorite, the redolent saffron bread.

Laurium, a company town like so many others ion this part of the Upper Peninsula's copper range, is characterized by "two-family" vertically elongated Cornish houses amid relics of long-abandoned copper mines. It's worth a drive-through for a look at what life was once like in this area of Michigan. And, before or after, a stop at the Country Kitchen to sample a dish that conjures up the past--the typical miner's lunch, the pasty--or other ethnic baked goods of Copper Country will make your excursion even more interesting.

Tops for pasties and pastries.

TONI'S COUNTRY KITCHEN, 79 Third Street, Laurium, MI 49913. In village center. Telephone (906) 337-0611. Hours: 7 a.m.-5 p.m. Monday-Saturday, June through October; 7 a.m.-5 p.m. Tuesday-Saturday, rest of the year. Closed Sunday and from December 25 through January 31. No alcoholic beverages. Credit cards and reservations not accepted.

DATE SANDWICH COOKIES
From Eric Frimodig, Toni's Country Kitchen

Place 1 pound pitted dates in a saucepan with liquid (half orange juice and half water) to cover. Simmer until dates are very tender and liquid is nearly absorbed. Add 2 tablespoons sugar and mash the dates well. In a mixing bowl cream together ½ cup butter or margarine, 1 cup brown sugar, 1 egg, and 1 teaspoon vanilla. Add 1 3/4 cups flour, ½ teaspoon baking soda, and ¼ teaspoon salt. Chill for 1 hour.

Sprinkle pastry board with granulated sugar, and roll out dough to ¼-inch thickness. Cut with donut cutter. Bake 8-10 minutes in preheated 400-degree oven. Cool. Spread date filling on the bottoms of half the cookie rounds. Place remaining cookies on top of the filling, bottom side down.

KEWEENAW MOUNTAIN LODGE

Very few Midwest, or even Michigan, tourists appear waaay uuup here in this part of our big, beautiful state. To be sure, the largest part of the adventure of eating at the Keweenaw Mountain Lodge is getting there and back. The winding drive towards the lodge is punctuated by a number of scenic stops, including the lovely Silver Falls and the town of Copper Harbor, charmingly reminiscent of those on the Maine coast. But the highlight without a doubt is Brockway Mountain Drive, a narrow blacktop road that winds along the often windy crest of one of the highest ridges forming the Keweenaw Peninsula. Travel writers and other visitors judge it to be the most scenic public roadway in the Midwest. From here, on a clear day you can see, if not forever, thousands of acres of rugged, undeveloped terrain and rocky shoreline, and you'll get a better idea of the magnitude of the largest of the Great Lakes, the well-named Lake Superior. Both coming and going to the lodge, you'll glimpse many of the relics of abandoned copper mines and near ghost towns with their Cornish-style company homes built for the miners.

The Keweenaw Mountain Lodge is located high on the north side of one of the largest and rockiest ridges in an attractive woodland setting near the east end of the peninsula. Begun as a Great Depression project by the CWA and completed by the WPA in 1936, the sprawling structure has literally been carved out of the wilderness. Clearing the land provided needed jobs for several hundred men over a period of two and a half years, during which time an estimated 187,000 trees were felled. The logs and poles were used in building the lodge and cabins; the limbs, tops, and stumps were made into firewood to supply fuel for families in the area; and the land cleared of timber is now a golf course. A charming aspect of the Keweenaw Mountain Lodge is the cabins, each with a bedroom or two and a fireplace that makes for especially pleasant evenings in chilly summer weather (but reserve as early as possible as they're often booked up weeks ahead).

The large, rustic-chic dining room with open rafters, paneled walls, two huge fireplaces at either end, and a circular lounge bar on the west are quite appropriate for this rugged northwoods setting. The menu primarily appeals to popular tastes: prime steaks and rib roast, barbequed ribs, Lake Superior trout and whitefish, and a generous salad bar. As we've noted, there's nothing much on the menu to stir the imagination. But the lodge certainly has attracted a faithful following over the years and is generally consistent in quality. New since our last edition are the Saturday evening smorgasbord and the Sunday brunch. The wines are modest in number and modestly priced.

While in the area, you won't want to miss visiting Copper Harbor, a resort village on a scenic inlet of Lake Superior. If you're here for more than a day and want some ethnic variety in cuisine you might try the Harbor Haus, a German eatery that friends tell us is well above average. From Copper Harbor you can take a day-long Lake Superior excursion to and from Isle Royale National Park. Campers and those interested in Michigan history will also enjoy the nearby Fort Wilkins State Park, site of a virtually undisturbed U.S. Army fort built in 1844 to "keep the peace" during the turbulent copper boom that opened the western Upper Peninsula to white settlement. Evening entertainments are few and far between, and one unusual and popular choice is to gawk at wild black bear from the protection of your car in especially prepared parking areas at the city dump (a way to test your environmental tolerance).

A sentimental Copper Country favorite.

THE KEWEENAW MOUNTAIN LODGE, U.S.41, Copper Harbor, MI 49918. One and a half miles south of town. Telephone (906) 289-4403. Hours: 7:30 a.m.-11 a.m. breakfast, 1 a.m.-5 p.m. luncheon, 5-9 p.m. dinner. Open mid-May to mid-October. Full bar service. Credit cards: MC, V.

"We may live without friends; we may live without books; but civilized man cannot live without cooks."

....Edward Robert Bullwer, Earl of Lytton

"Man is a cooking animal. The beasts have memory, judgment and all the faculties and passions as our own mind in a certain degree. But no beast is a cook."

....James Boswell

"Never consume more than your own weight at one sitting."

....Miss Piggy

SPECIAL RESTAURANTS
IN AND NEAR DETROIT

Like any large metropolitan area, Detroit and its suburbs offer numerous exciting dining possibilities. To include all these is beyond the scope or purpose of this book. If you intend to spend some time in Michigan's largest city, we suggest two guidebooks: "Restaurants of Detroit" by Molly Abraham and "Guide to Michigan Dining" by Sandra Silfven. Or, if you'll be in the city briefly, pick up a copy of Metropolitan Detroit or Detroit Monthly, magazines that carry restaurant listings.

What follows is a short alphabetical summary of 25 of our favorites, balancing price ranges, offering variety, and concentrating on places that suit our book's theme, adventurous eating. Each offers full bar service and accepts credit cards unless otherwise noted. The area code for all phone numbers is 313. Meals served are indicated by B (breakfast), L (lunch), and D (dinner).

ALDO's, 19143 Kelly, Detroit, 839-2180. Northern Italian cooking at its best. High moderate to expensive. D, no credit cards.

BAGLEY CAFE, 3354 Bagley Ave., Detroit, 842-1122. Turkish cuisine. No alcohol or credit cards. L, D; inexpensive.

BENJIE'S FISH AND SEAFOOD, 2650 Orchard Lake Rd., Sylvan Lake, 682-7730. Some 20 kinds of fish cooked to order; more than 100 wines by the glass. D; moderate. (Try the Atlantic sturgeon.)

THE BLUE NILE, 508 Monroe in Trapper's Alley, Detroit, 964-6699. Ethiopian fare. Use injera bread instead of silverware. Beer and wine. L, D; very reasonable.

CADIEUX CAFE, 4300 Cadieux, Detroit, 882-8560. The Belgian headquarters of Detroit. Sells more than 1500 pounds of mussels a week; Belgian rabbit on Sunday. L, D; inexpensive.

CHEZ RAPHAEL, 27000 Sheraton Dr., Novi, 348-5555. Creative French cuisine with inventive chef Keith Famie. Aura of a European country inn. L, D; expensive.

ELIZABETH'S, 227 Hutton, Northville, 348-0575. French country inn in an American farmhouse. Consistently superior offerings. D; expensive.

DA EDOARDO, 19767 Mack, Grosse Pointe Woods, 881-8540. Romantic trattoria. Great veal and spinach soup. D; high moderate to expensive.

THE GOLDEN MUSHROOM, 18100 W. 10 Mile Rd., Southfield, 559-4230. Milos Cihelka's a gifted chef. Great Continental classic dishes and a good wine list. L, D; very expensive.

LONDON CHOP HOUSE, 155 W. Congress, Detroit, 962-0278. The city's premier restaurant. Both classic and creative dishes. L, D; very expensive.

MATTIE'S BARBEQUE, 7504 W. McNichols, Detroit, 341-0832. Great ribs, soul food, and the homiest of home cooking. No cards or bar. B, L, D; inexpensive.

NEW HELLAS, 583 Monroe, Detroit, 961-5544. Oldest, most popular Greek eatery. Try the lamb chop or sea bass. L, D; inexpensive.

THE 1940 CHOP HOUSE, 1940 E. Jefferson, Detroit, 567-1940. Fortyish Art Deco decor. For beef eaters and bon vivants; great wine list. L, D; expensive.

NIPPON KAI, 511 W. 14 Mile Rd., Clawson, 288-3210. Sushi and traditional Japanese fare. L, D; moderate to expensive.

RESTAURANT DUGLASS, 29269 Southfield, Southfield, 424-9244. Showy, flamboyant, and exciting French food; Chef Duglass can be brilliant. L, D; very expensive.

THE ROYAL EAGLE, 1415 Parker, Detroit, 331-8088. "Gourmet Polish" food in Old World atmosphere. D; moderate.

THE SHEIK, 316 E. Lafayette, Detroit, 964-8441. May be the best Mideast cooking in the Western Hemisphere. L, D; moderate.

THE SOUP KITCHEN SALOON, 1585 Franklin, Detroit, 259-2643. City's oldest saloon and home of the blues. Being here is more important than eating here. L, D; inexpensive.

STAR OF DETROIT, 20 E. Atwater, Detroit, 1-800-782-7827 or 259-8190. Seasonal cruising on Detroit River; spectacular views, entertainment and dancing, American buffet dining. Great for families. L, D; expensive.

TRAFFIC JAM AND SNUG, 511 W. Canfield, Detroit, 831-9470. Informal, trendy, and imaginative. Unusual breads; dozens of wines by the glass and a wonderful changing menu. L, D; inexpensive.

TREATS, 4105 Orchard Lake Rd., Orchard Lake, 851-0060. No entrees--just "befores" (appetizers) and "afters" (desserts). Different, and very good! L, D; moderate.

VAN DYKE PLACE, 649 Van Dyke Pl., Detroit, 821-2620. Magnificent restored mansion. Offers American perspective on French cuisine. L, D; very expensive.

THE WHITNEY, 4421 Woodward Ave., Detroit, 832-5700. Romanesque estate beautifully renovated. A storybook, "must" dining experience in Detroit. L, D; expensive.

WOODBRIDGE TAVERN, 289 St. Aubin, Detroit, 259-0578. Authentic turn-of-the-century saloon with Dixieland music and singalongs. Great burgers, good times. L, D; inexpensive.

XOCHIMILCO, 3409 Bagley Ave., Detroit, 843-0179. Most popular Mexican place in town; the mountainous botana is a Detroit institution. L, D; inexpensive.

NOTABLE WINE LISTS

A number of restaurants outside of Detroit have cellars that will especially appeal to wine lovers. Here is our summary of those most interesting in terms of quality, quantity, theme, or price range. It is based on lists we were able to examine in detail and our personal notes but is not necessarily all inclusive. See our reviews of individual restaurants for more particulars. The eating places are listed in order of their appearance in the table of contents (based in turn on our map references, indicated in parentheses following each entry below). These are wine lists that the most learned oenologist we know, Harm J. de Blij, would appreciate.

TOSI'S (1)   A grand 250-item list including the finest assemblage of Italian wines we've seen anywhere. The house selections may be the best buys in the state; two Cruvinets, too. *

TABOR HILL (3)   Wines are limited to those made on the premises. The only restaurant in Michigan where you can see the vineyard, harvesting, processing, or bottling if you're there at the right time of year.

LITTLE RIVER CAFE (4)   Noteworthy in that more than 30 Michigan wines are offered, including Little River's own selection with its personalized label.

THE BLACK SWAN (5)   Not large but a very nice list, including some excellent wines.

OAKLEY'S IN THE HAYMARKET (6)   The finest list in the Kalamazoo area and one of the best in the state; about 200 offerings.

ARBOREAL INN (16)   More than 100 different

wines, mainly from France and California, but most less than 10 years old.

THE PIANO FACTORY (18)   Singular in that only seven of their 40 wines cost more than $10.

GIBSON'S (29)   A medium-sized, nicely composed cellar that is also a wine store. Prices tend to be reasonable.

THORNAPPLE VILLAGE INN (32)   Another medium-sized collection but with a terrific wine cellar, beautifully designed specifically for the visiting oenophile.

BEGGAR'S BANQUET (40)   An outstanding inventory of vintage and high-quality California wines.

COUSINS HERITAGE INN (48)   Limited to about 35 options but exceptional in diversity and quality, with a bargain or two here and there.

THE EARLE (49)   An extraordinary list of about 500 wines constituting a wide variety of sources, vintages, and prices; the most extensive collection we've seen outside of Detroit.

ESCOFFIER (50)   A moderate-sized compilation at present but currently being greatly expanded on the basis of the owners' considerable knowledge and skill.

DARBY'S (62)   Offers some of the world's great wines, along with the best choice of Cognacs we've seen in Michigan.

MICHIGAN BEAN COMPANY (71)   About 50 wines, numbering a few collectors' items and many priced less than $20.

JUSTINE (84)   An especially attractive ten-page list of about 200 wines; one of the most interesting cellars in central southern Michigan.

HOTEL FRANKFORT AND BROOKSIDE INN (97, 99)   The best collection of German wines (both red and white) we've seen in the state, personally selected and imported by the proprietor of Austrian descent.

LA BECASSE (101)   Forty well-chosen wines with practically all in the low to medium price range, ideally suited to this small country restaurant.

LEELANAU COUNTRY INN (102)   Distinctive

in that all of the 15 wines available are produced in Leelanau County and are priced less than $15.

THE TRILLIUM (111)   A very good cellar with a wide range of wines; the Cruvinet is an added attraction.*

SPENCER CREEK LANDING (112)   A well-rounded and affordable selection of nearly 50 different wines.

THE ROWE (116)   A distinguished list, reflecting quality rather than quantity, especially powerful in the area of red Bordeaux.

TAPAWINGO (117)   About 75 wines, most from France and California and many at reasonable prices, along with a few superb but expensive Bordeaux that we all love to talk about and too rarely, if ever, get to drink.

*Note on Cruvinets: The Trillium's wine list describes these French devices quite well; the Cruvinet is a "temperature-controlled dispensing system designed to serve fine wines by the glass while holding the unpoured portion in a virtually unopened condition." The restaurant can open as many bottles as the Cruvinet has spigots and can keep them in good condition for up to eight weeks.

"Give me books, fruit, French wine and fine weather and a little music played out of doors."
....John Keats

"Wine is one of the most civilized things in the world, and one of the material things of the world that has been brought to the greatest perfection and which offers a greater range of enjoyment and appreciation than, possibly, any other purely sensory thing which may be purchased."
....Ernest Hemingway

"No man having drunk old wine straightway desireth new: for he saith, The old is better."
....Saint Luke

353

Adventurous Eating in Michigan

A great gift for friends and relatives who enjoy travel and cooking

Those unusual, hard-to-find eating places are identified to save you time, money, and disappointment. Discover the state's most appealing settings, greatest values, and all the "extras" that contibute to adventures in eating.

Order additional copies for $11.95 each ($10.95 plus $1.00 for postage and handling). Must be prepaid; enclose check or money order payable to Beech Tree Press, 2673 Ramparte Path, Holt, Michigan 48842.

Want your copy or your gift autographed? Please let us know the name of the recipient and the special occasion, if any. (No additional charge for this personalized service.)

A Restaurant Guide and Cookbook

INDEX OF RECIPES

356

ABOUT THE AUTHORS

Marjorie Winters studied at the University of
Illinois and Northern Illinois University, where she
earned a master's degree in English, and until 1983
edited several academic journals and books at Michigan State University. More recently, she's been
concentrating on her love of food and cooking: as
a restaurant columnist, cookware buyer and demon-
strator, writer and editor of a cooking newsletter,
cooking teacher, and merchandiser for a national
wholesale food company. Her personal interests,
aside from writing and puttering over the stove,
are crossword puzzles, escapist literature, and travel
(she feels especially at home on a cruise ship).

Her husband and coauthor, Harold "Duke" Winters,
a Ph.D. from Northwestern University and since
1965 on the faculty of Michigan State University
as a Professor of Geography, has also been a visiting professor at Northwestern University, Simon
Fraser University, the University of British Colum-
bia, and the United States Military Academy at
West Point. He teaches a course in the geography
of Michigan and conducts research in glacial geo-
morphology and has numerous publications, many
in his profession's most prestigious journals. His
leisure-time pursuits include trout fishing, oenology,
and jazz.